Cognitive Psychology: Mind and Brain

Cognitive Psychology: Mind and Brain

Edited by Julian Hodges

CLANRYE INTERNATIONAL
www.clanryeinternational.com

Clanrye International,
750 Third Avenue, 9th Floor,
New York, NY 10017, USA

ISBN: 978-1-64726-158-0

Cataloging-in-Publication Data

Cognitive psychology : mind and brain / edited by Julian Hodges.
p. cm.
Includes bibliographical references and index.
ISBN 978-1-64726-158-0
1. Cognitive psychology. 2. Brain. 3. Mind and body. 4. Psychology. I. Hodges, Julian.
BF201 .C64 2021
153--dc23

For information on all Clanrye International publications visit our website at www.clanryeinternational.com

CLANRYE INTERNATIONAL

Contents

Preface

The scientific study which focuses on mental processes is known as cognitive psychology. The processes which are studied under this domain are language use, memory, creativity, perception and thinking. Cognition is subdivided into two different styles of processing, namely reasoning and intuition. Reasoning is based on conscious decisions and attitudes. It is slower and volatile. Intuition is faster than reasoning and automatic. It depends on formed habits and is difficult to change. Cognitive psychology finds applications in various fields such as social psychology, developmental psychology, abnormal psychology and educational psychology. This book presents researches and studies performed by experts across the globe. It provides significant information of this discipline to help develop a good understanding of cognitive psychology and related fields. Coherent flow of topics, student-friendly language and extensive use of examples make this book an invaluable source of knowledge.

Various studies have approached the subject by analyzing it with a single perspective, but the present book provides diverse methodologies and techniques to address this field. This book contains theories and applications needed for understanding the subject from different perspectives. The aim is to keep the readers informed about the progresses in the field; therefore, the contributions were carefully examined to compile novel researches by specialists from across the globe.

Indeed, the job of the editor is the most crucial and challenging in compiling all chapters into a single book. In the end, I would extend my sincere thanks to the chapter authors for their profound work. I am also thankful for the support provided by my family and colleagues during the compilation of this book.

Editor

1

An investigation of response competition in retrieval-induced forgetting

Gina A. Glanc[1*]

*Corresponding author: Gina A. Glanc, Department of Psychology & Sociology, Texas A&M University Corpus Christi, 6300 Ocean Drive, Corpus Christi, TX 78412, USA
E-mail: gina.glanc@tamucc.edu
Reviewing editor: Peter Walla, Webster Vienna Private University, Austria and University of Newcastle, Australia

Abstract: It has been demonstrated that retrieval practice on a subset of studied items can cause forgetting of different related studied items. This retrieval-induced forgetting (the RIF effect) has been demonstrated in a variety of recall studies and has been attributed to an inhibitory mechanism activated during retrieval practice by competition for a shared retrieval cue. The current study generalizes the RIF effect to recognition memory and investigates this competition assumption. Experiment 1 demonstrated an effect of RIF effect in item recognition with incidental encoding of category-exemplar association during the study phase. Experiment 2 demonstrated evidence of RIF with use of an independent retrieval cue during retrieval practice. Results from this study indicate that response competition may occur outside of the retrieval-practice phase, or may not be limited to situations where there is an overt link to a shared category cue.

Subjects: Cognitive Psychology; Consciousness & Cognition; Memory

Keywords: recognition memory; retrieval-induced forgetting; response competition; independent cues; memory inhibition; transfer appropriate processing

1. Introduction

Successful memory retrieval can serve to improve subsequent memory for the previously retrieved information (Allen, Mahler, & Estes, 1969; Carrier & Pashler, 1992; Gardiner, Craik, & Bleasdale, 1973; Gotts & Jacoby, 1974). Studies of retrieval-induced forgetting (RIF; Anderson, Bjork, & Bjork, 1994), however, have demonstrated that prior retrievals can make subsequent recall of semantically related information more difficult. This phenomenon is thought to be driven by competition for two or more items in memory for a shared retrieval cue. The commonly used retrieval-practice paradigm

ABOUT THE AUTHOR

Glanc's research focuses primarily on visual word recognition and how different aspects of the visual experience inform the memory process. She is largely interested in a multidisciplinary approach to memory research, investigating how phenomena from linguistics, cognitive, and even social psychology influence information processing.

PUBLIC INTEREST STATEMENT

Have you ever forgotten where you parked your car, and then could not remember where you parked today because you kept thinking about where you parked yesterday? This is related to a memory phenomenon known as retrieval-induced forgetting. Recollecting certain items from memory causes the subject to forget other, related items. This study aims to investigate how the human memory system works to create the retrieval-induced forgetting effect, and discusses how it may behave differently within different forms of memory, specifically, recall and recognition memory. Understanding effects such as this one will allow us to better understand why the memory system, while overall very accurate and efficient, fails us from time to time.

consists of three distinct phases: an initial study phase in which participants are given a series of category-exemplar pairs (e.g. Color—Pink, Color—Brown, and Fruit—Banana) for study, a retrieval-practice phase in which retrieval of a subset of the studied items is initiated, often through the use of a task such as word-stem completion (e.g. Color—Br__), and a final test phase in which participants are asked to remember the words from the original study list via a category-cued recall task (e.g. recall the study words from the following categories: Color, Fruit). RIF is demonstrated by contrasting memory performance on the final memory test between the two different types of items (e.g. practiced: Brown, and unpracticed: Pink) from practiced categories with performance on the baseline items from the non-practiced categories (Banana). Retrieval practice of a subset of items from practiced categories (e.g. Brown) results in impaired recall of the remaining items from those same practiced categories (e.g. Pink) as compared to control items from unpracticed categories (Banana). This RIF effect is quite robust, and has been demonstrated with a variety of materials and empirical manipulations (for reviews, see Anderson, 2003; Murayama, Miyatsu, Buchli, & Storm, 2014; Raaijmakers & Jakab, 2013; Storm & Levy, 2012).

To explain the memory impairment seen in RIF, Anderson et al. (1994) proposed a suppression-based retrieval mechanism. One of the basic assumptions of this hypothesis is that multiple items from practiced categories are in competition for activation by the shared retrieval cue (the category label) during retrieval practice, based on preexisting semantic relationships. This competition elicits suppression of non-target competing items in order to increase the probability of correct retrieval of the target items. The result of this suppression, however, is impaired recall of the suppressed items on the final memory test. Although Anderson et al.'s (1994) seminal research proposed an inhibition-based accounting of RIF, it is important to note that there has been considerable debate as to the nature of the underlying retrieval mechanism [see Storm and Levy (2012) for a summary of arguments supporting inhibition theory and Raaijmakers and Jakab (2013) for a summary of arguments against].

One of the critical properties in Anderson et al.'s (1994), theoretical account of RIF is its dependence on associative response competition. In additional studies, Anderson et al. (1994) found that unpracticed items from practiced categories are more likely to be suppressed when they are high-frequency exemplars of the category rather than low-frequency exemplars. This would indicate that items which compete most strongly with retrieval are more likely to be inhibited. Other researchers have provided additional evidence that RIF is a product of response competition. For example, Shivde and Anderson (2001) designed a RIF paradigm using homographs as categories. Exemplars of both their dominant and subordinate meanings were used. Words relating to the homograph's dominant meeting were inhibited more than words related to its subordinate meaning. Also, Storm, Bjork, and Bjork (2007) demonstrated that items on lists that participants are instructed to remember are more susceptible to the effects of RIF than items on lists that participants are instructed to forget (see also Bäuml & Samenieh, 2010, 2012).

Based on the above findings, the response competition assumption predicts that suppression elicited during retrieval practice is cue independent, and can be generalized to any item in memory that may compete with the target item, based on preexisting semantic relationships, for activation from the common retrieval cue (Anderson & Spellman, 1995). Evidence in support of this prediction has been found using an independent cue technique. This is a modified version of the retrieval-practice paradigm which has been expanded to include exemplars that could be related to more than one category label (e.g. Red—Blood, Red—Tomato and Food—Strawberry, Food—Crackers; Anderson & Spellman, 1995). It is important to note here that the exemplars Tomato and Strawberry, although studied with different category label cues, can actually each be considered members of both categories based on preexisting semantic relationships. Performance results from the final recall test typically show evidence of cross-category impairment. That is, when practiced items (Red—Blood) are related to exemplars from non-practiced categories (Food—Strawberry) impairment of the non-practiced items (Food—Strawberry) is seen on the final recall test. Based on these studies, it would appear that suppression does, in fact, generalize to any item in memory that might be activated by a practiced category label and therefore compete with the target item for retrieval.

Subsequent studies have also demonstrated cue-independent impairment when using independent (novel) cues during the final memory test (Anderson, 2003; Anderson & Bell, 2001; Anderson et al., 1994; Anderson, Bjork, & Bjork, 2000; Levy & Anderson, 2002; Saunders & MacLeod, 2006; Shivde & Anderson, 2001). To date, however, studies investigating the response competition and cue independence assumptions of RIF theory have resulted in a somewhat inconsistent body of literature in which some researchers have found additional evidence supporting cue-independent forgetting (Anderson, Green, & McCulloch, 2000; Anderson & Spellman, 1995; Hulbert, Shivde, & Anderson, 2011; Johnson & Anderson, 2004; MacLeod & Saunders, 2005; Saunders & MacLeod, 2006), while others have not (Camp, Pecher, & Schmidt, 2007; Perfect, Stark, Tree, Moulin, Ahmed, & Hutter, 2004; Williams & Zacks, 2001). Still other researchers have demonstrated that preexisting category-exemplar associations are not solely necessary in order for RIF to occur. For example, Jakab and Raaijmakers (2009) manipulated both study position and number of learning trials and found that, while both increased general recall performance, neither moderated the amount of RIF. Additionally, Tempel and Frings (2014) demonstrated that episodic categorization will also suffice to elicit the RIF effect by using non-word letter strings organized into arbitrary categories.

In light of the inconsistent results found in the literature regarding the response competition assumption and evidence found using independent retrieval cues, it is important to address effects of response competition in the retrieval-practice paradigm. As mentioned previously, it is commonly accepted that suppression occurs as a result of response competition for a shared retrieval cue which arises during the retrieval-practice phase. Therefore, the impairment seen for those competing items on a later memory test is a residual effect of the suppression elicited by earlier retrieval during the practice session, and not a direct result of competition occurring during retrieval of items during the memory test. Typically, the effects of retrieval-induced suppression have been found only in conditions where there is competition for a semantically shared retrieval cue; that is, in conditions which do not use individual item-specific information as a cue for item retrieval (Bäuml, 2008; Butler, Williams, Zacks, & Maki, 2001; Camp et al., 2007; Verde, 2009). Traditionally, in the standard retrieval practice paradigm, items are presented during the study phase in category—exemplar pairs, practiced as category—stem completion pairs, and then tested using category labels as retrieval cues. Thus, in this paradigm, the category label is a common retrieval cue used in all three phases of the paradigm. It may be predicted, therefore, that as long as category labels are used as both study and retrieval cues, competition will ensue, resulting in suppression of non-target items. If this competition is alleviated, then RIF should be attenuated and, if this competition is eliminated, then RIF should not occur at all. Some studies have investigated the response competition assumption of RIF by designing conditions in which competition is alleviated during the practice phase (Anderson, Green, et al., 2000; Anderson & McCulloch, 1999; Migueles & García-Bajos, 2007). In these studies, reducing competition resulted in less RIF seen on a final recall test.

The current study attempted to investigate the role of response competition by modifying the retrieval-practice paradigm in two novel ways: first, by presenting the study items without the presence of category labels and second, by utilizing an independent cue during the retrieval-practice phase. This manipulation was designed to eliminate response competition by de-emphasizing the semantic relationships between studied items. This should eliminate the need for suppression, thereby eliminating the RIF effect. In addition, a recognition test will be used for the final memory test to assess RIF. Most of the studies investigating RIF, including the ones mentioned above, have used final cued recall tests to assess RIF; however, some researchers have argued that recognition tests may provide an additional way of assessing both the assumptions of response competition and cue independence in RIF (Gómez-Ariza, Lechuga, Pelegrina, & Bajo, 2005; Hicks & Starns, 2004; Spitzer & Bäuml, 2007). Due to their item-specific nature, and the use of studied items themselves as cues, recognition tests should circumvent any episodic interference due to category-exemplar associations. Therefore, the argument has been made that observation of RIF seen using final recognition tests supports both the assumptions of response competition and cue independence (Román, Soriano, Gómez-Ariza, & Bajo, 2009; Spitzer & Bäuml, 2007, 2009; Starns & Hicks, 2004;

Veling & van Knippenberg, 2004; Verde, 2004). That is, response competition occurring during the retrieval-practice phase is caused by the preexisting semantic relationships between items competing for a shared cue (the category label). This competition causes the inhibition of competing items, and this inhibition is reflected in memory impairment for competing items on the final recognition test.

2. Experiment 1

The first experiment was an attempt to replicate RIF effects found in recall studies by other researchers, as well as to serve as an experimental baseline for Experiment 2. A retrieval-practice paradigm similar to the original one used by Anderson et al. (1994), was used in Experiment 1, with the exceptions that the study list included individual exemplars (e.g. Pink, Banana, Tulip, and Elbow), as is typically used in studies of item recognition, rather than category-exemplar pairs (e.g. Color—Pink, Fruit—Banana, Flower—Tulip, and Body Part—Elbow) and the final test was one of item recognition instead of cued recall. Based on the active suppression hypothesis, it was predicted that recognition hit rates would reflect the same empirical pattern as recall rates seen in previous studies. That is, it was expected that hit rates for practiced items would be significantly higher than hit rates for control items (unpracticed items from categories that were not practiced during the retrieval-practice phase), while at the same time it was expected that hit rates for unpracticed items from practiced categories would be significantly lower than hit rates for control items from unpracticed categories.

2.1. Method

2.1.1. Participants

Sixty-two students from introductory psychology classes participated to fulfill a class requirement.

2.1.2. Design

A standard retrieval-practice paradigm was utilized, consisting of three main phases: a study phase, a retrieval-practice phase, and a final test phase, with a distractor task separating the practice phase from the test phase. This design created three particular types of test items: practiced items from practiced categories (Rp+), non-practiced items from practiced categories (Rp−), and non-practiced items from non-practiced categories (Nrp). This results in a 2 × 3 repeated measures design, with factors including word status (old versus new) and practice condition (Rp+, Rp−, and Nrp). The dependent variable measured was the number of positive ("yes") responses in a standard yes/no test of item recognition.

2.1.3. Materials

Target stimuli consisted of 12 exemplars from eight common semantic categories (*Animal, Color, Fruit, Furniture, Weapon, Body Parts, Occupation*, and *Musical Instruments*), plus four exemplars from three additional categories (*Flower, Clothing*, and *Fabric*) which were used as buffer/filler items and not tested. Category labels were chosen to be as unrelated to each other as possible. For example, both *Vegetable* and *Fruit* were not used as categories, because exemplars from both could be considered belonging to an additional, related category *Food*. The words chosen for each category consisted of the 12 items with the largest response proportions for that category according to free association norms published by Van Overschelde, Rawson, and Dunlosky (2004). Items that contained the same first two letters as a previous list item in the same category were substituted with the next most qualified item in that category. Exemplars that could possibly fit into more than one category (e.g. *Orange*, which could be considered an exemplar for both the *Fruit* and *Color* categories) were omitted and replaced in the same fashion.

Experiment 1 presented the study items without the presence of a category label. The study list consisted of 54 exemplars, divided into six exemplars from each of the eight target categories, plus two primacy/recency buffers from the three buffer categories that were not tested. Practice booklets were designed for use during the retrieval-practice phase. Four of the eight categories were used for subsequent retrieval practice (designated Rp), while items from the remaining four categories did not receive additional retrieval practice (designated Nrp). The Rp categories were further divided into exemplars that were practiced (Rp+) and not practiced (Rp−). Recognition status (presented/new) and item status (Rp+, Rp−, Nrp) for each category and exemplar were counterbalanced, resulting in eight different study list/retrieval practice combinations, so that each item appeared equally as often as a presented or new item and equally as often in each item status (Rp+, Rp−, Nrp). Practice booklets contained 12 designated target items and three filler items (one item from each of the three buffer categories). A category name and the first two letters of a target exemplar (e.g. Fruit—Ap___) were printed in the center of each page and participants were instructed to complete the stem with a word that had been previously presented on the study list.

The final memory test consisted of a standard 96-item yes–no recognition test in which half of the items were old and half new. The initial order of test items for each group was randomly determined, and the test items were given in the same presentation order on the recognition test for all members of each group. Because each individual received a different retrieval practice booklet, the order of presentation of Rp+, Rp−, Nrp, and new items on the recognition test was counterbalanced so that each type of item appeared before the other types of items equally as often. This was done in an effort to balance effects of output interference.

2.1.4. Procedure

The study list consisted of 54 exemplars, divided into six exemplars from each of the eight target categories, plus two primacy/recency buffers from the three buffer categories that were not tested. The eight counterbalanced study list/retrieval practice combinations were presented to separate groups of participants. Each testing session consisted of a group of 15–20 students. Participants were seated in classroom style, and all study and test items were projected onto a large screen in the front of the room. The study list was presented one word at a time and each word remained on the screen for 2 s. Participants were instructed to pay equal attention to each word as it appeared on the screen, and were informed that a memory test for the study list would be given at the end of the session.

Following the initial study phase, participants completed a retrieval-practice phase consisting of a word stem completion task. Practice booklets contained 12 designated target items and three filler items (one item from each of the three buffer categories). A category name and the first two letters of a target exemplar (e.g. Fruit—Ap___) were printed in the center of each page and participants were instructed to complete the stem with a word that had been previously presented on the study list. The last three pages of the test booklet consisted of a distractor phase in which subjects completed a series of simple math problems. This task was designed to keep subjects occupied for a period of approximately 5 min.

When all participants had completed their test booklets, a memory test was presented on the screen one item at a time. The test items appeared one at a time, accompanied by the question "Did this item appear on the study list?" and remained on the screen for a duration of 6 s. Participants were given answer sheets and instructed to mark YES on the answer sheet if the test word had appeared previously on the study list and to mark NO if it had not appeared on the list. Following presentation of the last test item, all booklets and answer sheets were collected and the testing session ended.

2.2. Results

Hit and false-alarm rates are shown in Table 1. An α level of 0.05 was used as the standard of significance for all tests unless otherwise stated. A RIF effect was reflected in the pattern of recognition hit rates, which followed the order Rp+ > Nrp > Rp−. Retrieving items from a given category (Rp+) reduced the ability to recognize unpracticed words (Rp−) from the same practiced category during a later recognition test relative to baseline items (Nrp) from unpracticed categories.

Table 1. Mean proportion of positive recognition responses as a function of retrieval practice condition in Experiment 1

Retrieval practice condition	Item status			
	Old (hit rate)		New (false-alarm rate)	
		S.D.		S.D.
Rp+	0.92	0.09	0.15	0.11
Nrp	0.70	0.13	0.14	0.11
Rp−	0.65	0.16	0.15	0.11

Notes: Values are mean proportions of positive recognition responses made to presented (hit) and new (false-alarm) items. The false-alarm rates to new Rp+ and new Rp− items represent a common proportion ("yes" responses to new items from practiced categories).

2.2.1. Retrieval practice

In the retrieval practice phase, 87% of the items were correctly completed, indicating successful retrieval of target items.

2.2.2. Analysis of variance

An analysis of variance (ANOVA) on numbers of positive responses found significant main effects of both item status (old versus new), $F(1, 61) = 502.89$, MSe = 5.29, and practice condition, $F(2, 122) = 28.60$, MSe = 0.19, as well as a significant interaction between these two factors, $F(2, 122) = 624.71$, MSe = 18.57.

2.2.3. Hit rates

Mean performance in the test phase reflected a typical RIF effect for hit rates. That is, Rp+ items were recognized at higher proportion (92%) than Nrp (70%) items and Rp− items (65%), while Rp− items were recognized at a lower proportion than Nrp items and Rp+ items. The effect of practice condition was significant for hits, $F(2, 122) = 46.55$, MSe = 0.49. Pairwise comparisons of hit rates confirmed the differences: the hit rate for Rp+ items was significantly different from the hit rates for both Nrp items [$t(61) = 8.60$] and Rp− items [$t(61) = 7.91$], and the hit rate for Rp− items was significantly different from the hit rate for Nrp items, $t(61) = 2.01$.

2.2.4. Accuracy

In order to take false alarms into account, d' was compared to reflect overall recognition accuracy. The pattern of recognition accuracy was the same as the pattern for hit rates: Rp+ > Nrp > Rp−. The comparison of d' between Nrp and Rp+ items was found to be significant, $t(61) = 5.39$. The comparison of d' between Nrp and Rp− items was also found to be significant, $t(61) = 3.31$. This indicates that RIF was reflected in overall recognition accuracy as well as in recognition hit rates.

2.3. Discussion

The results seen here reflect both a benefit of retrieval practice for practiced (Rp+) items and an impairment of related, non-practiced (Rp−) items in later recognition as compared to baseline (Nrp) words from non-practiced categories. Recognition hit rates showed the same empirical pattern as performance rates seen in recall studies. Experiment 1 presented the study items without the presence of a category label. Participants, therefore, were expecting to see a list of individual words, not words that belong to specific categories, thereby de-emphasizing the importance of the category—exemplar association.

3. Experiment 2

Experiment 2 utilized an independent retrieval cue during the retrieval-practice phase in an attempt to circumvent the response competition proposed to give rise to retrieval-induced impairment of unpracticed competing items. For example, if retrieval practice occurs in the form of *Fruit—Banana* (or *Animal—Bear, Color—Blue*), then any unpracticed target items that would strongly compete with the target word (*Banana, Bear, Blue*) for the category label cue (*Fruit, Animal, Color*) would be suppressed during retrieval practice of the target word (*Banana, Bear, Blue*) and the result of this suppression would be evident in retrieval impairment of these competing items (e.g. *Apple, Dog, Red*) on the final memory test. However, it was predicted that recall elicited by an independent practice cue would not cause response competition during the retrieval-practice phase. That is, if the retrieval cue *Monkey* (or *Grizzly, Sky*) was used during the retrieval-practice phase to elicit retrieval of the target item *Banana* (*Bear, Blue*), then it would not be expected to cause suppression of the other exemplars from the *Fruit* (*Animal, Color*) category, as the cue *Monkey* (*Grizzly, Sky*) was not a commonly shared cue, making suppression unnecessary. Therefore, no evidence of RIF would be predicted if an independent cue was used during the practice phase.

3.1. Method

3.1.1. Participants

Eighty-two participants consisted of students from introductory psychology classes, who participated to fulfill a class requirement.

3.1.2. Design

The same 2 × 3 repeated measures design was used as in Experiment 1, with factors including word status (old versus new) and practice condition (Rp+, Rp−, and Nrp). The dependent variable measured was the number of positive ("yes") responses in a standard yes/no test of item recognition.

3.1.3. Materials

The target stimuli used during the presentation and testing phases were identical to those used in Experiment 1. The retrieval-practice phase used independent cues instead of category labels to elicit retrieval of the target items. Independent cues were defined as cues that were unrelated to the shared category cue, but sufficiently related to the practice target item to elicit retrieval. For example, the study list contained exemplars from the *Fruit* category, including *Banana*, *Apple* and *Cranberry*. For retrieval practice of the target item *Banana*, an independent cue, *Monkey*, was used instead of the shared category label *Fruit* (used in Experiment 1). Independent cues were chosen according to normative data from Nelson, McEvoy, and Schreiber (1998; Appendix B). Cues were chosen according to strength of the forward association connection between the cue and the target (the probability that the cue will elicit retrieval of the target item). The item with the strongest forward connection was chosen unless that item could be confused as a member of another category, in which case the next strongest item was chosen. For the small number of target items that did not have normative data listed, an independent cue was arbitrarily assigned by the experimenter.

3.1.4. Procedure

The current experiment used the same experimental procedure as used in Experiment 1 except that an independent cue was used instead of the category label during the retrieval-practice phase in order to directly assess the effect of response competition in the practice phase.

3.2. Results

Hit and false-alarm rates are shown in Table 2. A RIF effect was reflected in the pattern of recognition hit rates, which followed the order Rp+ > Nrp > Rp−. Retrieving items from a given category (Rp+) reduced the ability to recognize unpracticed words (Rp−) from the same practiced category during a later recognition test relative to baseline items (Nrp) from unpracticed categories.

3.2.1. Retrieval practice

In the retrieval practice phase, 78% of the items were correctly completed, indicating successful retrieval of target items.

Table 2. Mean proportion of positive recognition responses as a function of retrieval practice condition in Experiment 2

Retrieval practice condition	Item status			
	Old (hit rate)		New (false-alarm rate)	
		S.D.		S.D.
Rp+	0.94	0.09	0.16	0.17
Nrp	0.83	0.12	0.18	0.15
Rp−	0.76	0.15	0.16	0.17

Notes: Values are mean proportions of positive recognition responses made to presented (hit) and new (false-alarm) items. The false-alarm rates to new Rp+ and new Rp− items represent a common proportion ("yes" responses to new items from practiced categories).

3.2.2. Analysis of variance

An ANOVA on numbers of positive responses found significant main effects of both item status (old vs. new), $F(1, 81) = 460.86$, MSe = 24.62, and practice condition, $F(2, 162) = 18.30$, MSe = 0.15, as well as a significant interaction between these two factors, $F(2, 162) = 23.71$, MSe = 0.15.

3.2.3. Hit rates

Mean performance in the test phase reflected a typical RIF effect for hit rates. That is, Rp+ items were recognized at higher proportion (94%) than Nrp (83%) items and Rp− items (76%), while Rp− items were recognized at a lower proportion than Nrp items and Rp+ items. The effect of practice condition was significant for hits, $F(2, 162) = 30.67$, MSe = 0.30. Pairwise comparisons of hit rates confirmed the differences: the hit rate for Rp+ items was significantly different from hit rates for both Nrp items [$t(81) = 5.12$] and Rp− items [$t(81) = 7.17$], and the hit rate for Rp− items was significantly different from the hit rate for Nrp items, $t(81) = 3.14$.

3.2.4. Accuracy

As in Experiment 1, d' was compared to reflect overall recognition accuracy. The pattern of recognition accuracy was the same as the pattern for hit rates: Rp+ > Nrp > Rp−. The comparison of d' between Nrp and Rp+ items was found to be significant, $t(81) = 8.08$, $p < 0.01$. The comparison of d' between Nrp and Rp− items was also found to be significant, $t(81) = 2.87$, $p < 0.01$. This indicates that RIF was reflected in overall recognition accuracy as well as in recognition hit rates.

3.3. Discussion

Clear evidence of RIF was seen when independent cues were used for the retrieval-practice phase. This result, combined with the results from Experiment 1, draw into question the assumption that the impairment seen in RIF is caused by semantic competition for a shared retrieval cue that arises during the retrieval-practice phase.

It may be tempting, however, to assume that the evidence of RIF seen in the current experiment is the result of covert cueing by the participants, which could result in covert retrieval practice other than the type intended by the independent cue manipulation. For example, during the retrieval-practice phase it is possible that participants see the independent cue *Monkey*, which elicits retrieval of the studied item *Banana*. Along with this retrieval, participants may also remember that *Banana* was one of the "fruits" that they had seen on the study list. This would serve the same purpose as using the category cue itself as a retrieval cue and result in unintended retrieval competition. Although the effect of covert retrieval practice in RIF has not yet been directly addressed, there is some evidence from studies of part-list cueing and the list-strength effect that appear to indicate that most individuals do not engage in covert retrieval practice unless they are specifically encouraged to do so (Bäuml & Aslan, 2004; Verde, 2009). In the current study, the category labels were not used during presentation of the study list, so there was no direct encouragement for participants to use them for covert retrieval cues in the retrieval-practice phase. If covert retrieval practice is not a common occurrence, then it is not entirely persuasive as an explanation of the results seen in this study. In addition, Anderson (2003) hypothesized that covert cueing, because it provides the subject with multiple retrieval cues, should not inherently produce forgetting and may actually reduce, rather than enhance, the RIF effect in studies utilizing independent cues.

If covert cueing is occurring, it may be impossible to completely eliminate response competition among all of the items, as subjects' previous knowledge may interfere with the experimental manipulation when the study items have a strong semantic relationship. If response competition is not completely eliminated, then it could be expected that the independent cue manipulation would, at least, serve to de-emphasize (and thus weaken) the semantic connection between practiced items and result in an attenuation of the RIF effect. An examination of the means from the two experiments in Tables 1 and 2 shows the difference in performance between the two groups was minimal, and a direct statistical comparison confirms the difference in performance between the two groups was not significant.

4. General discussion

Evidence from the experiments presented here suggests that the RIF seen on a final recognition memory test may not be solely influenced by semantic response competition that occurs during the retrieval-practice phase. Evidence of RIF was seen in two experiments using an item recognition test in the final phase of the retrieval-practice paradigm. Both recognition hit rates and overall recognition accuracy were higher for practiced items from practiced categories (Rp+ items) than for items from unpracticed categories, but this increase in performance for practiced items was accompanied by a decrement in performance for unpracticed items from these same practiced categories (Rp− items). Recognition performance for the unpracticed items (Rp− items) showed hit rates that were significantly lower than both practiced items and control items from unpracticed categories (Nrp items). This RIF was seen even with the use of independent cues during the retrieval-practice phase. Rp− items continued to show evidence of impairment as opposed to Nrp items even though response competition that would normally take place during the retrieval-practice phase was circumvented by the use of non-shared retrieval cues.

4.1. Interference versus inhibition

These results seem to question the response competition assumption made by Anderson (2003) and Anderson et al. (1994) in his original explanation of RIF. According to this assumption, suppression occurs as a result of items in memory competing, based on pre-existing semantic relationships, for a shared retrieval cue (the category label) during the retrieval-practice phase. It follows from this hypothesis that if the retrieval cue used during the practice phase is an independent, rather than shared, cue, then competition would not ensue and suppression would not be necessary.

A discussion of an alternate explanation of RIF, based on non-inhibitory accounts, may be useful here. According to these accounts, successful memory retrieval is based on the relative strengths of associations between competing memory items and their retrieval cues. Retrieval practice of cue-target item increases the strength of the association between that particular cue-target combination, therefore producing associative interference on a subsequent memory test. This interference blocks retrieval of the unstudied items, resulting in impaired memory performance (Gillund & Shiffrin, 1984; Mensink & Raaijmakers, 1988; Raaijmakers & Shiffrin, 1981; Rundus, 1973). This is a result of strengthening of some of the studied items during retrieval practice. This strengthening of individual items would be predicted to occur regardless of the retrieval cue used. However, previous studies have shown that simply strengthening individual studied items (i.e. through repeated presentations) does not elicit RIF (Anderson, Bjork, et al., 2000; Bauml, 2002; Hulbert et al., 2011; Saunders, Fernandes, & Kosnes, 2009).

In their investigation into the RIF effect, Perfect et al. (2004) found evidence of memory impairment only when memory for the studied items was tested with their original study cues. These findings were interpreted as evidence of transfer-appropriate forgetting, and it was concluded that RIF is both context-, and cue-dependent. Subsequent recall studies have supported this hypothesis

(Camp et al., 2007; Camp, Pecher, Schmidt, & Zeelenberg, 2009). Results from the current study would appear to support a hypothesis of transfer-appropriate forgetting, as the criteria for transfer-appropriate forgetting were met in both Experiment 1 and Experiment 2: that is, the study conditions and final testing conditions did match, and significant RIF was found. It should be noted that these results are similar to those found in several recent recall studies questioning the inhibition account of RIF (Hanczakowski & Mazzoni, 2013; Jonker, Seli, & MacLeod, 2013; Raaijmakers & Jakab, 2012; Storm & Nestojko, 2010; but also see Grundgelger, 2014).

4.2. Recall versus recognition

As mentioned previously, results from Experiment 1 confirm evidence already seen in recall studies. Results from Experiment 2, however, do not show such agreement with similar manipulations done in recall studies. It was predicted that recall elicited by an independent practice cue would not cause response competition during the retrieval practice phase, thus eliminating (or reducing) memory impairment on the final recognition test. This hypothesis was not supported; however, as a significant RIF effect was still found even with the use of an independent cue. This finding, although contrary to prediction, may be seen as evidence of another property of RIF known as retrieval specificity (see Anderson, 2003; Hulbert et al., 2011, for a review).

According to retrieval specificity, RIF is dependent upon active retrieval of studied items. The cued recall tests typically used in RIF studies decidedly emphasize active recollection of studied items. Recognition decisions however, may not be based on conscious recollection to the same extent as recall performance (Verde & Perfect, 2011). That is, recognition decisions may also be influenced by relative familiarity of the test items. Single- and dual-process theorists have argued extensively over the differential contributions made by recollective and familiarity-based retrieval processes in recall and recognition decisions (see Ratcliff & McKoon, 2000, for a review). Other variables, such as normative word frequency, have been shown to affect recognition and recall processes differently (Gregg, 1976). Perhaps, the impairment seen in RIF is another example of this type of dissociation. Future research should focus on the differences seen in RIF between recall and recognition tasks in order to learn how and why it happens. This may provide a better picture of the actual mechanism underlying the effect.

Funding
The authors received no direct funding for this research.

Competing interests
The author declares no competing interests.

Author details
Gina A. Glanc[1]
E-mail: gina.glanc@tamucc.edu
[1] Department of Psychology & Sociology, Texas A&M University Corpus Christi, 6300 Ocean Drive, Corpus Christi, TX 78412, USA.

References

Allen, G. A., Mahler, W. A., & Estes, W. K. (1969). Effects of recall tests on long-term retention of paired associates. *Journal of Verbal Learning and Verbal Behavior, 8*, 463–470. doi:10.1016/S0022-5371(69)80090-3

Anderson, M. C. (2003). Rethinking interference theory: Executive control and the mechanisms of forgetting. *Journal of Memory and Language, 49*, 415–445. doi:10.1016/j.jml.2003.08.006

Anderson, M. C., & Bell, T. (2001). Forgetting our facts: The role of inhibitory processes in the loss of propositional knowledge. *Journal of Experimental Psychology: General, 130*, 544–570. doi:10.1037/0096-3445.130.3.544

Anderson, M. C., Bjork, E. L., & Bjork, R. A. (2000). Retrieval-induced forgetting: Evidence for a recall-specific mechanism. *Psychonomic Bulleting & Review, 7*, 522–530. doi:10.3758/BF03214366

Anderson, M. C., Bjork, R. A., & Bjork, E. L. (1994). Remembering can cause forgetting: Retrieval dynamics in long-term memory. *Journal of Experimental Psychology: Learning, Memory, and Cognition, 20*, 1063–1087. doi:10.1037/0278-7393.20.5.1063

Anderson, M. C., Green, C., & McCulloch, K. C. (2000). Similarity and inhibition in long-term memory: Evidence for a two-factor theory. *Journal of Experimental Psychology: Learning, Memory, and Cognition, 26*, 1141–1159. doi:10.1037/0278-7393.26.5.1141

Anderson, M. C., & McCulloch, K. C. (1999). Integration as a general boundary condition on retrieval-induced forgetting. *Journal of Experimental Psychology: Learning, Memory, and Cognition, 25*, 608–629. doi:10.1037/0278-7393.25.3.608

Anderson, M. C., & Spellman, B. A. (1995). On the status of inhibitory mechanisms in cognition: Memory retrieval as a model case. *Psychological Review, 102*, 68–100. doi:10.1037/0033-295X.102.1.68

Bauml, K.-H. (2002). Semantic generation can cause episodic forgetting. *Psychological Science, 13*, 356–360. doi:10.1111/j.0956-7976.2002.00464.x

Bäuml, K. -H. (2008). Inhibitory processes. In J. H. Byrne & H. L. Roediger III (Eds.), *Learning and memory:*

A comprehensive reference (pp. 195–220). Oxford: Elsevier. http://dx.doi.org/10.1016/B978-012370509-9.00155-8

Bäuml, K.-H., & Aslan, A. (2004). Part-list cuing as instructed retrieval inhibition. *Memory & Cognition, 31*, 610–617. doi:10.3758/BF03195852

Bäuml, K.-H. T., & Samenieh, A. (2012). Selective memory retrieval can impair and improve retrieval of other memories. *Journal of Experimental Psychology: Learning, Memory, and Cognition, 38*, 488–494. doi:10.1037/a0025683

Bäuml, K.-H. T., & Samenieh, A. (2010). The two faces of memory retrieval. *Psychological Science, 21*, 793–795. doi:10.1177/0956797610370162

Butler, K. M., Williams, C. C., Zacks, R. T., & Maki, R. H. (2001). Observation: A limit on retrieval-induced forgetting. *Journal of Experimental Psychology: Learning, Memory, and Cognition, 27*, 1314–1319. doi:10.1037/0278-7393.27.5.1314

Camp, G., Pecher, D., & Schmidt, H. G. (2007). No retrieval-induced forgetting using item-specific independent cues: Evidence against a general inhibitory account. *Journal of Experimental Psychology: Learning, Memory, and Cognition, 33*, 950–958. doi:10.1037/0278-7393.33.5.950

Camp, G., Pecher, D., Schmidt, H. G., & Zeelenberg, R. (2009). Are independent probes truly independent? *Journal of Experimental Psychology: Learning, Memory, and Cognition, 35*, 934–942. doi:10.1037/a0015536

Carrier, M., & Pashler, H. (1992). The influence of retrieval on retention. *Memory & Cognition, 20*, 633–642. doi:10.3758/BF03202713

Gardiner, J. M., Craik, F. I. M., & Bleasdale, F. A. (1973). Retrieval difficulty and subsequent recall. *Memory & Cognition, 1*, 213–216. doi:10.3758/BF03198098

Gillund, G., & Shiffrin, R. M. (1984). A retrieval model for both recognition and recall. *Psychological Review, 91*(1), 1–67. doi:10.1037/0033-295X.91.1.1

Gómez-Ariza, C. J., Lechuga, M. T., Pelegrina, S., & Bajo, M. T. (2005). Retrieval-induced forgetting in recall and recognition of thematically related and unrelated sentences. *Memory & Cognition, 33*, 1431–1441. doi:10.3758/Bf03193376

Gotts, A., & Jacoby, L. L. (1974). Encoding and retrieval processes in long-term retention. *Journal of Experimental Psychology, 102*, 291–297. doi:10.1037/h0035892

Gregg, V. (1976). Word frequency, recognition and recall. In J. Brown (Ed.), *Recall and recognition* (pp. 183–216). New York, NY: Wiley.

Grundgelger, T. (2014). Noncompetitive retrieval practice causes retrieval-induced forgetting in cued recall but not in recognition. *Memory & Cognition, 42*, 400–408. doi:10.3758/s13421-013-0372-z

Hanczakowski, M., & Mazzoni, G. (2013). Contextual match and cue-independence of retrieval-induced forgetting: Testing the prediction of the model by Norman, Newman, and Detre (2007). *Journal of Experimental Psychology: Learning, Memory, and Cognition, 39*, 953–958.

Hicks, J. L., & Starns, J. J. (2004). Retrieval-induced forgetting occurs in tests of item recognition. *Psychonomic Bulletin & Review, 11*, 125–130. doi:10.3758/BF03206471

Hulbert, J. C., Shivde, G., & Anderson, M. C. (2011). Evidence against associative blocking as a cause of cue-independent retrieval-induced forgetting. *Experimental Psychology, 59*, 11–21. doi:10.1027/1618-3169/a000120

Jakab, E., & Raaijmakers, J. G. W. (2009). The role of item strength in retrieval-induced forgetting. *Journal of Experimental Psychology: Learning, Memory and Cognition, 35*, 607–617. doi:10.1027/a0015264

Johnson, S. K., & Anderson, M. C. (2004). The role of inhibitory control in forgetting semantic knowledge. *Psychological Science, 15*, 448–453. doi:10.1111/j.0956-7976.2004.00700.x

Jonker, T. R., Seli, P., & MacLeod, C. M. (2013). Putting retrieval-induced forgetting in context: An inhibition-free, context-based account. *Psychological Review, 120*, 852–872. doi:10.1037/a0034246

Levy, B. J., & Anderson, M. C. (2002). Inhibitory processes and the control of memory retrieval. *Trends in Cognitive Sciences, 6*, 299–305. doi:10.1016/S1364-6613(02)01923-X

MacLeod, M. D., & Saunders, J. (2005). The role of inhibitory control in the production of misinformation effects. *Journal of Experimental Psychology: Learning, Memory, and Cognition, 31*, 964–979. doi:10.1037/0278-7393.31.5.964

Mensink, G.-J., & Raaijmakers, J. G. W. (1988). A model for interference and forgetting. *Psychological Review, 95*, 434–455. doi:10.1037/0033-295X.95.4.434

Migueles, M., & García-Bajos, E. (2007). Selective retrieval and induced forgetting in eyewitness memory. *Applied Cognitive Psychology, 21*, 1157–1172. doi:10.1002/acp.1323

Murayama, K., Miyatsu, T., Buchli, D., & Storm, B. C. (2014). Forgetting as a consequence of retrieval: A meta-analytic review of retrieval-induced forgetting. *Psychological Bulletin, 140*, 1383–1409. doi:10.1037/a0037505

Nelson, D. L., McEvoy, C. L., & Schreiber, T. A. (1998). *The University of South Florida word association, rhyme, and word fragment norms*. Retrieved from http://www.usf.edu/FreeAssociation/

Perfect, T. J., Stark, L.-J., Tree, J. J., Moulin, C. J. A., Ahmed, L., & Hutter, R. (2004). Transfer appropriate forgetting: The cue-dependent nature of retrieval-induced forgetting. *Journal of Memory and Language, 51*, 399–417. doi:10.1016/j.jml.2004.06.003

Raaijmakers, J. G. W., & Jakab, E. (2012). Retrieval-induced forgetting without competition: Testing the retrieval specificity assumption of the inhibition theory. *Memory & Cognition, 40*, 19–27. doi:10.3758/s13421-011-0131-y

Raaijmakers, J. G. W., & Jakab, E. (2013). Rethinking inhibition theory: On the problematic status of the inhibition theory for forgetting. *Journal of Memory and Language, 68*, 98–122. doi:10.1016/j.jml.2012.10.002

Raaijmakers, J. G. W., & Shiffrin, R. M. (1981). Search of associative memory. *Psychological Review, 88*, 93–134. doi:10.1037/0033-295X.88.2.93

Ratcliff, R., & McKoon, G. (2000). Memory models. In E. Tulving & F. I. M. Craik (Eds.), *The oxford handbook of memory* (pp. 571–581). New York, NY: Oxford University Press.

Román, P., Soriano, M. F., Gómez-Ariza, C. J., & Bajo, M. T. (2009). Retrieval-induced forgetting and executive control. *Psychological Science, 20*, 1053–1058. doi:10.1111/j.1467-9280.2009.02415.x

Rundus, D. (1973). Negative effects of using list items as recall cues. *Journal of Verbal Learning and Verbal Behavior, 12*, 43–50. http://dx.doi.org/10.1016/S0022-5371(73)80059-3

Saunders, J., Fernandes, M., & Kosnes, L. (2009). Retrieval-induced forgetting and mental imagery. *Memory & Cognition, 37*, 819–828. doi:10.3758/MC.37.6.819

Saunders, J., & MacLeod, M. D. (2006). Can inhibition resolve retrieval competition through the control of spreading activation? *Memory & Cognition, 34*, 307–322. doi:10.3758/BF03193409

Shivde, G., & Anderson, M. C. (2001). The role of inhibition in meaning selection: Insights from retrieval-induced forgetting. In D. Gorfein (Ed.), *On the consequences of meaning selection: Perspectives on resolving lexical ambiguity* (pp. 175–190). Washington, DC: American Psychological Association. doi:10.1037/10459-010

Spitzer, B., & Bäuml, K.-H. (2007). Retrieval-induced forgetting in item recognition: Evidence for a reduction in general memory strength. *Journal of Experimental Psychology: Learning, Memory, and Cognition, 33*, 863–875. doi:10.1037/0278-7393.33.5.863

Spitzer, B., & Bäuml, K.-H. (2009). Retrieval-induced forgetting in a category recognition task. *Journal of Experimental Psychology: Learning, Memory, and Cognition, 35*, 286–291. doi:10.1037/a0014363

Starns, J. J., & Hicks, J. L. (2004). Episodic generation can cause semantic forgetting: Retrieval-induced forgetting of false memories. *Memory & Cognition, 32*, 602–609. doi:10.3758/BF03195851

Storm, B. C., Bjork, E. L., & Bjork, R. A. (2007). When intended remembering leads to unintended forgetting. *The Quarterly Journal of Experimental Psychology, 60*, 909–915. doi:10.1080/17470210701288706

Storm, B. C., & Levy, B. J. (2012). A progress report on the inhibitory account of retrieval-induced forgetting. *Memory & Cognition, 40*, 827–843. doi:10.3758/s13421-012-0211-7

Storm, B. C., & Nestojko, J. F. (2010). Successful inhibition, unsuccessful retrieval: Manipulating time and success during retrieval practice. *Memory, 18*, 99–114. doi:10.1080/09658210903107853

Tempel, T., & Frings, C. (2014). Interference in episodic memory: Retrieval-induced forgetting of unknown words. *Psychological Research*. Retrieved August 27, 2014, from http://dx.doi.org/10.1007/s00426-014-0604-2

Van Overschelde, J. P., Rawson, K. A., & Dunlosky, J. (2004). Category norms: An updated and expanded version of the Battig and Montague (1969) norms. *Journal of Memory and Language, 50*, 289–335. doi:10.1016/j.jml.2003.10.003

Veling, H., & van Knippenberg, A. (2004). Remembering can cause inhibition: Retrieval-induced inhibition as cue independent process. *Journal of Experimental Psychology: Learning, Memory, and Cognition, 30*, 315–318. doi:10.1037/0278-7393.30.2.315

Verde, M. F. (2004). The retrieval practice effect in associative recognition. *Memory & Cognition, 32*, 1265–1272. doi:10.3578/BF03206317

Verde, M. F. (2009). The list strength effect in recall: Relative-strength competition and retrieval inhibition may both contribute to forgetting. *Journal of Experimental Psychology: Learning, Memory & Cognition, 35*, 205–220. doi:10.1037/a0014275

Verde, M. F., & Perfect, T. J. (2011). Retrieval-induced forgetting in recognition is absent under time pressure. *Psychonomic Bulletin & Review, 18*, 1166–1171. doi: 10.3758/s13423-011-0143-4

Williams, C. C., & Zacks, R. T. (2001). Is retrieval-induced forgetting an inhibitory process? *The American Journal of Psychology, 114*, 329–354. doi:10.2307/1423685

2

Antihistamines considerably modulate the cognitive and psychomotor performance of human volunteers

Rawshan Zannat[1], Mir Muhammad Nasir Uddin[2], Md. Atiar Rahman[3]*, Jannatul Aklima[3] and Md. Mamun Al Amin[4]

*Corresponding author: Md. Atiar Rahman, Department of Biochemistry and Molecular Biology, Faculty of Biological Sciences, University of Chittagong, Chittagong 4331, Bangladesh

E-mail: atiar@cu.ac.bd

Reviewing editor: Peter Walla, University of Newcastle, Australia

Abstract: This research investigated the modulating effects of antihistamines—Loratadine, Fexofenadine, Meclizine, and Chlorpheniramine on cognitive (executive function, memory, attention, emotion regulation), mood, psychomotor performance, and sedation in healthy human volunteers. Twenty healthy volunteers received Loratadine 10-mg, Fexofenadine 120-mg, Meclizine 50-mg, Chlorpheniramine Maleate 4-mg, and Placebo 250-mg starch tablet in a five-way crossover, double-blind study. Following each dose the participants were subjected to take a series of test of cognitive functions and psychomotor performances at defined interval. A certain amount of washout period was also maintained for each drug. The test battery included PennCNP—Full Battery Test, Psychology Experiment Building Language, Stanford Sleepiness Scale, and Brief Mood Introspection Scale. The test results These test results were analyzed by one-way and two-way ANOVAs. In general, antihistamines didn't show any statistically significant deviation from that of placebo. However, slight improvement was observed in word memory test (Both immediate

ABOUT THE AUTHOR

Md. Atiar Rahman has been working as an associate professor in the Department of Biochemistry and Molecular Biology at the University of Chittagong. Rahman has had his BSc honors and MSc in Biochemistry from the University of Dhaka, PhD from the United Graduate School of Agricultural Science Ehime University, Japan, and Post doctoral degree from KwaZulu Natal University, South Africa. He is a principal investigator of the Laboratory of Complentary and Alternative Medicine and Natural Product Research of the aforementioned department. Currently, he is carrying out the research to explore the novel and indigenous sources of phytomedicinal components as alternative therapeutics for non-communicable chronic diseases, especially type 2 diabetes, neurological disorders, and chemical-induced acute hepatic toxicity through intervention in animal models. He has published more than 60 papers in different reputed and peer-reviewed indexed journals. His current research is focused on neuropharmacology.

PUBLIC INTEREST STATEMENT

This research investigated the modulating effects of antihistamines—Loratadine, Fexofenadine, Meclizine, and Chlorpheniramine on cognitive (executive function, memory, attention, emotion regulation), mood, psychomotor performance, and sedation in healthy human volunteers. Antihistamines are pharmaceutical drugs widely used in relieving allergic symptoms. When histamine is overdosed among people suffering from seasonal allergic reactions, sedation and neurocognitive impairment is observed. Sedative effects can also contribute to impairment of cognitive and psychomotor performance. Right choice of antihistamine will maximize the productivity; minimize the losses of working hours and daytime in school and workplaces that will eventually result to contribute the economic growth. Right options of antihistamines for the people needed sharp motor functioning to work in a factory with life threatening machineries could be chosen in a wide flexibility. Choosing a better antihistamine will as well help them to avoid the interference of precise psychomotor function due to the sedative effect of antihistamine.

and delayed) by Chlorpheniramine; although it increased the reaction time in visual object learning test. Fexofenadine also increased performance in delayed word memory test. Meclizine showed significant reduction ($p < 0.05$) of reaction time in line orientation task. The subjects receiving Loratadine reported slightly unpleasant mood then control group. This study will contribute to choose antihistamine rightly maximizing the productivity; minimizing the losses of working hours and daytime in school and workplaces. Right options of antihistamines will make wider flexibility for the people needed sharp motor functioning to work in factory with life-threatening machineries achieving less sedation and psychomotor unimpairment.

Subjects: Bioscience; Food Science & Technology; Health and Social Care

Keywords: antihistamine; cognitive performance; psychomotor performance; mood; sleep

1. Introduction

Antihistamines are drugs that antagonize the effects of histamines. They are widely used in relieving allergic symptoms. They have adverse effects in the central nervous system (Gengo, 1996). They are mostly used to provide symptomatic relief from allergic symptoms caused by histamine release (Dridi, Ben Attia, Reinberg, & Boughattas, 2005). Sedative effects exerted by antihistamine impair cognitive, psychomotor performance (Marshall & Colon, 1993), working memory (Van Ruitenbeek, Vermeeren, & Riedel, 2010), learning (Vuurman, van Veggel, Sanders, Muntjewerff, & O'Hanlon, 1996), emotion (Arnone, Horder, Cowen, & Harmer, 2009), executive function (Tamura et al., 2010), attention (Conen, Theunissen, Vermeeren, & Ramaekers, 2011), and psychological functioning (Gauci, King, Saxarra, Tulloch, & Husband, 1993), mainly through histamine H1 receptors (H1Rs) (Watanabe, Timmerman, & Yanai, 2001). Allergic rhinitis interferes with our quality of living, because of its discomforts. Antihistamines are widely used in treating various allergic diseases. They can cross the blood-brain barrier and block histaminergic receptors and other neurotransmitters (e.g. serotonin, choline, noradrenaline) in the brain, and as a consequence produce sleepiness, drowsiness, fatigue, and sedation (Passalacqua et al., 1996; Snyder & Snowman, 1987), which lead to cognitive and psychomotor impairment (Hindmarch, 1995; Kay, 2000). There are three generation of antihistamine, first-generation antihistamines penetrate readily into the brain by crossing blood-brain barrier, in which they occupy 50–90% of the H1Rs (Tagawa et al., 2001) and impairs cognitive and psychomotor performance and have a sedative effect also (Theunissen, Vermeeren, van Oers, van Maris, & Ramaekers, 2004). Second-generation antihistamines also impair cognitive and psychomotor performance but have a low sedative effect (Bender, Berning, Dudden, Milgrom, & Tran, 2003; Kay & Harris, 1999) compared to first-generation. Third-generation antihistamines don't impair cognitive and psychomotor performances (Hindmarch, Shamsi, & Kimber, 2002) and do not have any sedative effects (Hindmarch, 2002).

Many studies showed certain effects of some antihistamines on human cognitive and psychomotor performance (Jauregui et al., 2013; Kay & Harris, 1999). Few studies also suggested that some antihistamine does not influence certain cognitive and psychomotor performance (Gupta, Kapoor, Gillani, Kapoor, & Gupta, 2004; Hindmarch, Shamsi, Stanley, & Fairweather, 1999).

Computerized neuropsychological (CNP) tests have been used in behavioral research for last two decades (Schlegel & Gilliland, 2007). Though many different test batteries have been developed and new batteries are introduced every year for clinical screening, but standardized psychometric measures are not yet available (Zygouris & Tsolaki, 2015). Paper and pencil-based neuropsychological tests are not fit in present time. PennCNP (The University of Pennsylvania Computerized Neuropsychological Test Battery) is suitable for evaluation of human behavior and performance. However, neuropsychological evaluation can provide information concerning normal brain functioning and allows monitoring the cognitive status of an individual, especially throughout older age (Canini et al., 2014). Therefore, its results are extremely important to trace a variety of normal functioning in the aging population. CNP also used for neurobehavioral evaluations of brain disorders. Application of neuropsychological batteries in psychiatric research has been initially slow, but more recently; it has become combined into efforts to understand the association of neural systems central nervous system (Censits, Danielragland, Gur, & Gur, 1997; Gur et al., 2001).

The main focus of this study is to explore the effect of antihistamines on common brain functions. Since these antihistamines may widely distribute in many brain areas and influence the activities associated with that particular area. Researches that have been conducted so far on this issue are very much tedious, imprecise, and insufficient as well. More specifically, no similar study has been conducted on Bangladeshi population till now. Therefore, specific and precise behavioral effects of antihistamines on human volunteers (Bangladeshi population) are still necessary to be investigated. We investigate the effects of antihistamines—Loratadine, Fexofenadine, Meclizine, and Chlorpheniramine on cognitive performance (emotion, attention, memory, executive function) and psychomotor performance on healthy human volunteers. This study also investigated activity of antihistamines on mood and alertness.

2. Methods

2.1. *Participants*

All of the participants (age: 18–24) which are situated in Chittagong district. Sample size of the study was total participants 100 (both male and female). These samples were selected by convenient sampling from the target population.

2.2. *Procedure*

This study was conducted on 100 participants. These participants were selected by convenient sampling method from targeted population (education level 14) that means undergraduate students which are situated in Chittagong district. Background of the volunteers was initially checked by university infirmary's chief medical officer for their physical conditions and exposure to other drugs and stress. The participants were given consent of participant sheet to be approved. After approval, a questionnaire for measuring sleepiness was provided to the volunteers. The volunteers took antihistamines randomly after returning back the questionnaire. The participant took it at bedtime and attended the computerized test in next day morning at 8 in psychological Laboratory, University of Chittagong. Their blood pressure and pulse rate were measured by a physician when they entered the laboratory first. Then they started the computerized neuropsychological test batteries in PennCNP (The University of Pennsylvania Computerized Neuropsychological Test Battery). After completing the test battery, they attended PEBL test. When participants completed the task, their blood pressure and pulse rate were measured once again by a physician. Finally, they were given a questionnaire for measuring mood. A Personal Information Form was used to collect information like—sex, age, educational background, and handiness in CNP test batteries. The whole process illustrated in Figure 1.

After collecting data from 100 participants, data were analyzed by proper statistical method.

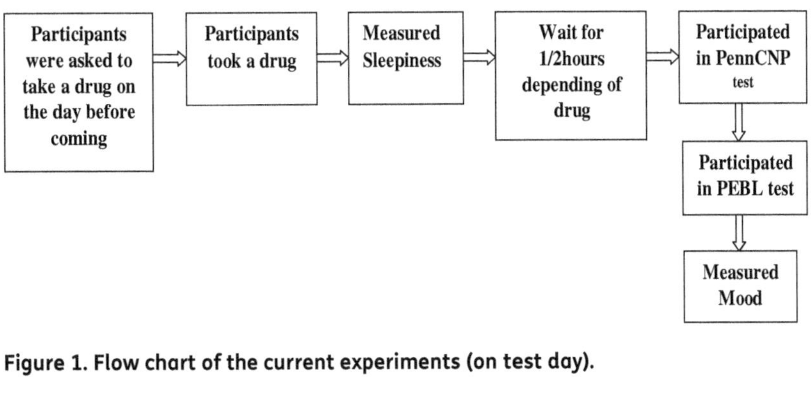

Figure 1. Flow chart of the current experiments (on test day).

2.3. Preparation of drugs and placebo

Inert placebo tablet (250-mg tablet made of starch) was used in this experiment. Chlorpheniramine maleate 4-mg Tablet (Histacin from Jayson pharma), Loratadine 10-mg Tablet (Oradin SK + F), Fexofenadine 120-mg Tablet (Fexo from Square Pharmaceuticals Ltd.), and Meclizine 50-mg Tablet (Vomec from Beximco Pharmaceuticals Ltd.) were given to the participants. Participants were not informed about the type of drug was given.

2.4. Measuring instruments

The University of Pennsylvania Computerized Neuropsychological test battery was used in the original study (PennCNP). The PennCNP comprises four computerized neuropsychological test batteries (executive function, memory, attention, and emotion regulation). In the study of the effect of antihistamines on cognitive and psychomotor performance, it has been made of a series of subjective and objective tests and examinations are given below:

(1) PennCNP—Full Battery Test.
(2) PEBL (Psychology Experiment Building Language).
(3) Stanford Sleepiness Scale (SSS).
(4) Brief Mood Introspection Scale (BMIS).

2.4.1. Motor Praxis (MPraxis)

The Motor Praxis (Gur et al., 2001) was designed as a measure of sensory-motor function. During the MPraxis test, the participant needed to move the computer mouse cursor over an ever-shrinking green box and clicked on it once each time it appeared on a different location on the test page.

2.4.2. Penn Facial Memory Test (CPF)

The Penn Facial Memory Test (Gur et al., 2001) is designed as a measure of facial memory. It consisted of 20 target faces and 20 non-target faces. The task trial was followed by immediate and delayed recognition trials, during which subjects were presented with the target faces mixed with 20 new faces. New faces were presented at each delayed. The participant's task was to decide whether they have seen the face before by selecting any one of a four-point scale: "definitely yes," "probably yes," "probably no," and "definitely no," The total number of true-positive responses and median reaction time for true-positive response were selected as cognitive performance measures.

2.4.3. Penn Word Memory Test (CPW)

The Penn Word Memory Test (Gur et al., 1993) was designed as a measure of word memory. It consisted of 20 target words and 20 non-target words. The task trial was followed by immediate and delayed recognition trials, during which subjects were presented with the target faces mixed with 20 new words. Procedure for administration and scoring of the task were identical to those for the facial recognition task.

2.4.4. Penn Continuous Performance Test—Number and Letter Version (PCPT-NL)

The Penn Continuous Performance Test—Number and Letter Version (Kurtz, Ragland, Bilker, Gur, & Gur, 2001) was designed as a measure of visual attention and vigilance in human. In this test, a series of red vertical and horizontal lines were flashed in a digital numeric frame-like as resembling a digital clock. The test was divided in two parts: one set of trials where the participant was looking for complete numbers and another was looking for complete letter followed by 3 min. Total number and letter of true-positive responses and median reaction time for true-positive response were selected as cognitive performance measures.

2.4.5. *Penn's Computerized Finger—Tapping Task (CTAP)*

The Penn's Computerized Finger—Tapping Task (Lezak, 2004) was designed as a measure of manual dexterity(Halstead, 1947; Reitan & Wolfson, 1993). In this task, participants used their dominant hand and non-dominant hand. The task consisted of 10 trials where five trials were dominant hand and another five trials were for the non-dominant hand. A total mean score of the dominant and non-dominant hand were selected as psychomotor performance.

2.4.6. *Penn Conditional Exclusion Task (PCET)*

The Penn Conditional Exclusion Task (Kurtz, Ragland, Moberg, & Gur, 2004; Kurtz, Wexler, & Bell, 2004) is measure of abstraction in executive function. It is form of the "Odd Man Out" model (Flowers & Robertson, 1985) where participants decided what object out of four objects did not belong with the other three. This test has three criteria for choosing an object, namely line thickness, shape, and size, respectively. The participants conducted 48 trials to find out 10 consecutive answers in each criterion. Total number of correct responses, median reaction time for correct response and error rate were selected as cognitive performance measures.

2.4.7. *Visual Object Learning Test (SVOLT)*

The Visual Object Learning Test (Glahn, Gur, Ragland, Censits, & Gur, 1997) was designed as a spatial analogy of the California Verbal Learning Test is measure of visual object learning and memory. It consisted 20 three-dimensional Euclidean shapes that were learning stimuli for both immediate and delayed recalls (delayed recall = SVOLTD). The total response, number, and median reaction time of true-positive responses were selected as cognitive performance measures for short- and long-term memory.

2.4.8. *Penn's Logical Reasoning Test (SPVRT)*

The Penn Logical Reasoning Test (Gur, Gur, Obrist, Skolnick, & Reivich, 1987) is the short version of the Penn Verbal Reasoning Test (PVRT) is a measure of verbal intellectual ability in human volunteer. The short PVRT has been developed at the University of Pennsylvania Neuropsychiatry Department. It was a multiple choice task in which the individual participant must answer eight questions which age-appropriate verbal analogy problem (R. C. Gur, J. D. Ragland, P. J. Moberg, T. H. Turner, et al., 2001).

2.4.9. *Penn Emotion Recognition Task (ER40)*

The Penn Emotion Recognition Task (Gur et al., 2002; Kohler, Turner, Gur, & Gur, 2004; Kohler et al. 2004) is a measure of emotion recognition. Participants were shown a series of 40 faces and it was a multiple choice task. It was taken from the University of Pennsylvania Emotion Recognition Task, 96 faces version, balanced for equality and intensity of emotion, age, gender, and ethnicity (Kohler et al. 2004).

2.4.10. *Letter-N-back (LNB2)*

The Letter-N-Back has been designed the Neuropsychiatry Department at the University of Pennsylvania (Ragland et al., 2002). It is measure of attention and working memory. In this task, participants were asked to give attention to flashing letters on the computer screen, one at a time, and to press the spacebar according to three different principles or rules: the 0-back, the 1-back, and the 2-back. Total number of correct responses, median reaction time for correct response, and reaction time of 0-Back, 1-Back, and 2-Back were selected as cognitive performance measures.

2.4.11. *Penn Abstraction Inhibition and Working Memory Task (AIM)*

The Penn Abstraction Inhibition and Working Memory Task is a measure of abstraction and concept formation, with and without working memory (Glahn, Cannon, Gur, Ragland, & Gur, 2000; Gur et al., 2001). It is divided into two separate question types, which the participant practices before starting the task. During the first question type, the participant sees two pairs of stimuli on the top of the page (adjusted to the left and to the right) and one single stimulus on the mid-bottom of the page. His/her task is to decide with which pair the stimulus on the bottom best belongs. The participant then clicks with the mouse on the pair he/she thinks fits the bottom stimulus the best and receives immediate feedback for his/her answer. Total number and median reaction time of true-positive responses of without working memory and with working memory were selected as cognitive performance measures memory.

2.4.12. Judgment of Line Orientation (CJOLO)

The Judgment of Line Orientation (Benton, Hannay, & Varney, 1975) is measure of Spatial orientation abilities based on the original paper-based task. Participants are shown a pair of lines on top of the screen and asked to click with the mouse on the letter label of the matching lines arranged in a coordinate array on the mid-bottom of the screen. Total number of correct responses and median reaction time for correct response were selected as cognitive performance measures.

2.4.13. Penn Emotion Discrimination Task (EDF40)

The Penn Emotion Discrimination Task (Erwin et al., 1992) is measure of emotion discrimination. Participants were shown 40 pairs of faces, one pair at a time. Each pair of faces consists of two pictures of the same person with or without a subtle, computer-generated difference in emotion expression, which might or may not represent a difference in the intensity of the emotion between the two faces. For each pair, the participant had to decide which face expressed the given emotion more intensely or whether they are equally emotional. Total number of correct responses, median reaction time of emotion discrimination and total number of correct response and median reaction time of happy and sad were selected as cognitive performance measures.

2.4.14. Change Detection Task

Psychology Experiment Building Language (PEBL) is a system designed for creating psychology and neuroscience experiments and tests. The change detection task measure the attention perception, motor, and executive function of brain. It is developed by Mueller, S.T. in 2011. In this test, participants have to press the space button as quickly as possible every time when she/he identify the changing object then click this object on the mouse. This test has given feedback "Correct" or "Incorrect" when click this object. After taking feedback, press the space button to start the next trial. The changing pattern has four ways that is changes in presence, location, size, and color of random circles among background field of circles was presented on the monitor in 20 trials.

2.4.15. Stanford Sleepiness Scale (SSS)

The Stanford Sleepiness Scale (SSS) is developed by Dement (1972), a great way to quickly assess how alert or sleepy of a person's feeling and discover the patterns of alertness by recording your "degree of sleepiness" at different times throughout the day. Using the seven-point scale below pick what best represents how participant are feeling and note the corresponding number on the chart. The scoring test-retest reliability was 0.88 and validity of mean SSS using the Wilkinson addition and vigilance tests was reported at correlation of 0.68.

2.4.16. Brief Mood Introspection Scale (BMIS)

The original version of the Brief Mood Introspection Scale (BMIS) was developed by (Mayer & Gaschke, 1988). This version was used to measure mood of the respondents in the present study. The BMIS scale is a freeware mood scale consisting of 16 mood-adjectives to which a person responds. The scale can yield measures of overall pleasant-unpleasant mood, arousal-calm mood, and it also can be scored according to positive-tired and negative-calm mood.

2.5. Data analysis

IBM SPSS Statistics 19 program, GraphPad Prism 6 and Microsoft Excel program (2013 version) was be used for analyzing the data. Collected data were presented in tables, graphs, and charts. Simple statistical tools, such as one-way ANOVA (and non-parametric) two-way ANOVA, Newman-Keuls comparison, and Tukey's multiple comparisons were used to interpret findings of the study. Emphasis was also being given on qualitative with quantitative data.

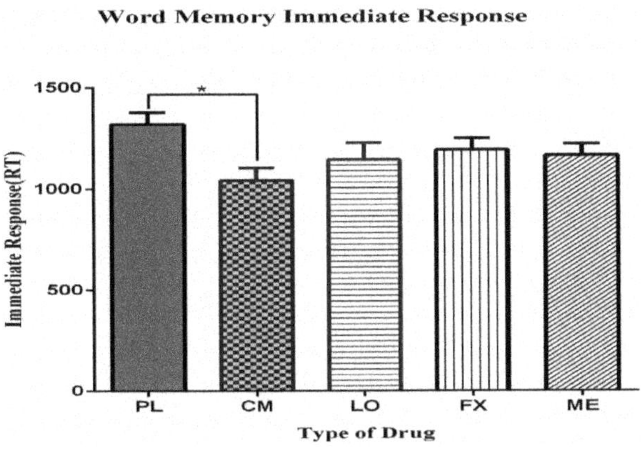

Figure 2. Effect of antihistamines on immediate recall word memory Task.

Notes: Horizontal axis represents antihistamines (PL = Placebo; CM = Chlorpheniramine Maleate; LO = Loratadine; FX = Fexofenadine; ME = Meclizine). Vertical axis represents reaction time in milliseconds. CM and FX group spent less time than the placebo group. Data are represented as Mean ± SEM (Standard Error of Mean). *Level of significance represented as $p < 0.05$.

3. Results

3.1. Effect on cognitive performance

Table 1 summarizes the effect of the antihistamines on the cognitive performances of the volunteers (Target identification and target location).

3.2. Immediate and delayed recall word memory test

In immediate word memory test, a one-way ANOVA was conducted to compare the effect of antihistamines between subjects and placebo on immediate recall word memory test. There was no significant effect of immediate recall word memory test on antihistamines at the $p < 0.05$ level for five conditions [$F(4, 88) = 0.44, p = 0.78$]. There was a significant effect of reaction time in immediate recall word memory test on antihistamines at the $p < 0.05$ level for the five conditions [$F(4, 88) = 2.39$, $p = 0.06$]. Neuman-Keuls multiple comparisons test showed that placebo group (M = 1,319, SD = 264.9) spent significantly ($p < 0.05$) higher time than the Chlorpheniramine Maleate group (M = 1,043; SD = 246.7) (Figure 2). In delayed word memory test, there was no significant effect of antihistamines on correct response in delayed recall word memory test at the $p < 0.05$ level for five conditions [$F(4, 82) = 0.26, p = 0.90$]. There was a significant effect of antihistamines on reaction time

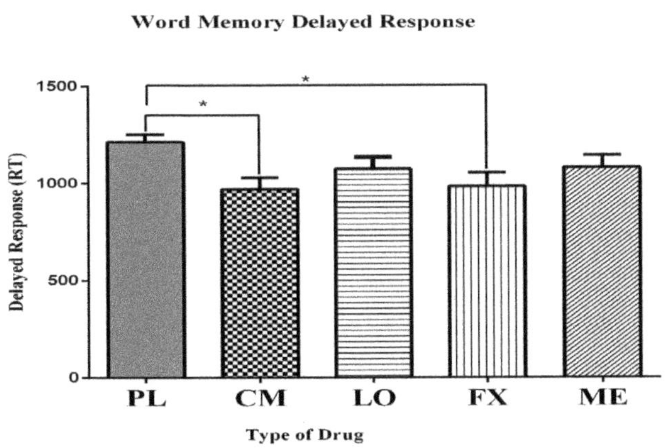

Figure 3. Effect of antihistamines on delayed recall word memory Task.

Notes: Horizontal axis represents antihistamines (PL = Placebo; CM = Chlorpheniramine Maleate; LO = Loratadine; FX = Fexofenadine; ME = Meclizine). Vertical axis represents reaction time in milliseconds. CM and FX group spent less time than the placebo group. Data are represented as Mean ± SEM (Standard Error of Mean). *Level of significance represented as $p < 0.05$.

Table 1. Effect of the antihistamines on the cognitive performances of the volunteers

	Placebo	Chlorpheniramine	Loratadine	Fexofenadine	Meclizine
Word-Memory test					
Immediate recall	18.80 ± 2.48	19.13 ± 1.54	18.44 ± 2.66	19.20 ± 1.32	18.79 ± 1.32
Immediate (RT)	1,319 ± 264.9	1,043 ± 246.7*	1,144 ± 352.3	1,193 ± 253.7	1,166 ± 242.4
Delayed recall	18.35 ± 2.52	18.42 ± 2.19	18.26 ± 2.42	18.75 ± 1.94	18.50 ± 1.62
Delayed (RT)	1,213 ± 178.5	970.3 ± 239.3*	1,075 ± 257.5	983.2 ± 291.9*	1,081 ± 251.5
Facial memory test					
Immediate recall	17.75 ± 3.77	17.84 ± 3.304	17.68 ± 2.81	18.40 ± 2.30	18.79 ± 1.65
Immediate (RT)	1,116 ± 212.3	990.7 ± 254.8	1,115 ± 307	1,042 ± 249.8	1,016 ± 245.8
Delayed recall	18.37 ± 1.98	18.39 ± 2.40	18.56 ± 2.18	18.89 ± 1.52	18.67 ± 1.72
Delayed (RT)	1,109 ± 264.6	1,025 ± 261.9	1,043 ± 271.5	1,047 ± 297.3	1,028 ± 272.5
Emotion test					
Emotion recognition (NF)	32.80 ± 4.65	32.89 ± 5.61	33.74 ± 2.60	33.35 ± 2.58	32.95 ± 6.78
Emotion recognition (RT)	1,697 ± 202.6	1,527 ± 249.9	1,609 ± 205.4	1,588 ± 224.9	1,488 ± 387.6
Emotion discrimination (CR)	15.89 ± 5.52	14.22 ± 5.01	16.11 ± 5.88	16.32 ± 6.07	14.95 ± 6.19
Emotion discrimination (RT)	2,289 ± 909.8	1,749 ± 765.4	217 ± 57.2	1,859 ± 638.7	1,867 ± 791.2
CR of happy	6.85 ± 3.23	5.78 ± 3.03	7.36 ± 3.91	6.90 ± 4.08	5.94 ± 3.61
RT of happy	2,136 ± 969.3	1,702 ± 836.4	2,191 ± 986.9	1,767 ± 686	1,895 ± 939.5
CR of sad	9.80 ± 3.16	9.31 ± 3.69	9.36 ± 3.27	10.05 ± 3.65	9.00 ± 2.91
RT of sad	2,274 ± 899.2	1,909 ± 932	2,156 ± 988.6	1,952 ± 729.2	1,909 ± 804.4
Change detection test					
Reaction time	14,992 ± 4,954	13,814 ± 5,326	12,425 ± 6,520	13,025 ± 5,044	14,245 ± 4,125
Number of times showed	30.35 ± 17.66	25.55 ± 16.65	25.53 ± 16.59	26.60 ± 13.62	23.95 ± 7.86
Abstract inhibition					
AI without WMCR)	25.3 ± 3.01	25.47 ± 2.93	25.58 ± 3.09	25. 90 ± 2.71	25.00 ± 3.49
AI without WM RT	1,947 ± 437.3	1,599 ± 361.3	1,887 ± 602.2	1,806 ± 460.8	1,773 ± 398.8
AI with WM (CR)	23.95 ± 3.14	23.00 ± 3.58	24.05 ± 3.34	23.70 ± 3.51	23.63 ± 3.09
AI with WM RT	1,370 ± 324.6	1,157 ± 326.6	1,316 ± 389.1	1,274 ± 352.7	1,219 ± 354.1
Letter-N-Back					
Response	26.60 ± 4.11	26.74 ± 4.01	26.58 ± 2.65	27.20 ± 2.09	27.32 ± 2.47
Reaction time	485.3 ± 68.90	503.1 ± 64.71	496.8 ± 99.42	479.3 ± 69.24	515.6 ± 95.70
0-Back	457.2 ± 34.12	456.4 ± 44.43	459.6 ± 50.19	464.4 ± 52.57	454.3 ± 45.93
1-Back	459.9 ± 55.61	486.3 ± 64.80	466.4 ± 68.41	470.4 ± 69.80	462.3 ± 67.17
2-Back	467.9 ± 50.66	504.6 ± 85.51	517.6 ± 130.3	488.2 ± 79.05	534.1 ± 105

(Continued)

Table 1. (Continued)

	Placebo	Chlorpheniramine	Loratadine	Fexofenadine	Meclizine
Line orientation task					
Correct response	1.64 ± 0.63	1.54 ± 0.97	1.50 ± 0.52	1.57 ± 0.85	1.54 ± 0.66
Reaction time	7,325 ± 2,970	6,692 ± 1,827	7,136 ± 1,511	7,603 ± 2,700	4,701 ± 2,361*
Number-Letter test					
Number correct	56.70 ± 9.92	57.47 ± 4.06	55.58 ±6.34	58.10 ± 3.66	57.00 ± 5.71
Number (RT)	451. ± 0.86	466.6 ± 36	458.2 ± 39.55	461.8 ± 35.55	451.9 ± 26.61
Letter correct	52.25 ± 13.42	55.21 ± 5.57	56.58 ± 4.77	55.40 ± 5.84	51.37 ± 12.95
Letter (RT)	471.7 ± 36.81	488.2 ± 29.77	472.9 ± 31.47	483.4 ± 34.64	488.6 ± 33.59
Conditional Exclusion Task					
Response	36.10 ± 12.26	39.42 ± 7.61	38.89 ± 13	41.95 ± 8.68	40.00 ± 7.51
Reaction Time	1,872 ± 401.6	1,663 ± 511.2	2,018 ± 498.2	1,856 ± 557.3	1,907 ± 504.8
Error rate	25.4 ± 10.98	29.79 ± 11.86	21.40 ± 13.35	16.53 ± 11.17	30.91 ± 13.12
Visual Object Learning Test					
Total response	1,167 ± 124.8	1,422 ± 479.9*	1,184 ± 127.5	1,190 ± 163.4	1,310 ± 207.9
Immediate recall	16.55 ± 2.67	16.89 ± 2.89	16.26 ± 3.09	16.25 ± 2.38	16.89 ± 2.54
Immediate (RT)	1,145 ± 151.3	1,201 ± 510.1	1,678 ± 322.7	1,137 ± 218.7	1,174 ± 296.9
Delayed recall	16.25 ± 2.51	16.42 ± 3.02	15.79 ± 2.72	15.65 ± 2.64	16.11 ± 2.98
Delayed (RT)	1,102 ± 136.9	1,096 ± 450.3	1,051 ± 230.1	1,010 ± 267.8	1,038 ± 300.6

Notes: CR = Correct Response, RT = Reaction Time, NF = Number of Face, WM = Working Memory, AI = Abstract Inhibition.

*Level of significance represented as $p < 0.05$.

in delayed recall word memory test at the $p < 0.05$ level for the five conditions [$F(4, 82) = 2.91$, $p = 0.03$]. Neuman-Keuls multiple comparisons test showed that placebo group ($M = 1,213$, $SD = 178.5$) spent significantly ($p < 0.05$) higher time than the Chlorpheniramine Maleate ($M = 970.3$, $SD = 239.3$) and Loratadine ($M = 983.2$, $SD = 291.9$) group (Figure 3).

3.3. Judgment of line orientation task

A one-way ANOVA between subjects was conducted to compare the effect of antihistamines and placebo. There was no significant effect of correct response in line orientation task of spatial

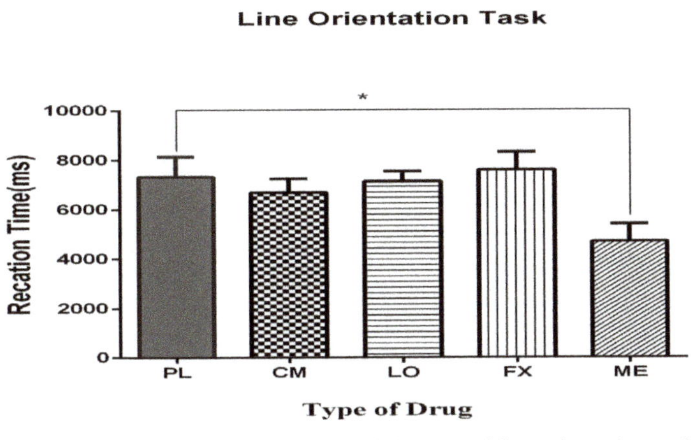

Figure 4. Effect of antihistamines on judgment of line orientation task.

Notes: Horizontal axis represents antihistamines (PL = Placebo; CM = Chlorpheniramine Maleate; LO = Loratadine; FX = Fexofenadine; ME = Meclizine). Vertical axis represents reaction time in milliseconds. ME group spent less time than the placebo group. Data are represented as Mean ± SEM (Standard Error of Mean). *Level of significance represented as $p < 0.05$.

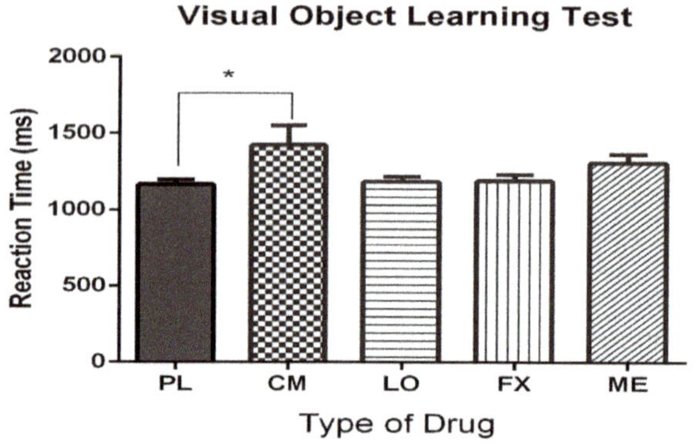

Figure 5. Effect of antihistamines on visual object learning Task.

Notes: Horizontal axis represents antihistamines (PL = Placebo; CM = Chlorpheniramine Maleate; LO = Loratadine; FX = Fexofenadine; ME = Meclizine). Vertical axis represents reaction time in milliseconds. CM group spent more time than the placebo group. Data are represented as Mean ± SEM (Standard Error of Mean). *Level of significance represented as $p < 0.05$.

orientation on antihistamines at the $p < 0.05$ level for the five conditions [$F(4, 94) = 0.07296$, $p = 0.9901$]. There was no significant difference between placebo and antihistamines on the context of reaction time in line orientation task at the $p < 0.05$ level for the five condition [$F(4, 58) = 2.848$, $p = 0.0318$]. Neuman-Keuls multiple comparisons test showed that placebo group ($M = 7{,}325$, SD = 2,970) spent significantly ($p < 0.05$) higher time than the Meclizine group ($M = 4{,}701$, SD = 2,361) (Figure 4).

3.4. Visual object learning test

A one-way ANOVA between subjects was conducted to compare the effect of antihistamines and placebo. There was no significant effect of total correct response time in visual object learning test of visual object learning and memory on antihistamines at the $p < 0.05$ level for the five conditions [$F(4, 72) = 2.904$, $p = 0.0275$]. Neuman-Keuls multiple comparisons test showed that placebo group ($M = 1{,}167$, SD = 124.8) spent significantly ($p < 0.05$) Lower time than the Chlorpheniramine Maleate group ($M = 1{,}422$, SD = 479.9) (Figure 5).

3.5. Effect on psychomotor performance

A one-way ANOVA between subjects was conducted to compare the effect of antihistamines on psychomotor performance in placebo. In this study, various psychomotor performances were assessed. The result of the cognitive performance is summarized in Table 2. There was no significant effect of psychomotor performance in antihistamine, i.e. Chlorpheniramine, Loratadine, Fexofenadine, and Meclizine.

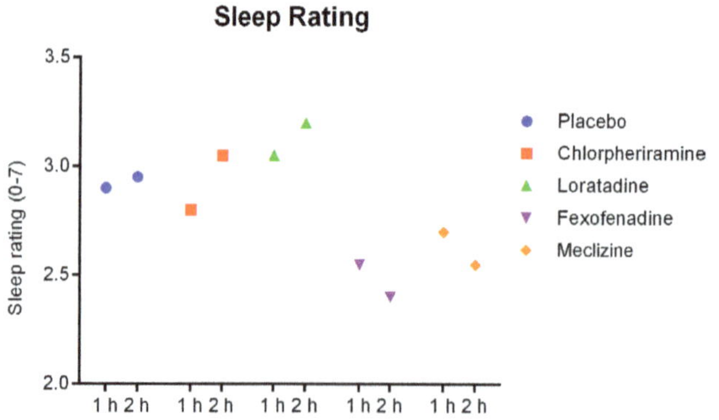

Figure 6. Effect of antihistamines on sleep.

Notes: There was no significant difference between placebo group and antihistamine group. Data are represented as Mean ± SEM (Standard Error of Mean). *Level of significance represented as $p < 0.05$.

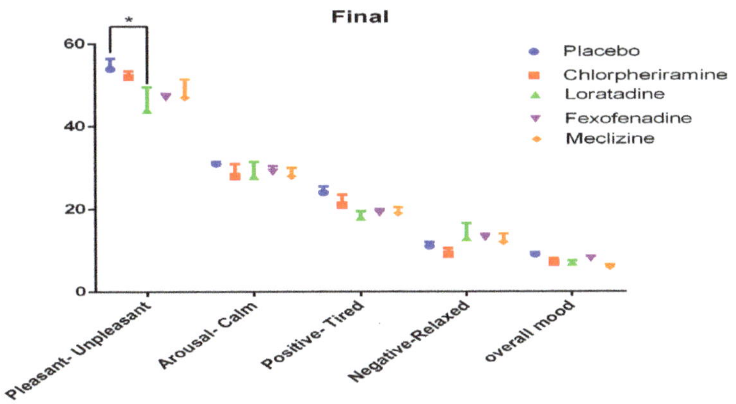

Figure 7. Effect of antihistamines on mood.

Notes: There was a significant difference between placebo group and Loratadine group. Data are represented as Mean ± SEM (Standard Error of Mean). *Level of significance represented as $p < 0.05$.

Table 2 Effect of the antihistamines on the psychomotor performances of the volunteers

Indexes	Placebo	Chlorpheniramine	Loratadine	Fexofenadine	Meclizine
Motor Praxis test					
Trial-1	854.2 ± 166.3	968.7 ± 348.1	931.4 ± 264.2	860.8 ± 306.2	891.4 ± 270.8
Trial-2	790.4 ± 154.1	849.1 ± 206.3	772.5 ± 131.9	799.2 ± 198.3	797.7 ± 195.7
Finger Tapping test					
Dominant hand	60.95 ± 7.997	61.26 ± 8.621	62.21 ± 9.028	59.80 ± 8.414	60.53 ± 8.356
Non-Dominant hand	54.05 ± 7.619	58.63 ± 17.77	55.58 ± 11.27	54.85 ± 8.922	55.47 ± 8.953

3.6. Effect on sleep

A two-way between subjects ANOVA was conducted to compare the effect of antihistamines and placebo on mood test. Five conditions were assessed to show that there was no significant sedative effect of antihistamines. It can be concluded that null hypothesis, i.e. there is no significant effect of sedation on antihistamine is accepted (Figure 6).

3.7. Effect on mood

A two-way between subjects ANOVA was conducted to compare the effect of antihistamines and placebo on mood test. Five conditions were assessed to show the effect of pleasant-unpleasant mood on antihistamine. The result reveals that one condition where $p < 0.05$ viz Loratadine is significant but the other four are not found to be significant. It can be concluded that null hypothesis, i.e. there is no significant effect of pleasant and unpleasant mood on antihistamine is partially accepted. Tukey's multiple comparisons test showed that the placebo group was in a better mood than Loratadine group on the aspect of pleasant-unpleasant mood (Figure 7).

4. Discussion

Many studies showed effects of antihistamine on human cognitive and psychomotor performance (Hindmarch et al., 1999; Jauregui et al., 2013; Kay & Harris, 1999) these results are different according to the generation of drugs. On the other hand, some other studies suggested that some antihistamine does not influence certain cognitive and psychomotor performance (Gupta et al., 2004; Hindmarch et al., 1999). Our present study was conducted to test the effect of antihistamine on the cognitive and psychomotor performance in a series of cognitive tasks using PennCNP—Full Battery Test and PEBL. The aim of the study was to investigate the effects of antihistamines Loratadine, Fexofenadine, Meclizine, and Chlorpheniramine on cognitive performance (emotion, attention, memory, and executive function), mood, psychomotor performance, and sedation in healthy volunteers.

Chlorpheniramine is a first-generation antihistamine meant to be used for the temporary relief of allergic symptoms. Chlorpheniramine 4 mg showed no effect on memory performance (Millet, Dreisbach, & Bryson, 1982). Chlorpheniramine Maleate performance was better to response than the placebo in word memory test. In our current study, no significant effect of the Chlorpheniramine on the cognitive performances of the volunteers was found. Only word memory and visual object learning task have a significant effect of cognitive performance. The word memory task has a positive effect and visual object learning has negative effect. Chlorpheniramine exposed volunteers took more time to perform the visual object learning task than placebo group. As a result in Chlorpheniramine impaired effect on the visual object learning (Simons, 1996) memory was found. The finding of the study showed that there was no significant effect of Chlorpheniramine in psychomotor performance. Chlorpheniramine did increase independently and individually measured signs of sedation than other antihistamines (e.g. Fexofenadine, Meclizine). The finding of this study showed there was no significant effect of Chlorphenamine on subjective mood and sleeping rate.

Loratadine is a second-generation antihistamine used to temporarily relieve the allergic symptoms of hay fever (allergy to pollen, dust, or other substances in the air) and other allergies. Loratadine 10 mg showed no effect on cognitive (Kay & Harris, 1999) and psychomotor performance (DuBuske, 2007; Hindmarch et al., 1999; Kay & Harris, 1999). Different study found that Loratadine did not impaired the performance of the memory-related task (Bender, McCormick, & Milgrom, 2001; Bradley & Nicholson, 1987), attention (Valk, Simons, Struyvenberg, Kruit, & van Berge Henegouwen, 1997), executive function (Philpot, 2000), and emotion same result was also found in our study. Ratings of sleepiness on the Stanford sleepiness scale were higher following the initial administration of Loratadine than rating for Chlorpheniramine and placebo. The sleepiness ratings increased in Loratadine group but not significant enough with compared to placebo. Loratidine 10-mg dose reported more sedation and unpleasant mood ($p < 0.05$) than the placebo group. Finally, Loratadine did not impair cognitive, psychomotor performance, and sleepiness but affected the mood.

Fexofenadine is a third-generation antihistamine used to relieve the allergic symptoms of seasonal allergic rhinitis. Fexofenadine 120 mg caused no significant effect in psychomotor performance including sensory motor ability, finger-tapping and cognitive function, including memory tasks such as word memory, facial memory, visual object learning memory, Letter-N-back for attention and working memory. Fexofenadine performance was better in response than placebo in the word memory test. The finding of the study indicated that Fexofenadine not impaired the memory, attention, executive function, emotion, and motor ability. Rating of sleepiness on the Stanford sleepiness scale were lower score of Fexofenadine than rating for Chlorpheniramine, Loratadine, Meclizine, and placebo. The sleepiness rating was decreased in Fexofenadine group but not significant enough with compared to placebo. With compared to five groups the lowest sleepiness rating was found in Fexofenadine and sleepiness also decreases per hour gradually. The mood score exhibited that the subject who received 120-mg dose of Fexofenadine, had no sedation and no mood effect than placebo group. Finally, Fexofenadine did not impair the cognitive, psychomotor performance, sleepiness and mood but influenced reaction time to perform the word memory task.

Meclizine is a first-generation antihistamine that antagonizes the effects of natural chemical histamine in the body. The result of the Meclizine 50 mg revealed no significant impairment on the psychomotor performance. The finding also indicated no significant impairment on the cognitive performance in word memory task, facial memory task, visual object learning memory, emotion recognition, logical reasoning, letter-N back, abstraction inhibition task, change detection task, emotion discrimination, and list learning task but only line orientation task influenced by meclizine. Rating of sleepiness on the Stanford sleepiness scale was lower than rating for Chlorpheniramine, Loratadine, and placebo. The sleepiness rating was decrease in Meclizine group but not have significant difference between Meclizine and placebo. The comparison of five groups indicated that the second lowest sleepiness rating was Meclizine and per hour gradually decrease the sleepiness. The mood score showed that the subject who received 50-mg dose of Meclizine reported no sedation and mood effect than placebo group. Finally, Meclizine did not impair cognitive, psychomotor performance and sleepiness and mood but influenced reaction time to performing the line orientation task.

5. Conclusion

The antihistamines didn't produce any disruptive effects on aspect of psychomotor and cognitive function. The study showed slight increase in cognitive function in case of FX and MC. CM exhibited better performance output then other antihistamines in most of the tests. None of the antihistamines varied significantly ($p < 0.05$) from placebo in increasing cognitive and psychomotor functions.

Acknowledgements
We would like to acknowledge the contribution of the PLCU (Psychological Laboratory of Chittagong University) team: Department of Psychology, Department of Pharmacy, and Department of Biochemistry in University of Chittagong, Chittagong, We would like to give them special thanks for providing all sorts of supports toward this study.

Funding
The University Grants Commission-Dean (UGC-Dean) project has funded for this research.

Competing interests
Authors declare that they don't have any competing interest.

Author details
Rawshan Zannat[1]
E-mail: rawshanzannat.kajal@gmail.com
ORCID ID: http://orcid.org/0000-0002-0269-6932
Mir Muhammad Nasir Uddin[2]
E-mail: nasirmir@cu.ac.bd
Md. Atiar Rahman[3]
E-mail: atiar@cu.ac.bd
ORCID ID: http://orcid.org/0000-0003-2902-7058
Jannatul Aklima[3]
E-mail: jannattulaklima@yahoo.com
Md. Mamun Al Amin[4]
E-mail: bd_pharmacy@yahoo.com
[1] Department of Psychology, University of Chittagong, Chittaagong 4334, Bangladesh.
[2] Department of Pharmacy, University of Chittagong, Chittagong 4331, Bangladesh.
[3] Department of Biochemistry and Molecular Biology, University of Chittagong, Chittagong 4331, Bangladesh.
[4] Queensland Brain Institute, University of Queensland, Queensland, Australia.

References

Arnone, D., Horder, J., Cowen, P. J., & Harmer, C. J. (2009). Early effects of mirtazapine on emotional processing. *Psychopharmacology, 203*, 685–691. doi:10.1007/s00213-008-1410-6

Bender, B. G., McCormick, D. R., & Milgrom, H. (2001). Children's school performance is not impaired by short-term administration of diphenhydramine or loratadine. *The Journal of Pediatrics, 138*, 656–660. doi:10.1067/mpd.2001.112647

Bender, B. G., Berning, S., Dudden, R., Milgrom, H., & Tran, Z. V. (2003). Sedation and performance impairment of diphenhydramine and second-generation antihistamines: A meta-analysis. *Journal of Allergy and Clinical Immunology, 111*, 770–776. doi:10.1067/mai.2003.1408

Benton, A., Hannay, H. J., & Varney, N. R. (1975). Visual perception of line direction in patients with unilateral brain disease. *Neurology, 25*, 907–910. http://dx.doi.org/10.1212/WNL.25.10.907

Bradley, C. M., & Nicholson, A. N. (1987). Studies on the central effects of the H1-antagonist, loratadine. *European Journal of Clinical Pharmacology, 32*, 419–421. doi:10.1007/BF00543979

Canini, M., Battista, P., Della Rosa, P. A., Catricalà, E., Salvatore, C., Gilardi, M. C., & Castiglioni, I. (2014). Computerized neuropsychological assessment in aging: Testing efficacy and clinical ecology of different interfaces. *Computational and mathematical methods in medicine, 2014*, Article ID 804723, 13. doi:10.1155/2014/804723.

Censits, D. M., Danielragland, J. D., Gur, R. C., & Gur, R. E. (1997). Neuropsychological evidence supporting a neurodevelopmental model of schizophrenia: A longitudinal study. *Schizophrenia Research, 24*, 289–298. http://dx.doi.org/10.1016/S0920-9964(96)00091-6

Conen, S., Theunissen, E. L., Vermeeren, A., & Ramaekers, J. G. (2011). Short-term effects of morning versus evening dose of hydroxyzine 50 mg on cognition in healthy volunteers. *Journal of Clinical Psychopharmacology, 31*, 294–301. doi:10.1097/JCP.0b013e318218943c

Dement, W., (1972). *Development and use of Stanford Sleepiness scale (SSS)*. Paper presented at the Psychophysiology.

Dridi, D., Ben Attia, M., Reinberg, A., & Boughattas, N. A. (2005). Rythmes circadiens des effets toxiques d'un antihistaminique H1 : la cétirizine chez la souris. *Pathologie Biologie, 53*, 193–198. doi:10.1016/j.patbio.2004.07.014

DuBuske, L. (2007). Desloratadine for chronic idiopathic urticaria. *American Journal of Clinical Dermatology, 8*, 271–283. http://dx.doi.org/10.2165/00128071-200708050-00002

Erwin, R. J., Gur, R. C., Gur, R. E., Skolnick, B., Mawhinney-Hee, M., & Smailis, J. (1992). Facial emotion discrimination: I. Task construction and behavioral findings in normal subjects. *Psychiatry Research, 42*, 231–240. http://dx.doi.org/10.1016/0165-1781(92)90115-J

Flowers, K. A., & Robertson, C. (1985). The effect of Parkinson's disease on the ability to maintain a mental set. *Journal of Neurology, Neurosurgery & Psychiatry, 48*, 517–529. http://dx.doi.org/10.1136/jnnp.48.6.517

Gauci, M., King, M. G., Saxarra, H., Tulloch, B. J., & Husband, A. J. (1993). A minnesota multiphasic personality inventory profile of women with allergic rhinitis. *Psychosomatic Medicine, 55*, 533–540. http://dx.doi.org/10.1097/00006842-199311000-00009

Gengo, F. M. (1996). Reduction of the central nervous system adverse effects associated with antihistamines in the management of allergic disorders: Strategies and progress. *Journal of Allergy and Clinical Immunology, 98*, S319–S325. http://dx.doi.org/10.1016/S0091-6749(96)80117-5

Glahn, D. C., Gur, R. C., Ragland, J. D., Censits, D. M., & Gur, R. E. (1997). Reliability, performance characteristics, construct validity, and an initial clinical application of a Visual Object Learning Test (VOLT). *Neuropsychology, 11*, 602–612. http://dx.doi.org/10.1037/0894-4105.11.4.602

Glahn, D. C., Cannon, T. D., Gur, R. E., Ragland, J. D., & Gur, R. C. (2000). Working memory constrains abstraction in schizophrenia. *Biological Psychiatry, 47*, 34–42. http://dx.doi.org/10.1016/S0006-3223(99)00187-0

Gupta, S., Kapoor, B., Gillani, Z., Kapoor, V., & Gupta, B. M. (2004). Effects of fexofenadine, cetirizine and diphenhydramine on psychomotor performance in adult healthy volunteer. *JK Science : Journal of Medical Education & Research, 6*, 201–205.

Gur, R. C., Gur, R. E., Obrist, W. D., Skolnick, B. E., & Reivich, M. (1987). Age and regional cerebral blood flow at rest and during cognitive activity. *Archives of General Psychiatry, 44*, 617–621. http://dx.doi.org/10.1001/archpsyc.1987.01800190037006

Gur, R. C., Jaggi, J. L., Ragland, J. D., Resnick, S. M., Shtasel, D., Muenz, L., & Gur, R. E. (1993). Effects of memory processing on regional brain activation: Cerebral blood flow in normal subjects. *International Journal of Neuroscience, 72*, 31–44. http://dx.doi.org/10.3109/00207459308991621

Gur, R. C., Ragland, J. D., Moberg, P. J., Turner, T. H., Bilker, W. B., Kohler, C., ... Gur, R. E. (2001). Computerized neurocognitive scanning: I. methodology and validation in healthy people. *Neuropsychopharmacology, 25*, 766–776. doi:10.1016/s0893-133x(01)00278-0

Gur, R. C., Sara, R., Hagendoorn, M., Marom, O., Hughett, P., Macy, L., & Gur, R. E. (2002). A method for obtaining 3-dimensional facial expressions and its standardization for use in neurocognitive studies. *Journal of Neuroscience Methods, 115*, 137–143. http://dx.doi.org/10.1016/S0165-0270(02)00006-7

Halstead, W. C. (1947). *Brain and intelligence: A quantitative study of the frontal lobes* (p. 170). Chicago: University of Chicago Press.

Hindmarch, I. (1995). Psychometric aspects of antihistamines. *Allergy, 50*, 48–54. http://dx.doi.org/10.1111/all.1995.50.issue-s24

Hindmarch, I. (2002). CNS effects of antihistamines: Is there a third generation of non-sedative drugs? *Clinical & Experimental Allergy Reviews, 2*, 26–31. doi:10.1046/j.1472-9725.2002.00031.x

Hindmarch, I., Shamsi, Z., Stanley, N., & Fairweather, D. B. (1999). A double-blind, placebo-controlled investigation of the effects of fexofenadine, loratadine and promethazine on cognitive and psychomotor function. *British Journal of Clinical Pharmacology, 48*, 200–206.

Hindmarch, I., Shamsi, Z., & Kimber, S. (2002). An evaluation of the effects of high-dose fexofenadine on the central nervous system: A double-blind, placebo-controlled study in healthy volunteers. *Clinical & Experimental Allergy, 32*, 133–139. http://dx.doi.org/10.1046/j.0022-0477.2001.01245.x

Jauregui, I., Ferrer, M., Montoro, J., Davila, I., Bartra, J., del Cuvillo, A., & Valero, A. (2013). Antihistamines in drivers, aircrew and occupations of risk. *Journal of Investigational Allergology and Clinical Immunology, 23*, 27–34.

Kay, G. G. (2000). The effects of antihistamines on cognition and performance. *Journal of Allergy and Clinical Immunology, 105*, S622–S627. http://dx.doi.org/10.1067/mai.2000.106153

Kay, G. G., & Harris, A. G. (1999). Loratadine: A non-sedating antihistamine. Review of its effects on cognition, psychomotor performance, mood and sedation. *Clinical & Experimental Allergy, 29*, 147–150. http://dx.doi.org/10.1046/j.1365-2222.1999.0290s3147.x

Kohler, C. G., Turner, T., Stolar, N. M., Bilker, W. B., Brensinger, C. M., Gur, R. E., & Gur, R. C. (2004). Differences in facial expressions of four universal emotions. *Psychiatry Research, 128*, 235–244. doi:10.1016/j.psychres.2004.07.003

Kohler, C. G., Turner, T. H., Gur, R. E., & Gur, R. C. (2004). Recognition of facial emotions in neuropsychiatric disorders. *CNS Spectrums, 9*, 267–274.

Kurtz, M. M., Ragland, J. D., Bilker, W., Gur, R. C., & Gur, R. E. (2001). Comparison of the continuous performance test with and without working memory demands in healthy controls and patients with schizophrenia. *Schizophrenia Research, 48*, 307–316. http://dx.doi.org/10.1016/S0920-9964(00)00060-8

Kurtz, M. M., Ragland, J. D., Moberg, P. J., & Gur, R. C. (2004). The penn conditional exclusion test: A new measure of executive-function with alternate forms for repeat administration. *Archives of Clinical Neuropsychology, 19*, 191–201. doi:10.1016/s0887-6177(03)00003-9

Kurtz, M. M., Wexler, B. E., & Bell, M. D. (2004). The penn conditional exclusion test (PCET): Relationship to the wisconsin card sorting test and work function in patients with schizophrenia. *Schizophrenia Research, 68*, 95–102. doi:10.1016/s0920-9964(03)00179-8

Lezak, M. D. (2004). *Neuropsychological assessment*. USA: Oxford University Press.

Marshall, P. S., & Colon, E. A. (1993). Effects of allergy season on mood and cognitive function. *Annals of Allergy, 71*, 251–258.

Mayer, J. D., & Gaschke, Y. N. (1988). The experience and meta-experience of mood. *Journal of Personality and Social Psychology, 55*, 102–111. http://dx.doi.org/10.1037/0022-3514.55.1.102

Millet, V. M., Dreisbach, M., & Bryson, Y. J. (1982). Double-blind controlled study of central nervous system side effects of amantadine, rimantadine, and chlorpheniramine. *Antimicrobial Agents and Chemotherapy, 21*, 1–4. doi:10.1128/aac.21.1.1

Passalacqua, G., Bousquet, J., Bachert, C., Church, M. K., Bindsley-Jensen, C., Nagy, L., & Canonica, G. W. (1996). The clinical safety of H1-receptor antagonists. *An EAACI position paper. Allergy, 51*, 666–675.

Philpot, E. E. (2000). Safety of second generation antihistamines. *Allergy and Asthma Proceedings, 21*, 15–20. doi:10.2500/108854100778249033

Ragland, J. D., Turetsky, B. I., Gur, R. C., Gunning-Dixon, F., Turner, T., Schroeder, L., & Chan, R. E. (2002). Working memory for complex figures: An fMRI comparison of letter and fractal n-back tasks. *Neuropsychology, 16*, 370–379. http://dx.doi.org/10.1037/0894-4105.16.3.370

Reitan, R., & Wolfson, D. (1993). *The Halstead-Reitan neuropsychological test battery: Theory and clinical applications*. Tucson, AZ: Neuropsychology Press.

Schlegel, R. E., & Gilliland, K. (2007). Development and quality assurance of computer-based assessment batteries.

Archives of Clinical Neuropsychology, 22, 49–61. http://dx.doi.org/10.1016/j.acn.2006.10.005

Simons, F. E. R. (1996). Learning impairment and allergic rhinitis. *Allergy and Asthma Proceedings, 17*, 185–189. doi:10.2500/108854196778996895

Snyder, S. H., & Snowman, A. M. (1987). Receptor effects of cetirizine. *Annals of Allergy, 59*, 4–8.

Tagawa, M., Kano, M., Okamura, N., Higuchi, M., Matsuda, M., Mizuki, Y., & Komemushi, S. (2001). Neuroimaging of histamine H1-receptor occupancy in human brain by positron emission tomography (PET): A comparative study of ebastine, a second-generation antihistamine, and (+)-chlorpheniramine, a classical antihistamine. *British journal of clinical pharmacology, 52*, 501–509.

Tamura, M., Larive, B., Unruh, M. L., Stokes, J. B., Nissenson, A., Mehta, R. L., & Chertow, G. M. (2010). Prevalence and correlates of cognitive impairment in hemodialysis patients: The frequent hemodialysis network trials. *Clinical Journal of the American Society of Nephrology, 5*, 1429–1438. doi:10.2215/cjn.01090210

Theunissen, E. L., Vermeeren, A., van Oers, A. C., van Maris, I., & Ramaekers, J. G. (2004). A dose-ranging study of the effects of mequitazine on actual driving, memory and psychomotor performance as compared to dexchlorpheniramine, cetirizine and placebo. *Clinical & Experimental Allergy, 34*, 250–258. http://dx.doi.org/10.1111/cea.2004.34.issue-2

Valk, P. J., Simons, R. M., Struyvenberg, P. A., Kruit, H., & van Berge Henegouwen, M. T. (1997). Effects of a single dose of loratadine on flying ability under conditions of simulated cabin pressure. *American Journal of Rhinology, 11*, 27–33. doi:10.2500/105065897781446838

Van Ruitenbeek, P., Vermeeren, A., & Riedel, W. J. (2010). Histamine H1 receptor antagonist cetirizine impairs working memory processing speed, but not episodic memory. *British Journal of Pharmacology, 161*, 456–466. doi:10.1111/j.1476-5381.2010.00907.x

Vuurman, E. F., van Veggel, L. M., Sanders, R. L., Muntjewerff, N. D., & O'Hanlon, J. F. (1996). Effects of semprex-D and diphenhydramine on learning in young adults with seasonal allergic rhinitis. *Annals of Allergy, Asthma & Immunology, 76*, 247–252. doi:10.1016/s1081-1206(10)63435-7

Watanabe, T., Timmerman, H., & Yanai, K. (2001, November 22–25). *Histamine research in the new millennium: Proceedings of the international sendai histamine symposium held in Sendai* (Vol. 1224). Elsevier Science Health Science Division.

Zygouris, S., & Tsolaki, M. (2015). Computerized cognitive testing for older adults: A review. *American Journal of Alzheimer's Disease and Other Dementias, 30*, 13–28. http://dx.doi.org/10.1177/1533317514522852

3

Test administrator effects on cognitive performance in a longitudinal study of ageing

Marieclaire Overton[1]*, Mats Pihlsgård[1] and Sölve Elmståhl[1]

*Corresponding author: Marieclaire Overton, Division of Geriatric Medicine, Lunds University, Skånes University Hospital, Jan Waldenströms gata 35, CRC Building 28, fl.13, SE-205 02 Malmö, Sweden

E-mail: marie_claire.overton@med.lu.se

Reviewing editor: Peter Walla, University of Newcastle, Australia

Abstract: In longitudinal studies, changes in participants' cognitive performances can partly be attributed to variations in the testing situation (testing specific factors), such as, different test administrators or different testing environments. Focusing on test administrator influence, testing specific factors were examined in a Swedish longitudinal study of ageing. Test scores from 6,686 examinations revealed significant test administrator effects on all instruments measuring speed of processing, episodic memory and spatial ability. 1.4–3.5% of the total variation in test scores was explained by the factor attributed to the test administrator. Further, results indicated task familiarity on speed scores, and fatigue attributable to the time of day of the testing session for memory and spatial ability. Participants tested in the testing centre performed significantly better than participants who received home visits. This study provides evidence that testing specific factors are tangible concerns in longitudinal ageing studies.

Subjects: Neuropsychology; Cognitive Psychology; Cognitive Neuropsychology; Behavioral Psychology; Developmental Psychology

Keywords: test administrator effects; ageing; instrumentation; cognitive performance; longitudinal research

1. Introduction

Ageing studies that examine cognition, have a tradition of using longitudinal data collecting because of the advantages of this design, of which the most important is that it directly measures within

ABOUT THE AUTHOR

Marieclaire Overton holds a MSc in psychology from Lund University. She is currently doing her PhD in ageing and cognition at the Division of Geriatric Medicine at Lund university. Her research is based on data from the longitudinal study of ageing "Good ageing in Skåne" (GÅS). She has previously worked with testing GÅS participants' cognitive abilities. Whilst working she became interested in investigating test administrators influence participants' test performance. Cognitive researchers use participants' test results to distinguish cognitively impaired groups of participants from cognitively healthy groups. It is thus important to investigate whether the test results are reliable and free from exterior influences.

PUBLIC INTEREST STATEMENT

Today, it is customary to use psychological testing to measure elders' mental health. Potentially, test results assess level of mental health, and whether they should receive mental health care. Our research suggests that certain exterior aspects in the testing situation may influence test results, causing an unfair assessment. For instance, the test administrator can unconsciously assist or in severe cases hinder the senior being tested. Also, the time of day and which type of environment the elder is tested in may also be influential. Luckily, these influences were found to be small. Even so, researchers and psychologist should be aware of possible sources of influences, so that routines that reduce exterior influences are applied. Routines may include the test administrator following a strict and standardised testing protocol. By applying routines appropriately, we can be fairly confident that seniors will face a fair assessment.

person cognitive change. Despite the advantages, this design involves methodological choices made by the researcher and other practical issues that can lead to implications when interpreting results (Ferrer & Ghisletta, 2011). Methodological choices include procedures such as having several versions of the same test and offering home visits to participants. Further, longitudinal studies consisting of several follow-up periods and large study samples may use more than one test administrator to collect cognitive data. (Guo, 2013; Hofer & Schaie, 2001). These studies usually extend over a large period of time, and therefore personnel are often replaced throughout the course of the study. Longitudinal investigators have then a two-folded possible source of change essential to measure. Firstly, the change in the examined factor (e.g. cognitive function), and secondly the change of the testing setting (e.g. a different test administrator) for the test occasions (Guo, 2013). Inaccurate interpretation of cognitive maturation tendencies could be a consequence of not considering the latter types of influences (Hofer & Schaie, 2001), e.g. inaccurately interpreting participant's cognitive deterioration at the subsequent testing occasion. Thus, change in the testing setting is a potential concern in longitudinal studies of ageing and its influence is fundamental to measure (Hofer & Schaie, 2001; Schmidt & Teti, 2005; Shadish, Cook, & Campbell, 2002). This paper focuses on investigating potential sources of influences on participants' cognitive performances, that are tied to testing procedures. In particular, it will discuss influences attributable to the practice of using multiple test administrators.

1.1. Test administrator influence

Level of cognition is imperative to measure, and standardised tests as well as standardised procedures are often implemented to collect cognitive data. Testing procedures contain a component of interaction between the test administrator and the participant. Previous research has verified that test administrators have an influence on participants' cognitive performances (test administrator influence). This influence can be partially avoided by using strict and standardised procedures of test administration (Rousson, Gasser, & Seifert, 2002; Sattler & Theye, 1967). However, despite standardised testing procedures, some underlying influence may still remain. Sattler and Theye (1967) describe three possible sources of test administrator influence. These are: *departures from standardised procedure*, e.g. adapting testing instructions, *situational variables*, e.g. using praise and discouragement and the *experimenter variable*, involving attributes of the test administrator. Ethnicity (Marx & Goff, 2005; Samuel, 1977), sex (Ortner & Vormittag, 2011; Samuel, 1977), prior experience of administrating (Hoyt & Kerns, 1999; Lim, 2011), expectancies on participant's behaviour (Rosenthal & Fode, 1963), personal reactions to participant attributions, e.g. the halo effect (Hoyt, 2000; Thorndike, 1920), and attitude (Bookout & Hosford, 1969) have all been suggested to influence participant's performance.

Hoyt and Kerns (1999) suggest that *rater bias* (a form of test administrator influence) is ascribable to the characteristics of the testing instrument in combination with the experimenter variable. In their meta-analysis, 47% of variance in rating scores was found attributable to a combination of the experience of the rater and the inferential level of the instrument's rating system. The largest variance of rater bias was established for inexperienced raters using highly inferential rating systems. However, there was still a substantial amount of variance (19%) in ratings although the ratings were conducted by experienced raters. Despite the convincing evidence of test administrator influences on cognitive performance, general discussions on the subject in longitudinal studies and in gerontological research have been somewhat neglected (Guo & Bollen, 2013; Ortner & Vormittag, 2011). Longitudinal studies often use multiple test administrators to collect data, and systematic differences in testing procedures between these test administrators may exist. Hence, it is important to examine whether and to what extent test administrator influence exists in these types of studies.

1.2. Testing specific factors

Procedural choices and practicalities can influence participant's cognitive performance and procedures may vary within participant but also vary between participants. Procedural choices and practicalities may include changes of the test administrator, cognitive test batteries, the time of day the person is tested and in which type of testing environment the person was tested.[1] All of these factors are tied to the specific testing situation and are therefore referred to as *testing specific factors*. Testing specific factors, reasons for implementing these and suggestions on how they influence performance

Table 1. Testing specific factors in the GÅS-study, implementation reason and suggested latent factors

Testing specific factors	Implementation reason	Latent factors
Multiple test administrators	Practical: Change in personnel throughout the study	Test administrator influence, e.g. experience of test administrator
Different test versions	Reduce practice effects on subsequent testing occasions	Different difficulty levels of the test versions
Different orders of test battery administration	To reduce potential systematic fatigue effects	Fatigue due to serial testing or alertness in the beginning of the testing session.
Time of day of testing	Practical: To test many participants in the same day	Fatigue due to differences in circadian rhythms.
Testing setting	To boost participant rate/minimise selection bias	Discomfort/comfort of the participant

are discussed below and displayed in Table 1. These types of procedures are often implemented to reduce problems related to large population samples and to longitudinal data collecting. For example, a different version of the same test at the subsequent testing occasion can be used to reduce practice effects (Salthouse, 2014). Additionally, changing orders in which the tests are presented in a test battery can be used to reduce potential systematic fatigue effects on participants' performances due to serial testing (Laukka et al., 2013). There might also be practical motivations behind implementation of specific procedures, such as testing participants at different times of day or the need to use multiple test administrators to collect data. Moreover, home visits may be offered to participants unable to come to the test centre in order to avoid losing participants that are too frail to come to the testing centre, thus boosting participant rates and reducing selection bias (Lissner et al., 2003).

Testing specific factors do not intrinsically influence participant's performance, but indirectly affect test scores, due to latent factors. Latent factors are the suggested explanations behind how testing specific factors cause alteration in performance. Previous research on the latent factors, related to the testing specific factors, is scarce. It has however been observed that variations in test scores due to different versions of the same tests were explained by differences in difficulty levels between test versions. Also, variation of the order of which a test is presented in the test battery is designed to measure and reduce the effects of fatigue due to serial testing (Laukka et al., 2013). Hence, test score differences between test orders can indicate fatigue or alertness of the participant. Past research has found that variations in test performances can be seen due to the time of day of the testing, where age of the participant particularly matters (Blatter & Cajochen, 2007; May, Hasher, & Foong, 2005; Schmidt, Collette, Cajochen, & Peigneux, 2007). These differences are described as fatigue or alertness of the participants due to individual differences in circadian rhythms. Home visits in comparison to testing in the clinic have been found to positively influence test scores on the Mini mental state examination (MMSE). This is explained by the participant being more comfortable when tested at home (Shievitz, Tudiver, Araujo, Sanghe, & Boyle, 1998).

1.2.1. The present study

The overall aim of this study was to inspect to what extent the use of multiple test administrators together with other testing specific factors could influence participant's cognitive test scores. This was done in a longitudinal study of ageing, that used multiple test administrators, implemented several testing specific procedural choices and used tests designed to measure multiple cognitive domains; speed of processing, episodic memory and spatial ability. The first specific aim was to examine the extent of potential test administrator influence on participant's test scores. This was done by examining if any of the explained variance in test scores was attributed to the practice of using multiple test administrators. The second aim was to examine potential influences on test scores of all testing specific factors included in the study, such as different versions of the same test or time of day of testing (all displayed in Table 1).

2. Method

2.1. Sample

Participants were recruited through the Good Ageing in Skåne study (GÅS: Gott åldrande i Skåne), which is an ongoing longitudinal study in the southern part of Sweden, covering five municipalities including both rural and urban areas. Participants were randomly invited from the general population using the National Population Registry (Ekström & Elmståhl, 2006). Participants were examined by a physician, registered nurse and psychological test administrator. Dementia was diagnosed by the examining physician according to the Diagnostic and Statistical Manual of Mental Disorders-IV criteria, and medical records. Two questionnaires about health and lifestyle were provided. Full examination took 7 h and was conducted at one of the study's test centres. In order to avoid losing participants, participants unable to come to the test centre were offered an examination in their home. So far, four data collection sessions are complete and the fifth is ongoing. Re-examination was performed every third year for participants above 78 years of age and every sixth year for participants below 78 years of age. New participants were recruited every sixth year. Additional descriptions of the study design have been provided elsewhere (Ekström & Elmståhl, 2006; Lagergren et al., 2004).

90% (8,204) of 9,107 participant observations provided data from at least one cognitive test in the test battery, see Figure 1. The 8,204 participant observations in this sample were acquired from 4,897 unique participants. The sample contains participants observations from participants examined up to five times (see Table 2). Reasons for not taking part in the psychological testing session included dementia, over medication, illness, participation merely via telephone interview, and refusal. Further exclusion was based on well-known factors that affect cognitive performance. Participants with missing scores or scores <24 on mini mental state examination (MMSE; Folstein, Folstein, & McHugh, 1975), moderately and severely depressed participants, participants that had very poor eyesight, and non-native speaking participants with language difficulties were excluded. The evaluations whether poor eyesight and language difficulties affected the execution of the test were made by the test administrator. Furthermore, the incomprehension of the instructions of a specific test, as judged by a test administrator, led to exclusion for each test individually, in total 31 participant observations were therefore excluded. The excluded group was older ($M = 80.60$, $SD = 10.63$) than the main sample of participants ($M = 71.34$, $SD = 10.12$), and more likely to have lower education (mean years of education = 9.13, $SD = 3.41$), compared to the main sample

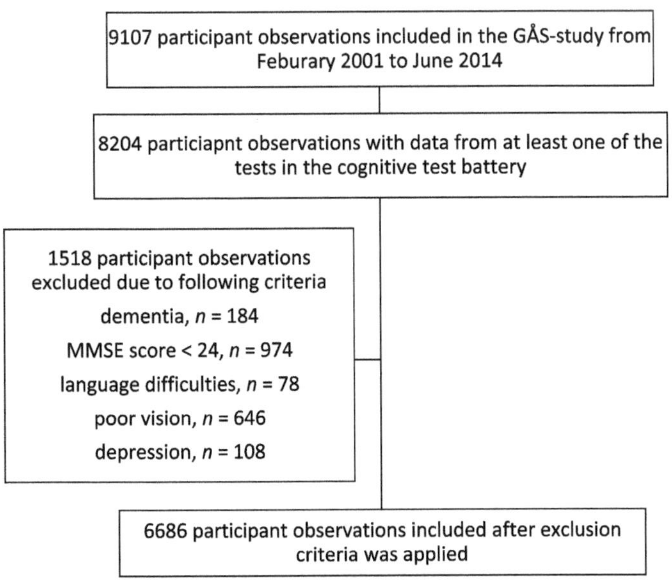

Figure 1. Flow chart of the sample with the exclusion criteria.

Note: MMSE = Mini mental state examination.

Table 2. Number of examination times for participants

	Number of participants	Percentage
Examination times		
1	2,611	53
2	1,523	31.1
3	542	11.1
4	184	3.8
5	37	.7
Total	4,897	100

Table 3. Sample characteristics after exclusion and descriptive statistics of participant observations and testing specific factors

	Mean	Standard deviation	Number of observations	Percentage
Age (years)	71.34	10.1		
Education (years)	10.90	3.79		
MMSE	27.62	1.69		
Sex				
Women			3,602	53.9
Men			3,084	46.1
Previous experience				
No experience at the time of examination			4,090	61.2
Previous experience			2,596	38.8
Time of day				
Morning			2,243	33.5
Prior lunch			2,820	42.2
Afternoon			1,618	24.2
Test order				
1			3,390	50.7
2			3,296	49.3
Test version				
1			2,248	33.6
2			2,219	33.2
3			2,219	33.2
Testing setting				
Test centre			5,921	88.6
Home visit			492	7.4

Notes: The 6,686 observations presented here were acquired from 4,090 distinct participants. MMSE = mini mental state examination.

(M = 10.90, SD = 3.79). There were more females in the excluded group (61% vs. 54%). After exclusion, 6,686 participant observations were included in the main sample. The following nine age groups were used; 60, 66, 72, 78, 81, 84, 87, 90, 93+. See main sample characteristics in Table 3. The study was approved by the regional ethics committee of Lund University (2002; registration No. LU 744-00) and all participants have provided written consent.

2.2. Test administrators

By June 2015, 21 (2 men, 19 women) test administrators have been involved in the study. Mean age was 32.8, median age was 30, age ranges from 25 to 50 years. The average duration of employment was 2.19 years, ranging between 0 and 10 years. Minimum requirement for serving as a test administrator was a bachelor's degree in behavioural sciences. The test administrators have tested between 42 and 1,503 participants.

Each administrator was provided with a detailed instruction handbook and had a minimum of two weeks training together with an experienced test administrator. The training weeks ended with a couple of practice sessions with a mock participant, before working with participants. The test administrator was observed by an experienced test administrator at the practice sessions, and during a real testing session. In addition, frequent meetings between test administrators and an experienced neuropsychologist took place every month, and more frequently if requested by the test administrator. This was to ensure standardised administration and consistency in test scoring. These meetings consisted of discussions of testing methodology and discussions of ambiguous responses from participants. To minimise expectancy effects, no information, prior to the testing session, on how returning participants performed on their last testing session was provided.

2.3. Cognitive assessment

The cognitive testing session was conducted by a test administrator and consisted of a standardised test battery, containing 12 neuropsychological tests, adapted for an older population. The examination time was about 1.5 h. Participants were either tested in the morning, between 8 and 10 am, or prior lunch, between 10 am and noon or in the afternoon, between 1 and 3 pm. To minimise systematic effects of fatigue due to serial testing, the test was administrated in two different orders in the test battery. To reduce practice effects, three different versions were provided for each test, and participants received different versions at consecutive visits. The three versions of all tests were constructed to be equally difficult and measure the same underlying cognitive function. Both test orders and test versions were divided equally between all participants. The battery included instruments that measured speed of processing, episodic memory, spatial ability, confidence judgments (Dahl, Allwood, Rennemark, & Hagberg, 2010), word comprehension (Dureman, 1960), and global cognitive function measured by MMSE (Folstein et al., 1975). Retest correlations for most of the tests were fairly high ($r = .51–.80$; median = .69), which indicates acceptable lower boundaries. However, for the test recognition ($r = .32$) and general knowledge ($r = .13$) the retest effect was low (Lövden et al., 2014). After testing, participants were interviewed about major life events, depression and coping strategies.

Depression was assessed by the Montgomery-Åsberg Depression Rating Scale. This scale was based on Comprehensive Psychiatric Rating Scale (CPRS; Montgomery & Asberg, 1979). The CPRS has repeatedly been used to assess depression in elderly populations (Bäckman, Hill, & Forsell, 1996; Pantzar et al., 2014). The scale consisted of ten questions regarding e.g. depression, anxiety, concentration and sleep deprivation. Each question had a scale from 0 to 6, with a total score of 60. According to Snaith, Harrop, Newby, and Teale (1986) scores of 0–6 indicated *free from depression*, 7–19 *mild depression*, 20–34 *moderate depression* and 35–60 *severe depression*.

2.3.1. Speed of processing

Two tests were included and designed to measure speed of processing, *the pattern comparison task* and the *digit cancellation task*. A structural equation model by Laukka et al. (2013) has found these two tests to be strongly correlated with each other. The pattern comparison task (Salthouse & Babcock, 1991) was a pencil and paper task with two separately administrated pages, consisting of 30 pairs of line-segment patterns, half of which were identical and half different, divided equally into two columns on each page. Participants had 30 s per page to identify as many identical pairs as possible. Three practice pattern-pairs were first completed to ensure comprehension of the task. Test score assessment was the total number of correctly classified patterns from both pages, maximum 60 correct patterns (Salthouse & Babcock, 1991). The digit cancellation task (Zazzo, 1974) was a pencil and paper task which originated from well-established cancellation tasks such as those used in Diller et al. (1974) and Lewis and Rennick (1979). The task consisted of one page with 11 rows of digits, ranging from 1 to 9, with one isolated practice row at the top of the page. There were 43 4's and the participant had 30 s to cross over as many of these as possible. Test score assessment was the total number of correctly crossed over digit "4".

2.3.2. Episodic memory

Two consecutive tests were designed to measure episodic memory, firstly *the free recall test* and secondly *the recognition test*. As for the speed of processing tests, a structural equation model showed that the free recall and recognition tests are strongly correlated. The test consisted of learning a word list, comprised of 16 unrelated concrete nouns (target words), with an immediate free recall trial and a forced yes/no recognition trial (Gardiner & Java, 1993). One at a time, words in a booklet were presented orally and visually for 5 s, in order to bypass visual and hearing problems, and to ensure registration of each word. Immediately after the presentation, participants were given two minutes for oral free recall. For the self-paced recognition task, the 16 target words intermixed with 16 interference words were presented in the same manner. Participants answered yes or no if they recognised a word or not. Of the interference words, four were perceptually similar, four were semantically similar and eight were unrelated to the target words. Following recognition of the word, participants were asked to choose between three alternatives. (1) If they remembered some specific detail ("remembered" item/source memory) from when the word was first presented to them. For example, whether they made an associative relation to the word, or inferred personal relevance to the word. (2) If they recognised the word as being familiar, but could not report a source memory for the word ("know" item based on familiarity). (3) If they were indecisive between alternative 1 and 2. Participants were requested to justify why they picked a specific alternative, confirming comprehension of the differences between remember/source memory and know/familiarity. Significant differences between the three versions have been found, participants performed somewhat better on version 1, compared to 2 and 3 in Laukka et al. (2013). Test score assessment for free recall was the total number of correctly recalled words, with a maximum of 16. For recognition scores, the recognised words were used, including both hits and false hits, combined into d-prime. d-prime is a concept originally stemming from signal detection theory, designed to distinguish between true hits and false hits (guessing), taking both hits and false hits into consideration (Snodgrass & Corwin, 1988).

2.3.3. Spatial ability

A *mental rotation test* (Rehnman & Herlitz, 2006) was designed to measure spatial ability. 10 series of 4 two-dimensional (quasi three-dimensional) figures of the Shepard and Metzler type (Shepard & Metzler, 1971) were presented in a booklet, one at a time. Each figure consisted of 10 cubes and there were three different versions of the 10 x 4 series. Each series contained one original figure placed to the left of three figures. One of the figures to the right was the same as the original figure but rotated to a specific angle. The two remaining figures were distractors, and could not be rotated to be congruent with the original figure. Participants were requested to choose between the three figures to the right and, as fast as possible, pick the correct rotated original figure. If the participant had not answered after 35 and 45 s, respectively, they were encouraged to do so. Three practice series were completed prior to the test in order to ensure comprehension. Test score assessment was divided into two elements, speed and accuracy. Speed was measured by seconds required for the participant to point at the correct figure.[2] Each task had a difficulty rating, which was the proportion of correct answers obtained when the test was assigned to a group of participants.[3] A difficult task endured a lower percentage of correct responses. Difficulty rating was considered when assessing speed response for each series (10 x participant). Two out of 30 tasks were missing difficulty ratings due to subsequent changes of the test after the difficulty ratings were produced, and therefore could not be used in the analysis. Accuracy was measured by number of correct responses, divided by the number of tasks in each version the participant had completed. The majority of participants completed all 10 tasks.

2.4. Statistical analyses

The data were analysed using a series of linear mixed models using IBM SPSS Statistics 22. The equation used for the mixed models was the following. The outcome (dependent variable of interest, i.e. the test score) y_{ijk} (corresponding to participant *i* meeting with test administrator *j* at visit *k*) is assumed to satisfy the relation:

$$y_{ijk} = \text{Prediction}_{ik} + \varepsilon_i + \varepsilon_j + \varepsilon_{ijk}.$$

The Prediction_{ik} represents nine predictors (independent variables as fixed effects) and the error terms ε_i, ε_j (random effects) and ε_{ijk} are assumed to follow independent zero mean Gaussian distributions with variances σ_1^2, σ_2^2 and σ_3^2, respectively. This assumption leads to the correlation $\frac{\sigma_1^2}{\sigma_1^2+\sigma_2^2+\sigma_3^2}$ between two measurements coming from one participant and $\frac{\sigma_2^2}{\sigma_1^2+\sigma_2^2+\sigma_3^2}$ between two measurements corresponding to one test administrator. There were in total five categorical predictors related to testing setting; time of day of the testing, the test order, versions of the test, testing setting. For speed of mental rotation, difficulty level of the task was included instead of test version. There were also three categorical predictors related to the participant; age group, sex, and previous experience of cognitive testing. Years of education of the participant was included as a continuous predictor. The testing specific factors were further assessed by estimated marginal means, adjusted for multiple testing using the Sidak-method. Cohen's *d* effect sizes were reported for each test (Cohen, 1992).

3. Results

3.1. Test administrator effects

There was a significant random effect of the test administrators for all the cognitive tests ($p < .01$), see Table 4 for detailed statistics. The variance components analysis revealed that the proportion of variance of the random intercept corresponding to test administrator was (.37/(.37 + 3.92 + 9.07)) = .028 for digit cancellation. This suggests that about 2.8%, of the total variation in the participant scores for digit cancellation, was ascribed to the test administrators, see Table 8 for further variance calculations. This entails that the total variance in the participants' test scores, determined by the factor corresponding to the test administrators, was between 1.4 and 3.5%.

3.2. Testing specific factor effects

Results showed that different testing specific factors were associated with particular cognitive tests (see Tables 5–8). When examining the estimated marginal means, significant differences between test versions were found for all the cognitive tests, except for accuracy for mental rotation. For digit cancellation, participants performed worse on version one in comparison to version three and for pattern comparison participants performed worse on version three in comparison to version two. Participants tested with version three of the episodic memory tests recalled significantly fewer words, and had poorer d'prime scores than those participants who received version one and two. Better performance scores were found when the speed of processing task was administrated as the second speed task in the test battery. A similar significant tendency was found for speed of mental rotation, i.e. having the mental rotation tasks further into the test battery was beneficial for a faster response, compared to having the mental rotation test at the very beginning of the test battery. Estimated marginal means showed that participants performed better on the recognition test in the morning testing sessions compared to before lunch, or in the afternoon and, in comparison to afternoon sessions, participants performed better before lunch. However, the reverse effect was seen for speed of mental rotation, where participants were slower when solving the task in morning compared to before lunch and in the afternoon. Participants that were tested at home performed worse on both speed of processing tasks and memory tasks compared to the participants that were tested at the testing centre. For accuracy of mental rotations scores, there were no significant effects of any of the testing specific factors contributing to participants' test scores.

Table 4. Variance estimates for different tests and variance components and percentage of variance corresponding to test administrator

Random effects	Variance estimate	Standard error	Wald Z	p-value	Percentage of variance
Digit cancellation					
Test administrator	.369	.129	2.86	.004**	2.8
Participant	9.07	.282	32.1	.001***	
Residual	3.92	.118	33.2	.001***	
Pattern comparison					
Test administrator	1.32	.437	2.82	.005**	3.5
Participant	22.3	.746	29.9	.001***	
Residual	11.7	.355	32.9	.001***	
Free recall					
Test administrator	.065	.029	2.26	.024*	1.4
Participant	1.92	.099	19.4	.001***	
Residual	2.59	.077	33.8	.001***	
Recognition					
Test administrator	.021	.008	2.52	.012*	2.6
Participant	.314	.017	18.4	.001***	
Residual	.473	.014	34.1	.001***	
Speed of mental rotation					
Test administrator	1.64	.573	2.68	.007**	1.5
Participant	27.8	.851	32.7	.001***	
Residual	71.6	.569	125.9	.001***	
Accuracy of mental rotation					
Test administrator	.0006	.0002	2.49	.013*	1.9
Participant	.008	.0007	11.6	.001***	
Residual	.024	.0007	34.5	.001***	

*Significant at the $p < .05$ level.
**Significant at the $p < .01$ level.
***Significant at the $p < .001$ level.

In addition, the analyses revealed poorer test performances with an increase in age (see Table 9). Length of education had a positive effect on all test scores. Moreover, women had better test scores than men on all cognitive tests, except for mental rotation, where men were both faster and had more correct responses. Previous experience of testing situation was favourable for tests scores of digit cancellation and speed of mental rotation. The correlation of test scores stemming from the same participants were large for all tests, varying between .248 and .680, suggesting that about 24.8–68% of the total variance in the participant's test scores was explained at the participant level.

Table 5. Statistics for time of day with estimated means, *F*-values and *p*-values for fixed effects and effect sizes of pairwise comparisons

Tests	Estimated marginal means† (*SE*)			*df*			*F*-value	*p*-value	Cohen's *d*		
	Morn.	P. lunch	Aftern.	Morn.	P. lunch	Aftern.			Morn. vs. P. lunch	Morn. vs. Aftern.	P. lunch vs Aftern.
Digit cancellation	15.3 (.172)	15.4 (.171)	15.5 (.173)	48.9	48.0	50.5	1.32	.268	.012	.014	.029
Pattern comparison	23.5 (.301)	23.6 (.3)	23.8 (.303)	40.8	49.1	42.2	1.54	.214	.081	.047	.029
Free recall	6.15 (.09)	6.11 (.89)	6.02 (.091)	68.1	66.2	73.4	1.81	.164	.021	.059	.038
Recognition	2.75 (.043)	2.67 (.43)	2.6 (.044)	46.9	45.8	49.4	14.4	.001***	.089	.168	.079
Speed of mental rotation	16.7 (.335)	16.2 (.333)	16.2 (.337)	36.4	35.8	37.6	6.28**	.002**	.046	.051	.006
Accuracy of mental rotation	.604 (.008)	.596 (.008)	.598 (.008)	62.3	60.4	67.3	1.28	.278	.045	.033	.011

Notes: Morn. = Morning, P. lunch = Prior lunch, Aftern. = Afternoon.

†Estimated means are evaluated at 10.9 years of education for all tests except speed of mental rotation which is evaluated at 11.14 years.

**Significant at the $p < .01$ level.

***Significant at the $p < .001$ level.

Table 6. Statistics for test order with estimated means, *F*-values and *p*-values for fixed effects and effect sizes of pairwise comparisons

Tests	Estimated marginal means† (*SE*)		*df*		*F*-value	*p*-value	Cohen's *d*
	Order 1	Order 2	Order 1	Order 2			Order 1 vs. 2
Digit cancellation	15.3 (.169)	15.6 (.17)	46.1	46.8	12.4	.001***	.082
Pattern comparison	24.3 (.297)	23.0 (.298)	38.6	39.0	87.8	.001***	.226
Free recall	6.07 (.086)	6.11 (.087)	59.1	60.4	.425	.515	.017
Recognition	2.66 (.042)	2.69 (.42)	41.9	42.6	1.99	.158	.036
Speed of mental rotation	15.8 (.331)	16.9 (.331)	34.9	35.0	42.8	.001***	.010
Accuracy of mental rotation	.598 (.008)	.6 (.008)	54.15	54.2	.228	.633	.011

†Estimated means are evaluated at 10.9 years of education for all tests except speed of mental rotation which is evaluated at 11.14 years.

***Significant at the $p < .001$ level.

Table 7. Statistics for test versions with estimated means, *F*-values and *p*-values for fixed effects and effect sizes of pairwise comparisons

Tests	Estimated marginal means† (*SE*)			*df*			*F*-value	*p*-value	Cohen's *d*		
	Version 1	Version 2	Version 3	Version 1	Version 2	Version 3			Version 1 vs. 2	Version 1 vs. 3	Version 2 vs. 3
Digit cancellation	15.5 (.169)	15.4 (.17)	15.3 (.17)	46.4	46.8	47.0	6.02	.001***	.039	.071	.034
Pattern comparison	23.6 (.297)	23.9 (.298)	23.4 (.298)	39.0	39.4	39.4	8.52	.001***	.052	.038	.09
Free recall	6.3 (.088)	5.8 (.088)	6.17 (.88)	64.8	64.8	64.8	42.2	.001***	.234	.06	.173
Recognition	2.65 (.043)	2.72 (.043)	2.66 (.043)	45.0	45.1	45.2	5.24**	.005**	.078	.007	.071
Speed of mental rotation	N/A	N/A	N/A	N/A	N/A	N/A	2,236	.001***	N/A	N/A	N/A
Accuracy of mental rotation	.593 (.008)	.605 (.008)	.599 (.008)	60.0	60.6	60.6	2.38	.93	.061	.033	.033

Note: The covariate difficulty level is only relevant for mental rotation speed, all remaining tests have test version as covariate instead.

†Estimated means are evaluated at 10.9 years of education for all tests except speed of mental rotation which is evaluated at 11.14 years.

**Significant at the $p < .01$ level.

***Significant at the $p < .001$ level.

Table 8. Statistics for testing setting with estimated means, *F*-values and *p*-values for fixed effects and effect sizes of pairwise comparisons

Tests	Estimated marginal mean† (*SE*)		*df*		*F*-value	*p*-value	Cohen's *d*
	Test centre	Home visit	Test centre	Home visit			Test centre vs. home visit
Digit cancellation	16.1 (.159)	14.8 (.204)	36.1	96.6	64.9	.001***	.356
Pattern comparison	24.9 (.28)	22.4 (.354)	30.8	77.51	87.2	.001***	.43
Free recall	6.34 (.077)	5.85 (.118)	38.1	199.1	19.2	.001***	.173
Recognition	2.74 (.039)	2.61 (.054)	30.0	114.9	6.87	.001***	.139
Speed of mental rotation	16.2 (.313)	16.5 (.394)	27.9	69.9	1.23	.268	.034
Accuracy of mental rotation	.598 (.007)	.6 (.011)	35.5	174.5	.862	.011*	.862

†Estimated means are evaluated at 10.9 years of education for all tests except speed of mental rotation which is evaluated at 11.14 years.

*Significant at the $p < .05$ level.

***Significant at the $p < .001$ level.

Table 9. *F*-values and *p*-values for fixed effects for individual differences

Tests	Individual differences							
	Age		Sex		Education		Previous experience	
	F-value	*p*-value	*F*-value	*p*-value	*F*-value	*p*-value	*F*-value	*p*-value
Digit cancellation	107.1	.001***	44.2	.001***	97.66	.001***	9.8	.002**
Pattern comparison	192.2	.001***	19.7	.001***	255.1	.001***	3.45	.064
Free recall	46.5	.001***	225	.001***	169.5	.001***	.53	.467
Recognition	3.53	.001***	78.4	.001***	66.5	.001***	.177	.674
Speed of mental rotation	31.9	.001***	5.69	.001***	31.36	.001***	22.6	.001***
Accuracy of mental rotation	16.7	.001***	320	.001***	104	.001***	1.37	.242

**Significant at the $p < .01$ level.

***Significant at the $p < .001$ level.

4. Discussion

The aims of this study were to investigate the influence of the test administrator and testing specific factors on test scores in a longitudinal study. Results showed a significant amount of test administrator influence on participant's test scores, where 1.4–3.5% of the variations in test scores were explained on a test administrator level. Influences of other testing specific factors, such as test version, test order, time of day and testing setting were found to significantly influence the majority of test scores measuring different cognitive functions.

4.1. Test administrator influence

In regard to previous research on underlying causes of test administrator influence, it is likely that the test administrator influence found here is partially related to experimenter variables (Sattler & Theye, 1967), e.g. experience, age and sex of the test administrator. This study included female and male test administrators, with large variation in testing experience (42–1,503 participants) and age range (25–50 years). Inexperience of test administrators has previously explained discrepancies in test scores (Hoyt & Kerns, 1999). However, separate analyses involving only experienced test administrators also showed a test administrator effect (data not shown). It thus seems reasonable to conjecture that experience of the test administrator does not account for all test administrator influence on test scores in our sample of test administrators. Although there was a large age discrepancy between test administrators, 71% of the administrators were between 25 and 33 (median 30), which is a rather small variation in age, making it difficult to draw conclusions of whether the age of the test administrator was an influential factor or not. Similarly, with two male and 18 female test administrators, we cannot assess the influence of the sex of the test administrator.

Additionally, we cannot rule out that the experimenter variables interact with other factors, e.g. concerning the characteristics of the participant. For instance, Ortner and Vormittag (2011) found that female participants performed better on verbal general knowledge test when tested by a female test administrator.

Sattler and Theye (1967) discuss that departures from standardised procedures, are more prominent in ageing studies than in studies using younger participants. Level of overall cognition declines with advancing age (Salthouse, 2009), and therefore samples of elder participants may require supplementary test instructions to comprehend the task at hand. This can lead to departures from standardised testing instructions when testing older participants. One test administrator might handle the elder's incomprehension differently from its colleague, and therefore systematic test administrator influences occur more often in studies examining elderly samples, compared to those focusing on younger samples. Future research could focus on test administrator influence in relation to the age of the sample, bringing insight to whether ageing studies should routinely inspect for test administrator influence.

Furthermore, differences in the magnitude of test administrator influence were observed between different types of tests. The largest proportion of the total variance attributed to test administrator was found for the speed of processing instruments and recognition, the smallest for mental rotation and free recall. The fact that the variance attributed to test administrator is positive for all tests may indicate that regardless of the type of test and what underlying cognitive function it is intended to capture, test administrator influence may exist in test scores.

The extent of test administrator influences on cognitive test scores in longitudinal studies has not been studied. Reasons for this include that rigid routines of test administration are usually applied, to purposely eliminate test administrator influence. Likewise, because of the complicated nature of test administrators influences and their underlying causes, investigators may struggle to comprehend to what extent test administrator influences exist in their data (Hoyt, 2000), leading to a hesitation in exploring such influences. Although this paper can only speculate why there is administrator influence on test scores, it demonstrates that despite rigid routines, variability in participants' performance is attributable to the test administrator, accounting for up to 4% of the variance.

4.2. Testing specific influences

There were four major findings of influences attributable to the testing specific factors. Firstly, no negative effect of the second test order was found, implying that serial testing was not mentally tiring for the participants. One could also then presume that our test battery was not strenuous for our participants. On the contrary, participants performed better on the speed of processing and the speed of mental rotation task further into the testing battery, signifying *task familiarity* or *immediate practice effects*. It has previously been suggested that participants perform better on tasks that they have already completed, because they fully comprehend what the test requires the second time they receive a similar test (Goldberg, Harvey, Wesnes, Snyder, & Schneider, 2015).

Secondly, there were effects of time of day for the recognition test, and best performances were found for morning sessions. Additionally, participants tested in the afternoon and prior lunch performed better than participants tested in the morning on the speed of mental rotation test. Differences in test scores ascribed to time of day have previously been explained by circadian rhythm influences on cognition, and participants tested at matched peak circadian periods show better cognitive performances than those tested at off-peak time of day (Blatter & Cajochen, 2007). These results have been found for a wide range of cognitive tasks, measuring different types of memory, executive functioning, and attention (Schmidt et al., 2007). However, not all types of performances on cognitive tasks are influenced equally (Blatter & Cajochen, 2007). Differences in task duration, cognitive load (high vs. low), and difficulty level could explain why we found specific time of day effects exclusively on recognition and speed of mental rotation, and not for the remaining tests. For example, less cognitively demanding tasks (e.g. the speed of processing tasks used here) have been found to be less affected by influences of circadian rhythms (Yoon, May, & Hasher, 1999). In regard to our elderly sample, May et al. (2005) also found that morning testing sessions, compared to testing sessions later in the day, were beneficial for performances on instruments measuring memory for individuals between 60 and 75 years old.

Thirdly, there were significant differences between test versions of all the cognitive tests except for accuracy of mental rotation. Differences between test versions of the episodic memory test have previously been presented in SNAC-Kungsholmen study (Laukka et al., 2013), and explained by variations in difficulty levels. Researchers that use different versions of the same instrument should routinely inspect and report methodological diversities, in order to reduce reactive effects.

Fourthly, participants tested in their home environment performed worse than those tested in the test centre. Many distractions may exist in a home environment influencing the scores negatively, such as uncontrollable background noise, distractions from home care assistance and so forth. Yet, these results are inconsistent with previous results from Shievitz et al. (1998), who found that geriatric participants tested at home scored significantly better on the MMSE than when tested in a clinical setting. Selection bias can provide insight to these contradictory results. Participants that receive home visits are those individuals that are not well enough to come to the testing centre. Although we applied a rather strict exclusion criterion, a selection of the most unfit may still remain in the home visit group, leading to poorer scores in this group in comparison to the testing centre group.

In sum, testing specific factors can be relevant for most cognitive performances, however future research is needed to confirm these results.

4.3. Limitations and strengths

One limitation in our study was not to include any potential influencing factors related to experimenter variables (characteristics of the test administrator) in the statistical analyses, making it impossible to draw conclusions regarding the impact of these factors. However, the main aim of this study was to solely examine the extent to which test administrator influence could exist in a longitudinal ageing study. Moreover, further potentially relevant information concerning the characteristics of test administrator, such as ethnicity or personality traits, was not accessible in our study. Neither was information regarding situational variables, e.g. praise or discouragement of the participant's performance during testing, and if this was used systematically by particular test administrators. Another weakness was not inspecting interactions of testing specific factors. For example, the effect on test score of a difficult test version may be different in the morning compared to the afternoon.

Strengths of the study include using a large random sample from the general population, covering both urban and rural areas, with multiple follow-ups and including diverse cognitive testing instruments. This increases generalisability of the results. Furthermore, by examining test administrator influence through a random effect, the sample of test administrators are statistically assumed to come from a hypothetical population of test administrators, which could also increase generalisability (Searle, 1971). Another strength, are our procedures of data collection, enabling an ability to measure and evaluate specific confounding factors. For example, two different orders of the test battery allow us to investigate fatigue effects due to serial testing on particular tests. Also, by documenting when the participant was tested, investigation of fatigue due to the time of day could be carried out.

Reducing test administrator bias on test scores is crucial in order to acquire internal validity, and ensure reliable cognitive instruments. High quality training of administrators, and good standardisation, of the instruments reduce these types of weaknesses (Rousson et al., 2002). Our study applied these types of precautions, such as training, extensive test manuals and regular meetings between test administrators. Furthermore, this study used acceptably reliable instruments. Still, there were differences in test scores attributable to the test administrators. It is however plausible that the effects are relatively small due to the very fact that rigid routines were applied. Therefore, it seems worthwhile to continue with these types of practices. Moreover, investigators should examine their data for systematic test administrator effects, alternatively use computer-based instruments, when appropriate. On a further note, systematic test administrator influences in cross-sectional data could also be of a concern, and our results could be applicable to cross-sectional studies using multiple test administrators to collect data.

When considering what type of procedural choices to implement, and practicalities to take into account, it is important to consider their impact on the outcome. For example, the results indicate that there were no effects of fatigue due to serial testing, therefore two orders of the testing battery could be excessive. The time of day was seen to influence test scores and therefore future studies should consider whether it is possible to test all participants at the same time of day. Comparing results from participants tested at home to those tested at the testing centre is also a challenge. Weighing the benefits of reducing selection bias against the potential influence of differences in testing environment warrants further investigation.

4.4. Concluding remarks

This study has provided evidence that the practice of using multiple test administrators to collect cognitive data is a tangible concern in longitudinal studies of ageing. The effects of test administrator influence on test scores are noteworthy, even though the magnitude of these effects is relatively small. We found that time of day, serial testing, different versions of the same test, and testing setting can also cause implications in interpretation of test scores. In summary, these results endorse Guo's (2013) assertion that researchers must consider both individual change and variation in testing settings when analysing longitudinal data.

Funding
The authors received no direct funding for this research.

Competing Interests
The authors declare no competing interest.

Author details
Marieclaire Overton[1]
E-mail: marie_claire.overton@med.lu.se
ORCID ID: http://orcid.org/00-0001-6708-6273
Mats Pihlsgård[1]
E-mail: mats.pihlsgard@med.lu.se
ORCID ID: http://orcid.org/0000-0002-3934-9387
Sölve Elmståhl[1]
E-mail: solve.elmstahl@med.lu.se
ORCID ID: http://orcid.org/0000-0001-7153-5414
[1] Division of Geriatric Medicine, Lunds University, Skånes University Hospital, Jan Waldenströms gata 35, CRC Building 28, fl.13, SE-205 02 Malmö, Sweden.

Notes

1. Other testing specific factor may exist than the ones mentioned here, these are relevant for our study.
2. That the time it takes for the participant to point at the incorrect figure is irrelevant here.
3. Over 200 students in a pilot study, who responded to 20 tasks each, of all three versions.

References

Bäckman, L., Hill, R. D., & Forsell, Y. (1996). The influence of depressive symptomatology on episodic memory functioning among clinically nondepressed older adults. *Journal of Abnormal Psychology, 105*, 97–105. doi:10.1037/0021-843X.105.1.97

Blatter, K., & Cajochen, C. (2007). Circadian rhythms in cognitive performance: Methodological constraints, protocols, theoretical underpinnings. *Physiology & Behavior, 90*, 196–208. doi:10.1016/j.physbeh.2006.09.009

Bookout, D. V., & Hosford, R. E. (1969). Administration effects on the S-329 of the GATB using three experimental treatments. *Journal of Employment Counseling, 6*, 124–133. doi:10.1002/j.2161-1920.1969.tb00523.x

Cohen, J. (1992). A power primer. *Psychological Bulletin, 112*, 155–159. doi:10.1037/0033-2909.112.1.155

Dahl, M., Allwood, C., Rennemark, M., & Hagberg, B. (2010). The relation between personality and the realism in confidence judgements in older adults. *European Journal of Ageing, 7*, 283–291. doi:10.1007/s10433-010-0164-2

Diller, L., Ben-Yishay, Y., Gerstman, L. J., Goodkin, R., Gordon, W., & Weinberg, J. (1974). *Studies in cognition and rehabilitation in hemiplegia* (Rehabilitation Monograph No.50). New York, NY: New York University Medical Center.

Dureman, I. (1960). *SRB: 1*. Stockholm: Psykologiförlaget.

Ekström, H., & Elmståhl, S. (2006). Pain and fractures are independently related to lower walking speed and grip strength: Results from the population study "Good Ageing in Skåne". *Acta Orthopaedica, 77*, 902–911. doi:10.1080/17453670610013204

Ferrer, E., & Ghisletta, P. (2011). Methodological and analytical issues in the psychology of ageing. In W. Schaie & S. L. Willis (Eds.), *Handbook of the psychology of ageing* (7th ed., pp. 25–39). London: Academic Press. http://dx.doi.org/10.1016/B978-0-12-380882-0.00002-4

Folstein, M. F., Folstein, S. E., & McHugh, P. R. (1975). "Mini-mental state". *Journal of Psychiatric Research, 12*, 189–198. doi:10.1016/0022-3956(75)90026-6

Gardiner, J. M., & Java, R. I. (1993). Recognizing and remembering. In A. F. Collins, S. E. Gathercole, M. A. Conway, & P. E. Morris (Eds.), *Theories of memory* (pp. 163–188). Hove: Erlbaum.

Goldberg, T. E., Harvey, P., Wesnes, K. A., Snyder, P. J., & Schneider, L. S. (2015). Practice effects due to serial cognitive assessment: Impliactions for preclinical Alzheimer's disease randomized controlled trials. *Cognitive & Behavioral Assessment, 1*, 103–111. doi:10.1016/j.dadm.2014.11.003

Guo, S. (2013). Correction of rater effects in longitudinal research with a cross-classified random effects model. *Applied Psychological Measurement, 38*, 37–60. doi:10.1177/0146621613488821

Guo, S., & Bollen, K. A. (2013). Research using longitudinal ratings collected by multiple raters: One methodological problem and approaches to its solution. *Social Work Research, 37*, 85–98. doi:10.1093/swr/svs029

Hofer, M. S., & Schaie, K. W. (2001). Longitudinals studies in ageing research. In J. E. Birren & K. W. Schaie (Eds.), *Handbook of the psychology of ageing* (5th ed., pp. 53–77). San Diego, CA: Academic Press.

Hoyt, W. T. (2000). Rater bias in psychological research: When is it a problem and what can we do about it? *Psychological Methods, 5*, 64–86. doi:10.1037/1082-989X.5.1.64

Hoyt, W. T., & Kerns, M. (1999). Magnitude and moderators of bias in observer ratings: A meta-analysis. *Psychological Methods, 4*, 403–424. doi:10.1037/1082-989X.4.4.403

Lagergren, M., Fratiglioni, L., Hallberg, I. R., Berglund, J., Elmståhl, S., Hagberg, B., ... Wimo, A. (2004). A longitudinal study integrating population, care and social services data. The Swedish national study on ageing and care (SNAC). *Ageing Clinical Experimental Research, 16*, 158–168. http://dx.doi.org/10.1007/BF03324546

Laukka, E. J., Lövdén, M., Herlitz, A., Karlsson, S., Ferencz, B., Pantzar, A., ... Bäckman, L. (2013). Genetic effects on old-age cognitive functioning: A population-based study. *Psychology and Ageing, 28*, 262–274. doi:10.1037/a0030829

Lewis, R. F., & Rennick, P. M. (1979). *Manual for the repeatable cognitive-perceptual-motor battery*. Grosse Pointe Park, MI: Axon.

Lim, G. S. (2011). The development and maintenance of rating quality in performance writing assessment: A longitudinal study of new and experienced raters. *Language Testing, 28*, 543-560. doi:10.1177/0265532211406422.

Lissner, L. M., Skoog, I., Andersson, K., Beckman, N., Sundh, V., Waern, M., ... Björkelund, C. (2003). Participation bias in longitudinal studies: Experience from the population study of women in Gothenburg, Sweden. *Scandinavian Journal of Primary Health Care, 21*, 242–247. doi:10.1080/02813430310003309-1693

Lövden, M., Köhnke, Y., Laukka, E. J., Kalpouzos, G., Salami, A., Li, T. Q., ... Bäckman, L. (2014). Changes in perceptual speed and white matter microstructure in the corticospinal tract are associated in very old age. *Neuroimage*, 15, 520–530. doi:10.1016/j.neuroimage.2014.08.020

Marx, D. M., & Goff, P. A. (2005). Clearing the air: The effect of experimenter race on target's test performance and subjective experience. *British Journal of Social Psychology, 44*, 645–657. doi:10.1348/014466604X17948

May, C. P., Hasher, L., & Foong, N. (2005). Implicit memory, age, and time of day. *Psychological Science, 16*, 96–100. doi:10.1111/j.0956-7976.2005.00788.x

Montgomery, S. A., & Asberg, M. (1979). A new depression scale designed to be sensitive to change. *The British Journal of Psychiatry, 134*, 382–389. doi:10.1192/bjp.134.4.382

Ortner, T. M., & Vormittag, I. (2011). Test administrator's gender affects female and male students' self-estimated verbal general knowledge. *Learning and Instruction, 21*, 14–21. doi:10.1016/j.learninstruc.2009.09.003

Pantzar, A., Laukka, E. J., Atti, A. R., Fastbom, J., Fratiglioni, L., & Bäckman, L. (2014). Cognitive deficits in unipolar old-age depression: A population-based study. *Psychological Medicine, 44*, 937–947. doi:10.1017/S0033291713001736

Rehnman, J., & Herlitz, A. (2006). Higher face recognition ability in girls: Magnified by own-sex and own-ethnicity bias. *Memory, 14*, 289–296. doi:10.1080/09658210500233581

Rosenthal, R., & Fode, K. L. (1963). Psychology of the scientist: V. Three experiments in experimenter bias monograph supplement 3-V12. *Psychological Reports, 12*, 491–511. doi:10.2466/pr0.1963.12.2.491

Rousson, V., Gasser, T., & Seifert, B. (2002). Assessing intrarater, interrater and test-retest reliability of continuous measurements. *Statistics in Medicine, 21*, 3431–3446. doi:10.1002/sim.1253

Salthouse, T. A. (2009). When does age-related cognitive decline begin? *Neurobiology of Ageing, 30*, 507–514. doi:10.1016/j.neurobiolageing.2008.09.023

Salthouse, T. A. (2014). Ageing cognition unconfounded by prior test experience. *The Journals of Gerontology Series B: Psychological Sciences and Social Sciences, 65*, 698–705. doi:10.1093/geronb/gbu063

Salthouse, T. A., & Babcock, R. L. (1991). Decomposing adult age differences in working memory. *Developmental Psychology, 27*, 763–776. doi:10.1037/0012-1649.27.5.763

Samuel, W. (1977). Observed IQ as a function of test atmosphere, tester expectation, and race of tester: A replication for female subjects. *Journal of Educational Psychology, 69*, 593–604. doi:10.1037/0022-0663.69.5.593

Sattler, J. M., & Theye, F. (1967). Procedural, situational, and interpersonal variables in individual intelligence testing. *Psychological Bulletin, 68*, 347–360. doi:10.1037/h0020194

Schmidt, C., Collette, F., Cajochen, C., & Peigneux, P. (2007). A time to think: Circadian rhythms in human cognition. *Cognitive Neuropsychology, 24*, 755–789. doi:10.1080/02643290701754158

Schmidt, K. R. T., & Teti, D. M. (2005). Issues in the use of longitudinal and cross-sectional designs. In D. M. Teti (Ed.), *Handbook of research methods in developmental science* (pp. 3–20). Malden, MA: Blackwell Publishing.

Searle, S. R. (1971). *Linear models*. New York, NY: Wiley.

Shadish, W. R., Cook, T. D., & Campbell, D. T. (2002). *Experimental and quasi-experimental designs for generalized causal inference*. Boston, MA: Houghton Mifflin Harcourt.

Shepard, R. N., & Metzler, J. (1971). Mental rotation of three-dimensional objects. *Science, 171*, 701–703. doi:10.1126/science.171.3972.701

Shievitz, A. L., Tudiver, F., Araujo, A., Sanghe, P., & Boyle, E. (1998). Do elderly people score better on cognitive tests at home? *Canadian Familiy Physician, 44*, 1652–1656.

Snaith, R., Harrop, F., Newby, D., & Teale, C. (1986). Grade scores of the Montgomery-Asberg depression and the clinical anxiety scales. *The British Journal of Psychiatry, 148*, 599–601. doi:10.1192/bjp.148.5.599

Snodgrass, J. G., & Corwin, J. (1988). Pragmatics of measuring recognition memory: Applications to dementia and amnesia. *Journal of Experimental Psychology, 1*, 35–50. doi:10.1037/0096-3445.117.1.34

Thorndike, E. L. (1920). A constant error in psychological ratings. *Journal of Applied Psychology, 4*, 25–29. doi:10.1037/h0071663

Yoon, C., May, C. P., & Hasher, L. (1999). Ageing, circadian arousal patterns, and cognition. In N. Schwarz, D. Park, B. Knauper, & S. Sudman (Eds.), *Ageing, cognition and self reports* (pp. 117–143). Washington, DC: Psychological Press.

Zazzo, R. (1974). *Test des deux barrages. Actualités pédagogiques et psychologiques [Test of the two dams. News pedagogical and psychological]* (Vol. 7). Neuchâtel: Delachaux et Nestlé.

4

Dual-tasking and aging—About multiple perspectives and possible implementations in interventions for the elderly

Magnus Liebherr[1,2]*, Patric Schubert[1], Johannes Schiebener[2], Stephanie Kersten[1] and Christian T. Haas[1]

*Corresponding author: Magnus Liebherr, Faculty of Health and Social Sciences, Institute of Complex Health Research, Hochschule Fresenius, University of Applied Sciences, Idstein, Germany; Department of General Psychology, University of Duisburg-Essen, Duisburg, Germany

E-mail: magnus.liebherr@hs-fresenius.de

Reviewing editor: Peter Walla, University of Newcastle, Australia

Abstract: It is well known that dual-tasking is adversely affected by physiological degenerative processes. Furthermore, the completion of a secondary task while walking is frequently discussed as a key contributor for falls in the elderly. Age-related differences in both activated neural structures and human behavior are indicated in numerous previous studies. Besides a general overview of dual-tasking and aging, this article reviews studies aiming at improving gait or postural control in older adults using dual- or multi-task interventions. Approximately, 130 parameters out of 17 illustrated studies presented significant changes after dual-task-specific interventions regarding gait, postural control/balance, and falls. On the one hand, the article at hand shows highly consistent results in all of the dual-task intervention studies analyzed, indicating significant improvements related to postural control, gait, falls, or the performance of a secondary task. On the other hand, the results represent a heterogeneous structure and a gap between theoretical aspects and practical use. To optimize the use of dual-task, a systematization of underlying tasks is inevitable and should be focused on in further research.

ABOUT THE AUTHOR

Magnus Liebherr is a PhD student at the University of Duisburg-Essen, General Psychology: Cognition, and is working at the Institute of Complex Health Research, Hochschule Fresenius, University of Applied Sciences (Idstein, Germany). His main fields of interest comprise information processing, executive functions, the simultaneously processing of different demands, and the process of aging. In his current projects, he focuses on the influence of various demands on cognitive processing, using both behavioral and neurophysiological measurements. The investigated demands include additional motor and cognitive tasks as well as individual factors such as aging. Together with the Cognitive Neuroscience Lab at the University of South Australia (Adelaide), Magnus Liebherr investigates the possibilities of using neurophysiological measurements within "real-world" scenarios in order to get a deeper understanding of the underlying neurophysiological mechanisms of daily situations.

PUBLIC INTEREST STATEMENT

We are driving a car while calling a friend, standing in the railway while reading the newspaper, or working on the computer while watching TV. The complexity of our daily life is growing permanently, whereas the ability to handle these situations decreases during the process of aging. Focusing on the simultaneously "talking while walking", previous studies revealed an increased risk of falling in the elderly, respectively. Based on these findings, and in order to improve the abilities of our aging society to handle these situations, diverse interventions have been developed. While the results consistently indicated improvements in gait, falls, and the performance of a secondary task after finishing the programs, the relation between underlying neurophysiological mechanisms and practical use is still less understood. The present review sheds light on both existing interventions and the underlying neurophysiological mechanisms in order to get a better understanding of its relation and to create a basis for future approaches.

Subjects: Behavioral Sciences; Psychological Science; Behavioral Neuroscience; Aging

Keywords: dual-task; aging; behavior; gait; postural control

1. Introduction

Dual-task situations nowadays are of increasing relevance. The extent of successful execution depends on many factors and is adversely affected by physiological degenerative processes (Korteling, 1993; Verhaeghen, Steitz, Sliwinski, & Cerella, 2003). Next to the effects on dual-task performance, both motor and cognitive tasks are significantly affected as single components, during the process of aging (MacPherson, Phillips, & Della Sala, 2002; Mattay et al., 2002; Seidler et al., 2010). Against this background, studying dual-task effects on the elderly has become an emerging field of research, especially in the context of gait and postural control (Shumwas-Cook & Woollacott, 2000; Woollacott & Shumway-Cook, 2002). Using dual-task paradigms sheds light on both the influence of age-related changes in terms of stability of apparently simple motor tasks (Woollacott & Shumway-Cook, 2002), as well as the performance of the secondary cognitive tasks (Li, Lindenberger, Freund, & Baltes, 2001; Smolders, Doumas, & Krampe, 2010). Hence, the inevitability of completing further tasks while walking (reading signs, talking to another person, etc.) could be seen as a key contributor of falls and gait impairments in the elderly (Korteling, 1993; Lundin-Olsson, Nyberg, & Gustafson, 1997; Verhaeghen et al., 2003). In this context, Shumway-Cook et al. (2007) investigated age-specific performance of complex walking tasks of 1,227 persons (aged 20–95). The authors found a larger decline in gait speed at age 65 and older, as well as greater differences between the performance of simple and complex walking tasks in older participants compared to younger adults. Furthermore, there was an increased number of older adults who walked under simple low-challenge conditions, but were unable to walk under complex conditions. Investigating cognitive and sensorimotor performance, Li et al. (2001) found greater age-related differences of dual-task costs in memory performance than in walking which is in accordance with the results of Smolders et al. (2010). While Li et al. (2001) suggested that older adults prioritized walking over memory, a conclusion can be drawn on the assumptions of Hausdorff, Yogev, Springer, Simon, and Giladi (2005). Here, the authors speculated that during the process of aging, walking (as automated, rhythmic motor task) becomes a more cognitive task.

Considering the daily relevance of handling dual-task situations as well as the stated reduction of performance during the process of aging, it seems to be obvious that an integration of the dual-task paradigm into training and intervention programs might be useful in order to improve the ability of walking and postural control in older people (Bock, 2008). Although, numerous studies and reviews investigated age-related differences in dual-task performance (e.g. Beurskens & Bock, 2012 for review), the present article aims a more global insight (not limited, e.g. on the motor task “gait”) in the effects of combining cognitive and motor tasks in older adults. Here, we focus on the underlying neurophysiological structures, as well as the influence of motor–cognitive task combinations on both the performance of the cognitive and the motor components. Complementing this consideration, we shed light on studies that aimed preventing falls and improved gait and/or postural control in the elderly using interventions based on motor and cognitive task combinations.

2. Dual-tasking and aging

As already stated in the introduction, the process of aging determines the performance of dual-tasking. The following sections emphasis a general insight into the underlying mechanisms as well as age-related changes.

2.1. Underlying structures in dual-tasking

For better understanding the effects of performing an additional task on behavioral parameters, we would give an insight in how the brain processes these additional demands. Therefore, within this chapter, we reviewed literature that investigated neuronal structures, which were activated in performing dual-tasks, but more importantly, age-related differences. Principally, the activation of structures underlying the process of dual-task could be classified in three different patterns: (1) increase

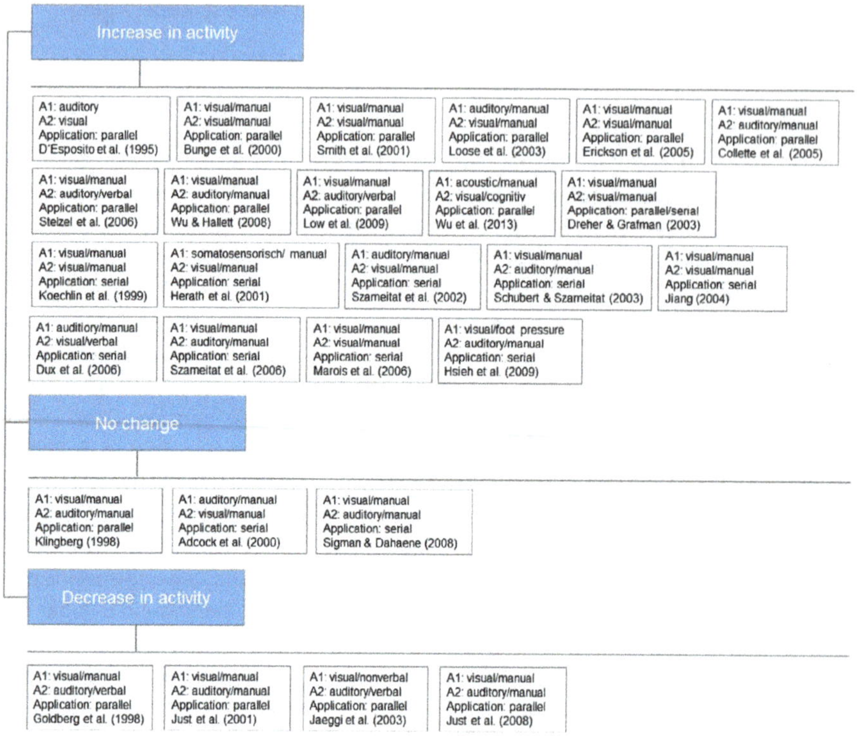

Figure 1. Dual-task studies showing either increased, decreased, or no activation.

in activity of structures, already activated under single-task conditions or additional structures; (2) no change in activity; and (3) decrease of neural activity compared to single-task condition. Within Figure 1 are studies focusing on the underlying structures assigned to one of the three categories. Studies reporting a decrease of neural activity in the dual-task compared to single-task condition identified both a specific (Goldberg et al., 1998; Just et al., 2001; Just et al., 2008) as well as a general decrease in activity. While we considered 27 studies, 20 studies reported an increase of activity in dual-task situations. To give an idea about the structures showing a dual-task-related increase in activity or be additionally activated, Figure 2 comprises the results of the 20 studies mentioned above. Here, a large variance of the activated structures during the performance of dual-tasks becomes apparent. Therefore, it is necessary to consider the characteristics of combined tasks in relation to the activated structures. This highlights a problem, which occurred repeatedly at different points in this article.

The dual-task paradigm does not consist of two clearly defined tasks.

While most studies concentrate on the combination of two cognitive tasks, some studies investigate additionally the performance of motor tasks. Here, Wu, Liu, Hallett, Zheng, and Chang (2013) used a dual-task setting consisting of a motor (self-paced tapping) and a cognitive (visual letter counting) task in order to determine additionally activated brain structures during dual-tasking. Structures indicated by Wu et al. (2013) differ clearly from both the results illustrated in Figure 2 as well as the discussion about the prefrontal cortex as a general mechanism for solving dual-task problems (e.g. D'Esposito et al., 1995). Also studies investigating exclusively cognitive task combinations showed an activation of structures not exclusively located in the prefrontal cortex (Szameitat, Schubert, Müller, & von Cramon, 2002). Besides task-related influences (which should be reviewed in detail in a future article), the types of response need to be considered: for example motor (trigger/button) (Dux, Ivanoff, Asplund, & Marois, 2006; Herath, Klingberg, Young, Amunts, & Roland, 2001; Jiang, 2004; Schubert & Szameitat, 2003; Stelzel, Schumacher, Schubert, & D'Esposito, 2006;

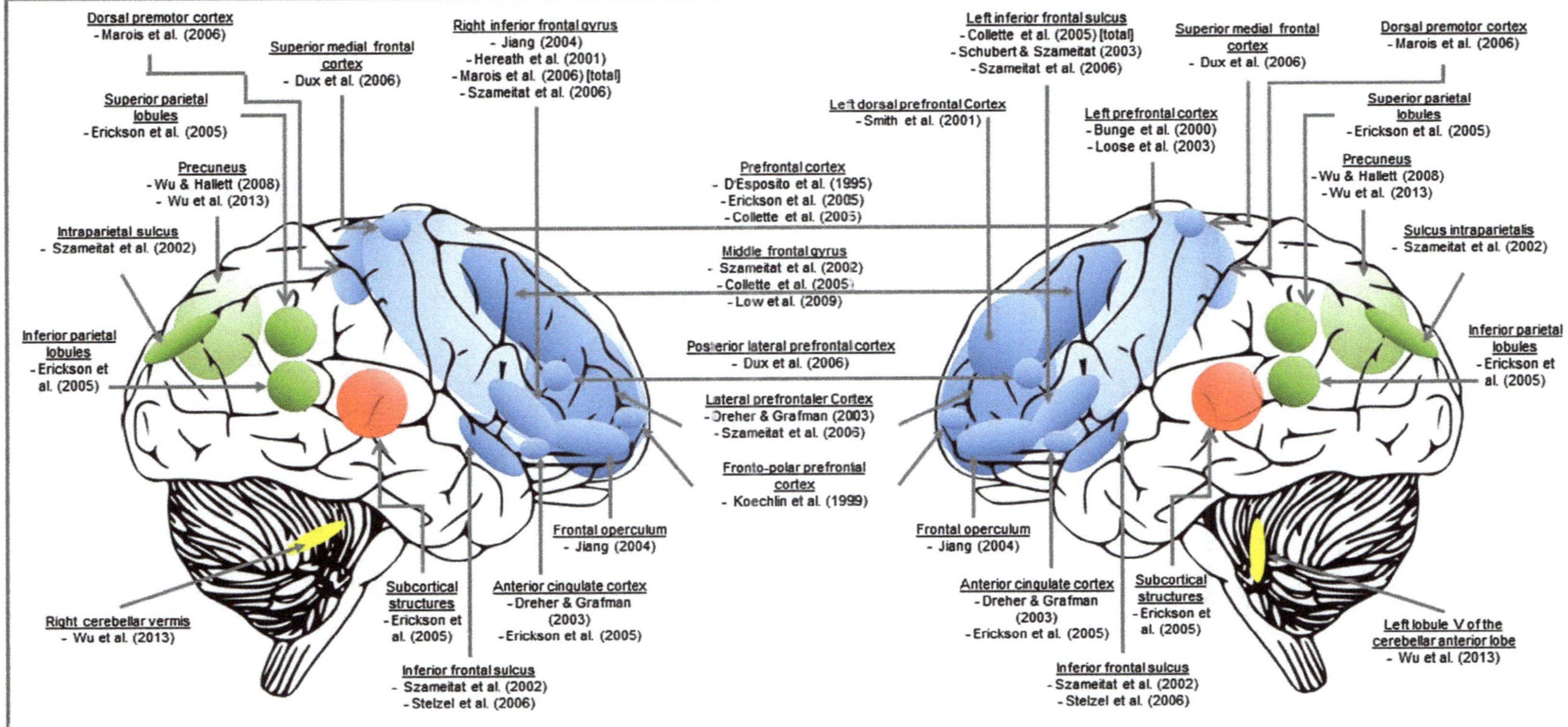

Hsieh et al. (2009): Inferior frontal gyrus, anterior insula, orbitofrontal cortex, lateral prefrontaler cortex, supplementary motor cortex, anterior & posterior cingulate gyrus, right superior parietal lobe, right intraparietal sulcus, right precuneus, and right cuneus

Figure 2. Brain structures showing increased activation in dual-compared to single-task condition.

Szameitat et al., 2002) or verbal (Dux et al., 2006; Stelzel et al., 2006) response which has been used in the illustrated studies. This short overview and the stated aspects demonstrate the necessity for further investigations. Here, numerous dual-task situations should be analyzed within one experiment in order to get a deeper insight into the underlying pattern of activation.

Focusing on age-related differences, the following section gives an overview about previous neuroimaging findings. Here, Chmielewski, Yildiz, and Beste (2014) measured brain activity in 14 healthy late middle-aged adults (mean age 60.51 ± 3.34) and 14 young participants (mean age 24.37 ± 2.89), by utilizing the psychological refractory period test. While behavioral data showed an increasing reaction time in late middle-aged participants compared to young subjects, the fMRI data revealed more activation in the occipital regions in late middle-aged subjects compared to younger subjects. Furthermore, during more complex conditions, late middle-aged participants showed lower activations in the middle frontal and superior frontal gyrus. Using visual task combinations with a manual response (movement of right index or right second finger) in an fMRI study, Hartley, Jonides, and Sylvester (2011) identified an involvement of a medial prefrontal network and a lateral frontal–parietal network, largely similar in both younger and older adults. In the older group, a polar prefrontal area seemed to be responsible for top-down management of task goals. Another fMRI study (Van Impe, Coxon, Goble, Wenderoth, & Swinnen, 2011) investigated age-related dual-task effects using both auditory and visuomotor tasks. Here, the authors reported an age-associated increase in brain activation only in the single visuomotor task setting (frontoparietal network). In dual-task situations, both groups showed additional activation in the supplementary motor area/pre-supplementary motor area, anterior insula, and inferior precentral gyrus showing no age-related differences. Using functional magnetic resonance imaging and diffusion tensor imaging, Madden et al. (2010) examined aged-related differences in task switching. The authors concluded that the functional connectivity of frontoparietal activation might be seen as a potential source of age-related decline in executive control.

Results in imaging studies allow for drawing conclusions from activated brain structures to both general abilities as well as age-related differences of performing dual-task. However, the opposite is true in behavioral studies. Here, assumptions regarding the performance of dual-tasking resulting from human behavior are considered.

2.2. Influence of dual-tasking on cognitive behavior in aging

In the field of dual-tasking, classical neuropsychological studies mostly focus on the combination of two cognitive tasks. Based on the well-known psychological refractory period (PRP) (Telford, 1931; Welford, 1952), these experiments often combine simple reaction tasks (visual or auditory) with different stimulus onset asynchronies (SOAs). In varying SOAs, it is found that a decrease in SOA leads to an increased reaction time (RT) of task 2 (PRP-effect) (Kahneman, 1973), whereas the effect on the first task is much smaller (Smith, 1969) and sometimes essentially absent (Pashler, 1994; Pashler & Johnston, 1989). In contrast, Hein and Schubert (2004) reported a significant increase in both RT 1 and RT 2 in older participants during short SOA conditions. While this study used SOAs between 50 ms and 800 ms, SOAs in the study of Glass et al. (2000) varied between 50 ms and 1,000 ms. Besides an overall reduction of reaction time, the authors also reported a significant SOA effect for both task 1 and task 2 (size of effect in task 1 was rather small compared to the effect of task 2) in older adults. While Glass et al. (2000) and Hein and Schubert (2004) concentrated on the examination of different SOA conditions, Vaportzis, Georgiou-Karistianis, and Stout (2013) investigated the simultaneous performance of choice reaction time tasks paired with digit tasks. The authors indicated different behavioral strategies (between younger and older adults) depending on complexity and difficulty of tasks. Compared to younger participants, older adults were significantly slower, but had a lower error rate in performing simple reaction time tasks. However, the opposite was true in the complex choice reaction time tasks. Using neuropsychological tests, Holtzer, Stern, and Rakitin (2005) examined age-related differences in performing dual-tasks in 16 older adults (aged 65–85) and 16 younger adults (19–31). On the one side, the authors pointed out the important role attention placed in mediating dual-task performance. On the other side, they suggested that compromised central executive might be causal for the decline in dual-task performance. While related studies considered the influence of dual-tasking as cross-sectional investigations, Göthe, Oberauer, and Kliegl (2007) investigated age differences in parallel processing of two cognitive operations through practice (longitudinal approach). The results show that after eight training phases, 9 out of 12 young people were able to process the given tasks, but none of the older adults reached the criterion of parallel processing.

In addition to the effect of performing two cognitive tasks simultaneously, the combination of a motor and a cognitive task needs to be considered. Here, Marsh and Geel (2000) found a significant deterioration in the cognitive RT task during the performed dual-task in older adults. The authors combined a primary quiet standing task (under four conditions) with a secondary verbal reaction time task. In addition, Redfern, Müller, Jennings, and Furman (2002) combined simple standing with randomly implied perturbations, while performing visual and acoustic RT tasks. Regarding cognitive behavior, RT in older participants was shown to be more influenced by perturbation compared to younger ones. While these studies concentrated on quiet standing, Sparrow, Bradshaw, Lamoureux, and Tirosh (2002) and Srygley, Mirelman, Herman, Giladi, and Hausdorff (2008) combined different cognitive tasks with the performance of walking. Here, Sparrow et al. (2002) compared 6 young (26.3) and 12 healthy older (71.1) adults in terms of reaction time in three different cognitive tasks while walking. Results showed no age-related differences in single cognitive task conditions, whereas during the simultaneous performance of walking, older adults showed significant longer reaction times in the visual and auditory/visual condition, but not in the auditory condition. Single-task conditions in the study of Sparrow et al. (2002) were analyzed in upright standing, whereas Srygley et al. (2008) investigated cognitive single-tasks in a sitting position. Thereby, Srygley et al. (2008) also used three different cognitive tasks: (1) serial three subtractions, (2) serial seven subtractions, and (3) phoneme monitoring. Older adults showed much larger effect of walking on cognitive performance compared to younger subjects. Furthermore, a current study by Jabourian et al. (2014) indicated gait velocity as an indicator of cognitive performance in healthy middle-aged adults. The authors found both a lower cognitive performance and longer walking time in older subjects compared to younger ones. With respect to these results and the stated findings by Li et al. (2001), which discussed the prioritization of walking over memory in older subjects, it might be necessary to additionally consider the influence of dual-tasks on motor behavior.

2.3. *Influence of dual-tasking on motor behavior in aging*

Maintaining motor function especially during the influence of additional demands is adversely effected during the process of aging. In this context, Hollman, Kovash, Kubik, and Linbo (2007) investigated parameters of gait during walking while simultaneously performing a cognitive task in three groups (sixty older, middle-aged, young adults). The older group walked slower and had an increased variability in stride velocity compared to the middle-aged and young participants. The authors suggested that the impaired walking performance was associated with impaired cognitive performance in dual-task walking. In the same manner, Dubost et al. (2006) found a decrease in gait velocity and an increase in variability in healthy elderly subjects when walking under dual-task conditions in comparison to free walking. These results are supported by further studies (e.g. Lindenberger, Marsiske, & Baltes, 2000; Priest, Salamon, & Hollman, 2008). According to a study by Springer et al. (2006), each combination of a secondary task with a walking task lead to decreased gait variability in each group (healthy young, healthy elderly non-fallers, and healthy elderly fallers). The authors did not find a difference between younger and older non-fallers. However, a significant difference became apparent when the elderly faller group was taken into account. It might be speculated that with a decrease in executive function, resources to manage the simultaneous processing of conflicting tasks decline. This tendency could be found in postural control studies as well (Brown, Shumway-Cook, & Woollacott, 1999; Shumway-Cook, Woollacott, Kerns, & Baldwin, 1997; Teasdale, Bard, LaRue, & Fleury, 1993). For instance, it has been reported that muscle activity while reacting on platform perturbations is significantly affected by a secondary task, and that this effect is more pronounced in the elderly (Rankin, Woollacott, Shumway-Cook, & Brown, 2000). As stated by Shumway-Cook et al. (1997), higher discriminative effects between healthy younger and healthy elderly subjects come along with increased task complexity which confirms with other investigative studies (Bernard-Demanze, Dumitrescu, Jimeno, Borel, & Lacour, 2009; Shumwas-Cook & Woollacott, 2000). A competing result is presented by Prado, Stoffregen, and Duarte (2007), who in fact reported an impact of a dual-task design on postural control parameters, but there was no difference between young subjects and elderly subjects when performing the dual-task setting. However, in postural control studies, the main challenge for researchers is the great variety of available parameters which partly leads to contradictional interpretations (Fraizer & Mitra, 2008; Lacour, Bernard-Demanze, & Dumitrescu, 2008). In general, it may be conjectured that strategies underlying postural control with a dual-task paradigm are different in younger compared to older subjects and are based on different task prioritizations (Bernard-Demanze et al., 2009). Within this background, the consideration of effects of dual-tasks-based interventions on gait or postural control seemed to be essential for (1) a better understanding of the underlying modes of action, as well as (2) the development of optimal concepts of intervention.

2.4. Dual-task-based interventions in the elderly

As described in previous chapters, the process of aging leads to a change in activation patterns of involved brain structures, as well as a decline in performance of motor and/or cognitive behavior in dual-task situations. This chapter will review studies investigating the effect of dual-task-based interventions on gait or postural control in the elderly. While numerous interventions unconsciously include dual-tasks, we considered only studies which described interventions explicitly as dual-task. Here, studies could be classified due to the characterization of its intervention: (1) stepping exercises (Yamada, Aoyama, Tanaka, Nagai, & Ichihashi, 2011; Yamada, Aoyama, Hikita et al., 2011), (2) exercises with combined walking and cognitive tasks (You et al., 2009), (3) balance training (Granacher et al., 2010; Melzer & Oddsson, 2013; Plummer-D'Amato et al., 2012; Silsupadol, Shummay-Cook et al., 2009, Silsupadol, Lugade et al., 2009), (4) balance exercises based on activities of daily living (Halvarsson et al., 2011, 2013), (5) computerized training (Li et al., 2010), (6) music-based rhythmic training (Trombetti et al., 2011), (7) combined strength, agility, and balance training (Hiyamizu, Morioka, Shomoto, & Shimada, 2012; Uemura et al., 2012), and (8) dance videogame training (Pichierri, Coppe, Lorenzetti, Murer, & de Bruin, 2012; Pichierri, Murer, & de Bruin, 2012; Schoene et al., 2013). Table 1 shows a short characterization of the interventions of considered studies. In relation to the identified studies, balance training has been the most common constituent of dual-task interventions in the elderly with respect to improving gait or postural control. Within these five studies, two studies (Granacher et al., 2010; Melzer & Oddsson, 2013) investigated the combination of exclusively motor tasks, whereas three (Plummer-D'Amato et al., 2012; Silsupadol, Lugade et al., 2009, Silsupadol, Shummay-Cook et al., 2009) examined the effect of simultaneously training motor and cognitive tasks. While both Silsupadol, Shummay-Cook et al. (2009) and Plummer-D'Amato et al. (2012) used balance and gait as motor components, Silsupadol and Lugade et al. (2009) integrated only balance exercises into their intervention program. Both studies of (Silsupadol, Lugade et al., 2009, Silsupadol, Shummay-Cook et al., 2009) additionally focused on different attention strategies. Here, group I was instructed to focus on both cognitive and motor tasks during the whole training, whereas group II was instructed to focus one half of the training on motor and one half of it on cognitive task performance. A comparison of the underlying results of the dual-task studies focusing on balance training shows that only these interventions (Silsupadol, Lugade et al., 2009, Silsupadol, Shummay-Cook et al. 2009) recorded significant changes in gait under dual-tasking. While the condition of fixed priority instruction shows only short-term improvements (Silsupadol, Shummay-Cook et al., 2009) or changes similar to single-task training (Silsupadol, Lugade et al., 2009), the condition of variable priority instruction was more effective in improving both motor and cognitive performance under dual-task (Silsupadol, Lugade et al., 2009) and in maintaining the training effect at the 12-week follow-up (Silsupadol, Shummay-Cook et al., 2009).

While balance training has a long tradition as part of prevention and rehabilitation programs (e.g. Chang et al., 2004 for review), current interventions include more and more video or computerized training (e.g. Kueider, Parisi, Gross, & Rebok, 2012 for review). In the context of dual-task interventions (to improve gait and postural control in the elderly), Pichierri, Coppe et al. (2012), Pichierri,

Table 1. Studies investigated interventions based on dual-task paradigm

Reference	Intervention
Granacher et al. (2010)	60 min, three times a week balance training consisted of postural stabilization tasks, intensified by including additional motor interference tasks
Hiyamizu et al. (2012)	60 min, twice a week strength and balance training, calculation task, visual search task, and verbal fluency task were performed simultaneously during balance training
Pichierri, Coppe et al. (2012)	60 min, twice a week cognitive motor intervention with progressive resistance training, progressive postural balance training, and progressive dance video gaming
Schoene et al. (2013)	15–20 min, 2–3 sessions per week videogame-based stepping exercise with additional cognitive load
Trombetti et al. (2011)	60 min, once a week various music-based multi-task exercises; basic exercise consisted of walking in time to the music and responding to change in the music's rhythmic patterns
Yamada, Aoyama, Tanaka et al. (2011)	50 min, once a week aerobic, strength, flexibility, and balance exercise, stepping exercise while performing fluency task, enumerating words within a category or letter
Halvarsson et al. (2011)	45 min, three times a week exercises comprised elements that represent daily activities; dual/multi-task exercises included counting, reading a newspaper, doing up/undoing buttons, and carrying a tray while walking
Li et al. (2010)	60 min computerized dual-task cognitive training; adaptive feedback on the computer screen indicating the participant's current performance
Pichierri, Murer et al. (2012)	40 + 10–15 min (game dancing), twice a week progressive resistance training, progressive postural balance training, and additional dance video game
Silsupadol, Shummay-Cook et al. (2009)	45 min, three times a week dual-task balance and gait training with fixed priority instruction
Uemura et al. (2012)	30 min, once a week stretching, agility, and strength exercises; executive motor tasks where performed with cognitive tasks: COP shift exercise, start-stop exercise, and switch exercise
You et al. (2009)	30 min, five times a week cognitive gait intervention
Halvarsson et al. (2013)	45 min, three times a week exercises comprised elements that represent daily activities; the dual/multi-tasks included counting, reading a newspaper, doing up/undoing buttons, and carrying a tray while walking
Melzer and Oddsson (2013)	60 min, twice a week balance training consisted of postural stabilization tasks, intensified by including additional motor interference tasks
Plummer-D'Amato et al. (2012)	45 min, once a week balance, gait, and agility activities; dual-task training includes cognitive tasks with simultaneous balance and gait activities
Silsupadol, Lugade et al. (2009)	45 min, three times a week dual-task balance training with fixed priority instruction
Yamada, Aoyama, Hikita et al. (2011)	20 min, twice a week DVD exercise included basic exercise section and dual-task stepping exercise

Murer et al. (2012), and Schoene et al. (2013) included dance videogames in their intervention programs, whereas Li et al. (2010) investigated a computerized exercise program. While interventions based on dance videogames obviously include a motor component, the intervention program investigated by Li et al. (2010) was the only 1 out of 17 studies found which combined two cognitive tasks in order to improve motor behavior in the elderly. Here, participants were trained to make two-choice decisions to visually presented stimuli. The results showed a significant improvement during single-support balance and double-support dynamic balance in the training group, whereas the control group reported no appreciable improvements (Li et al., 2010). Considering parameters of gait, significant changes during the intervention were only observed by Pichierri, Coppe et al. (2012), Pichierri, Murer et al. (2012) (within computerized or video-based dual-task training). Both Pichierri,

Coppe et al. (2012), Pichierri, Murer et al. (2012) investigated obviously the same intervention program, comprising a 12-week cognitive motor exercise program with progressive strength and balance training and supplemented with additional dance video gaming. Studies differ in measurement systems that were used, as well as the interventions applied to the control group. While the control group in the study of Pichierri, Murer et al. (2012) completed the same program as the intervention group except of dance video gaming, no intervention was applied to the control group in the study conducted by Pichierri, Coppe et al. (2012). While Pichierri, Coppe et al. (2012) and Pichierri, Murer et al. (2012) combined a dance video game with traditional strength and balance training, Schoene et al. (2013) investigated a video game training exclusively. Here, the authors found a significant improvement in the intervention group compared to controls (regarding choice stepping reaction time, physiological profile assessment, postural sway, and contrast sensitivity). Other components (strength and balance training), also integrated in the studies of Pichierri, Coppe et al. (2012) and Pichierri, Murer et al. (2012), were further investigated in a study with a combined cognitive motor intervention without video game (Hiyamizu et al., 2012). As well, the intervention program studied by Uemura et al. (2012) was based on strength training with additional stretching and agility components. Similar to Hiyamizu et al. (2012), motor tasks were combined with additional cognitive tasks. While Uemura et al. (2012) reported significant changes in walking time (under dual-task), COP displacement, and reaction time, people assigned to the intervention group in the study of Hiyamizu et al. (2012) reached significant improvement only in the rate of stroop task.

Up to now, the considered dual-task interventions that have been based on balance components have mostly integrated isolated tasks with no direct references to everyday life. In contrast, Halvarsson et al. (2011, 2013) investigated a dual-task balance exercise training focusing elements based on activities of daily living. Here, short-term effects were reported by Halvarsson et al. (2011), whereas the study by Halvarsson et al. (2013) investigated effects in a long-term determination. Significant improvements were reported in numerous gait parameters (in both single and dual-task walking) both subsequently to the intervention (Halvarsson et al., 2011) and in the nine-month follow-up (Halvarsson et al., 2013). Regarding the 15-month follow-up, a significant improvement was only reported in the self-perceived fear of falling; however, gait speed remained significantly higher in the training group compared to the control group (Halvarsson et al., 2013).

Another form of combining classic exercise components in a dual-task setting was investigated by Yamada, Aoyama, Hikita et al. (2011), Yamada, Aoyama, Tanaka et al. (2011). Here, classic exercises (balance, strength, aerobic) were combined with dual-task seated stepping exercises in a DVD group training (Yamada, Aoyama, Hikita et al., 2011) and a conventional group training (Yamada, Aoyama, Tanaka et al., 2011). While the training group in the DVD group training received a significant improvement only in the dual-task walking time and dual-task time lag, the conventional group training reported significant changes in numerous gait parameters (i.e. cadence, speed, and cost) under cognitive and manual task conditions with an additional improvement in performing the cognitive task. Furthermore, an improvement in the cognitive component during dual-task training was reported by You et al. (2009). Participants were trained with combined walking and cognitive exercises over a six-week period. Although a main component of the intervention was walking exercises, there were no significant changes in gait parameters. Instead of this, Trombetti et al. (2011) reported significant changes in gait parameters under single- and dual-task conditions. Here, community-dwelling individuals older than 65 years participated in a music-based rhythmic training program. The intervention program is based on various multi-task exercises (walking, handling of objects, balance, and/or upper body movements) performed to the rhythm of piano music. Besides the gait changes, the intervention group showed significant fewer falls and a lower risk of falling, as well as significant changes in parameters of balance (i.e. displacement A-P, angular velocity A-P, and/or duration).

The relevant aspects of considered studies investigating dual-task exercises in order to improve gait and/or postural control in healthy older adults could be summarized as follows:

- Treatment durations ranged from four weeks (e.g. Plummer-D'Amato et al., 2012) to six months (e.g. Trombetti et al., 2011).
- The effect of intervention was measured in all studies immediately after the last treatment session. One study reported a long-term follow-up with a retention period of 6 months (Trombetti et al., 2011), another one with 9 or 15 months (Halvarsson et al., 2013).
- Regarding the outcome measures, 14 studies used a combination of clinical assessments and biomechanical analyses of gait or postural control (Granacher et al., 2010; Halvarsson et al., 2011, 2013; Hiyamizu et al., 2012; Li et al., 2010; Melzer & Oddsson, 2013; Pichierri, Murer et al., 2012; Plummer-D'Amato et al., 2012; Schoene et al., 2013; Silsupadol, Shumway-Cook et al., 2009; Trombetti et al., 2011; Yamada, Aoyama, Hikita et al., 2011, Yamada, Aoyama, Tanaka et al., 2011; You et al., 2009). Only three studies applied tools of gait analyses exclusively (Pichierri, Coppe et al., 2012; Silsupadol, Lugade et al., 2009; Uemura et al., 2012).
- Approximately, 130 parameters (spatio-temporal gait parameter, parameters of the center of pressure, etc.) out of the 17 illustrated studies presented significant changes immediately after the intervention, as well as the two investigations with follow-up period regarding gait, postural control/balance, and falls. However, with respect to informative values, it is obvious that these parameters comprise very different aspects of the underlying physiological processes.

3. Discussion

Movement is ubiquitous in human behavior. While individually perceived as simple and automated single-task processes, neurophysiological findings, however, demonstrate the hidden complex structure of daily single-task movements (e.g. walking or standing). Postural control, for instance, as one of the most common requirements in everyday life involves complex processes that require dynamic integration of visual, proprioceptive, and vestibular sensory information (Massion, 1994; Mergner & Rosemeier, 1998). This problem becomes amplified during the process of aging. Zwergal et al. (2012) reported an age-associated shift from automatic (subcortical level) to attentional control (cortical level) of locomotion and stance in elderly people. Therefore, it is likely that with the process of aging, influence in brain functions between locomotion and a conscious secondary task increases. In this conjunction, evidence has been accumulated directly (Annweiler et al., 2013) and indirectly (Lajoie, Teasdale, Bard, & Fleury, 1996). To counteract these processes, training seems to be an efficient method (Wollesen & Voelcker-Rehage, 2013).

But does the dual-task paradigm have the potential of increasing the performance of daily tasks such as postural control and gait?

The present review shows highly consistent results as far as approximately 130 parameters were identified out of all investigated dual-task intervention studies indicating significant improvements related to postural control, gait, falls, or the performance of a secondary task. On the one hand, this manifests the importance of dual-task training. On the other hand, 14 interventions summarized in eight categories from the 17 studies represent a heterogeneous structure. The included interventions characterized by both the exclusive application of motor (Granacher et al., 2010) or cognitive (Li et al., 2010) tasks, as well as a combination of both forms (Halvarsson et al., 2011, 2013; Hiyamizu et al., 2012; Li et al., 2010; Melzer & Oddsson, 2013; Pichierri, Coppe et al., 2012; Pichierri, Murer et al., 2012; Plummer-D'Amato et al., 2012; Schoene et al., 2013; Silsupadol, Lugade et al., 2009, Silsupadol, Shummay-Cook et al., 2009; Trombetti et al., 2011; Uemura et al., 2012; Yamada, Aoyama, Hikita et al., 2011; Yamada, Aoyama, Tanaka et al., 2011; You et al., 2009). Hereby, it is assumed that the interference in context of the dual-task paradigm depends on the similarity or confusability of the mental representations involved in each task (Navon & Miller, 1987). The intervention evaluated by Trombetti et al. (2011) appeared to be unique. Combining motor tasks with changing rhythms, it could be speculated that the implied music supports the automated process of walking. It has been shown that healthy older adults walked faster in time to music and exhibited no changes in spatio-temporal variability (Wittwer, Webster, & Hill, 2013). Regarding automatism, some aspects need to be emphasized. Practicing dual-task (Ruthruff, Johnston, & Van Selst, 2001) or combining relatively simple or automated processes (Riby, Perfect, & Stollery, 2004) leads to the same effect: reduced central interference in dual-tasking. It can be assumed that a decline of variability of the concurrent secondary task during training also leads to a reduced interference. Therefore, seated stepping exercises (Yamada, Aoyama, Hikita et al., 2011, Yamada, Aoyama, Tanaka et al., 2011) might tend to be an automated process compared to others which are characterized by a more ambitious content.

The integration of new technology such as video games (Pichierri, Coppe et al., 2012, Pichierri, Murer et al., 2012; Schoene et al., 2013) and computer programs (Li et al., 2010) into training might have the potential of overcoming many of the current barriers to physical activity (Biddiss & Irwin, 2010; Jorgensen, Laessoe, Hendriksen, Nielsen, & Aagaard, 2012). On the one hand, different aspects such as motivational effects, as well as the independence of the application, the standardization, and high variability, promote these new technologies. On the other hand, especially these aspects may lead to the risk of an exclusive consideration of the "effect" of an intervention without displaying attention to the "original stimulus" of combined tasks. Within dual-task, it seems to be a general problem to focus exclusively on the effects in terms of physiological output parameters rather than investigating the original stimulus. In the present review, this phenomenon is reflected in the lack of applying specific stimuli in the interventions, despite showing consistently significant results. However, to obtain optimal output parameters, it is necessary to examine the internal processes of the stimulus. In this context, the theories of dual-tasking (capacity sharing, bottleneck, and/or crosstalk) and further hybrid forms commonly have been used to describe the interference of internal central processes (Pashler & Johnston, 1998). Beside these theoretical constructs, imaging studies provide the opportunity of gaining an understanding of the localization of dual-task processes. However, a consideration of the individual task and its systematization with respect to brain imaging hardly seems to be possible (Takeuchi et al., 2013). But in order to optimize the use of dual-tasking, a systematization of underlying parts is inevitable. To ensure this systematization, conclusions from the effect of the stimulus have to be drawn. To obtain such a pattern, in future research, a gradual augmentation of task complexity has to be pursued. One approach could be to vary sensory modalities of the secondary task and to keep the primary motor task constant (Liebherr et al., 2015). Henceforth, a further comparison between different age groups is necessary to get an insight into the alterations of dual-task processability with aging. Further research should be conducted with regard to the remarks of the present review.

Funding
The authors received no direct funding for this research.

Competing Interests
The authors declare no competing interest.

Author details
Magnus Liebherr[1,2]
E-mail: magnus.liebherr@hs-fresenius.de
Patric Schubert[1]
E-mail: patric.schubert@hs-fresenius.de
Johannes Schiebener[2]
E-mail: johannes.schiebener@uni-due.de
Stephanie Kersten[1]
E-mail: stephanie.kersten@hs-fresenius.de
Christian T. Haas[1]
E-mail: haas@hs-fresenius.de
[1] Faculty of Health and Social Sciences, Institute of Complex Health Research, Hochschule Fresenius, University of Applied Sciences, Idstein, Germany.
[2] Department of General Psychology, University of Duisburg-Essen, Duisburg, Germany.

References
Annweiler, C., Beauchet, O., Bartha, R., Wells, J. L., Borrie, M. J., Hachinski, V., & Montero-Odasso, M. (2013). Motor cortex and gait in mild cognitive impairment: A magnetic resonance spectroscopy and volumetric imaging study. *Brain, 136*, 859–871. doi:10.1093/brain/aws373

Bernard-Demanze, L., Dumitrescu, M., Jimeno, P., Borel, L., & Lacour, M. (2009). Age-related changes in posture control are differentially affected by postural and cognitive task complexity. *Current Aging Science, 2*, 139–149. doi:10.2174/1874609810902020135

Beurskens, R., & Bock, O. (2012). Age-related deficits of dual-task walking: A review. *Neural Plasticity, 2012*. doi:10.1155/2012/131608

Biddiss, E., & Irwin, J. (2010). Active video games to promote physical activity in children and youth. *Archives of Pediatrics & Adolescent Medicine, 164*, 664–672. doi:10.1001/archpediatrics.2010.104

Bock, O. (2008). Dual-task costs while walking increase in old age for some, but not for other tasks: An experimental study of healthy young and elderly persons. *Journal of NeuroEngineering and Rehabilitation, 5*, 1–9. doi:10.1186/1743-0003-5-27

Brown, L. A., Shumway-Cook, A., & Woollacott, M. H. (1999). Attentional demands and postural recovery: The effects of aging. *The Journals of Gerontology Series A: Biological Sciences and Medical Sciences, 54*, M165–M171. doi:10.1093/gerona/54.4.M165

Chang, J. T., Morton, S. C., Rubenstein, L. Z., Mojica, W. A., Maglione, M., Suttorp, M. J., ... Shekelle, P. G. (2004).

Interventions for the prevention of falls in older adults: Systematic review and meta-analysis of randomized clinical trials. *BMJ, 328*, 680. doi:10.1136/bmj.328.7441.680

Chmielewski, W. X., Yildiz, A., & Beste, C. (2014). The neural architecture of age-related dual-task interferences. *Frontiers in Aging Neuroscience, 6*, 1–26. doi:10.3389/fnagi.2014.00193

D'Esposito, M. D., Detre, J. A., Alsop, D. C., Shin, R. K., Atlas, S., & Grossman, M. (1995). The neural basis of the central executive system of working memory. *Nature, 378*, 279–281. doi:10.1038/378279a0

Dubost, V., Kressig, R. W., Gonthier, R., Hermann, F. R., Aminian, K., Najafi, B., & Beauchet, O. (2006). Relationships between dual-task related changes in stride velocity and stride time variability in healthy older adults. *Human Movement Science, 25*, 372–382. doi:10.1016/j.humov.2006.03.004

Dux, E. P., Ivanoff, J., Asplund, C. L., & Marois, R. (2006). Isolation of a central bottleneck of information processing with time resolved fMRI. *Neuron, 52*, 1109–1120. doi:10.1016/j.neuron.2006.11.009

Fraizer, E. V., & Mitra, S. (2008). Methodological and interpretive issues in posture-cognition dual-tasking in upright stance. *Gait Posture, 27*, 271–279. doi:10.1016/j.gaitpost.2007.04.002

Glass, J. M., Schumacher, E. H., Lauber, E. J., Zurbriggen, E. L., Gmeindl, L., Kieras, D. E., & Meyer, D. E. (2000). Aging and the psychological refractory period: Task-coordination strategies in young and old adults. *Psychology and Aging, 15*, 571–595. doi:10.1037/0882-7974.15.4.571

Göthe, K., Oberauer, K., & Kliegl, R. (2007). Age differences in dual-task performance after practice. *Psychology and Aging, 22*, 596–606. doi:10.1037/0882-7974.22.3.596

Granacher, U., Muehlbauer, T., Bridenbaugh, S., Bleiker, E., Wehrle, A., & Kressig, R. W. (2010). Balance training and multi-task performance in seniors. *International Journal of Sports Medicine, 31*, 353–358. doi:10.1055/s-0030-1248322

Halvarsson, A., Franzén, E., Farén, E., Olsson, E., Oddsson, L., & Ståhle, A. (2013). Long-term effects of new progressive group balance training for elderly people with increased risk of falling—A randomized controlled trial. *Clinical Rehabilitation, 27*, 450–458. doi:10.1177/0269215512462908

Halvarsson, A., Oddsson, L., Olsson, E., Farén, E., Pettersson, A., & Ståhle, A. (2011). Effects of new, individually adjusted, progressive balance group training for elderly people with fear of falling and tend to fall: A randomized controlled trial. *Clinical Rehabilitation, 25*, 1021–1031. doi:10.1177/0269215511411937

Hartley, A. A., Jonides, J., & Sylvester, C. C. (2011). Dual-task processing in younger and older adults: Similarities and differences revealed by fMRI. *Brain and Cognition, 75*, 281–291. doi:10.1016/j.bandc.2011.01.004

Hausdorff, J. M., Yogev, G., Springer, S., Simon, E. S., & Giladi, N. (2005). Walking is more like catching than tapping: Gait in the elderly as a complex cognitive task. *Experimental Brain Research, 164*, 541–548. doi:10.1007/s00221-005-2280-3

Hein, G., & Schubert, T. (2004). Aging and input processing in dual-task situations. *Psychology and Aging, 19*, 416–432. doi:10.1037/0882-7974.19.3.416

Herath, P., Klingberg, T., Young, J., Amunts, K., & Roland, P. (2001). Neural correlates of dual task interference can be dissociated from those of divided attention: An fMRI study. *Cerebral Cortex, 11*, 796–805. doi:10.1093/cercor/11.9.796

Hiyamizu, M., Morioka, S., Shomoto, K., & Shimada, T. (2012). Effects of dual task balance training on dual task performance in elderly people: A randomized controlled trial. *Clinical Rehabilitation, 26*, 58–67. doi:10.1177/0269215510394222

Hollman, J. H., Kovash, F. M., Kubik, J. J., & Linbo, R. A. (2007). Age-related differences in spatiotemporal markers of gait stability during dual task walking. *Gait Posture, 26*, 113–119. doi:10.1016/j.gaitpost.2006.08.005

Goldberg, T. E., Berman, K. F., Fleming, K., Ostrem, J., Van Horn, J. D., Esposito, G., ... Weinberger, D. R. (1998). Uncoupling cognitive workload and prefrontal cortical physiology: A PET rCBF study. *NeuroImage, 7*, 296–303. doi:10.1006/nimg.1998.0338

Holtzer, R., Stern, Y., & Rakitin, B. C. (2005). Predicting age-related dual-task effects with individual differences on neuropsychological tests. *Neuropsychology, 19*, 18–27. doi:10.1037/0894-4105.19.1.18

Jabourian, A., Lancrenon, S., Delva, C., Perreve-Genet, A., Lablanchy, J. P., & Jabourian, M. (2014). Gait velocity is an indicator of cognitive performance in healthy middle-aged adults. *PLOS one, 9*, e103211. doi:10.1371/journal.pone.0103211

Jiang, Y. (2004). Resolving dual-task interference: An fMRI study. *NeuroImage, 22*, 748–854. doi:10.1016/j.neuroimage.2004.01.043

Jorgensen, M. G., Laessoe, U., Hendriksen, C., Nielsen, O. B., & Aagaard, P. (2012). Efficacy of Nintendo Wii training on mechanical leg muscle function and postural balance in community-dwelling older adults: A randomized controlled trial. *The Journals of Gerontology Series A: Biological Sciences and Medical Sciences, 68*, 845–852. doi:10.1093/gerona/gls222

Just, M. A., Carpenter, P. A., Keller, T. A., Emery, L., Zajac, H., & Thulborn, K. R. (2001). Interdependence of nonoverlapping cortical systems in dual cognitive tasks. *NeuroImage, 14*, 417–426. doi:10.1006/nimg.2001.0826

Just, M. A., Keller, T. A., & Cynkar, J. (2008). A decrease in brain activation associated with driving when listening to someone speak. *Brain Research, 1205*, 70–80. doi:10.1016/j.brainres.2007.12.075

Kahneman, D. (1973). *Attention and effort*. Englewood Cliffs, NJ: Prentice Hall.

Korteling, J. E. (1993). Effects of age and task similarity on dual task performance. *Human Factors: The Journal of the Human Factors and Ergonomics Society, 35*, 99–113. Retrieved from http://hfs.sagepub.com/content/35/1/99.full.pdf

Kueider, A. M., Parisi, J. M., Gross, A. L., & Rebok, G. W. (2012). Computerized cognitive training with older adults: A systematic review. *PLOS one, 7*, e40588. doi:10.1371/journal.pone.0040588

Lacour, M., Bernard-Demanze, L., & Dumitrescu, M. (2008). Posture control, aging, and attention resources: Models and posture-analysis methods. *Neurophysiologie Clinique/Clinical Neurophysiology, 38*, 411–421. doi:10.1016/j.neucli.2008.09.005

Lajoie, Y., Teasdale, N., Bard, C., & Fleury, M. (1996). Upright standing and gait: Are there changes in attentional requirements related to normal aging? *Experimental Aging Research, 22*, 185–198. doi:10.1080/03610739608254006

Li, K. Z. H., Lindenberger, U., Freund, A. M., & Baltes, P. B. (2001). Walking while memorizing: Age-related differences in compensatory behavior. *Psychological Science, 12*, 230–237. doi:10.1111/1467-9280.00341

Li, K. Z. H., Roudaia, E., Lussier, M., Bherer, L., Leroux, A., & McKinley, P. A. (2010). Benefits of cognitive dual-task training on balance performance in healthy older adults. *The Journals of Gerontology Series A: Biological Sciences and Medical Sciences, 65*, 1344–1352. doi:10.1093/gerona/glq151

Liebherr, M., Schubert, P., Kersten, S., Dietz, C., Franz, L., & Haas, C. T. (2015, January). *Dual-task—Immersion in the interactions of simultaneously performed tasks.* Paris: Paper presented at the International Congress on Cognitive Neuroscience.

Lindenberger, U., Marsiske, M., & Baltes, P. B. (2000). Memorizing while walking: Increase in dual-task costs from young adulthood to old age. *Psychology and Aging, 15*, 417–436. doi:10.1037/0882-7974.15.3.417

Lundin-Olsson, L., Nyberg, L., & Gustafson, Y. (1997). "Stops walking when talking" as a predictor of falls in elderly people. *Lancet, 349*, 617. doi:10.1016/S0140-6736(97)24009-2

MacPherson, S. E., Phillips, L. H., & Della Sala, S. (2002). Age, executive function, and social decision making: A dorsolateral prefrontal theory of cognitive aging. *Psychology and Aging, 17*, 598–609. doi:10.1037/0882-7974.17.4.598

Madden, D. J., Costello, M. C., Dennis, N. A., Davis, S. W., Shepler, A. M., Spaniol, J., ... Cabeza, R. (2010). Adult age differences in functional connectivity during executive control. *NeuroImage, 52*, 643–657. doi:10.1016/j.neuroimage.2010.04.249

Marsh, A. P., & Geel, S. E. (2000). The effect of age on the attentional demands of postural control. *Gait Posture, 12*, 105–113. doi:10.1016/S0966-6362(00)00074-6

Massion, J. (1994). Postural control system. *Current Opinion in Neurobiology, 4*, 877–887. doi:10.1016/0959-4388(94)90137-6

Mattay, V. S., Fera, F., Tessitore, A., Hariri, A. R., Das, S., Callicott, J. H., & Weinberger, D. R. (2002). Neurophysiological correlates of age-related changes in human motor function. *Neurology, 58*, 630–635. doi:10.1212/WNL.58.4.630

Melzer, I., & Oddsson, L. L. E. (2013). Improving balance control and self-reported lower extremity function in community-dwelling older adults: A randomized control trial. *Clinical Rehabilitation, 27*, 195–206. doi:10.1177/0269215512450295

Mergner, T., & Rosemeier, T. (1998). Interaction of vestibular somatosensory and visual signals for postural control under terrestrial and microgravity conditions—A conceptual model. *Brain Research Reviews, 28*, 118–135. doi:10.1016/S0165-0173(98)00032-0

Navon, D., & Miller, J. (1987). Role of outcome conflict in dual task interference. *Journal of Experimental Psychology: Human Perception and Performance, 13*, 435–448. doi:10.1037/0096-1523.13.3.435

Pashler, H. (1994). Dual task interference in simple tasks: Data and theory. *Psychological Bulletin, 116*, 220–244. doi:10.1037/0033-2909.116.2.220

Pashler, H., & Johnston, J. (1989). Chronometric evidence for central postponement in temporally overlapping tasks. *The Quarterly Journal of Experimental Psychology, 41*, 19–45. doi:10.1080/14640748908402351

Pashler, H., & Johnston, J. C. (1998). Attentional limitations in dual-task performance. In H. Pashler (Ed.), *Attention* (pp. 230–257). Hove: Psychology Press.

Pichierri, G., Coppe, A., Lorenzetti, S., Murer, K., & de Bruin, E. D. (2012). The effect of a cognitive-motor intervention on voluntary step execution under single and dual task conditions in older adults: A randomized controlled pilot study. *Clin Interv Aging, 7*, 175–184. doi:10.2147/CIA.S32558

Pichierri, G., Murer, K., & de Bruin, E. D. (2012). A cognitive-motor intervention using a dance video game to enhance foot placement accuracy and gait under dual task conditions in older adults: A randomized controlled trial. *BMC Geriatr, 12*, 1–14. doi:10.1186/1471-2318-12-74

Plummer-D'Amato, P., Cohen, Z., Daee, N. A., Lawson, S. E., Lizotte, M. R., & Padilla, A. (2012). Effects of once weekly dual task training in older adults: A pilot randomized controlled trial. *Geriatrics & Gerontology International, 12*, 622–629. doi:10.1111/j.1447-0594.2011.00825.x

Prado, J. M., Stoffregen, T. A., & Duarte, M. (2007). Postural sway during dual tasks in young and elderly adults. *Gerontology, 53*, 274–281. doi:10.1159/000102938

Priest, A. W., Salamon, K. B., & Hollman, J. H. (2008). Age-related differences in dual task walking: A cross sectional study. *Journal of Neuroengineering and Rehabilitation, 5*, 1–8. doi:10.1186/1743-0003-5-29

Rankin, J. K., Woollacott, M. H., Shumway-Cook, A., & Brown, L. A. (2000). Cognitive influence on postural stability: A neuromuscular analysis in young and older adults. *The Journals of Gerontology Series A: Biological Sciences and Medical Sciences, 55*, M112–M119. doi:10.1093/gerona/55.3.M112

Redfern, M. S., Müller, M. L. T. M., Jennings, J. R., & Furman, J. M. (2002). Attentional dynamics in postural control during perturbations in young and older adults. *The Journals of Gerontology Series A: Biological Sciences and Medical Sciences, 57A*, B298–B303. doi:10.1093/gerona/57.8.B298

Riby, L., Perfect, T., & Stollery, B. (2004). The effects of age and task domain on dual task performance: A meta-analysis. *European Journal of Cognitive Psychology, 16*, 863–891. doi:10.1080/09541440340000402

Ruthruff, E., Johnston, J. C., & Van Selst, M. (2001). Why practice reduces dual-task interference. *Journal of Experimental Psychology: Human Perception and Performance, 27*, 3–21. doi:10.1037/0096-1523.27.1.3

Schoene, D., Lord, S. R., Delbaere, K., Severino, C., Davies, T. A., & Smith, S. T. (2013). A randomized controlled pilot study of home-based step training in older people using videogame technology. *PLOS one, 8*, e57734. doi:10.1371/journal.pone.0057734

Schubert, T., & Szameitat, A. J. (2003). Functional neuroanatomy of interference in overlapping dual tasks: An fMRI study. *Cognitive Brain Research, 17*, 733–746. doi:10.1016/S0926-6410(03)00198-8

Seidler, R. D., Bernard, J. A., Burutolu, T. B., Fling, B. W., Gordon, M. T., Gwin, J. T., ... Lipps, D. B. (2010). Motor control and aging: Links to age-related brain structural functional, and biochemical effects. *Neuroscience & Biobehavioral Reviews, 34*, 721–733. doi:10.1016/j.neubiorev.2009.10.005

Shumwas-Cook, A., & Woollacott, M. (2000). Attentional demands and postural control: The effect of sensory context. *Journals of Gerontology-Biological Sciences and Medical Sciences, 55*, M10–M16. doi:10.1093/gerona/55.1.M10

Shumway-Cook, A., Guralnik, J. M., Phillips, C. L., Coppin, A. K., Ciol, M. A., Bandinelli, S., & Ferrucci, L. (2007). Age-associated declines in complex walking task performance: The walking InCHIANTI toolkit. *Journal of the American Geriatrics Society, 55*, 58–65. doi:10.1111/j.1532-5415.2006.00962.x

Shumway-Cook, A., Woollacott, M., Kerns, K. A., & Baldwin, M. (1997). The effects of two types of cognitive tasks on postural stability in older adults with and without a history of falls. *The Journals of Gerontology Series A: Biological Sciences and Medical Sciences, 52*, M232–M240. doi:10.1093/gerona/52A.4.M232

Silsupadol, P., Lugade, V., Shumway-Cook, A., van Donkelaar, P., Chou, L. S., Mayr, U., & Woollacott, M. H. (2009). Training-related changes in dual-task walking performance of elderly persons with balance impairment: A double-blind, randomized controlled trial. *Gait Posture, 29*, 634–639. doi:10.1016/j.gaitpost.2009.01.006

Silsupadol, P., Shumway-Cook, A., Lugade, V., van Donkelaar, P., Chou, L. S., Mayr, U., & Woollacott, M. H. (2009). Effects of single-task versus dual-task training on balance performance in older adults: A double-blind, randomized controlled trial. *Archives of Physical Medicine and Rehabilitation, 90*, 381–387. doi:10.1016/j.apmr.2008.09.559

Smith, M. C. (1969). The effect of varying information on the psychological refractory period. *Acta Psychologica, 30*, 220–231. doi:10.1016/0001-6918(69)90052-3

Smolders, C., Doumas, M., & Krampe, R. T. (2010). Posture and cognition interfere in later adulthood even without concurrent response production. *Human Movement Science, 29*, 809–819. doi:10.1016/j.humov.2009.07.009

Sparrow, W. A., Bradshaw, E. J., Lamoureux, E., & Tirosh, O. (2002). Ageing effects on the attention demands of walking. *Human Movement Science, 21*, 961–972. doi:10.1016/S0167-9457(02)00154-9

Springer, S., Giladi, N., Peretz, C., Yogev, G., Simon, E. S., & Hausdorff, J. M. (2006). Dual-tasking effects on gait variability: The role of aging, falls, and executive function. *Movement Disorders, 21*, 950–957. doi:10.1002/mds.20848

Srygley, J. M., Mirelman, A., Herman, T., Giladi, N., & Hausdorff, J. M. (2008). When does walking alter thinking? Age and task associated findings. *Brain Research, 1253*, 92–99. doi:10.1016/j.brainres.2008.11.067

Stelzel, C., Schumacher, E. H., Schubert, T., & D'Esposito, M. (2006). The neural effect of stimulus-response modality compatibility on dual-task performance: An fMRI study. *Psychological Research, 70*, 514–525. doi:10.1007/s00426-005-0013-7

Szameitat, A. J., Schubert, T., Müller, K., & von Cramon, D. Y. (2002). Localization of executive functions in dual-task performance with fMRI. *Journal of Cognitive Neuroscience, 14*, 1184–1199. doi:10.1162/089892902760807195

Takeuchi, H., Ysuyuki, T., Nouchi, R., Hashizume, H., Sekiguchi, A., Kotozaki, Y., ... Kawashima, R. (2013). Effects of multitasking-training on gray matter structure and resting state neural mechanisms. *Human Brain Mapping, 35*, 1–15. doi:10.1002/hbm.22427

Teasdale, N., Bard, C., LaRue, J., & Fleury, M. (1993). On the cognitive penetrability of posture control. *Experimental Aging Research, 19*, 1–13. doi:10.1080/03610739308253919

Telford, C. W. (1931). The refractory phase of voluntary and associative responses. *Journal of Experimental Psychology, 14*, 1–36. doi:10.1037/h0073262

Trombetti, A., Hars, M., Herrmann, F. R., Kressig, R. W., Ferrari, S., & Rizzoli, R. (2011). Effect of music-based multitask training on gait, balance, and fall risk in elderly people: A randomized controlled trial. *Archives of Internal Medicine, 171*, 525–533. doi:10.1001/archinternmed.2010.446

Uemura, K., Yamada, M., Nagai, K., Tateuchi, H., Mori, S., Tanaka, B., & Ichihashi, N. (2012). Effects of dual task switch exercise on gait and gait initiation performance in older adults: Preliminary results of a randomized controlled trial. *Archives of Gerontology and Geriatrics, 54*, e167–e171. doi:10.1016/j.archger.2012.01.002

Van Impe, A., Coxon, J. P., Goble, D. J., Wenderoth, N., & Swinnen, S. P. (2011). Age-related changes in brain activation underlying single- and dual-task performance: Visuomanual drawing and mental arithmetic. *Neuropsychologia, 49*, 2400–2409. doi:10.1016/j.neuropsychologia.2011.04.016

Vaportzis, E., Georgiou-Karistianis, N., & Stout, J. C. (2013). Dual task performance in normal aging: A comparison of choice reaction time tasks. *PLOS one, 8*, e60265. doi:10.1371/journal.pone.0060265

Verhaeghen, P., Steitz, D. W., Sliwinski, M. J., & Cerella, J. (2003). Aging and dual-task performance: A meta-analysis. *Psychology and Aging, 18*, 443–460. doi:10.1037/0882-7974.18.3.443

Welford, A. T. (1952). The psychological refractory period and the timing of high speed performance: A review and a theory. *British Journal of Psychology, 43*, 2–9. doi:10.1111/j.2044-8295.1952.tb00322.x

Wittwer, J. E., Webster, K. E., & Hill, K. (2013). Music and metronome cues produce different effects on gait spatiotemporal measures but not gait variability in healthy older adults. *Gait Posture, 37*, 219–222. doi:10.1016/j.gaitpost.2012.07.006

Wollesen, B., & Voelcker-Rehage, C. (2013). Training effects on motor-cognitive dual-task performance in older adults. *European Review of Aging and Physical Activity, 11*, 5–24. doi:10.1007/s11556-013-0122-z

Woollacott, M., & Shumway-Cook, A. (2002). Attention and the control of posture and gait. A review of an emerging area of research. *Gait Posture, 16*, 1–14. doi:10.1016/S0966-6362(01)00156-4

Wu, T., Liu, J., Hallett, M., Zheng, Z., & Chang, P. (2013). Cerebellum and integration of neural networks in dual-task processing. *Neuroimage, 15*, 466–475. doi:10.1016/j.neuroimage.2012.10.004

Yamada, M., Aoyama, T., Hikita, Y., Takamura, M., Tanaka, Y., Kajiwara, Y., ... Tanaka, B. (2011). Effects of a DVD-based seated dual task stepping exercise on the fall risk factors among community-dwelling elderly adults. *Telemedicine and e-Health, 17*, 768–772. doi:10.1089/tmj.2011.0054

Yamada, M., Aoyama, T., Tanaka, B., Nagai, K., & Ichihashi, N. (2011). Seated stepping exercise in a dual-task condition improves ambulatory function with a secondary task: A randomized controlled trial. *Aging Clinical and Experimental Research, 23*, 386–392. doi:10.1007/BF03337763

You, J. H., Shetty, A., Jones, T., Shields, K., Belay, Y., & Brown, D. (2009). Effects of dual-task cognitive-gait intervention on memory and gait dynamics in older adults with a history of falls: A preliminary intervention. *NeuroRehabilitation, 24*, 193–198. doi:10.3233/NRE-2009-0468

Zwergal, A., Linn, J., Xiong, J., Brandt, T., Strupp, M., & Jahn, K. (2012). Aging of human supraspinal locomotor and postural control in fMRI. *Neurobiology of Aging, 33*, 1073–1084. doi:10.1016/j.neurobiolaging.2010.09.022

5

Music-evoked autobiographical memories (MEAMs) in Alzheimer disease: Evidence for a positivity effect

Lola L. Cuddy[1], Ritu Sikka[1*], Kristen Silveira[1], Sean Bai[1] and Ashley Vanstone[1]

*Corresponding author: Ritu Sikka, Department of Psychology, Queen's University, 62 Arch Street, Humphrey Hall, Room 232, Kingston, Ontario, Canada

E-mail: ritu.sikka@queensu.ca

Reviewing editor: Peter Walla, University of Newcastle, Australia

Abstract: We present a study designed to assess the presence of the positivity effect in music-evoked autobiographical memories or MEAMs. In particular, we sought to determine whether the positivity effect was evident in cases of Alzheimer's disease (AD), where a preserved memory for music in AD might also be reflected in an ability to retrieve memories associated with music. The positivity effect refers to instances where, compared to younger adults, older adults reveal a relative preference in attention and memory for positive over negative information. It is considered to be a hallmark of healthy aging. Three groups of participants—20 younger adults, 20 older adults, and 20 adults with mild-to-moderate AD—were asked to listen to familiar musical excerpts and describe any memories evoked by the excerpts. Word usage and topics in the memory transcripts were analyzed, as well as ratings of the memories provided by the participants in order to detect any positive bias or absence-of-negativity bias in older as compared to younger adults. Self-ratings yielded the strongest evidence. Compared with young adults, MEAMs for both groups of older adults were self-rated as less specific, but more vivid, more positive and less negative. In general, the characteristics of MEAMs reflected the effects of age rather than disease. For AD, MEAMs may reveal a sense of self-identity that has been preserved despite the ravages of neural degeneration.

ABOUT THE AUTHOR

Lola Cuddy is the director of the Music Cognition Laboratory at Queen's University in Kingston, Ontario, Canada. Lola also serves on the Scientific Advisory Board for the *International Conference for the Perception and Cognition of Music* and is the editor of the journal *Music Perception*, an interdisciplinary journal of music perception, cognition, and performance. Lola is interested in the perceptual, cognitive, and emotional processes involved in music appreciation and understanding. She has studied topics such as the effects of music lessons on nonmusical cognitive skills, aging and music, amusia following stroke, and sparing of musical and related autobiographical memories in Alzheimer's disease. After testing over 200 people—young adults, older adults, and adults with dementia—on a variety of music and cognitive tests, she has shown that musical memories are present for many people throughout the various stages of dementia.

PUBLIC INTEREST STATEMENT

Alzheimer's is an incurable brain disease that can rob a person of memory and personality. The diagnosis of Alzheimer's has devastating consequences not only for the person with the disease, but also for family, friends, and caregivers. However, not all mental faculties are equally destroyed in the progress of the disease. Here, we show that music can be used to evoke personal memories of a past life. Music-evoked memories of our Alzheimer's participants were similar to those of healthy older adults. Both Alzheimer's and healthy older participants rated their memories as both more positive and less negative than did young adults, revealing sparing in Alzheimer's of an effect known as the ***positivity effect***, whereby adults become overall more positive in life with age. Understanding the sparing of music-related memories in Alzheimer's is useful when creating rehabilitation programs to encourage communication with individuals with Alzheimer's.

Subjects: Memory; Psychology of Music; Gerontology/Ageing; Dementia; Cognitive Neuroscience of Memory; Quality of Life; Dementia & Alzheimer's Disease

Keywords: Alzheimer's disease; positivity effect; music; memories; autobiographical memories; music-evoked autobiographical memories; MEAMs

1. Introduction

The neurodegenerative disease Alzheimer's disease (AD) affects some 46.8 million people worldwide and is predicted to reach 131.5 million by the year 2050 according to the 2015 World Alzheimer Report (Prince et al., 2015). Behavioral hallmarks of the disease include memory and language impairment, with serious consequences for interpersonal communication and the sense of self and well-being in AD. Given the unrelenting progress of the disease and the fact that there is no cure, a diagnosis of AD is a devastating situation for both patients and caregivers alike. Methods for improving communication have the potential to improve quality of life in AD and thereby alleviate caregiver burden.

Music has long been thought to be a therapeutic means of reaching out to persons with AD and encouraging responses from such persons. Music is seen as an important component of dementia care and treatment. However, empirical studies where the efficacy of a treatment group (music therapy) has been compared with a nontreatment group have yielded mixed or inconclusive results (Vink, Bruinsma, & Scholten, 2003). Music intervention studies therefore yield a limited view of music efficacy, one that needs to be enhanced with a larger picture of music cognition and the brain.

We offer an alternative and complementary approach to the power of music, which is to focus on the implications of a particular research finding: Musical memories—familiarity for music heard in one's past—are preserved in healthy aging and also in the early stages of AD (Cuddy et al., 2012; Fornazzari et al., 2006; Hsieh, Hornberger, Piguet, & Hodges, 2011; Omar, Hailstone, & Warren, 2012). Musical memories are sometimes spared, despite severe cognitive impairment, even in the later stages of AD (Cuddy & Duffin, 2005; Vanstone & Cuddy, 2010). Research on spared systems can help us better understand and identify the mechanisms and neural substrates of the neurodegenerative process (Jacobsen et al., 2015). It may also provide directives for care management.

Musical memories may be associated with other, nonmusical, memories that are previous personal experiences, or autobiographical memories. Music-evoked autobiographical memories are known as MEAMS (Janata, Tomic, & Rakowski, 2007). To elicit MEAMs, musical excerpts are played to participants who are asked to describe any memory from their recent or remote past that was brought to mind by the music. The paradigm differs from the usual autobiographical memory test in that the latter requires a voluntary and directed memory search for a particular experience at a particular time following an explicit test instruction (e.g. the autobiographical memory interview or AMI: Kopelman, Wilson, & Baddeley, 1989). By contrast, MEAMs are simply memories of past personal events that come to mind spontaneously and effortlessly, triggered by a perceptual cue or a current thought and, as such, may be considered involuntary memories (Berntsen, 1996, 1998; Rasmussen & Berntsen, 2009). An oft-cited literary example of an involuntary memory is Proust's narrator in *Remembrance of Times Past,* where the taste of a madeleine arouses earlier episodes in his life.

MEAMs have been collected and the contents described for young adults by Janata and colleagues (Janata et al., 2007), for healthy older adults and persons with AD by El Haj and colleagues (El Haj, Fasotti, & Allain, 2012; El Haj, Postal, & Allain, 2012) and for patients with acquired brain injury (Baird & Samson, 2014). Compared to memories retrieved in silence, MEAMs are typically specific, positive, and automatic (El Haj et al., 2012).

The study by El Haj et al. (2012) obtained MEAMs from 12 patients diagnosed with probable (mild) AD and 12 matched healthy older controls. The music presented to all participants was either

Vivaldi's *Four Seasons* or self-selected "Chosen" music, tested in separate conditions and compared against memories elicited in a separate "Silence" condition. El Haj et al. reported an enhancement of positive emotional words in the MEAMs, particularly evident for the AD patients. Such a finding is intriguing for two reasons. First, it is remarkable that AD patients responded with MEAMs, given the known deterioration of autobiographical memory accompanying the disease (El Haj, Kapogiannis, & Antoine, 2016; Greene, Hodges, & Baddeley, 1995). Second, although it might well be expected that the music would influence emotion in a positive way (for a review, see Croom, 2015), the memories evoked by music may have revealed an additional and potentially informative influence known as the *positivity effect* (Kennedy, Mather, & Carstensen, 2004).

1.1. The positivity effect

In general, the positivity effect refers to instances where, compared to younger adults, older adults reveal a relative preference in attention and memory for positive over negative information (Mather & Carstensen, 2005; Reed & Carstensen, 2012). The effect may be uncovered in a variety of experimental paradigms, tasks, and stimuli (Reed, Chan, & Mikels, 2014). The positivity effect can be evidenced either through older adults recalling memories with more positive or less negative content than younger adults (e.g. Schlagman, Schulz, & Kvavilashvili, 2006); for recognition of musical excerpts, see Parks & Dollinger, 2014). Alternatively, it can be evidenced through older adults rating all memories either more positively or less negatively than younger adults, regardless of memory content (e.g. Schlagman et al., 2006).

It is considered by many to be a hallmark of successful aging. Opinions vary as to whether the positivity effect in old age is an adaptive or nonadaptive process (Reed & Carstensen, 2012). On the one hand, it may be a nonadaptive process, a natural and fixed consequence of cognitive decline because in aging brains, cognitive flexibility decreases and the networks for processing emotion are compromised (e.g. Wurm, 2011). On the other, it may reflect a controlled process where cognitive resources are recruited to adapt to changing lifestyle and time-limited goals. It has also been proposed as a disease-avoidance mechanism, following from the observation of a stronger positivity bias for attractive faces among older adults with health problems, relative to those without health problems (Zebrowitz, Franklin, & Palumbo, 2015). These authors argue that older adults in generally poor health feel vulnerable to disease and thus show voting preferences for attractive faces and avoidance of unattractive faces that may be associated with poor health.

According to socioemotional selectivity theory (SST: Carstensen, 1992, 1995), the goals and expectations in old age, as opposed to the young, direct cognitive processing to emotion regulation, emotional meaning, and well-being. Young adults perceive time as open-ended and focus on preparatory goals, such as seeking new experiences, friends, and knowledge. In contrast, the goals of older adults involve emotional satisfaction obtained through the emotional regulation of negative affect and the enhancement of positive affect. Older adults focus on emotional information in order to optimize well-being relatively quickly. Behavioral evidence for this effect converges with neurobiological findings of age-related changes to the noradrenergic system which may alter the mechanisms of emotional memory (for a review, see Mammarella, Di Domenico, Palumbo, & Fairfield, 2016). Greater activity of the system during aging means that "healthy older adults are able to circumvent or minimize the experience of negative emotions and stabilize or even enhance positive emotional experiences" (p. 61).

Further support for the thought that the positivity effect is a controlled process comes from evidence that older adults who performed poorly on tests of executive control or who were distracted with a divided attention task during memory encoding were less likely to exhibit the positivity effect (Mather & Knight, 2005). Recent research by Belleville, Chertkow, and Gauthier (2007) suggests that executive control is one of the first areas of cognitive decline in AD. Thus, it would be particularly interesting if older adults with AD still exhibit the positivity effect—a (likely) controlled emotion regulation process.

1.2. The positivity effect, music, and AD

In a recent review, Baird and Samson (2015) point out that music is perhaps unique in its power to elicit memories and emotions. Given this "island of preservation" (Baird & Samson, 2015, p. 209) in otherwise cognitively impaired persons, it would seem likely that the positivity effect may also be present in AD. However, no clear evidence has indicated whether the positivity effect is preserved in the MEAMs of patients diagnosed with AD. As MEAMs capture a personal past and self-identity they may, for persons with AD, offer a special means of communication with music therapists and care givers. Implications for preserving the well-being of AD patients may follow.

As noted above, either emotional processing or, alternatively, the cognitive control required for emotion regulation is involved with the positivity effect. Either may be damaged in AD, leading to the prediction that the positivity effect would be reduced or eliminated in AD. For example, a positivity effect was not observed in mild AD patients viewing familiar neutral faces and novel fearful human facial expressions (Wright, Dickerson, Feczko, Negeira, & Williams, 2007). The researchers used functional magnetic resonance imaging to examine and compare amygdala responses in young and elderly controls; the groups did not significantly differ from each other. The patients, however, showed greater amygdala activation in response to both the neutral familiar faces and the fearful novel faces. Wright et al. (2007) interpret their findings according to pathological changes in either the amygdala or prefrontal regions that modulate amygdala activity, such that amygdala activation becomes less specific or hyper-responsive in mild AD patients. This activation is clinically meaningful as patients are more irritable and agitated or aggressive when they are overly reactive to irrelevant neutral or negative stimuli. According to Scheibe and Carstensen (2010, p. 5), "It is intriguing to assume that in [AD patients] cognitive control processes are no longer effective in inhibiting amygdala activation in response to negative stimuli." Lack of control processes would eliminate the selective bias toward positive information, or the positivity effect. Moreover, in the review by Mammarella et al. (2016), it is noted that weaker noradrenergic activity in AD may lead to reduced or null effects of emotion and reduced positivity effects in memory.

For music, the results obtained by El Haj and colleagues have provided suggestive evidence for a possible link between AD and the positivity effect. El Haj et al. (2012) reported that a group of AD persons produced more positive words in their MEAMs than did elderly age-matched controls. The study did not include a younger adult group so an assessment of the positivity effect is not possible. As well, the AD group produced more negative words than the elderly controls, a finding indicating that emotional words overall, not just positive words, were more prevalent in the AD MEAMs—again a finding that does not allow a conclusion that a positivity effect was present. El Haj et al. (2012) did include a younger group of participants and in that study, rather than calibrating the word count of positive and negative words, the researchers collected emotional ratings of MEAMs on a five-point scale ranging from "1-very negative," to "5-very positive." The mean rating for elderly controls was higher than for younger controls, indicating a positivity effect in healthy aging, but the mean rating for the AD group in this case, was lower than the mean rating for the age-matched controls and was similar to the younger controls. Thus, the two studies do not reveal clear evidence of a positivity effect in AD.

1.3. The present study

El Haj and colleagues have provided strong evidence that music evokes memories more effectively than do specific instructions to recall in silence. Thus, our focus in the present study is not the comparison of music and silence. Rather, we follow the direction of the study by Janata et al. (2007), undertaken with young adults, to explore further the properties of memories aroused by music; we include the effects of aging and neurodegenerative disease. We present a study designed to assess the presence of the positivity effect in MEAMs with 20 healthy older adults and 20 persons with AD. The data from these two groups were compared with those from a group of 20 young adults.

The expectation that a positivity effect would be found with healthy adults was derived from three proposals arising from the studies cited above: (1) that music-perceptual cues arouse involuntary memories; (2) that involuntary memories involve less cognitive control (fewer demands on executive and attentive resources) than voluntary memories, and (3) fewer demands on memory-retrieval resources release cognitive resources for emotional control in aging, leading to the positivity effect.

The expectation regarding AD participants is less clear. As noted above, the cognitive damage associated with AD may result in a lack of emotional control. However, if cognitive demands for memory retrieval are lightened in the production of involuntary memories, emotional control of memories may be possible and the positivity effect may emerge.

Additional features of the study include:

(1) Choice of musical excerpts: The musical excerpts presented to participants were familiar instrumental tunes—unlike most previous work which used songs as stimuli. Instrumental tunes allow us to gauge whether music alone is successful in evoking MEAMs, whereas songs with lyrics confound the role of music and words. Familiarity was determined by pilot work.
(2) Number of excerpts: Twelve instrumental tunes (rather than one or two as in previous work with AD and MEAMs) were employed so that we could examine the relation between number of MEAMs evoked and cognitive status in AD, and could extend our results beyond the single pieces used in earlier studies.
(3) Response measures: Three different response measures were used to assess the content of MEAMs. We could therefore examine whether evidence for a positivity effect was measure-dependent or whether measures converged. The first measure was the word count obtained by the Linguistic Inquiry Word Count software, (LIWC: Tausczik & Pennebaker, 2009), which provides a tally of both positive (e.g. "love, nice, sweet") and negative (e.g. "hurt, ugly, nasty") words. The second was the distribution of content topics according to the categorical scheme for the distribution of topics in involuntary diary entries by Schlagman et al. (2006). Schlagman et al. identified both positive (e.g. "Holidays," "Going out") and negative ("Accidents/illness") topics. The third was a self-rating of the valence of each MEAM on each of two scales, one reflecting the positivity of the memory, the other the negativity. The use of two scales allowed participants to respond, if they chose, that the memory contained both positive and negative aspects (i.e. mixed emotions; see Hunter, Schellenberg, & Schimmack, 2010).
(4) Mood-congruence hypothesis: The mood-congruency hypothesis predicts that emotional valence of the memories will be strongly related to current mood, especially in older people who tend to report more positive affect (Schlagman et al., 2006). Mood was assessed by administering the Positive and Negative Affect Scale (PANAS; Watson, Clark, & Tellegen, 1988) before and after collecting MEAM data.

2. Method

2.1. Participants

MEAM data from three groups of volunteer participants are presented: 20 younger adults (YA), 20 older adults (OA), and 20 adults with a diagnosis of probable AD. All participants were native English speakers.[1] Length of formal music training ranged from less than 1 to over 10 years; the modal years of training for OA and AD was less than one year and slightly more for YA at 4–7 years. (The availability of music in the high schools in this area makes it virtually impossible to find a YA with less than 1 year of training). The minimum level of education for all groups was high school attendance; the modal level of education was high school completion. Exclusion criteria were severe hearing loss, a known history of substance abuse, and a history of severe psychiatric disorders, stroke, head injury, or major neurological disorder other than a diagnosis of dementia in the AD group. Hearing was not formally assessed, but all participants were able to hear well enough to have a regular conversation. All participants in the OA and AD groups (except four AD who resided in long-term care facilities) were community-dwelling adults and not living in an institution. Participants were compensated $10/hour for their participation (approximately $10 for YA and $15 for OA and AD). This study was approved by the Queen's University General Research Ethics Board.

2.1.1. Younger adults

YA ($n = 20$; 10 females) were undergraduate university students recruited through advertisements on campus. Their age range was 19–24 years ($M = 21.2$, SD = 1.2).

2.1.2. Older adults

OA ($n = 20$; 11 females) were recruited through advertisements in community newspapers and appropriate seniors' organizations. They ranged in age from 66 to 83 years ($M = 73.1$, SD = 5.2). A minimum score of 28 out of 30 on the Mini-Mental State Examination (MMSE; Folstein, Folstein, & McHugh, 1975) was required for participation. Two of the OA participants from an initial set of 22 were excluded due to MMSE scores below 28.

2.1.3. Alzheimer's disease

A total of 24 AD participants was recruited though a geriatric medicine outpatient clinic and an inpatient geriatric ward for physical rehabilitation. Recruitment personnel were asked to locate interested participants with mild-to-moderate AD.

Participants met the criteria for probable AD as defined by the Diagnostic and Statistical Manual for Mental Disorders (4th ed., text rev., DSM-IV-TR; American Psychiatric Association, 2000) and the National Institute of Neurological and Communicative Disorders and Stroke-Alzheimer's Disease and Related Disorders Association (NINCDS-ADRDA) criteria (McKhann et al., 1984). Cases of "mixed" dementia ($n = 4$, AD plus cerebrovascular involvement such as minor infarcts) were included given that they met the criteria of dementia of the AD type, and that, in the judgment of the referring geriatrician, AD, not cerebrovascular involvement, was responsible for their cognitive impairment.

Of the 24 participants, 20 (termed "responders"; 10 females) provided at least 1 MEAM and 4 (termed "nonresponders"; 2 females) were unable to provide any MEAMs. There were no easily identified demographic or diagnostic factors (on referral) on which to discriminate nonresponders from responders—that is, factors that would place the nonresponders in a clearly distinct group. For example, the age range and MMSE status of the nonresponders fell within the range of the responders. The age range of the responders was 63–89 years ($Mdn = 77.5$), and MMSE scores out of 30 ranged from 8 to 29 ($Mdn = 21.0$). Nonresponders ranged in age from 71 to 84 years ($Mdn = 74.0$), and had MMSE scores ranging from 9 to 20 ($Mdn = 16.5$). Both groups lacked music training (responders and nonresponders mode = "less than 1 year," range = "less than 1 year" to "4–7 years"). Data from only responders were entered into further analysis of MEAMs.

2.2. Stimuli

Twelve excerpts from instrumental tunes were selected based on pilot testing in our laboratory where the melodies for the tunes were assessed for familiarity in both younger and older adults. All tunes had a familiarity rating below 2.1 on a scale from "1" to "3," where "1" was "very familiar" and "3" was "very unfamiliar" These tunes were also considered pleasant as shown by a mean rating below 2.5 on a scale from "1" to "5," where "1" was "very pleasing" and "5" was "very displeasing." The tunes were required to have a mean rating, for both YA and OA, above "2" on a familiarity scale from "0" to "3," where "3" was "very familiar." Each tune excerpt was 30 s in length, with a 2-s fade-in and fade-out. Tune duration was adopted from Janata et al. (2007) and extensive pilot work that ensured that 30 s was adequate to recover a MEAM in younger and older participants. The excerpts were in their original instrumentation downloaded as mp3 files from commercially available internet sources. Examples of tunes were "The Sorcerer's Apprentice" by Paul Dukas and "In the Mood" by Glen Miller. The full set is given in the Appendix A.

2.3. Procedure

YA and OA, as well as 5 out of the 20 AD responders, were tested in a quiet laboratory (sound-isolated rooms), whereas the remaining 15 AD were tested in their place of residence, either their own homes or a quiet ward room. The session began with administration of a standard lab questionnaire to capture demographic data and participant's musical background, followed by the MMSE for OA and AD. The participant's mood at the moment was then assessed using the Positive and Negative Affective Schedule (PANAS; Watson et al., 1988). The PANAS is a standardized questionnaire consisting of two 10-item scales describing different feelings and emotions. Examples of items on the positive scale are "excited," "enthusiastic," and "alert"; examples from the negative scale are "distressed," "upset," and "nervous." The participant was asked to read each item and then rate a number from "1" or "very slightly or not at all" to "5" or "extremely," to "the extent you feel right now." YA and OA answered with pencil and paper. The items were read aloud to AD adults by the test administrator who then recorded their responses.

The PANAS was followed by the music and memories session. The excerpts were played in random order without replacement though the speakers of a laptop for YA and OA participants and on an iPod with computer speakers for AD. The entire session was recorded using a Sony HDR-CX200 video camera.

At the start of the music and memories session participants were informed that music may evoke memories from their past that "come to mind spontaneously" without any explicit effort to recall them. They were told that these memories could be from the distant or recent past, could be specific or general, and could have a vague or vivid image. The participants were instructed to listen to each excerpt and, for each excerpt in turn, to elaborate immediately on the first memory from their past that spontaneously arose while the excerpt played or after it stopped. If no memories had arisen by the time the excerpt finished playing, or shortly thereafter, they were asked to indicate this by simply saying "No memory." After the tune stopped, if participants had not already begun describing a memory, then the test administrator asked if they had had any memories. After a participant's initial description, the test administrator provided one prompt: "Is there anything more you could add to that?"

After the participant finished a memory description, a series of questions followed concerning the valence, specificity, vividness, and age of the memory. Visual rating scales were presented to YA and OA or read to AD by the test administrator. Four valence scales were presented first. Participants were instructed to rate on a scale from "0" to "3," how positively, and on a second scale from "0" to "3," how negatively, they felt about the memory now. On a third and fourth scale, they recorded how positively, and how negatively, they felt about the memory at the time of the event. It was explained to the participants that both positive and negative feelings, or neither, might occur toward the event. The participant was then asked if the memory was specific (a single event) or general (a repeated event or multiple events). The vividness of the memory was specified on a visual scale from 1 to 7, with "1" representing low vividness. Finally, the participant was asked to provide an estimate of his/her age at the time of the memory. These questions were repeated for each memory.

After all excerpts were played and any corresponding memories recorded, the PANAS was administered for a second time. The memories were later transcribed to a text file for content analysis.

The testing session was followed by a collection of supplementary measures intended for AD participants:

(1) The informant version of the Music Engagement Questionnaire (Vanstone, Wolf, Poon, & Cuddy, 2015), completed by the caregiver.
(2) The Familiarity Decision Test (FDT; Liegeois-Chauvel, Peretz, Babai, Laguitton, & Chauvel, 1998) to assess long-term familiarity with well-known tunes, and Distorted Tunes Test (DTT; Drayna, Manichaikul, de Lange, Snieder, & Spector, 2001) to assess the ability to detect pitch distortions in familiar tunes.
(3) The Animal Naming task (Rosen, 1980), a test of semantic fluency where the participant is asked to name as many animals as possible within a one-minute period. The semantic fluency

test has been shown to predict the retrieval of autobiographical memories (Benjamin, Cifelli, Garrard, Caine, & Jones, 2015).

(4) Dementia Severity Rating Scale (DSRS; Clark & Ewbank, 1996), an informant-based questionnaire for assessing disease severity with a possible score range of 0–54 (0 = no impairment, 54 = maximum impairment).

(5) The Montreal Cognitive Assessment (MoCA; Nasreddine et al., 2005) as a verification of the MMSE results. The correlation between MMSE and MoCA results was high, $\rho(n = 23) = 0.87$, $p < 0.0005$.

(6) The Geriatric Depression Scale (GDS; Sheikh & Yesavage, 1986), a screen that has been validated for detecting depression in the elderly, including those with mild to moderate dementia (0–5 is considered a normal score, and the maximum possible score is 15).

Each participant was then debriefed to conclude the testing.

3. Results

As our focus is the examination of music-evoked autobiographical memory, we conducted a preliminary review of the data to ensure that our data base consisted of autobiographical memories. All responses to the excerpts were categorized as either an autobiographical memory (MEAM) or as nonautobiographical (nonMEAM) by two independent judges. The criterion for a MEAM was that the response should include reference to the self in some manner—that is, following instructions, the memory contained a description involving the participant's "real life."

MEAMs occurred in all participant groups; groups did not differ in the frequency of MEAM responses relative to all responses. The median percent of responses categorized as MEAMs was 100% for both OA and AD with YA slightly but not significantly lower at 90%, $U = 340$, $N = 60$, $p = 0.293$). Overall, nonMEAMs were relatively rare (36/472 of total responses or 7%). MEAMs were entered into further data analysis.

Each MEAM was categorized by the same two independent judges as either episodic or semantic and for those deemed episodic, further as specific or general. A memory was considered episodic if it included information on the time or place of the event. An episodic memory, in turn, was marked as specific if it referred to a single event and as general for a repeated or extended event. A semantic MEAM was a response that reflected knowledge of one's past self but with no reference to the time or place of a personal event or episode.

Agreement between the two judges was good ($\kappa = 0.79$, 95% 95% CI [0.74, 0.84]). Disagreements were resolved by discussion.

3.1. Occurrence and characteristics of MEAMs

The measures reported in Tables 1a and 1b (upper and lower sections of Table 1) are the relative occurrence of MEAMS and certain characteristics of these obtained MEAMs. All measures in Table 1a were either extracted from the memory descriptions (first two rows) or provided directly by participants (remaining entries). Measures in Table 1b are the results of categorization of memories by independent judges.

For relative occurrence (Table 1a), the dependent variable was the percent (out of a total of 12) of excerpts yielding MEAMS, calculated for each participant. Characteristics of these MEAMS, again calculated as an average for each participant were: word count per MEAM; age of the participant when the memory occurred (given as an age range in "years from" and "years to"); percent of MEAMs rated by the participant as specific; and vividness of the MEAMs on a seven-point scale.

Table 1a presents the median and the range of values across participants for each of the above measures. Between-group differences (overall differences among YA, OA, and AD) were assessed

Table 1a. Descriptive measures for music-evoked memories

OA vs. AD	OA (n = 20) Median (range)	AD (n = 20) Median (range)	Mann–Whitney test	
			U-statistic	*p*-value
Percent of tunes with MEAMs	67 (17–100)	42 (8–100)	117	0.024
Word count per MEAM	95 (15–298)	82(11–208)	188	0.758
Age of memory—Years from	25 (16–50)	20 (4–54)	139	0.096
Age of memory—Years to	34 (18–65)	26 (5–58)	139	0.102
Percent specific	50 (22–100)	10 (0–100)	80	0.001**
Vividness rating	5.5 (3.1–7.0)	6.0 (1.5–7.0)	1687	0.383
YA vs. OA + AD	YA (n = 20) Median (range)	OA + AD (n = 40) Median (range)	*U*-statistic	*p*-value
Percent of tunes with MEAMs[a]	67 (42–83)	58 (8–100)	264	0.031
Word count per MEAM	73 (26–226)	89 (11–298)	352	0.452
Age of memory- From	14 (8–17)	23 (4–54)	77	<0.001**
Age of memory-To	14 (8–18)	31 (5–65)	31	<0.001**
Percent specific	67 (38–100)	33 (0–100)	211	0.003*
Vividness rating	4.6 (2.7–5.8)	5.6 (1.5–7.0)	173	<0.001**

[a]When the median of both groups is 0, the *U*-statistic and *p*-value are not calculated (i.e. the two groups are not compared).

*$p < 0.05$ according to Bonferroni correction.

**$p < 0.01$ according to Bonferroni correction.

Table 1b. Episodic and episodic-specific memory categorization

OA vs. AD	OA (n = 20) Median (range)	AD (n = 20) Median (range)	Mann–Whitney test	
			U-statistic	*p*-value
Percent episodic	88 (36–100)	83 (0–100)	185	0.698
Percent episodic specific	27 (0–100)	20 (0–100)	127	0.046
YA vs. OA + AD	YA (n = 20) Median (range)	OA + AD (n = 40) Median (range)	Mann–Whitney test	
			U-Statistic	*p*-value
Percent episodic	89 (40–100)	83 (0–100)	317	0.184
Percent episodic specific	50 (20–100)	17 (0–100)	167	<0.001**

**$p < 0.01$ according to Bonferroni correction.

through an omnibus analysis followed by two orthogonal contrasts. The first contrast was OA versus AD, which tested the effect of the disease as the difference between two groups of comparable age but differing in cognitive status. The second was YA versus (OA + AD) which tested the effect of age as the difference between a young versus older group irrespective of cognitive status of the latter. The normality of the distributions was checked by the Shapiro–Wilk test. The assumption of normality was violated in multiple distributions; thus, nonparametric tests were applied to determine the statistical significance of differences.

For five of the measures in Table 1a, that is, for all measures except the word count per MEAM, the Kruskal–Wallis H test revealed significant differences among the groups (for five measures, $9.88 < \chi^2(2\ df) < 35.40$, all $p < 0.007$). The right-hand columns of Table 1a show the results of the

Mann–Whitney test for the significance of the orthogonal contrasts. The table also notes the outcomes that were significant given the Bonferroni correction for multiple tests.

For the OA versus AD contrast (presented at the top of Table 1a), the only measure that was significantly different after the Bonferroni correction was applied, was the percent of MEAMs identified by participants as specific, with OA being higher than AD (50 versus 10%). For the YA versus (OA + AD) contrast (bottom of Table 1a) the age range of the memory, percent of MEAMs identified as specific, and vividness rating were all significantly different. Memories for YA tended to have occurred in early adolescence; memories for OA and AD tended to occur in early adulthood (the "reminiscence bump" first demonstrated by Rubin, Wetzler, and Nebes (1986)). The younger group reported their memories to be more specific, but less vivid, than the combined older groups. In sum, for the measures in Table 1a, the effects of age were more prevalent than the effects of the disease.

For AD, but not OA, the age range at which the memory was said to occur was negatively correlated with percent of excerpts yielding MEAMs ("age from" $\rho(n = 20) = -0.62$, $p = 0.004$; "age to" $\rho(n = 20) = 0.44$, $p = 0.051$). In other words, for AD, a larger number of MEAMs was associated with earlier memories.

Table 1b reports the percent of MEAMs judged episodic and the percent of all episodic memories judged specific as opposed to general; statistical analysis followed the procedures adopted for Table 1a. The Kruskal–Wallis H test revealed statistical differences among groups for the latter measure only (for percent episodic $\chi^2(2\ df) = 1.91$, $p = 0.386$; for percent episodic-specific $\chi^2(2\ df) = 16.35$, $p < 0.01$). Here again, the orthogonal contrasts in the right-hand column of Table 1b show that the effect of age is more evident than the effect of the disease, with, as might be expected, specific episodic memories less available in older age.

3.2. AD nonresponders and supplementary tests

It was noted in the recruitment of AD participants (see above) that neither age, MMSE status, nor years of music training, accounted for nonresponding. The nonresponders did not form a distinct group on the PANAS scales (positive affect scores for responders ranged from 16 to 45 and for nonresponders 22 to 38; negative affect scores for responders were from 10 to 15 and for nonresponders from 11 to 19). They did not show a greater tendency toward depression on the GDS than nonresponders (GDS range for responders was 0–7 and for nonresponders 1–2).

The supplementary tests were administered at the end of the testing protocol to AD participants. Not all participants were available or willing to complete the supplementary session, and in the case of the informant questionnaires, not all informants submitted their forms. However, despite the reduced *N* we examined the responses as an exploratory means of providing guidelines for future research. In particular, we looked for clues why some AD persons were unable to produce memories to the excerpts.

Inspection of the results of the supplementary tests indicated that musical memory and attraction to music did not predict inability to respond. However, the DSRS questionnaire revealed greater functional impairment in nonresponders (responders $Mdn = 16.0$, range = 0–31; nonresponders $Mdn = 31.0$, range = 25–39; $U = 7.0$, $n_1 = 14$, $n_2 = 4$, $p = 0.025$). The total absence of MEAMs in the nonresponders may have been due to a higher severity of impairment than that revealed by their MMSE or diagnostic status.

For the AD responders, none of the supplementary tests was indicative of the percent of excerpts yielding MEAMs, even though there was considerable variability in this responsiveness. Individual participant scores varied from 8 to 100% for evocation of MEAMs—see Table 1a. Although the DSRS discriminated responders from nonresponders, it did not predict responsivity within the responder group ($\rho(n = 14) = -0.13$, $p = 0.653$).

Table 2. Assessing the positivity effect using positive and negative words from LIWC analysis

OA vs. AD	OA ($n = 20$) Median (range)	AD ($n = 20$) Median (range)	U-statistic	p-value
Percent positive words	3.14 (0.00–6.25)	3.96 (0.00–16.67)	197	0.989
Percent negative words	0.45 (0.00–1.22)	0.37 (0.00–9.09)	170	0.429
YA vs. OA + AD	YA ($n = 20$) Median (range)	OA + AD ($n = 40$) Median (range)	U-statistic	p-value
Percent positive words	2.48 (0.45–4.54)	3.35 (0.00–9.16.67)	246	0.016
Percent negative words	0.67 (0.00–2.72)	0.43 (0.00–9.09)	279	0.057

3.3. Positivity effect

This section continues the content analysis of MEAMs with a specific focus on the evidence for greater positive affect and lower negative affect among older participants. Three different analyses were conducted, comparing across groups: (1) a computational word count of the proportion of both positive and negative emotion words relative to all words contained in the MEAMs; (2) the proportion of both positive and negative content categories reported in the MEAMs according to the content categorization system of Schlagman et al. (2006); (3) the subjective rating of positivity and negativity of a memory provided by the participants themselves. The analyses are presented in order of ascending confidence that can be placed on a positivity effect.

3.3.1. Word count analysis

Table 2 shows for each group of participants the results of the word count analysis conducted by text analysis software, the Linguistic Inquiry Word Count. The LIWC vocabulary contains 406 positive emotion words and 499 negative emotion words. The data shown in Table 2 are the median percent (and range) across participants of words classified as positive or negative according to the count.

According to the LIWC count, emotion words were rare. Positive words accounted for less than 4% of all words expressed; negative words for less than 1% of all words. Numerically, YA expressed fewer positive words and more negative words than the older groups and OA expressed more negative words than AD. However, the Kruskal-Wallis test was not significant for either positive or negative words. For positive words, the contrast YA versus (OA + AD) was significant, but has to be interpreted with caution. All in all, given the low count of emotion words, we conclude that the word count analysis was not a productive means of examining a positivity effect.

3.3.2. Content categories

Table 3 shows the assignment of content of MEAMs according to the Schlagman et al. (2006) categorical analysis for involuntary diary memories. The first column is the category label ascribed by Schlagman et al. There are three main columns, one each for YA, OA, and AD The first two columns in each main column represent the frequency and percentage of MEAMs in each category. Assignment was done by two independent raters who read each MEAM and allotted it to a category. Agreement among raters was moderate, Cohen's $\kappa = 0.59$ ($p < 0.001$), 95% CI (0.54, 0.65). Disagreements arose when the memory involved more than one category; they were resolved by discussion as to which category was best represented.

Inspection of Table 3 reveals that the categories most popular across groups were similar to those for Schlagman et al. (2006) and for MEAMs collected by Janata et al. (2007), e.g. Persons, Leisure/Sports, Object/Places. A log-linear procedure was applied to compare group differences in distribution across all categories with an expected MEAM count greater than 1. An initial model of complete independence was used to test the hypothesis that the MEAM counts were distributed similarly in the two groups under consideration. The categories did not differ between OA and AD, as the independence model fit the data well, $LR(7) = 4.89$, $p = 0.673$, and all adjusted residuals between ±1.51. For comparison of YA and (OA + AD), the independence model was rejected, $LR(11) = 60.09$, $p < 0.001$. Group-category interactions corresponding to cells with adjusted residuals above 2 were then added to the independence model in order to create the most parsimonious partial independence

Table 3. Descriptive statistics for MEAMs based on the Schlagman et al. (2006) categories. The four columns in each group represent (1) frequency, (2) percentage, (3) mean positivity ratings, and (4) mean negativity ratings for memories in each content category

Content category	Frequencies (percentages) positivity and negativity ratings											
	YA (n = 20), MEAMs (n = 162)				OA (n = 20), MEAMs (n = 154)				AD (n = 20), MEAMs (n = 104)			
	Freq	(%)	Pos	Neg	Freq	(%)	Pos	Neg	Freq	(%)	Pos	Neg
1. Person	22	(12.9)	1.66	0.41	18	(11.5)	2.47	0.11	18	(16.5)	2.75	0.19
2. Accidents/Illness	0	(0)	N/A	N/A	1	(0.6)	2.00	1.00	0	(0)	N/A	N/A
3. Stressful Events	10	(5.9)	0.75	1.80	2	(1.3)	1.50	1.50	0	(0)	N/A	N/A
4. Holidays	3	(1.8)	2.67	0.17	1	(0.6)	3.00	0.50	0	(0)	N/A	N/A
5. Conversations	1	(0.6)	3.00	0.50	1	(0.6)	1.50	1.00	0	(0)	N/A	N/A
6. Leisure/Sports	44	(25.9)	1.87	0.32	39	(24.8)	2.47	0.32	35	(32.1)	2.52	0.20
7. Objects/Places	16	(9.4)	1.66	0.38	18	(11.5)	2.25	0.19	7	(6.4)	2.79	0.43
8. Going Out	15	(8.8)	1.87	0.20	41	(26.1)	2.34	0.27	27	(24.8)	2.40	0.08
9. Work/University	11	(6.5)	1.68	0.59	1	(0.6)	2.50	0.50	0	(0)	N/A	N/A
10. Romance	0	(0)	N/A	N/A	2	(1.3)	2.50	0	1	(0.9)	1.50	1.00
11. School	26	(15.3)	1.35	0.62	6	(3.8)	2.25	0	6	(5.5)	2.50	0.25
12. Deaths/Funerals	1	(0.6)	0	2.50	1	(0.6)	0.00	3.00	1	(0.9)	1.50	1.50
13. Miscellaneous	0	(0)	N/A	N/A	0	(0)	N/A	N/A	0	(0)	N/A	N/A
14. Special occasions	18	(10.6)	2.18	0.32	20	(12.7)	2.58	0.38	12	(11.0)	2.80	0.10
15. Births	0	(0)	N/A	N/A	0	(0)	N/A	N/A	0	(0)	N/A	N/A
16. Traveling/Journeys	2	(1.2)	2.25	0.50	2	(1.3)	2.50	0.50	0	(0)	N/A	N/A
17 War/Army	1	(0.6)	2.00	1.00	4	(2.5)	2.00	0.63	2	(1.8)	1.75	0.50
Totals	170	(100)	1.76	0.72	157	(100)	2.12	0.66	109	(100)	2.28	0.47

model that fit the data well, $LR(7) = 4.56$, $p = 0.713$, with all remaining adjusted residuals between ±1.56. The following categories had significantly different percentages in YA and the combined older groups: "Stressful events" (YA 5.9%, Older 0.8%), "Going out" (YA 8.8%, Older 25.6%), "Work/University" (YA 6.5%, Older 0.4%), and "School" (YA 15.3%, Older 4.5%). Of these categories that were different between the groups, "Going out" is the only category classified by Schlagman et al. (2006) as positive, and "Stressful events" the only negative. Differences found here in both categories are in the direction of a positivity effect.

Categories considered positive by Schlagman et al. (2006) were "Holidays," "Going out," "Romance," and "Special occasions." The MEAM data were pooled across these categories to form a Percent Positive Categories score for each participant. Median scores for each group are shown in Table 4. Medians for positive categories were significantly different according to the Kruskal–Wallis

Table 4. Assessing the positivity effect using percent of positive and negative memories according to the categorical system of Schlagman et al. (2006)

OA vs. AD	OA (n = 20) Median (range)	AD (n = 20) Median (range)	U-statistic	p-value
Percent positive categories	41 (13–100)	42 (0–100)	184	0.678
Percent negative categories	0 (0–20)	0 (0–100)	N/A[a]	N/A[a]
YA vs. OA + AD	YA (n = 20) Median (range)	OA + AD (n = 40) Median (range)	U-statistic	p-value
Percent positive categories	16 (0–50)	41 (0–100)	212	0.003**
Percent negative categories	0 (0–30)	0 (0–100)	N/A[a]	N/A[a]

[a]When the median of both groups is 0, the U-statistic and p-value are not calculated (i.e. the two groups are not compared).

**$p < 0.01$ according to Bonferroni correction.

Table 5. Assessing the positivity effect using participant self-ratings

OA vs. AD	OA (n = 20) Median (range)	AD (n = 20) Median (range)	U-statistic	p-value
Present positivity ratings	2.22 (1.33–3.00)	2.54 (1.00–3.00)	154	0.221
Present negativity ratings	0.14 (0.00–1.25)	0.00 (0.00–1.50)	162	0.301
Past positivity ratings	2.50 (1.40–3.00)	2.62 (0.00–3.00)	160	0.277
Past negativity ratings	0.26 (0.00–1.63)	0.00 (0.00–3.00)	159	0.277
YA vs. OA + AD	YA (n = 20) Median (range)	OA + AD (n = 40) Median (range)	U-statistic	p-value
Present positivity ratings	1.70 (1.00–2.44)	2.40 (1.00–3.00)	147	<0.001**
Present negativity ratings	0.32 (0.00–1.20)	0.09 (0.00–1.50)	288	0.068
Past positivity ratings	1.73 (0.14–2.44)	2.50 (0.00–3.00)	107	<0.001**
Past negativity ratings	0.55 (0.00–1.38)	0.10 (0.00–3.00)	193	0.001**

**p < 0.01 according to Bonferroni correction.

H test (χ^2(2 df) = 9.4, p < 0.01) In Table 4, it may be seen that memories in positive categories were significantly more represented for OA and AD than for YA.

Categories considered negative by Schlagman et al. (2006) were "Accident/illness," "Stressful events," and "Deaths/funerals." Instances of negative categories in all groups were too rare to allow reliable statistical analysis. The median percent of pooled negative categories was zero for all groups.

In summary, the results in Tables 3 and 4 support a positivity effect where memories of positive topics are more frequent for older than for younger adults.

3.3.3. Subjective ratings

Table 5 shows for each group the median (and range) of ratings given to MEAMs by participants on the scales of positivity and negativity. The higher the value (with an upper limit of "3"), the more intense the reported feeling of a positive or a negative emotion attached to the memory Participants rated their feelings at the time of the memory and also how they felt about it at the present. Past and present positivity ratings were stable and not significantly different for all groups (Wilcoxon Z = 1.49, N = 60, p = 0.135). Past and present negativity ratings were, however, significantly different (Wilcoxon Z = 3.25, n = 60, p = 0.001); for all groups, the negativity attributed to a past event memory appears somewhat diminished in the present.

Overall group differences emerged in the ratings for the Kruskal–Wallis test. For positive ratings for the past, χ^2(2 df) = 21.63, p < 0.001; for the present, χ^2(2 df) = 16.96, p < 0.001. For negative ratings from the past, the χ^2(2 df) = 11.69, p < 0.01; for the present, the significance level failed to reach a conventional value, χ^2(2 df) = 4.18, p = 0.124.

In Table 5, it can be seen that YA memories were rated, on average, as significantly less positive than the OA and AD groups combined. The YA also rated their memories as more negative in the past than these older groups. The direction of these differences also held across all Schlagman et al. categories (Table 4, bottom line).

The subjective ratings support an effect of age rather than that of disease, and of the three above measures most clearly reflect a positivity effect.

3.4. Mood assessment (PANAS)

Table 6 shows the results of the PANAS scale. Two participants (one OA, one AD) declined to respond so N is reduced to 19 for OA and AD. Scores are out of a possible total of 50 (10 items × a top rating

Table 6. PANAS measures of positive and negative mood across two administrations of the test

OA vs. AD	OA (n = 19) Median (range)	AD (n = 19) Median (range)	U-statistic	p-value
Average positive mood ratings (before and after)	32.5 (13.0–47.5)	34.0 (15.5–45.0)	170	0.773
Average negative mood ratings (before and after)	10.5 (10.0–12.5)	11.0 (10.0–14.5)	141	0.258
YA vs. OA + AD	YA (n = 20) Median (range)	OA + AD (n = 39) Median (range)	U-statistic	p-value
Average positive mood ratings (before and after)	28.3 (14.0–38.0)	33.3 (13.0–47.5)	197	0.003*
Average negative mood ratings (before and after)	12.3 (10.0–20.0)	10.5 (10.0–14.5)	182	0.001**

*$p < 0.05$ according to Bonferroni correction.

**$p < 0.01$ according to Bonferroni correction.

of "5" per item) and a minimum of 10. Median scores are combined across the two administrations of the positive and the negative scale because no differences were found between the two administrations of the scale for any group (a result reflecting the test-retest stability of the PANAS instrument as a measure of trait mood).

Median scores for positive affect ranged from 28.3 to 34.0. Median scores for negative affect scores were relatively low (10.5–12.3). The mean score for the development sample of the PANAS was 29.7 (SD = 7.9) for positive affect and 14.8 (SD = 6.2) for negative affect (Watson et al., 1988). Our sample was similar to the development sample in positive affect but possibly was less negative.

The Kruskal-Wallis H test showed group differences for both the positive PANAS ($\chi^2(2\ df) = 9.1$, $p = 0.011$) and the negative PANAS ($\chi^2(2\ df) = 12.1$, $p < 0.01$. Median scores for positive affect differed significantly between YA and combined OA and AD; the latter group had higher scores. Negative affect scores were, however, significantly higher (reflecting greater negativity of mood) for the YA compared to the older groups.

Within groups, PANAS positive and negative affect scores for YA and OA were not significantly correlated with present or past, positive or negative subjective ratings, indicating that the positivity or negativity of the memories recalled was likely not due to the mood congruence effect. AD, however, did show a correlation of the positive PANAS affect score to the present positivity rating ($\rho(n = 19) = 0.55$, $p = 0.015$), as well as the negative PANAS affect score to both the present positivity ($\rho(n = 19) = -0.66$, $p = 0.002$) and past positivity ($\rho(n = 19) = -0.71$, $p = 0.001$) ratings, such that the AD participants, to some degree, either recalled mood-congruent memories or at least matched the memory valence ratings to their mood.

3.5. Age within OA and AD

As noted above, age effects were demonstrated by the difference in responding between YA in their early 20s and the older adults in their 70s (OA and AD). We also looked at possible age effects within our older groups as the AD group was slightly but significantly older ($N = 40$; Mann-Whitney $U = 102$, $p < 0.01$) than the OA group, though the range of ages was comparable. The difference in median age arises from the fact that within the range, the age distributions were positively skewed in the OA group, negatively skewed in the AD group. Nonparametric (Spearman) correlations were conducted within groups between age and the dependent variables on which the positivity effect was assessed: Table 2 (positive and negative words); Table 4 (positive and negative categories); and Table 5 (positive and negative ratings for the present and the past). No correlation was significant ($N = 20$; $-0.13 < \rho < 0.31$, all $p > 0.18$), a result indicating that age between approximately 60 and 90 did not predict greater positivity or less negativity. Age differences were therefore not implicated in the positivity effect comparisons for OA and AD.

4. Discussion

We have successfully replicated and extended earlier findings that music is an effective perceptual cue for evocation of autobiographical memories (MEAMs). Our paradigm (following Janata et al., 2007) investigated memories spontaneously arising from musical cues, as opposed to memories obtained by direct questioning during music exposure (e.g. the Autobiographical Interview; Irish et al., 2006). We extended the procedure of El Haj et al. (2012) in that we collected memories elicited by a variety of familiar instrumental excerpts. We have thus also shown that MEAMs do not require the presence of song lyrics or even preferred music; rather, "pure" instrumental music generally familiar in the culture is sufficient to evoke memories.

The majority of AD participants tested here not only recovered memories, but also as a group responded similar to healthy controls on a number of measures—percent excerpts evoking memories, length (word count) of the memories, selection of memory topics, recency (age from and to) of the memories, rated vividness, and rated positivity of the memories. As well, independent estimates of the percent of memories judged as specific episodes were also similar for AD and OA. As far as our analyses reached into the evidence for memory evocation and memory content, AD participants displayed the effects of age, but not of disease.

Other features of the data also reflect the effect of age more than the disease. These are rated vividness (Table 1a) and percent of memories categorized as episodic-specific by independent raters (Table 1b). The implication is that, with perhaps the exception of percent rated specific, the phenomenological reliving of episodic events may be preserved in AD. AD were similar to OA on these features; vividness, in fact, was rated as even higher by OA and AD than YA. Such an implication runs counter to conclusions that retrieval of phenomenological features is compromised in AD (El Haj, Antoine, Nandrino, & Kapogiannis, 2015; El Haj et al., 2016) with accompanying decline in autobiographical memory, and loss of sense of self and identity. The findings cited by El Haj and colleagues do not refer to MEAMs, however. They refer to the standard assessments of autobiographical memory in silence. We propose, therefore, an alternative explanation that stronger reliving is evoked by spontaneous memories such as those associated with musical cues. See Larsson and Willander (2009) for a similar conclusion regarding the use of odor cues to trigger memories.

Importantly, we have now shown for the first time that the music-evoked memories in aging and AD reveal a positivity effect—that is, in old age and AD, compared to young adults, the topics of memories are more positive and the rated valence of memories is both more positive and less negative. The presence of the positivity effect strengthens the claim that musical cues arouse involuntary memories (El Haj et al., 2012).

To address the finding of the positivity effect in AD, three points are relevant. The first is that the functions of autobiographical memory are varied, but most accounts refer to the preservation of self-identity and self-knowledge. For example, Harris, Rasmussen, and Berntsen (2014) propose four classes of memory function—which they label reflective, generative, ruminative, and social—and link them to the ways people "make meaning of their selves, their environment and this social world more generally" (p. 559). The result of impairment of this ability in AD is a compromised sense of self and identity (El Haj, Antoine, Nandrino, & Raffard, 2015). See also Eustache et al. (2013) who found impairments in self-knowledge with AD patients, which the authors attribute to the patients' episodic memory deficits. Second, the evoking of involuntary autobiographical memories from perceptual cues may be an automatic process. Whereas, a dedicated memory search places high demands on executive control, attention, and other cognitive processes involved in the search, involuntary memories may be aroused despite the degenerative loss of executive control and attention in AD. Third, the positivity effect uncovered here may be the result of the lower cognitive demands associated with involuntary memories and, in accordance with SST, may free additional cognitive resources to control emotional responses to memories. Thus, despite the difficulties associated with emotional control processes in AD (Henry, Rendell, Scicluna, Jackson, & Phillips, 2009) there may be instances where an apparent preservation of emotion regulation is evident. In sum, the positivity effect in AD may signal a positive and controlled sense of self that has been spared the ravages of the disease.

Several issues arise from the above conclusions concerning (1) the similarities and differences between OA and AD, including mood-congruence; (2) the nonresponders among the AD participants; (3) the selection of musical excerpts; and (4) the status of music as a memory retrieval cue. These issues will be addressed in turn. First, although the similarities overall found here between OA and AD, and the differences with YA, were striking, it is acknowledged that there were certain differences between AD and OA in the memory protocols. Memories were rated as more specific by OA than AD participants and current further analyses of the video transcripts (Belyea, Sikka, Chan, & Cuddy, 2016) suggest that although OA and AD reacted similarly in many ways to the excerpts (e.g. smiling, laughing, nodding) other visible musical reactions (e.g. humming, singing, tapping) were more frequent in AD than OA. Other differences, such as those that might be uncovered through linguistic analysis of the transcripts, warrant further investigation.

Moreover, the similarity of AD and OA with regard to the positivity effect does not mean that similar mechanisms are involved. Mood (as assessed by the PANAS scales) was not a predictor of rated MEAM valence in OA, yet it was for AD Thus, for AD, mood may have either (1) enhanced decisions about the valence of memories, decisions based on possibly compromised cognitive processes, or (2) enhanced sensitivity to memories with positive content or information. Therefore, the found positivity effect does not necessarily indicate that music increases deliberate selection of positive memories. Behaviorally, though, if music allows or encourages patients' sensitivity to mood-congruent positive memories, playing music for patients could possibly reduce the irritability and agitation/aggression stemming from their usual sensitivity and responsivity toward negative and neutral information (e.g. Wright et al., 2007). In terms of broader implications, even if the positivity effect is not necessarily a process involving cognitive effort in AD, these results show that MEAMs are likely to be a source of positive reminiscence and life satisfaction for AD.

Second, we noted that not all AD persons responded with MEAMs. Several AD participants, whom we termed "nonresponders," were unable to produce a single memory to the instrumental excerpts. This finding was unexpected, given the willingness of most of our AD participants to respond, but it is not unknown: El Haj et al. (2012) reported that two AD participants and one OA participant had no memories triggered by music. Nonresponders in the present study appeared to have crossed a diagnostic line not easily identified by neuropsychological testing and clinical assessment. The one test that separated nonresponders from responders was the DSRS, which is completed by an informant familiar with the day to day behavior of the AD participant. Scores suggested greater functional impairment among nonresponders. Yet DSRS scores were not predictive of number of memories evoked among the responders, and so cannot account for individual differences in responsivity to the musical excerpts. Future research with a larger sample could explore beyond our present tests to detect the correlates of nonresponding and thereby to discover processes or links that are broken if memories cannot be evoked by music in AD.

Third, the musical excerpts cues used here were not self-selected but experimenter-selected after extensive pilot work to ensure above-average familiarity (and its co-variate pleasantness) of excerpts with both YA and OA. Whereas, preferred music, or self-selected music, may be an optimal choice for music-therapeutic interventions, the use of individualized musical stimuli in MEAM studies is arguably not optimal. The self-selection procedure loses experimental control of known acoustical parameters that influence, in part, emotional responding to music (for example, see Dean & Bailes, 2016). In the current study, all groups received the same acoustical stimuli so that the differences in groups, on which evidence for the positivity effect rests, could not be attributed to differences induced by acoustical parameters.

Finally, we did not set out to find, neither do we claim, that music is unique in its power to evoke positive memories. Nevertheless, the ubiquitous nature of music, its strong ties with emotion, and its preserved familiarity in OA and AD, all point to its potential value as a practical and effective adjunct to care and rehabilitation. Positive memories that support a positive sense of self can be explored for purposes of communication with music therapists, caregivers, and family. As well, the present findings support theoretical proposals of functional neuroanatomical connections between brain networks for music and large-scale networks supporting autobiographical memory (Janata, 2009; Peck, Girard, Russo, & Fiocco, 2016). Understanding behavioral patterns of loss and sparing—such as music and memory—can help narrow the search for the neural substrates of this connectivity and so facilitate understanding of the AD disease process.

In conclusion, the findings have both theoretical and practical relevance. In support of earlier research, we have further documented the finding that music is an effective cue for retrieval of autobiographical memories in AD. Moreover, we support the theoretical proposal that such memories are representative of involuntary memories, being memories spontaneously aroused by a sensory cue (music) rather than responses to specific instructions requiring voluntary recall. As such, they are more vivid, specific, and positive. A practical implication for care and rehabilitation is that music may be beneficially employed to assist the person with AD to recall details of a personal past and perhaps restore communication with family members. That MEAMs are generally positive suggests that reminiscence experiences through MEAMs will also be generally positive and that music can still be enjoyed despite the cognitive impairments accompanying AD.

The current project was not designed to assess different explanations of the positivity effect—top-down or bottom-up accounts of its emergence through aging. It is particularly intriguing, nevertheless, to speculate that music provides an avenue for assessing a spared mechanism of emotional arousal and processing in AD. If that is the case, further research in the sparing of emotional processes in AD (e.g. Gagnon, Gosselin, Provencher, & Bier, 2012) is warranted with a view to assessing the origin of the positivity effect in AD, possibly engaging automatic emotional responding associated with posterior brain regions (Grady, 2012; Kramer, Humphrey, Larish, Logan, & Strayer, 1994).

The results could be further strengthened by a replication in a larger scale study where extensive behavioral and neurobiological assessments are conducted to examine positivity effects within the aging process. It would be informative to collect data across the lifespan so that the development of the positivity effect could be traced in a quantitative manner. Aging effects in our data were evident over decades of life but not over a short range within old age. It would also be informative to gather information about the participants' socio-musical experiences, as more and greater such experiences likely lead to the availability of more memories. Finally, as noted above, a subsequent study could be conducted to analyze the transcripts for evidence whether the positivity effect in AD is related to linguistic or behavioral characteristics of the respondents.

Support for the positivity effect in older age and AD will be welcome news for caregivers and therapists. Reminiscence through music can be used to enhance wellbeing through a focus on positive memories of the past. See El Haj et al., (2015, p. 188), for a critical commentary on reminiscence therapy. Evidence of the validity of the therapy in AD is mixed, but music as a cue for recall has not yet been rigorously studied in this context.

Positivity in older age comes with a caution. Although it may enhance well-being in both healthy older and neurally compromised adults, it could also lead to impoverished decision-making in financial and social situations. Too high a level of positivity could leave a person vulnerable to fraud and deceit (Scheibe & Carstensen, 2010). Future research could address the issue of adaptive vs. nonadaptive levels of positivity.

Acknowledgments

We would like to acknowledge the contribution of Deanna Choi, Alex Duncan, Janice Lee, Mike O'Grady, Hannah Ramsay, Kevin Shabahang, and Emma Walton to this study. We would also like to thank Dr A. Garcia and Dr S. Gill from the Division of Geriatrics, Department of Medicine, Queen's University, Kingston, Ontario and the staff of Helen Henderson Care Centre in Amherstview, Ontario for assistance with recruitment of AD participants.

Funding

This research was supported by a Discovery Grant from NSERC, and a grant from the GRAMMY foundation.

Competing Interests

The author declares no competing interest.

Author details

Lola L. Cuddy[1]
E-mail: lola.cuddy@queensu.ca
Ritu Sikka[1]
E-mail: ritu.sikka@queensu.ca
ORCID ID: http://orcid.org/0000-0001-5814-3643
Kristen Silveira[1]
E-mail: silveira@uvic.ca
Sean Bai[1]
E-mail: 0syb@queensu.ca
Ashley Vanstone[1]
E-mail: a.vanstone@queensu.ca

[1] Department of Psychology, Queen's University, 62 Arch Street, Humphrey Hall, Room 232, Kingston, Ontario, Canada.

Note

1. One AD participant had German as her native language, but she spoke English fluently and expressed familiarity with the tunes in the study, and so her data were retained in the sample.

References

American Psychiatric Association. (2000). *Diagnostic and statistical manual of mental disorders* (4th ed., text rev.). Washington, DC: American Psychiatric Association.

Baird, A., & Samson, S. (2014). Music evoked autobiographical memory after severe acquired brain injury: Preliminary findings from a case series. *Neuropsychological Rehabilitation, 24*, 125–143. doi:10.1080/09602011.2013.858642

Baird, A., & Samson, S. (2015). Music and dementia. In E. Altenmüller, S. Finger, & F. Boller (Eds.), *Progress in brain research* (Vol. *217*, pp. 207–235). Amsterdam: Elsevier. doi:10.1016/bs.pbr.2014.11.028

Belleville, S., Chertkow, H., & Gauthier, S. (2007). Working memory and control of attention in persons with Alzheimer's disease and mild cognitive impairment. *Neuropsychology, 21*, 458–469. doi:10.1037/0894-4105.21.4.458

Belyea, A. D., Sikka, R., Chan, J., & Cuddy, L. L. (2016, November). *Visible responses to music-evoked autobiographical memories in Alzheimer's disease.* Poster session presented at the 12th annual Canadian Undergraduate Conference on Healthcare, Kingston, ON.

Benjamin, M. J., Cifelli, A., Garrard, P., Caine, D., & Jones, F. W. (2015). The role of working memory and verbal fluency in autobiographical memory in early Alzheimer's disease and matched controls. *Neuropsychologia, 78*, 115–121. doi:10.1016/j.neuropsychologia.2015.10.006

Berntsen, D. (1996). Involuntary autobiographical memories. *Applied Cognitive Psychology, 10*, 435–454. http://dx.doi.org/10.1002/(ISSN)1099-0720

Berntsen, D. (1998). Voluntary and involuntary access to autobiographical memory. *Memory, 6*, 113–141. doi:10.1080/741942071

Carstensen, L. L. (1992). Social and emotional patterns in adulthood: Support for socioemotional selectivity theory. *Psychology and Aging, 7*, 331–338. http://dx.doi.org/10.1037/0882-7974.7.3.331

Carstensen, L. L. (1995). Evidence for a life-span theory of socioemotional selectivity. *Current Directions in Psychological Science, 4*, 151–156. http://dx.doi.org/10.1111/cdir.1995.4.issue-5

Clark, C. M., & Ewbank, D. C. (1996). Performance of the dementia severity rating scale: A caregiver questionnaire for rating severity in Alzheimer disease. *Alzheimer Disease & Associated Disorders, 10*, 31–39.

Croom, A. M. (2015). Music practice and participation for psychological well-being: A review of how music influences positive emotion, engagement, relationships, meaning, and accomplishment. *Musicae Scientiae, 19*, 44–64. doi:10.1177/1029864914561709

Cuddy, L. L., & Duffin, J. M. (2005). Music, memory, and Alzheimer's disease: Is music recognition spared in dementia, and how can it be assessed? *Medical Hypotheses, 64*, 229–235. doi:10.1016/j.mehy.2004.09.005

Cuddy, L. L., Duffin, J. M., Gill, S. S., Brown, C. L., Sikka, R., & Vanstone, A. D. (2012). Memory for melodies and lyrics in Alzheimer's disease. *Music Perception, 29*, 479–491. doi:10.1525/MP.2012.29.5.479

Dean, R. T., & Bailes, F. (2016). Modeling perceptions of valence in diverse music: Roles of acoustic features, agency, and individual variation. *Music Perception, 34*, 104–117. doi:10.1525/mp.2016.34.1.104

Drayna, D., Manichaikul, A., de Lange, M., Snieder, H., & Spector, T. (2001). Genetic correlates of musical pitch recognition in humans. *Science, 291*, 1969–1972. doi:10.1126/science.291.5510.1969

El Haj, M., Antoine, P., Nandrino, J. L., & Kapogiannis, D. (2015). Autobiographical memory decline in Alzheimer's disease, a theoretical and clinical overview. *Ageing Research Reviews, 23*, 183–192. doi:10.1016/j.arr.2015.07.001

El Haj, M., Antoine, P., Nandrino, J. L., & Raffard, S. (2015). Self-defining memories during exposure to music in Alzheimer's disease. *International Psychogeriatrics, 27*, 1719–1730. doi:10.1017/S1041610215000812

El Haj, M., Fasotti, L., & Allain, P. (2012). The involuntary nature of music-evoked autobiographical memories in Alzheimer's disease. *Consciousness and Cognition, 21*, 238–246. doi:10.1016/j.concog.2011.12.005

El Haj, M., Postal, V., & Allain, P. (2012). Music enhances autobiographical memory in mild Alzheimer's disease. *Educational Gerontology, 38*, 30–41. doi:10.1080/03601277.2010.515897

El Haj, M., Kapogiannis, D., & Antoine, P. (2016). Phenomenological reliving and visual imagery during autobiographical recall in Alzheimer's disease. *Journal of Alzheimer's Disease, 52*, 421–431. doi:10.3233/JAD-151122

Eustache, M. L., Laisney, M., Juskenaite, A., Letortu, O., Platel, H., Eustache, F., & Desgranges, B. (2013). Sense of identity in advanced Alzheimer's dementia: A cognitive dissociation between sameness and selfhood? *Consciousness and Cognition, 22*, 1456–1467. doi:10.1016/j.concog.2013.09.009

Folstein, M. F., Folstein, S., & McHugh, P. (1975). "Mini-mental state": A practical method for grading the cognitive state of patients for the clinician. *Journal of Psychiatric Research, 12*, 189–198. http://dx.doi.org/10.1016/0022-3956(75)90026-6

Fornazzari, L., Castle, T., Nadkarni, S., Ambrose, M., Miranda, D., Apanasiewicz, N., & Phillips, F. (2006). Preservation of episodic musical memory in a pianist with Alzheimer disease. *Neurology, 66*, 610–611. doi:10.1212/01.WNL.0000198504.41315.B1

Gagnon, L., Gosselin, N., Provencher, V., & Bier, N. (2012). Perception and emotional judgments of music in dementia of the Alzheimer type: A short case study. *Music Perception, 29*, 509–519.

Grady, C. L. (2012). The cognitive neuroscience of ageing. *Nature Reviews Neuroscience, 13*, 491–505. doi:10.1038/nrn3256

Greene, J. D. W., Hodges, J. R., & Baddeley, A. D. (1995). Autobiographical memory and executive function in early dementia of Alzheimer type. *Neuropsychologia, 33*, 1647–1670. doi:10.1016/0028-3932(95)00046-1

Harris, C. B., Rasmussen, A. S., & Berntsen, D. (2014). The functions of autobiographical memory: An integrative approach. *Memory, 22*, 559–581. doi:10.1080/09658211.2013.806555

Henry, J. D., Rendell, P. G., Scicluna, A., Jackson, M., & Phillips, L. H. (2009). Emotion experience, expression, and regulation in Alzheimer's disease. *Psychology and Aging, 24*, 252–257. doi:10.1037/a0014001

Hsieh, S., Hornberger, M., Piguet, O., & Hodges, J. R. (2011). Neural basis of music knowledge: Evidence from the dementias. *Brain, 134*, 2523–2534. doi:10.1093/brain/awr190

Hunter, P. G., Schellenberg, E. G., & Schimmack, U. (2010). Feelings and perceptions of happiness and sadness induced by music: Similarities, differences, and mixed emotions. *Psychology of Aesthetics, Creativity, and the Arts, 4*, 47–56. doi:10.1037/a0016873

Irish, M., Cunningham, C. J., Walsh, J. B., Coakley, D., Lawlor, B. A., Robertson, I. H., & Coen, R. F. (2006). Investigating the enhancing effect of music on autobiographical memory in mild Alzheimer's disease. *Dementia and Geriatric Cognitive Disorders, 22*, 108–120. doi:10.1159/000093487

Jacobsen, J.-H., Stelzer, J., Fritz, T. H., Chételat, G., La Joie, R., & Turner, R. (2015). Why musical memory can be preserved in advanced Alzheimer's disease. *Brain, 138*, 2438–2450. doi:10.1093/awv148

Janata, P. (2009). The neural architecture of music-evoked autobiographical memories. *Cerebral Cortex, 19*, 2579–2594. doi:10.1093/cercor/bhp008

Janata, P., Tomic, S. T., & Rakowski, S. K. (2007). Characterisation of music-evoked autobiographical memories. *Memory, 15*, 845–860. doi:10.1080/09658210701734593

Kennedy, Q., Mather, M., & Carstensen, L. L. (2004). The role of motivation in the age-related positivity effect in autobiographical memory. *Psychological Science, 15*, 208–214. doi:10.1111/j.0956-7976.2004.01503011.x

Kopelman, M. D., Wilson, B. A., & Baddeley, A. D. (1989). The autobiographical memory interview: A new assessment of autobiographical and personal semantic memory in amnesic patients. *Journal of Clinical and Experimental Neuropsychology, 11*, 724–744. doi:10.1080/01688638908400928

Kramer, A. F., Humphrey, D. G., Larish, J. F., Logan, G. D., & Strayer, D. L. (1994). Aging and inhibition: Beyond a unitary view of inhibitory processing in attention. *Psychology and Aging, 9*, 491–512. doi:10.1037/0882-7974.9.4.491

Larsson, M., & Willander, J. (2009). Autobiographical odor memory. *Annals of the New York Academy of Sciences, 1170*, 318–323. doi:10.1111/j.1749-6632.2009.03934.x http://dx.doi.org/10.1111/j.1749-6632.2009.03934.x

Liegeois-Chauvel, C., Peretz, I., Babai, M., Laguitton, V., & Chauvel, P. (1998). Contribution of different cortical areas in the temporal lobes to music processing. *Brain, 121*, 1853–1867. http://dx.doi.org/10.1093/brain/121.10.1853

Mammarella, N., Di Domenico, A., Palumbo, R., & Fairfield, B. (2016). Noradrenergic modulation of emotional memory in aging. *Ageing Research Reviews, 27*, 61–66. doi:10.1016/j.arr.2016.03.004

Mather, M., & Carstensen, L. L. (2005). Aging and motivated cognition: The positivity effect in attention and memory. *Trends in Cognitive Sciences, 9*, 496–502. doi:10.1016/j.tics.2005.08.005

Mather, M., & Knight, M. (2005). Goal-directed memory: The role of cognitive control in older adults' emotional memory. *Psychology and Aging, 20*, 554–570. doi:10.1037/0882-7974.20.4.554

McKhann, G., Drachman, D., Folstein, M. F., Katzman, R., Price, D., & Stadlan, E. M. (1984). Clinical diagnosis of Alzheimer's disease: Report of the NINCDS-ADRDA Work Group under the auspices of Department of Health and Human Services Task Force on Alzheimer's Disease. *Neurology, 34*, 939–939. doi:10.1212/WNL.34.7.939

Nasreddine, Z. S., Phillips, N. A., Bédirian, V., Charbonneau, S., Whitehead, V., Collin, I., ... Chertkow, H. (2005). The montreal cognitive assessment, MoCA: A brief screening tool for mild cognitive impairment. *Journal of the American Geriatrics Society, 53*, 695–699. doi:10.1111/j.1532-5415.2005.53221.x

Omar, R., Hailstone, J. C., & Warren, J. D. (2012). Semantic memory for music in dementia. *Music Perception, 29*, 467–477. doi:10.1525/MP.2012.29.5.467

Parks, S. L., & Dollinger, S. C. (2014). The positivity effect and auditory recognition memory for musical excerpts in young, middle-aged, and older adults. *Psychomusicology: Music, Mind, and Brain, 24*, 298–308. doi:10.1037/pmu0000079

Peck, K., Girard, T. A., Russo, F., & Fiocco, A. J. (2016). Music and memory in alzheimer's disease and the potential underlying mechanisms. *Journal of Alzheimer's Disease, 51*, 949–959. doi:10.3233/JAD-150998

Prince, M., Wimo, A., Guerchet, M., Gemma-Claire, A., Wu, Y.-T., & Prina, M. (2015). World Alzheimer Report 2015. *Alzheimer's Disease International.* doi:10.1111/j.0963-7214.2004.00293.x

Rasmussen, A. S., & Berntsen, D. (2009). The possible functions of involuntary autobiographical memories. *Applied Cognitive Psychology, 23*, 1137–1152. doi:10.1002/acp

Reed, A. E., & Carstensen, L. L. (2012). The theory behind the age-related positivity effect. *Frontiers in Psychology, 3*, 339. doi:10.3389/fpsyg.2012.00339

Reed, A. E., Chan, L., & Mikels, J. A. (2014). Meta-analysis of the age-related positivity effect: Age differences in preferences for positive over negative information. *Psychology and Aging, 29*(1), 1–15. doi:10.1037/a0035194

Rosen, W. G. (1980). Verbal fluency in aging and dementia. *Journal of Clinical Neuropsychology, 2*, 135–146. doi:10.1080/01688638008403788

Rubin, D. C., Wetzler, S. E., & Nebes, R. D. (1986). Autobiographical memory across the lifespan. In D. C. Rubin (Ed.), *Autobiographical memory* (1st ed., pp. 202–222). New York, NY: Cambridge University Press. doi:10.1017/CBO9780511558313.018 http://dx.doi.org/10.1017/CBO9780511558313

Scheibe, S., & Carstensen, L. L. (2010). Emotional aging: Recent findings and future trends. *Journal of Gerontology: Psychological Sciences.* doi:10.1093/geronb/gbp132

Schlagman, S., Schulz, J., & Kvavilashvili, L. (2006). A content analysis of involuntary autobiographical memories: Examining the positivity effect in old age. *Memory, 14.* doi:10.1080/09658210544000024

Sheikh, J. I., & Yesavage, J. A. (1986). Geriatric Depression Scale (GDS): Recent evidence and development of a shorter version. *Clinical Gerontologist: The Journal of Aging and Mental Health, 5*, 165–173.

Tausczik, Y. R., & Pennebaker, J. W. (2009). The psychological meaning of words: LIWC and computerized text analysis methods. *Journal of Language and Social Psychology, 29*, 24–54. doi:10.1177/0261927X09351676

Vanstone, A. D., & Cuddy, L. L. (2010). Musical memory in Alzheimer disease. *Aging, Neuropsychology and Cognition, 17*, 108–128. doi:10.1080/13825580903042676

Vanstone, A. D., Wolf, M., Poon, T., & Cuddy, L. L. (2015). Measuring engagement with music: Development of an informant-report questionnaire. *Aging & Mental Health, 20*, 474–484. doi:10.1080/13607863.2015.1021750

Vink, A. C., Bruinsma, M. S., & Scholten, R. J. S. (2003). Music therapy for people with dementia (Review). *The Cochrane Library*. doi:10.1002/14651858.CD003477.pub2

Watson, D., Clark, L. A., & Tellegen, A. (1988). Development and validation of brief measures of positive and negative affect: The PANAS scales. *Journal of Personality and Social Psychology, 54*, 1063–1070. doi:10.1037/0022-3514.54.6.1063

Wright, C. I., Dickerson, B. C., Feczko, E., Negeira, A., & Williams, D. (2007). A functional magnetic resonance imaging study of amygdala responses to human faces in aging and mild alzheimer's disease. *Biological Psychiatry, 62*, 1388–1395. doi:10.1016/j.biopsych.2006.11.013

Wurm, L. H. (2011). Decreasing complexity of affective space in older adults lower on cognitive control: Affective effects in a nonaffective task and with nonaffective stimuli. *Psychology and Aging, 26*, 716–730. doi:10.1037/a0022513

Zebrowitz, L. A., Franklin, R. G., & Palumbo, R. (2015). Ailing voters advance attractive congressional candidates. *Evolutionary Psychology, 13*, 16–28.

Appendix A

Musical Excerpts (30 s)

Excerpt	Composer	Title	Start bar number
1	Khachaturian, Aram	Sabre Dance from Gayane	3
2	Miller, Glen	In the Mood	1
3	Irish Traditional Music	The Irish Washerwoman / The Washwoman	1 (pickup beat)
4	Boccherini, Luigi	Minuet from String Quintet in E Major, Op.11, No.5 (G275)	1
5	Mexican Folk Dance	La Raspa	1
6	Dukas, Paul	The Sorcerer's Apprentice (L'Apprenti Sorcier)	72
7	Thomas, Werner	The Chicken Dance	1
8	Tchaikovsky, Peter Ilich	Trepak (Russian Dance) from The Nutcracker	1
9	Vivaldi, Antonio	Concerto No.1. La Primavera, Spring, Frühling. Op.8, No.1, RV 269, Allegro	1 (pickup beat)
10	Strauss, Johann	An der schönen blauen Donau op. 314 ("Blue Danube Waltz")	45
11	Wagner, Richard	Bridal March (Lohengrin)	1
12	Beethoven, Ludwig von	Symphony No. 5 in C minor, Op. 67, 1st movement	1

6

Brain changes during a shamanic trance: Altered modes of consciousness, hemispheric laterality, and systemic psychobiology

Pierre Flor-Henry[1], Yakov Shapiro[1]* and Corine Sombrun[2]

*Corresponding author: Yakov Shapiro, Department of Psychiatry, University of Alberta, Edmonton, Canada
E-mail: yshapiro@shaw.ca
Reviewing editor: Peter Walla, University of Newcastle, Australia

Abstract: There have been a number of electrophysiological and neuroimaging studies in "altered" states of consciousness including dissociative conditions, hypnosis, and meditation; however, the nature and clinical significance of trance states remain elusive. Alterations of consciousness that accompany trance can shed light on the brain networks contributing to the experience of autobiographical self; the subjective demarcation of "self" from others and reality at large; and normative vs. pathological domains of self-experience. Shamanic trance is a volitional, self-induced state of consciousness that historically served the purposes of social cohesion and healing interventions in diverse tribal settings. We present the first neurophysiological study of a normal subject, who has received extensive training in the Mongolian shamanic tradition and is capable of self-inducing a trance state without external sensory stimulation. Quantitative EEG mapping and LORETA (low resolution electromagnetic tomography) source imaging indicate that shamanic state of consciousness (SSC) involves a shift from the normally dominant left

ABOUT THE AUTHORS

Prof Pierre Flor-Henry is an internationally recognized expert in the fields of hemispheric laterality and spectral EEG imaging, with over 120 publications in the field. The annual Flor-Henry Lectures international conference has been established in his honor in Edmonton, Canada.

Prof Yakov Shapiro specializes in the field of psychotherapy/psychopharmacology integration and teaches courses on evolutionary psychiatry, neuroscience of psychotherapy, and psychobiology of self-experience at the University of Alberta, Canada.

Corine Sombrun was the first Westerner to achieve the status of ugdan (female shaman) in the Mongolian shamanic tradition, and has published extensive phenomenological accounts of the field. She is involved in ongoing research in shamanic trance states.

PUBLIC INTEREST STATEMENT

Shamanic states of consciousness (SSC) go back to the dawn of the middle Paleolithic "cognitive revolution" some 70,000 years ago. They represent humanity's most ancient spiritual tradition that lies at the core of religion and culture as we know them today. A diverse set of findings in neurophysiology and cultural anthropology research suggest that altered modes of consciousness can shed light on the brain mechanisms contributing to the experience of unitary "self" and normative vs. pathological domains of self-experience.

We present the first neurophysiological study of a normal subject and our co-author, who had received extensive training in the Mongolian shamanic tradition and is capable of inducing a shamanic trance state at will. We integrate original research with extensive literature review and suggest a unified psychobiological model for "altered" modes of consciousness. This model incorporates objective, subjective, and intersubjective science within a broad evolutionary framework. It provides a non-reductionist account of psychological, biological, and social determinants of self-experience that helps bridge Western and traditional healing techniques.

analytical to the right experiential mode of self-experience, and from the normally dominant anterior prefrontal to the posterior somatosensory mode. These findings have implications for the psychobiology of the normative conscious mode of awareness and neurophysiological processes contributing to dissociative, psychotic, and transpersonal domains of self-experience. They may be used as a foundation to bridge Western and traditional healing techniques.

Subjects: Social & Cultural Anthropology; Evolutionary Psychology; Integrative Psychotherapy; Behavioral Neuroscience; Neuropsychiatry

Keywords: altered states; consciousness; EEG; first-person neuroscience; psychotherapy; psychobiology; shamanic; self

1. Introduction

> Our normal waking consciousness, rational consciousness as we call it, is but one special type of consciousness, whilst all about it, parted from it by the flimsiest of screens, there lie potential forms of consciousness entirely different. ... No account of the universe in its totality can be final which leaves these other forms of consciousness quite discarded. How to regard them is the question, for they are so discontinuous with ordinary consciousness. (William James, "Varieties of religious experience", 1902)

The category of *altered states of consciousness* (ASCs), to which trance experiences belong, forms the second domain of conscious experience in addition to ordinary states of consciousness (OSCs). Trance is defined as a "temporary marked alteration in the state of consciousness or loss of customary sense of personal identity" (International Classification of Disorders, 1992), which can be either normative or pathological. The normative end of the ASC spectrum involves alterations in the autobiographical sense of self, from expanded states of absorption (such as creative flow and meditative practices) to hypnotic trance; culture- and religion-specific practices including shamanic states of consciousness (SSC); and various modes of extra-sensory perception. Drug-induced psychedelic trances, synesthesias, savant capacities, and near-death experiences lie in the middle of the scale, while pathological ASC conditions include dissociative trance disorder, lycanthropy and related cultural practices, dissociative conditions such as Dissociative Identity Disorder (DID) and psychogenic fugues, and neuropsychiatric syndromes, such as temporal lobe epilepsy, schizophrenia, and affective psychoses where the sense of self may be radically altered or lost. One important corollary is that trance and altered states are not necessarily associated with psychopathology and may in fact be therapeutic (Money, 2000).

Both ordinary and altered domains of conscious experience can be conceptualized as a function of arousal vs. absorption extending from normality to psychopathology (Figure 1). The *arousal axis* extends from sleep and dreaming to normal wakefulness to heighted excitement and pathological self states involved in catatonia or manic psychosis. The orthogonal *absorption axis* incorporates

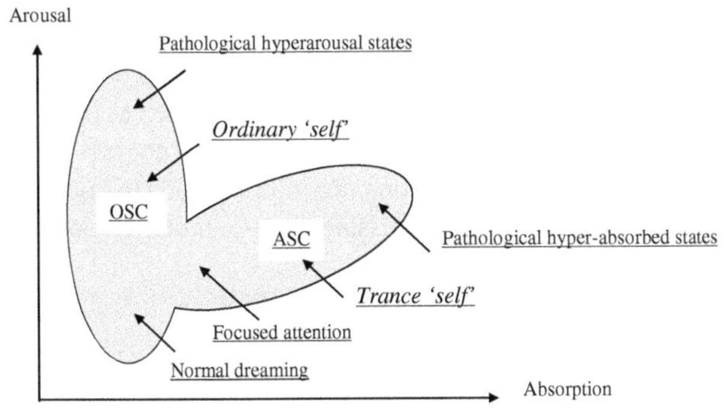

Figure 1. Ordinary (OSC) vs. altered (ASC) states of consciousness as a function of arousal/absorption.

normative self states of relaxed wakefulness progressing to focused attention, and pathological states of derealization/depersonalization, autoscopy, dissociative fugue, and DID. While the normal autobiographical self is identified with the dominant linguistic hemisphere (left in dextral population), there is evidence that some of the "altered states" phenomena may result from intrusions of non-dominant right hemispheric content into waking awareness (Persinger, 1993).

Contrary to the prevalent Western belief, ASCs are extremely common: anthropological studies show that of the 488 societies studied worldwide, over 90% were found to have an institutionalized form of ASCs, and 57% of these were possession trances (Oohashi et al., 2002). A recent cross-sectional study of normal British population (Pechey & Halligan, 2012) estimated the prevalence of anomalous experiences at 48%. Culture-bound religious and/or spiritual beliefs are a major factor determining their specific context. Within a particular social group, altered states can be experienced as either pathological (such as possession trance) or beneficial (such as meditative and shamanic practices). In fact, from the perspective of some meditative practices such as Zen Buddhism, it is the normative "dual" state of consciousness that fragments our perception into inner and outer reality and contributes to suffering and psychopathology. The expressed goal of many meditative practices therefore lies in achieving a non-dual state of unitary awareness (Berman & Stevens, 2015). Conversely, the Western rational tradition tends to pathologize ASC phenomena based on reductionist and behaviorist medical models, although there has been an increasing number of anthropological and neurobiological studies in recent years attempting to clarify their normative phenomenology and neurobiological mechanisms (Jilek, 2005; Vaitl et al., 2005).

There is a common mode of consciousness that may serve to bridge ordinary and altered self-experience. It is related to various types of focused attention, where conscious awareness is narrowed on either inner or outer content to the exclusion of wider self/world awareness. These states range from the everyday experience of focusing on a task at hand; to absent-mindedness (internal focus to the exclusion of environmental cues); to peak experiences and "flow states" (Csikszentmihalyi, 1996) linked to creativity or musical performance; to hyper-focused attention practices such as meditation and hypnotic trance. Narrowed attention states can be conceptualized as a form of "normative dissociation" induced by either external triggers or internal-imaginative processes (Seligman & Kirmayer, 2008).

Psychoevolutionary understanding of normative dissociation states suggests an adaptive function akin to the "freezing" response in dealing with inescapable threat, where neither fight nor flight alternatives are available. The resultant uncoupling from self/world awareness results from a deficit in normal integration of perceptions, feelings, thoughts, and experiences into verbal reflective consciousness, with consequent alterations in the coherent autobiographical narrative self. Dissociative states dampen autonomic and emotional reactivity, resulting in a combination of focused hypervigilance characterized by "simultaneous multisensory scanning of relevant information from the environment" while detaching from one's self and the world at large, which may manifest as depersonalization/derealization (Seligman & Kirmayer, 2008). Experiences of early physical or psychological trauma may facilitate the development of dissociative defenses leading to trauma spectrum disorders, such as predisposition to chronic/complex post-traumatic stress disorder (PTSD, Herman, 1992), borderline personality states, and dissociative spectrum syndromes such as psychogenic amnesias and DID. It is important to note that such dissociative processes are characterized by *both* deficits in normative integration of self/world experiences *and* rich internally driven imagery, which can be experienced in multiple sensory modalities. In discussing the traumatic etiology of pathological trance states, Castillo (2003) notes:

> Some people can withdraw from reality by means of profound spontaneous trances, usually secondary to stress or psychological trauma, and create a fantasy experience by narrowly focusing their attention on imaginary structures or remembered traumatic events while blocking out external reality. (pp. 13–14)

The International Classification of Disorders (ICD) first listed the proposed criteria for Dissociative Conversion Disorder in 1989, and officially included it in ICD-10 (1992). The Diagnostic and Statistical Manual of Psychiatric Disorders (DSM) listed a proposed diagnosis of Dissociative Trance Disorder in DSM-IV (1994). Both classifications differentiated between trance and possession (defined as "single or episodic alteration in the state of consciousness characterized by the replacement of customary sense of personal identity by a new identity... attributed to the influence of a spirit, power, deity, or other person"). To be considered pathological, trance and possession states must occur involuntarily, cause significant distress or impairment to the individual, and not be a part of a culturally or religiously accepted practice. A comprehensive literature review by During, Elahi, Taieb, Moro, and Baubet (2011) for the period between 1988 and 2010 identified 402 case reports satisfying the criteria for DTD, with a 2:1 predominance of possession subtype (69%), a mean age of 25.2 years at the time of the first episode, and equal sex ratio.

A critical distinction between normative vs. pathological ASCs is the capacity for voluntary control in the service of a specific goal (Etevenon, 2010). This is one of the distinguishing features of meditative, shamanic, and other non-pathological trance states. Specifically, the historic ability of shamanic practitioners to enter trance as a way of bridging systemic social interactions with their increasingly complex inner representations distinguishes them from dissociative or psychotic conditions. In spite of an earlier tendency to label shamanic experiences as primitive and pathological, later studies link them to cohesion and evolution of sociability in tribal groups (Krippner, 2002; Stephen & Suryani, 2000). The resulting integration of cognitive and intuitive modes of experience may have promoted the evolution of culture and religion as we know them today (Winkelman, 2010).

The purpose of this study is to:

(1) Clarify to what extent shamanic trance states may represent psychopathology vs. an anomalous but non-pathological mode of brain functioning. We therefore compared detailed spectral EEG parameters of our experimental subject and co-author in both normal and trance states with pre-recorded banks of normal, schizophrenic, manic, and depressed female dextral subjects.
(2) Demonstrate specific alterations in brain function that accompany shamanic trance state using the experimental subject as her own control. We hypothesized that the relatively non-verbal and highly sensory experiences of the trance would be accompanied by a shift from the normally dominant left hemispheric verbal mode of conscious awareness to a relative predominance of right hemispheric activation previously demonstrated to accompany altered states (Krippner & Combs, 2002; Persinger, 1993).

2. Phenomenology of the shamanic state of consciousness

Shamanic States of Consciousness are a distinct sub-category of ASCs characterized by lucid but narrowed awareness of physical surroundings, expanded inner imagery, modified somatosensory processing, altered sense of self, and an experience of spiritual travel to obtain information necessary for solving a particular individual or social problem. It is best understood not as a religion but as a set of ethnically defined healer/medium practices systematically utilizing ASCs for the purpose of healing and tribal group cohesion, such as persistent health problems, within-group conflicts, and threats to the group as a whole (Wright, 1989). Shamanic states are therefore purposeful and volitional unlike psychotic or dissociative conditions. A recent review by Frecska, Hoppál, and Luna (2016) defines SSCs as "a form of focused and expanded consciousness, closer to meditative states, in which the participant intentionally shifts his or her awareness from ordinary perception toward a different 'input', which seems to originate from 'within'" (p. 157). Winkelman (2010) similarly conceptualizes SSCs as a hyper-focused "integrative state" that transcends the limits of the ordinary "rational self" and helps identify the sources of discord within the individual, their tribal group, and wider environment, not unlike the techniques of dream analysis and free association in the Western psychoanalytic and Jungian traditions (Knox, 2009).

Anthropological evidence demonstrates that shamanic traditions are a universal form of cultural practices around the globe and may represent humanity's earliest spiritual practice, predating all known religions (VanPool, 2009). Based on commonalities to shamanic practices of Australian aborigines, who became culturally isolated between 50,000 and 65,000 years ago, shamanism can be traced to the middle Paleolithic period at the onset of the Cognitive Revolution around 70,000 BP (Peters, 1989). There are several broad domains of shamanic practices including African; Siberian/Mongolian; native South and North American (seen as descendants of the Siberian tradition); and Asian-Pacific, including Australian aborigines. The origin of the "shaman" term stems from the Evenki people in the Tungus region of southwestern Siberia (*"šamán"* meaning "one who knows"). The term "shamanistic" (as opposed to "shamanic") practice is reserved for utilizing shamanic trance techniques outside of their original sociocultural context, such as in Western industrial societies.

While shamanic practices are diverse and may include the use of psychoactive drugs (such as ayahuasca and peyote), drumming, dancing, or environmental triggers (such as Native sweat lodge ceremonies), one common pathway involves the phenomenon of a "shamanic journey"—the intentional induction of an altered state of consciousness to facilitate individual growth or adaptive functioning in a tribal group. Nishimura (1987) described three types of shamanic journeys, although they are not always distinct:

(1) *Ecstatic trance*, in which the shaman's spirit purportedly leaves the body and communicates with animal or other spirits in their domains,
(2) *Possession trance*, in which animal or other spirits enter the shaman's body, sometimes to the exclusion of his or her own self, and
(3) *Dreamlike trance*, in which the shaman remains in possession of the self and meets animal or other spirits in a shared domain.

The phenomenon of a "shamanic call", or initiation into the shaman's role, is worth mentioning here. Several common pathways have been described in the literature including a violent personal crisis, intense anxiety, and social withdrawal accompanied by "dreams, visions or inner voices" (Wright, 1989). While in the Western cultures these symptoms may accompany the prodromal phase of a psychotic illness, a tribal group member identified to possess "shamanic gifts" would then proceed with shamanic initiation and training. There is evidence that shamanic trance capacity is not culture-bound but may represent "an inherent psychobiological predisposition ... perhaps universal in the species" (Noll, 1983). One of the authors (C.S) has been researching digital musical loops derived from the shamanic drum beat, and achieved over 80% trance induction response in normal college population (personal communication). In fact, the ability to convert sensorimotor imagery into symbolic stories inherent in shamanic practices may have been pivotal to the gradual emergence of abstract thinking and the evolutionary success of *Homo sapiens sapiens* (Krippner, 2000).

In their contextual variable analysis, Houran, Lange, and Crist-Houran (1997) describe eight experiential categories common to altered and SSC states, the first four corresponding to sensory modalities (*visual, auditory, olfactory,* and *tactile*), with additional categories of *sensed presence, intense emotionality,* unexplained *object movement,* and *erratic functioning of complex machinery* (such as unaccountable malfunction of electrical or mechanical equipment in the vicinity). The authors cite Walsh (1989) stating that "the experiential content of the shamanic journey is complex and coherent...highly structured, meaningful, consistent with the shaman's learned cosmology and the purpose of the specific session, and [apparently] under partial voluntary control" (p. 60). They conclude that shamanic experiences are not limited to psychopathology or a biologically determined set of archetypal perceptions but rather represent a constructivist synthesis of the individual's beliefs and specific cultural factors within the tribal group.

3. Psychophysiology of altered and shamanic states of consciousness

Similar neurophysiological markers have been documented in diverse trance states including yoga and shamanic practices; Zen Buddhist and transcendental meditation; psychedelic experiences associated with hallucinogenic drugs; mediumship/psychography; hypnosis; and shamanic states. These include:

(1) Generalized shift toward right hemisphere dominance (Krippner & Combs, 2002). This may represent a core feature of ASCs resulting from right hemispheric activation and homologous trans-callosal inhibition of contralateral left hemispheric functions responsible for ordinary, ego-bound states of consciousness.

(2) Greater proportion and amplitude of alpha band (8–13 Hz) activity with anterior–posterior synchronization (Banquet, 1973). These oscillations are thought to originate from thalamo-cortical feedback loops responsible for somatosensory binding (Cahn & Polich, 2006). Subjective correlates include relaxed wakefulness, creativity, and free association.

(3) Increased theta power and short, synchronous bursts of high-voltage theta waves (4–7 Hz), which are distinct from those observed in drowsiness/sleep states and correlate with subjective reports of blissful awareness accompanied by rich visual imagery and dissolution of ego boundaries (Wright, 1989). Theta frequencies are thought to represent coherent limbic activity in the septal areas, amygdala, and hippocampal projections to association cortices responsible for emotional, cognitive, and memory information processing (Kirenskaya, Novototsky-Vlasov, & Zvonikov, 2011), and may represent inhibitory influence on the prefrontal association cortices.

(4) Increased gamma power thought to represent diffuse cortical activation and integrative conscious information processing (Lehmann et al., 2001).

(5) Synchronization of EEG activity between left and right frontal lobes, which may be accompanied by progressive frontal hypoactivation in deeper forms of trance (Dietrich, 2003).

(6) Generalized shift toward parasympathetic dominance and release of endogenous opioids, which may be responsible for the subjective reports of ecstasy and decreased pain perception (Krippner & Combs, 2002).

There is extensive data involving lateralized effects in altered self experience. Right hemisphere activation has been linked to a diverse range phenomena including autoscopy, depersonalization/derealization, out-of-body experiences, and voluntarily altered states such as self-dissolution meditation (Lehmann et al., 2001). Persinger (1993) used the construct of *vectorial cerebral hemisphericity* to provide neurophysiological evidence for right hemispheric intrusion phenomena, which are perceived as subjectively ego-alien, coming as it were from "outside" of the conventional left hemispheric, linguistically based mode of self-awareness. He states: "The right hemispheric intrusions are experienced as sensed presences that are described as 'impressions', 'entities', 'ghosts', 'old hags', cosmic consciousness and spiritual beings; the experiences are maximally affective and minimally linguistic and are judged more frequently as unpleasant ..." (p. 916). In subsequent works, Cook and Persinger (1997) pioneered the transcranial magnetic stimulation (rTMS) paradigm and were successful in replicating such presence phenomena in normal college population with a complex magnetic field simulating amygdaloid neuronal firing patterns. Interestingly, visual correlations of the "presences" were most frequently encountered in the left visual field, supporting their right hemispheric origin.

Sabourin et al.'s (1990) spectral EEG analysis of hypnotic trance showed that highly hypnotizable subjects generated more theta power at all occipital, central, and frontal locations, more pronounced in the anterior regions. These frequencies are inhibitory in nature and correlate with enhanced attention and imagery, the highly hypnotizable group also reporting higher absorptive attentional skills. The authors suggest that increased fronto-central theta power may represent *class II inhibition*, with "selective deactivation of particular responses so that a continuing excitatory state becomes directed or patterned" (by contrast, class I or global inhibition relates to general inactivity and drowsiness). According to Michel, Lehmann, Henggeler, and Brandeis (1992), the associated state of hippocampal-septal hypersynchrony linked to hippocampal sources correlates with a "transpersonal mode" of experience accompanied by expanded consciousness and creative thought.

A recent study by Kirenskaya et al. (2011) showed sharply elevated coherence between distributed brain regions in alpha and theta bands among highly hypnotizable subjects. In addition, the authors demonstrated increased posterior-frontal coherence in beta and gamma (38–42 Hz) bands, suggesting that highly hypnotizable subjects preferentially engage in hypnotic trance imagery rather than verbal processing. These findings are consistent with the observations of increased global gamma coherence in the naturalistic conditions of ayahuasca-induced trance (Stuckey, Lawson, & Luna, 2005). Since beta and gamma activity is thought to be predominantly cortically generated, these findings suggest that distributed cortical hyper-coherence correlates with the subjective reports of intense synesthetic experiences and dissolution of ego boundaries. More specifically, Lehmann et al. (2001) have shown increased right posterior gamma sources in subjects practicing visual meditations vs. increased right anterior gamma sources in meditative self-dissolution, and left central gamma sources in verbal-based mantra meditations.

Flor-Henry, Lind, and Kole (2013) demonstrated relative right brain activation and left/frontal hypofunction in males with cannabis-induced psychosis, with increased beta and gamma sources in the left temporo-parietal region. In an earlier discussion of dissociative and stable hysteria syndromes, Flor-Henry (1983) concluded that in view of the evidence already available at that time, the fundamental problem was a defect in sensorimotor integration evidenced by bilateral frontal dysfunction ($R > L$) that comes as a consequence of altered left-dominant systems producing a secondary disorganization of the contralateral hemisphere.

Neuroimaging studies of psychedelic-induced altered states (Carhart-Harris et al., 2012) show evidence of default mode network (DMN) inhibition in transition from normal waking consciousness. Surprisingly, the profound consciousness alterations under the influence of psilocybin are only associated with *decreases* in the regional blood flow specific to the hub regions of sensory and self-referential information processing in the thalamus, anterior and posterior cingulate, and medial prefrontal cortex. The authors suggest that psychedelic effects are primarily due to the release from DMN inhibition leading to "unconstrained cognition". A recent fMRI study by Lutz, Brühl, Scheerer, Jäncke, and Herwig (2016) in long-term meditators similarly showed decreased activation of the cortical midline structures involved in the DMN during subjective experiences of mindful awareness, coupled with increased activation in somatosensory regions.

The first specific fMRI study of shamanic trance by Michael Hove's team at Harvard (2015) showed higher neural network connectivity in posterior cingulate (PCC), dorsal anterior cingulate cortex, and left insula. These findings point to co-activation of the default network for internally oriented cognitive states, and modulatory control networks which help focus attention on the relevant internal stimuli. There was an associated finding of perceptual (auditory) decoupling, which would serve to close down external sensory channels. Parallel findings of PCC activation were noted in experienced mindfulness meditators and normal dreaming (Ives-Deliperi, Solms, & Meintjes, 2011), although decreased control network activity in REM states results in involuntary dreaming experience rather than voluntary, lucid visions of a shamanic trance. While the rate of drum beat of four beats per second (4 Hz) to induce the trance state in the study is consistent with the previous suggestions of an auditory driver for increased theta power, the authors rather suggest the mechanism of gating and suppression of the highly predictable sensory input leading to decreased cortical activity. By contrast, they observe that "an unpredicted rhythmic shift is commonly used to end the shamanic journey and helps disengage from the trance and reengage with the sensory world" (p. 6). They conclude that a shamanic journey should be seen as "a goal-directed exploratory state, wherein nascent and previously disparate mental contents can be stimulated, evaluated, and integrated," and suggest that "shamanic trance involves a reconfiguration of connectivity between brain regions that is consistent across individuals and thus cannot be dismissed as an empty ritual" (p. 7).

In this paper, we present the first detailed spectral EEG study of a normal subject who was trained to induce a shamanic trance and is presently able to enter it without the sound of the drum. She was the first Westerner to achieve the designation of *udgan* (a Mongolian female shaman).

4. Case history

The subject and one the authors (C.S) is an only child born in Draguignan, in the south of France. She spent her early years in Ouagadougou (Burkina Faso) in Africa. She underwent a near-death experience in Africa at the age of 11 months due to an allergic reaction to smallpox vaccine. After her parents' divorce at the age of eight, she was raised by her mother in France; her father stayed in Africa and she visited him for summer holidays. She studied musicology, piano, and composition, and after winning national and international competitions in 1986, she received a scholarship from the Franco-Quebecois Youth Office to study with multimedia performers and composers in Montreal.

Following a traumatic episode in 1999 when her partner of 10 years died, she moved to London, England where she pursued a career as a pianist/composer and worked as a reporter for BBC World Service. In 2001, during a report on Mongolia ("Mongolian mysteries" aired on BBC World Service in 2002), the sound of a shamanic drum induced a violent crisis when she could no longer control her movements. A Dakhad shaman (one of the 31 ethnic Mongolian groups) recognized her as having unique shamanic gifts and invited her to apprentice for Shaman training (Sombrun, 2004). She traveled to Mongolia near the Siberian frontier for the following eight years, being taught shamanic practices by an ugdan Enkhetuya belonging to the Tsaatans ethnic group. In 2009, C.S became the first Westerner to achieve the status of *udgan* herself.

In 2005, C.S traveled to New Mexico to meet with Harlyn Geronimo, a medicine man and great-grandson of the famous Apache warrior. According to the Apache legend, this Indian tribe had originated in Mongolia (this is consistent with paleoanthropological and genetic data on the Bering land bridge migration route from Eastern Siberia to Alaska between 12,000 and 14,000 years ago—Wang et al., 2007). In 2008, C.S continued with her research on the migration of Mongolian tribes and went to Alaska where she met Athabascan Indians, presumed ancestors of the Apaches and descendants of the Mongols.

C.S. first experienced a spontaneous trance at the age of six, when she and her parents were attending a tribal funeral ceremony in Burkina Faso. She remembers being completely absorbed by the music, her mother later telling her that she began to shake, which spread to all of her body. Following her spontaneous trance experience in Mongolia, she came to Prof. P. Flor-Henry's Clinical Diagnostic and Research Centre at Alberta Hospital Edmonton in Canada in an attempt to elucidate the physiological mechanisms underlying her ability to induce a shamanic trance.

C.S continues to compose music, give lectures, and research the mechanisms of SSCs. She is involved in ongoing research in shamanic trance states with Pr Edward Frenkel (University of California, Berkeley, USA), Pr Francis Taulelle (KU Leuven, Belgium), Pr Patrick Lemoine (Lyon University, France and Peking University, China) and Pr Marc Henry (Strasbourg University, France). She designed a digital sound loop with Elie D. Lequemener modeled from original musical pieces played to induce trance by shamans. During a course on trance and creativity in December 2015, it was played to students of Beaux-Arts in Nantes, with 16 out of 20 students undergoing a trance induction and subsequently returning to their normal state. Follow-up study is presently in progress. These findings demonstrate that trance states may be much more common than what is generally accepted, representing an underused potentiality rather than an exceptional gift or psychopathology.

5. Methodology

5.1. Subjects

Our experimental subject's spectral EEG parameters were compared to the bank of previously investigated control groups of normal, schizophrenic, manic, and depressed dextral female subjects (the numbers vary slightly due to the removal of cases with EEG artifacts in various frequencies). When tested at the age of 45, our subject was within the age range of manic (mean age 44.87 ± 12.32 years) and depressed (37.39 ± 10.94) age groups, but slightly older than the schizophrenic (mean age 35.33 ± 8.82 years) and normal control samples (mean age of 25.57 ± 8.37 years). However, the normalization of the cross-spectral matrix from each subject by its trace (total EEG power in the band) was used to eliminate any dependence of EEG power on age. Specifically, Klimesch (1999) documented that with increasing age, absolute power in the alpha and theta oscillations decreases while upper alpha power increases, and overall alpha power increases from early childhood to adulthood and then progressively decreases with age. Consequently, the peak alpha frequency of the subject, controls, and comparison schizophrenic, manic, and depressed populations was analyzed.

Comparison subjects were all unmedicated at the time of their data recordings. All subjects were completely right handed as determined by the handedness questionnaires (see the experimental protocol in Koles, Lind, & Flor-Henry, 2004). The pretest interview was used to exclude illicit drug use, medication, alcohol abuse, migraine or other neurological disorders, comorbid psychiatric disorders, birth complications, and head trauma. In addition, the Quick Diagnostic Interview Schedule, the Basic Personality Inventory, and the Multidimensional Aptitude Battery, which provides verbal, performance, and full-scale IQ, were administered to all patients and controls.

EEGs were recorded from all subjects during a passive condition, eyes open (EO) or eyes closed (EC), and a spatial cognitive task, dot localization (DL). At least 3 min of recording was obtained from each subject. During the passive condition, the subjects were told to relax, think of nothing in particular, and fix their gaze on a point across the room. The DL task contained 25 items, each consisting of two vertically arranged open rectangles, the top rectangle containing a pair of dots and the bottom rectangle, slightly offset to either the right or the left, containing an array of numbers. The offset of the bottom rectangle differed randomly among items such that half of the items were offset to either the right or the left side. Subjects were asked to indicate which two numbers in the lower rectangle corresponded to the location of the dots in the upper rectangle. Item difficulty is determined by the size of the number arrays, which varied in five levels, from 8 to 50 numbers. The experimental subject in this study was tested in both EO and EC conditions in her normal state, but only in the EC condition during the trance, which was necessary for trance induction.

The research protocol as outlined above was reviewed by the Ethics Review Committee of the Alberta Hospital Edmonton and found to be acceptable within the limitations of human experimentation. No third-party consents were necessary since our experimental subject is one of the co-authors for this project.

5.2. Recordings

EEG recordings were obtained using a 43-lead stretchable electrode cap containing tin electrodes. The 43 electrode sites represented standard electrode positions described in the American Electroencephalography Society Guidelines. The lead sites were AF_3, AF_4, FC_5, FC_6, FC_1, FC_2, C_3, C_4, C_1, C_2, TP_7, TP_8, CP_5, CP_6, CP_1, CP_2, P_3, P_4, P_1, P_2, PO_3, PO_4, AF_z, F_z, FC_z, C_z, CP_z, P_z, PO_z, FP_1, FP_2, F_7, F_8, F_3, F_4, FT_7, FT_8, T_7, T_8, P_7, P_8, O_1, and O_2. All leads were referenced to the left ear, then converted to average reference, and the impedance at each electrode was adjusted to be below 5 KΩ. Three additional channels were recorded: the electrocardiogram (EKG), a bipolar recording over the external canthus to the supra-orbit of the right eye to monitor vertical and horizontal eye movements (EOG), and one bipolar electromyogram (EMG) channel recorded from the temporomandibular region on the right and left sides. All channels were amplified using a Grass Neurodata system and digitized with a 12-bit RC Electronics analog to digital converter at a rate of 256 samples/s. The band pass was set at

3–80 Hz with the high pass controlled by a Grass Model 12A5 two-pole Butterworth filter with the 3 dB point set at 3 Hz. The anti-aliasing filter was an eight-pole Bessel function filter with the 3 dB point set at 80 Hz.

5.3. Spectral analysis

The digitized EEG records were visually edited offline in the attempt to select 20 non-overlapping, 1-s data segments corresponding to correct responses to the tasks. These were selected randomly from all of the one-second segments available from the subject. Segments that contained voltage spikes, large eye movements, or muscle activity were not selected for analysis. Only those patients and subjects who were able to contribute the 20 segments were admitted into the study.

The Fast Fourier Transform (FFT) was applied to each row of the data matrix formed by the 46 EEG, EKG, EMG, and EOG channels (as rows) and 256 time samples (as columns) collected during each second. Prior to the application of the FFT, each row of the data matrix was preprocessed by applying a 50% Hamming taper. With 256 samples in each one-second segment, the frequency resolution of the FFT along the columns of each transformed data matrix, $V(\mathrm{f})$ was 1 Hz spanning the range of frequencies from 0 to 255 Hz. The selected columns from the transformed data matrices were characterized in terms of their cross-spectra. The cross-spectral matrices $\Sigma(\alpha)$ and $\Sigma(\beta)$ were formed as:

$\Sigma(\alpha) = V(\alpha)\,V^{\mathrm{T}}(\alpha)$ and $\Sigma(\beta) = V(\beta)\,V^{\mathrm{T}}(\beta)$, where $V(\alpha)$ and $\Sigma(\beta)$ are the alpha and beta columns from $V(\mathrm{f})$ and T is the complex conjugate transpose. An average 46×46 complex-valued cross-spectral matrix over the 20 segments available from each subject was then calculated for each frequency band and for each of the EO, EC, and DL conditions.

The correlated effects of the EKG, EOG, and EMG with the EEG were removed using the matched filtering technique, resulting in 43×43 cross-spectral matrices for each subject/frequency band/condition. Each matrix was then normalized by dividing all of its elements by its trace (the sum of its diagonal elements). This procedure was implemented in order to remove the confounding effects of skull thickness on EEG power. For more technical details, please refer to Koles et al. (2004).

6. Results

6.1. Psychological testing

- Quick Diagnostic Interview Schedule:
  - No psychiatric disorders.
- Basic Personality Inventory:
  - Normal on all 12 personality dimensions.
- Eysenck Personality Inventory:
  - Neuroticism: 0 percentile
  - Extraversion: 40th percentile.

The experimental subject does not have any psychiatric history and has never required any psychotropic medication or psychotherapy.

6.2. Spectral EEG findings

6.2.1. Centroid analysis

In her normal state, the subject is similar to 80 normal dextral female controls, in all frequency bands. This is true for both the EO and EC conditions, as well as when engaging in the non-dominant hemisphere DL task.

Table 1. EEG frequency bands and sub-bands as defined in this study	
Delta	2–3 Hz
Theta	4–7 Hz
Alpha	8–13 Hz
Beta 1 (low beta)	14–20 Hz
Beta 2 (high beta)	21–50 Hz
Gamma	38–42 Hz
EMG	50–64 Hz

In the trance state, all measurements were taken in the EC condition, which was necessary for trance induction. The EEG frequency bands as used in this study are summarized in Table 1. Centroid analysis shows that the subject's trance EEG is similar to normal dextral female controls in alpha, theta, and delta bands but statistically different in low and high beta frequency bands (13–20 Hz and 21–50 Hz), with $p < 0.04$ and $p < 0.01$, respectively (Figure 2(A)). Discriminant function comparison with unmedicated dextral females with schizophrenia ($n = 18$); mania ($n = 19$); depression ($n = 84$); and control ($n = 80$) reveals that in the trance state only, the subject's scores were fully outside the normal range and clustered within the depression and schizophrenia groups in the high beta band (Figure 2(B) and 2(D)); and within the mania group in the delta and high beta bands (Figure 2(C)).

6.2.2. Quantitative EEG mapping

In the trance state, the subject shows reduced coherence in the right hemisphere and increased coherence in the left hemisphere in the low beta band compared to the controls (Figure 3(A)). In the high beta band, the pattern is of increased anterior-posterior coherence (fronto-central and occipital, Figure 3(B)). Of particular interest is the presence of two symmetrical foci of increased power

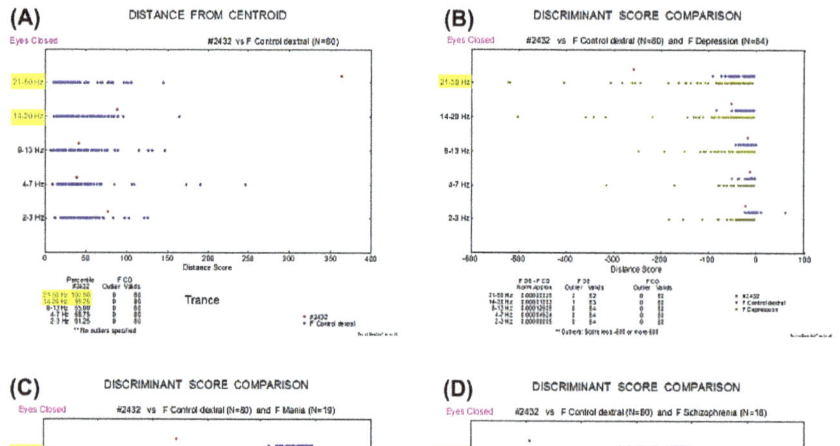

Figure 2. Centroid analysis. (A) Centroid analysis of the subject in the trance state (red) vs. 80 normal dextral female controls (blue). (B) Discriminant score comparison of the subject in the trance state (red) vs. 80 normal dextral female controls (blue) and 84 females with depression (yellow). (C) Discriminant score comparison of the subject in the trance state (red) vs. 80 normal dextral female controls (blue) and 19 females with mania (yellow). (D) Discriminant score comparison of the subject in the trance state (red) vs. 80 normal dextral female controls (blue) and 18 females with schizophrenia (yellow).

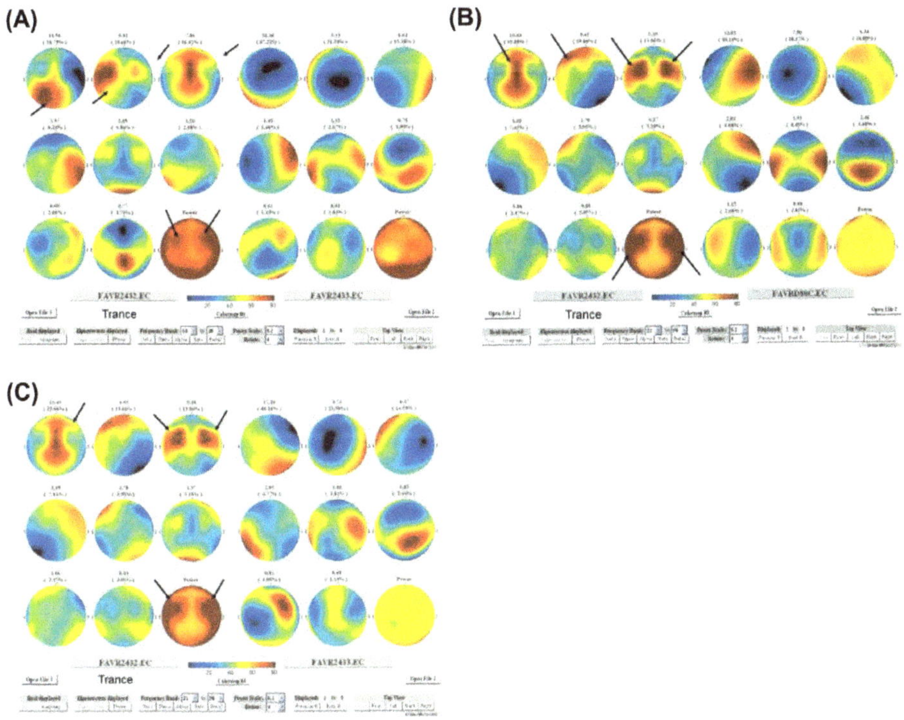

Figure 3. Quantitative EEG mapping of the subject in the trance state (left 3 × 3 maps) vs. 78 normal dextral female controls (right 3 × 3 maps): (A) Low beta band, EC condition. (B) High beta band, EC condition. (C) The subject in the trance state (left 3 × 3 maps) vs. in her normal state (right 3 × 3 maps): high beta band, EC condition.

bilaterally in the centro-temporal regions, which is completely absent in the control condition. This may suggest a trance-specific disruption of inter-hemispheric integration.

Inspection of the EEG map when the subject is in the trance compared to her normal state (eyes closed—Figure 3(C)) shows a dramatic increase in power in the low and high beta bands, which is bilaterally symmetrical in the mid-temporal/central regions and in the lateral convexity extending across the fronto-parietal zones. In the trance state, the three most significant coherence configuration factors that account for 68% of the variance in the 21–50 Hz band, and 50% in the 14–20 Hz band are characterized by increased midline coherence in the fronto-temporo-parietal regions; increased left fronto-temporal foci; and symmetrical foci of increased coherence in the medial-central temporal regions, respectively.

6.2.3. LORETA source analysis

In the normal state, the subject shows increased sources in the right frontal regions in delta, theta, alpha, and low and high beta bands compared to the 78 normal dextral female controls (Figure 4(A)–(E)). There are additional gamma sources in the right post-central gyrus (Figure 4(F)). The anatomical origins of the LORETA sources compared to 78 normal female controls are shifted from anterior to posterior-frontal pre-central gyrus in the subject's normal state, and further to post-central gyrus and parietal locations in the trance state.

In the trance state, there are increased unilateral sources in the right hemisphere in the delta and theta bands compared to the 78 normal dextral female controls (Figure 5(A)–(B)). These originate from the right inferior temporal lobe (delta) and right parietal lobe (theta). In the alpha band, the sources are increased in both hemispheres, originating in superior temporal gyrus (Figure 5(C)). A similar configuration of symmetrically increased sources in both hemispheres is found in both low and high beta and in gamma bands: frontal for the low beta, and parietal for the high beta and gamma bands (Figure 5(D)–(F)).

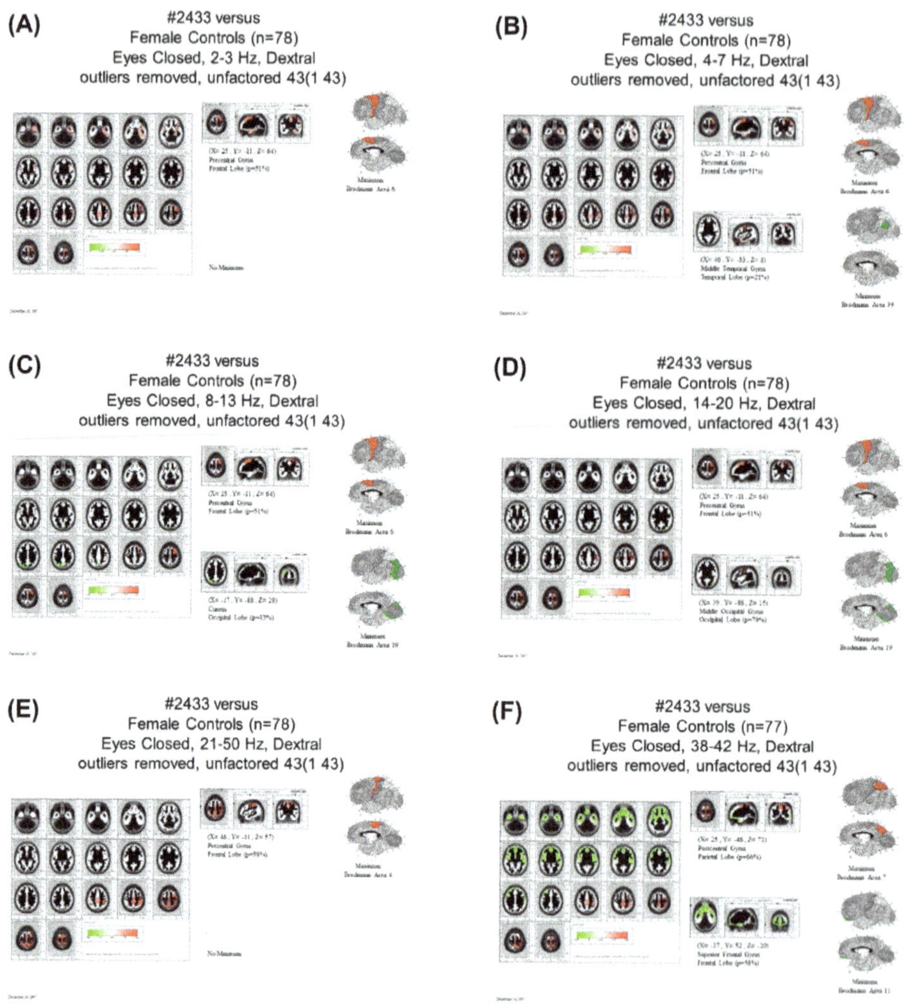

Figure 4. LORETA power source distribution of the subject in the normal state vs. 78 normal dextral female controls, EC condition: (A) Delta band; (B) Theta band; (C) Alpha band; (D) Low beta band; (E) High beta band; (F) Gamma band.

Specific localization of LORETA power sources in the trance state by the frequency bands compared to 78 dextral female controls demonstrated the following patterns:

Delta sources (2–3 Hz): Increased unilaterally, maximally in the right temporal lobe (originates in inferior temporal gyrus, Broadmann area (BA) 20—Figure 5(A)).

Theta sources (4–7 Hz): Increased in the right fronto-temporo-parietal areas (originates in posterior central gyrus, BA 40—Figure 5(B)).

Alpha sources (8–13 Hz): Increased bilaterally in the fronto-temporo-parieto-occipital areas, maximally in the temporal lobe (originates in superior temporal gyrus bilaterally, BA 22—Figure 5(C)).

Low beta sources (14–20 Hz): Increased bilaterally in the fronto-parieto-occipital areas, maximally in frontal lobe (originates in precentral gyri bilaterally), BA 6 (Figure 5(D)).

High beta sources (21–50 Hz): Increased bilaterally in the fronto-temporo-parietal areas, maximally in the parietal lobe (originates in post-central gyri), BA 2 (Figure 5(E)). There is evidence of

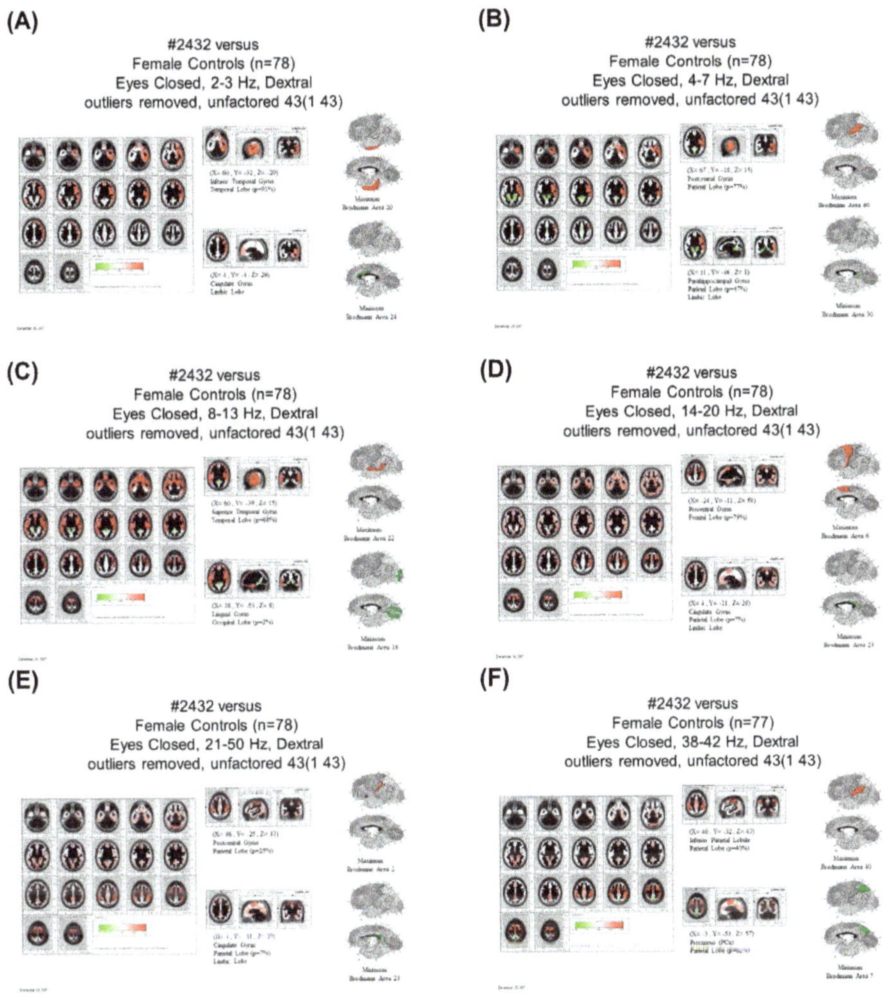

Figure 5. LORETA power source distribution of the subject in the trance state vs. 78 normal dextral female controls, EC condition: (A) Delta band; (B) Theta band; (C) Alpha band; (D) Low beta band; (E) High beta band; (F) Gamma band.

increased coherence in same regions in both normal (EC) and trance conditions (Figures 4(E) and 5(E)), representing a progression of the same pattern, which is accentuated in the trance state.

Gamma sources (38–42 Hz): Increased bilaterally in the fronto-temporo-parietal areas, maximally in the inferior parietal lobule (BA 40)—Figure 5(F).

Alpha power ratios (log *R/L*) show consistent relative right brain activation in parietal (P4-P3), mid- and posterior temporal (T4-T3, T6-T5), and frontal (F8-F7) areas (Table 2).

Table 2. Lateralized log *R/L* alpha power ratios in normal vs. trance state

	Normal (relative left brain activation)	Trance (relative right brain activation)
P4–P3	0.924	−0.250
T4–T3	0.727	−0.247
F8–F7	0.182	−0.318
T6–T5	1.047	−0.217

In summary, the pattern of EEG changes observed during the trance state suggests altered neurophysiological organization in the right hemisphere, inhibitory in nature, maximal in temporo-parietal areas, associated with impaired inter-hemispheric connectivity, and a generalized increase in cortical beta sources. In the transition from the normal to the trance state, there is evidence of an antero-posterior shift, from frontal (delta, theta, alpha, and low and high beta) and parietal post-central (gamma) in the normal state to inferior temporal/parietal (delta), parietal post-central (theta), superior temporal gyrus (alpha), frontal and precentral gyrus (low beta), parietal, post-central gyrus (high beta), and inferior temporal lobule (gamma) during the trance. The underlying neurophysiological changes, preexisting in the right frontal region, may explain the subject's unintentional first experiences of the trance, and relate to the fact that at the age of 11 months, following an allergic reaction to smallpox, she became comatose and had a brief cardiac arrest.

7. Discussion

The diverse levels of evidence reviewed to this point range from phenomenological accounts of altered states to anthropological and ethnocultural observations to electrophysiological and neuroimaging data. Brain neuroplasticity stands at the crossroads between subjective and cultural experience, allowing us to conceptualize an emergent discipline of *neuroanthropology*. In his recent review, Northoff (2010) commented that there *is* "bidirectional traffic between subject and environment that is mirrored in brain's neuronal activity... which allows ourselves to constitute ourselves as humans and to create the different environments investigated in anthropology" (p. 749). The challenge for the general reader and researcher alike is to integrate these highly specialized threads into an integrated model that may shed light on the mechanisms of trance and ASCs.

Northoff and Heinzel (2006a) made a seminal distinction between conventional "third-person neuroscience" focusing on observable changes in brain function vs. "first-person neuroscience," in which the contents of the subjective experience are carefully linked to objective observations on a case-by-case basis. They comment that "empirical investigations of brain states focus exclusively on neuronal states and presuppose therefore only the third-person perspective"; however, "in order to reveal the true neuronal correlates of mental states, first- and third-person perspective must be linked to each other, resulting in the systematic 'science of experience'." In utilizing this paradigm, we offer parallel subjective and objective correlates of the subject's shamanic trance experience, which will serve as a foundation for the integrated psychobiological model of *SSC*, and by extension the entire category of altered states and their relation to normative conscious processes.

7.1. The subjective perspective

7.1.1. Experience of trance from 12/10/2007

It was a very light trance, because I was asked not to move a lot. My nose began to tremble as it used to do in the beginning of each trance (now I am able not to move at all). Then my hands and my arms started shaking lightly. An inner vision of a wolf face, very close to my face, came soon after. Then an owl (two close representations are joined). I have to add that these visions were not seen as precisely as they are with our eyes. It may happen that the visions are quite similar to how we see with our eyes, but sometimes it's more like the feeling of a presence than the image of it. But despite the fact that I don't really see it, I "know" what or who it is. During that trance too, I perceived some soft sounds and a bit of a song that I didn't know.

7.1.2. Changes in perception and body awareness

I find myself in a completely dark place (I don't know if it is the reason why the shamans call it "black world"). The first impression is the loss of time perception, like being in a timeless space. My strength is increased a lot (I can hold and beat the drum, which weighs 8 kg, for hours without any difficulties). My perception of pain is considerably reduced. For instance, at the beginning of my practice, my body hurt a lot because I had to manipulate the drum made of thick wood. But amazingly each trance was painless, while when I was back to my normal state, I felt a lot of pain in every part of my body. Another effect of the trance is the loss of the perception of cold and heat.

My eyes (closed during every trance) have visions like geometrical patterns, places or entities called spirits by the shamans. They can appear to me as men, or women, or animal patterns, that I can suddenly speak with. I feel like I can also detect discords in my environment. When discord is present, my nose can "smell" it. Or, I guess, it is not the odor but the information at the root of the odor. My hands act like they are responding to these discords by performing gestures that I have absolutely no control over. I also can feel forms (more often like balls) in the air. My hands can turn around, try to soften them or to move them gently. I sing songs I have never sang or even learned, I speak unknown languages, and I perform very complex sounds that I am unable to perform in my normal state.

7.1.3. Changes in thinking and emotional state

My sense of self seems to be receding because I don't feel like I am myself anymore; I lose the perception of who I am, or who I used to be. I suddenly feel like the animal or the entity I am supposed to be possessed by. As I am a wolf, for example, I can feel paws in place of my hands and a muzzle in place of my nose. I don't speak anymore but howl like a wolf. About the emotional changes, I'd like to say that I can feel I am incredibly at peace but at the same time possess the strength of "a fierce warrior" when it happens that I have to fight what I see as a harmful entity.

7.2. The objective perspective

The novel contribution of this study is our cardinal observation of the right and posterior shift in the transition to shamanic trance state, with markedly increased fronto-central coherence in the excitatory high beta band bilaterally, extending posteriorly to include parietal and occipital regions. Previous observations (Tsakiris, Costantini, & Haggard, 2008) identify right temporo-parietal junction as a specific substrate in maintaining a coherent sense of one's body ("me" vs. "not me"). Coupled with bilaterally increased power sources in the central temporal regions suggesting a discrete disruption of inter-hemispheric integration, these changes may underlie alterations in the default bodily and autobiographical sense of self that depends on integrated functions of the verbal left and experiential right modes of awareness.

A seminal study of left vs. right hemispheric modes of cognitive processing was undertaken by Vadim Deglin in St. Petersburg (1996), utilizing a false syllogism paradigm before and after unilateral ECT treatments. Under the conditions of the right hemisphere post-ECT suppression ("left self" mode), all linguistic tasks were solved quickly and with more confidence than in the control condition; however, the solutions were limited to the internal consistency of the proposition rather than its correspondence to external reality. For example, in solving a false syllogism:

(a) Winter is cold in tropical countries
(b) Ecuador is a tropical country
(c) Is it cold in Ecuador in winter, or not?

the subject would provide a *theoretical answer* and insist that it is cold in Ecuador "because it says so." By contrast, under the conditions of the left hemisphere post-ECT suppression ("right self" mode), the same subject would provide an empirical answer and reject the syllogism as wrong because "everyone knows that tropical countries don't have cold winters." The authors concluded that "under left hemisphere suppression and reciprocal activation of the right hemisphere, when empirical thought dominates, false premises evoke negative emotional responses. Under right hemisphere suppression and reciprocal activation of the left hemisphere, when theoretical thought dominates, false premises are calmly accepted" (p. 303).

While these findings are consistent with the importance of right frontal regions in reality testing (Lehmann et al., 2001), Newberg and d'Aquili (2000) also identified specific lateralized regions responsible for conscious information processing. The left *causal operator* is responsible for analytical understanding of both external sensory and internal associative information input in the superior parietal lobule and anterior frontal convexity of the dominant hemisphere, and the right *holistic operator* is responsible for generating gestalt understanding of the information input and its correspondence to external reality in the posterior superior parietal lobule of the non-dominant hemisphere (Figure 6).

The novel findings in our study identify an altered balance in the subject's right- vs. left-based modes of awareness, progressing from normal to shamanic trance state. In the normal condition, there is evidence of increased right hemispheric frontal/pre-central power sources in delta and beta bands, and right parietal/post-central sources in gamma band, coupled with increased coherence in the right parietal-occipital and fronto-temporal regions accounting for 40% of the variance, and decreased coherence in the left hemispheric sources accounting for 23%. This is consistent with previous studies of experienced meditators who show persistent changes in the resting, non-meditating state, likely as a result of entrainment of the relevant cortical circuitry following habitual meditation practice (Tei et al., 2009). Such entrainment may also allow for voluntary control of otherwise pathological trance states, and agrees with phenomenological accounts of shamanic practitioners shifting at will between ordinary vs. altered ways of perceiving physical and social reality. The findings of similarities on discriminate function analysis between our subject and depressed, manic, and schizophrenic populations in the high beta band may therefore be related to a disruption in left hemispheric fronto-temporal integration resulting in the release from contralateral inhibition and homologous right hemispheric overactivation, which may represent a common factor in schizophrenic/dissociative psychopathology and in the shamanic trance state. However, the cardinal observation in this study is that the corresponding electrophysiological changes are limited to the trance condition and to a specific band frequency, the subject maintaining the capacity to return to her normal state at will. This capacity for voluntary induction and termination of seemingly pathological brain states coupled with the availability of the internally derived trance information for subsequent analytical processing is the defining characteristic of functional trance states and SSCs, which distinguishes them from psychopathology.

Our observation of increased fronto-central delta, theta, and alpha power sources is also consistent with Carhart-Harris' et al. (2012) evidence of DMN inhibition in psychedelic states and reduced duration of default mode conceptual processing in Zen meditation implicating alterations in attentional networks (Pagnoni, Cekic, & Guo, 2008). The DMN and attentional networks impose top-down control on the lower cortical and limbic networks, effectively gating sensory, affective, and associative information processing into established patterns of self-referential templates in order to minimize prediction errors (Northoff et al., 2006b). The shamanic mode of consciousness may therefore correspond to an altered pattern of self-referential processing due to a release from the ordinary top-down inhibitory control mechanisms, resulting in a wider range of association networks coming into conscious awareness, similar to psychedelic and lucid dream states.

The resultant increase in cortical-subcortical connectivity is evidenced by the bilateral increase in fronto-temporal alpha power and increased fronto-temporal and parieto-occipital low/high beta and gamma sources. Among other functions, alpha oscillations have been shown to underlie temporal attention to visual stimuli (Hanslmayr, Gross, Klimesch, & Shapiro, 2011), and gamma activity may reflect the binding function of diverse aspects of object representation in conscious awareness. These objective data are consistent with our subject's subjective reports of altered self-experience, intense consciously accessible inner imagery, and somatosensory alterations suggesting a shift from verbally driven, ego-bound mode of ordinary consciousness (OSC) toward more visual and somatosensory "right experiential mode" prevalent in altered states. The analysis of alpha power ratios pre- and post-trance induction correspondingly shows relative left brain dominance during the subject's normal conscious state shifting to marked right brain dominance in the trance state.

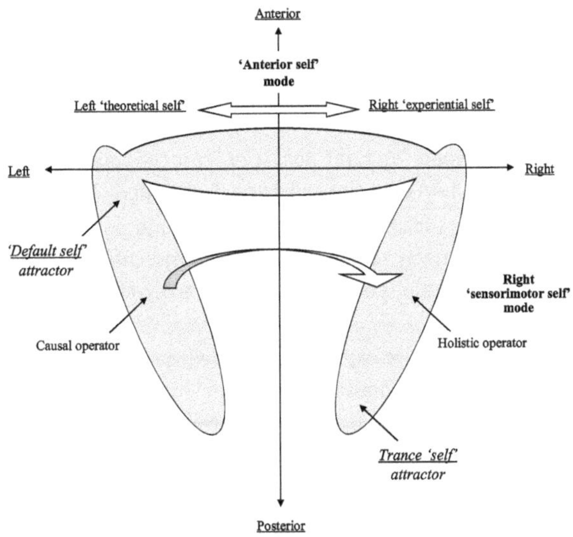

Figure 6. Posterior–anterior and lateral axes in normal and altered states of consciousness.

7.3. The unified psychobiological model

Our findings point at a unified clinical model of altered state experiences based on a shift from the left hemisphere-dominant, verbally based, serial mode of information processing in normative conscious awareness to right hemisphere-dominant, somatosensory-based, parallel mode of information processing in ASC states (Figure 6). We can conceptualize this shift occurring on two separate axes:

The lateral axis (inter-hemispheric right to left hemispheric processing): increasing information complexity through integration and modulation of implicit experiential and somatosensory-affective experiences into explicit verbal conscious awareness.

(1) Ordinary left hemisphere-dominant "analytical self" mode allows for a normative conscious state of dual awareness (OSC) with a sense of autobiographical self extended in time, symbolic information processing, abstract capacity, and linear cause–effect attribution. Based on lateralized inhibition of right hemispheric systems through evolutionarily newer left dorsolateral networks.

(2) Internally or externally induced release from left hemispheric inhibition results in a shift to the right "experiential self" mode (Figure 6), with altered states of awareness (ASCs) accompanied by non-verbal, timeless perception of reality grounded in experiential-gestalt rather than theoretical-analytical domain. Represents uncoupling of the right hemispheric "holistic operator" from the normally dominant left hemispheric "causal operator" networks, manifested in the homologous right hemispheric contralateral overactivation in the fronto-temporo-parietal areas and subjective intrusion of the right hemispheric content into waking awareness.

The posterior-anterior axis (subcortical/primary association areas to anterior cortical midline structures): increasing information complexity through the coalescent autobiographical sense of "dual self" possessed of intentionality and willful action planning.

(1) Ordinary prefrontal-dominant "anterior self" mode allows for "me—not-me" distinction, with an experience of separate self possessing thoughts and emotions interacting with separate others and larger independent reality, as well as subjecticve sense of "free will". Based on top-down inhibition of lower affective-somatosensory systems through evolutionarily newer prefrontal cortical structures.

(2) Internally or externally induced release from prefrontal inhibition results in a shift to the posterior "sensorimotor self" mode, with ASCs accompanied by rich imagery, intense affective experiences,

> synesthesias, dissolution of ego boundaries, and cosmic feelings of "oneness" with the Universe. Manifested by relative hypofrontality and "decreased activity and connectivity in the brain's key connector hubs, enabling a state of unconstrained cognition". (Carhart-Harris et al., 2012)

The combined picture suggests a correlation between the right-posterior "trance" consciousness mode with the phylogenetically older, reflexive X-system of social cognition (Lieberman, 2007) characterized by implicit, parallel information processing facilitated by high arousal and unaffected by cognitive load. Its outputs are experienced as subjectively real, with blurred demarcation between self and "not-self." By contrast, the left-prefrontal "default" consciousness mode correlates with the phylogenetically newer, reflective C-system characterized by explicit, serial information processing inhibited by high arousal and cognitive load. Its outputs are experienced as self-generated and distinct from external reality, resulting in dual self/not-self awareness.

We believe that the findings of this study and the proposed psychobiological model have wide-ranging implications for cognitive science and consciousness research. Based on the above model, consciousness and self-awareness are best conceptualized as a *process of experience* rather than discrete "states of consciousness", whether normal or pathological. Conscious awareness represents a fluid equilibrium between anterior/posterior and right/left modes of experience that constantly shift depending on the individual psychobiology, external information input, and cultural paradigms (Han et al., 2013). The illusion of fixed "states of consciousness" and a subjective self are based on habitually established patterns of information processing that can be conceptualized as *attractor dynamics* encoding diverse patterns of self-experience (Shapiro, 2015). From the dynamical systems perspective, attractors represent adaptive algorithms that carried a survival value in the course of *Homo sapiens* evolution; they determine default patterns of organizing our perceptual, affective, cognitive, and relational experience, and acting on it. Attractor-bound events are fundamentally process oriented, and are best conceptualized as dynamic "modes of conscious experience" rather than static "ordinary" vs. "altered" states.

The "default self" mode of consciousness can therefore be conceptualized as a periodic attractor that involves sleep–wakefulness phases and predominantly operates within the left-anterior analytical network domain (Figure 6). In contrast, the "trance self" mode represents a point attractor that operates within the right-posterior experiential/sensorimotor network domain. The transition between default and trance attractor modes is facilitated by the release of the normative left-hemispheric contralateral and prefrontal inhibition under the conditions of meditative or psychedelic trance techniques. Shamanic and altered modes of consciousness may thus represent a learned voluntary capacity to step aside from the analytical conscious attractor dynamics (default self-awareness) and access alternate ways of experiencing internal and external reality that has been conceptualized as a "nonlocal-intuitive" perspective (Frecska et al., 2016).

7.4. Implications for psychiatry

In psychiatry, the longstanding separation into biological vs. psychosocial modalities is rapidly growing obsolete: both psychopharmacogical and psychotherapeutic interventions effect biological changes in the brain, both are administered in the context of a therapeutic relationship, and both are inseparable from the patient's subjective experience of the treatment. Conversely, there is consistent evidence that alterations in subjective experience, such as learning and psychotherapy, can induce lasting changes in brain structure and function by effecting epigenetic changes that modify the very synaptic networks that give rise to our subjective experience (Kandel, 1998; Shapiro, John, Scott, & Tomy, 2016a, 2016b). In the words of Nobel laureate Eric Kandel, "insofar as psychotherapy or counseling is effective and produces long-term changes in behavior, it presumably does so through learning, by producing changes in gene expression that alter the strength of synaptic connections" (p. 460).

In addition, a wide range of treatments that would have been considered esoteric only a decade ago, such as mindfulness, hypnotherapy, meditation, and psychedelic and altered state experiences, demonstrate effectiveness in a wide range of depressive, anxiety, and trauma-based syndromes (Masson & Bernoussi, 2014; Pathania, 2015). A recent review of mindfulness practices in mental health (Kok & Singer, 2017) suggests that they are associated with increased positivity of affect, feelings of warmth toward others, metacognitive awareness, and decreased thought distraction. Mindfulness-based stress relaxation (MBSR) and mindfulness-based cognitive therapy (MBCT) have been shown to increase alpha and theta band activity in prefrontal and anterior cingulate networks (Chiesa & Serretti, 2010). Sensorimotor therapy approaches utilize non-verbal, body-oriented modalities to process intense trauma memories (Ogden, Minton, & Pain, 2006), and research into unconscious processes in mental health and psychopathology highlights the essential role of implicit cognition, affective processing, and social cuing that happen outside of verbal conscious awareness and provide the basis for automatic emotional regulation and attachment dynamics (Schore, 2011).

While in Western psychiatry trance experiences have been largely been viewed as pathological or esoteric, there are diverse cultural traditions where altered modes of consciousness serve the function of healing and self-exploration. With the current resurgence of interest in integrative medicine and complementary healing techniques, understanding the psychobiology of trance states may not only help to "de-pathologize" them in the eyes of medical practitioners but also use them as another therapeutic tool in the psychiatric treatment provision.

8. Conclusion

At the onset of this study, we posed two key questions:

(1) Do shamanic trance states represent psychopathology or an anomalous but non-pathological mode of brain functioning?
(2) What specific alterations in brain function accompany shamanic trance states? Specifically, are shamanic states characterized by a shift from the normally left hemisphere-dominant mode of conscious awareness to a relative predominance of right hemispheric activation?

The evidence from this study and systematic analysis of existing neurophysiological, neuroimaging, and phenomenological data on the altered modes of consciousness strongly suggest that while there are some parallels to spectral EEG changes in clinical populations, shamanic trance is not a psychopathological condition and cannot be reduced to psychotic or dissociative clinical phenomena. In addition, we corroborated not only generalized right hemispheric dominance during shamanic trance but also a specific shift from the normative anterior prefrontal to the right posterior mode of awareness. There is now enough emerging evidence to begin constructing a comprehensive psychobiological model of trance states, which can inform both the wider field of basic consciousness research and clinical work with pathological consciousness alterations.

The concept of first-person neuroscience can be extended to incorporate *systemic psychobiology* (Shapiro & Scott, in press), where brain/mind is seen as a dynamic, nonlinear system with multi-level emergent properties that interact through both bottom-up and top-down causal loops in a continuous diathesis with our internal, physical, and cultural environments. Approaching cognitive science from the perspective of systemic psychobiology allows us to transcend the reductionist brain/mind and nature/nurture dichotomies by utilizing parallel dynamics between four emergent levels of complexity:

(1) "Third-person" level of observable neural network processes.
(2) The emergent "first-person" level of subjective experience with associated patterns of perception, feeling, thinking, and intentionality in the course of individual lifespan (emergence of consciousness).

(3) The emergent "second-person" level of intersubjective experience with associated relational patterns of individual and group interactions.
(4) The emergent social level of cultural experience associated with stable patterns of interpreting objective and subjective reality that are influenced by the individuals but transcend the individual lifespan.

Our model suggests that subjective conscious experience in ordinary and altered domains, and the brain mechanisms that give rise to them, cannot be understood in isolation from each other and their larger social and cultural contexts. Both brain scientists and clinicians as well as cultural anthropologists have to resist the temptation of reductionist linear models, whether brain, mind or society based. To understand the individual, we must integrate the fluid dynamic of objective third-person data with subjective systems of meaning and the cultural context that gives rise to them. In this view, individual conscious processes are inseparable from their intersubjective milieu and relational, social, and cultural contexts. Therefore, any meaningful exploration of brain changes contributing to conscious experience has to be based on unifying objective, subjective, and intersubjective science in health and psychopathology.

The shift to the evolutionarily older, right hemisphere-dominant mode of awareness may help transcend the established left hemisphere "theoretical" constructs informed by our developmental and cultural interactions, and allow for a novel, gestalt experience of physical and social reality leading to qualitatively different awareness of the problem under consideration (such as our subject's synesthetic "smell of discord"). The systematic use of the right hemispheric "experiential" mode may thus serve as a tool in allowing SSC practitioners to operate within largely non-verbal, associative awareness, which they tend to experience in visual and somatosensory modalities. Psychoanalytic and Jungian traditions have long emphasized the importance of attending to the unconscious content of experience, and there has been a recent shift in Western schools of psychotherapy from largely verbal to more experiential, nonlinear approaches that integrate affective, somatic, and intersubjective domains (Lyons-Ruth, 2001). These perspectives may help us bridge traditional and Western concepts of psychopathology and mental health treatment, and integrate the current bio-opsychosocial orientation in psychiatry within a wider evolutionary foundation of systemic psychobiology that incorporates objective, subjective, and intersubjective science.

It is the authors' sincere hope that more research within the systemic psychobiology framework may help not only to elucidate the neural correlates of ordinary and altered conscious experience, but also to bring about an emergent, non-reductive paradigm of the systematic "science of experience" in neuroscience and clinical psychiatry. To paraphrase William James' introductory epigraph, no scientific account of the universe in its totality can be final when it leaves out the phenomenon of conscious experience.

Funding
The authors received no direct funding for this research.

Competing Interests
The authors declare no competing interest.

Author details
Pierre Flor-Henry[1]
E-mail: flor-henry@shaw.ca
Yakov Shapiro[1]
E-mail: yshapiro@shaw.ca
Corine Sombrun[2]
E-mail: csombrun@orange.fr
[1] Department of Psychiatry, University of Alberta, Edmonton, Canada.
[2] Les Beaux Arts, Paris, France.

References
Banquet, J. P. (1973). Spectral analysis of the EEG in meditation. *Electroencephalography and Clinical*

Neurophysiology, 35, 143–151. http://dx.doi.org/10.1016/0013-4694(73)90170-3

Berman, A. E., & Stevens, L. (2015). EEG manifestations of nondual experiences in meditators. *Consciousness and Cognition, 31*, 1–11. http://dx.doi.org/10.1016/j.concog.2014.10.002

Cahn, B. R., & Polich, J. (2006). Meditation states and traits: EEG, ERP, and neuroimaging studies. *Psychological Bulletin, 132*, 180. http://dx.doi.org/10.1037/0033-2909.132.2.180

Carhart-Harris, R. L., Erritzoe, D., Williams, T., Stone, J. M., Reed, L. J., Colasanti, A., ... Hobden, P. (2012). Neural correlates of the psychedelic state as determined by fMRI studies with psilocybin. *Proceedings of the National Academy of Sciences, 109*, 2138–2143. http://dx.doi.org/10.1073/pnas.1119598109

Castillo, R. J. (2003). Trance, functional psychosis, and culture. *Psychiatry: Interpersonal and Biological Processes, 66*, 9–21. http://dx.doi.org/10.1521/psyc.66.1.9.20285

Chiesa, A., & Serretti, A. (2010). A systematic review of neurobiological and clinical features of mindfulness meditations. *Psychological Medicine, 40*, 1239–1252. http://dx.doi.org/10.1017/S0033291709991747

Cook, C. M., & Persinger, M. A. (1997). Experimental induction of the "sensed presence" in normal subjects and an exceptional subject. *Perceptual and Motor Skills, 85*, 683–683. http://dx.doi.org/10.2466/PMS.85.6.683-693

Csikszentmihalyi, M. (1996). *Creativity*. New York, NY: Harper Perennial.

Deglin, V. L., & Kinsbourne, M. (1996). Divergent thinking styles of the hemispheres: How syllogisms are solved during transitory hemisphere suppression. *Brain and Cognition, 31*, 285–307. http://dx.doi.org/10.1006/brcg.1996.0048

Dietrich, A. (2003). Functional neuroanatomy of altered states of consciousness: The transient hypofrontality hypothesis. *Consciousness and Cognition, 12*, 231–256. http://dx.doi.org/10.1016/S1053-8100(02)00046-6

During, E. H., Elahi, F. M., Taieb, O., Moro, M. R., & Baubet, T. (2011). A critical review of dissociative trance and possession disorders: Etiological, diagnostic, therapeutic, and nosological issues. *The Canadian Journal of Psychiatry, 56*, 235–242. http://dx.doi.org/10.1177/070674371105600407

Etevenon, P. (2010). Meditation as a state of consciousness: A personal account. *Human Cognitive Neurophysiology, 3*, 1–26.

Flor-Henry, P. (1983). *Cerebral basis of psychopathology*. Boston: John Wright PSG .

Flor-Henry, P., Lind, J. C., & Kole, Z. J. (2013). Neurophysiological aspects of cannabis induced psychosis. Paper presentation, Joint Meeting of the EEG and Clinical Neuroscience Society, The International Society of Brain Electromagnetic Topography, International Society of Neuroimaging in Psychiatry, and the Evoked Potentials International Conference, Bristol, Tennessee, USA, Sept 12–15. *Clin EEG* Neuroscience, 44, 76.

Frecska, E., Hoppál, M., & Luna, L. E. (2016). Nonlocality and the shamanic state of consciousness. *NeuroQuantology, 14*, 155–165.

Han, S., Northoff, G., Vogeley, K., Wexler, B. E., Kitayama, S., Michael, E. W., & Varnum, M. E. W. (2013). A cultural neuroscience approach to the biosocial nature of the human brain. *Annual Review of Psychology, 64*, 335–359. http://dx.doi.org/10.1146/annurev-psych-071112-054629

Hanslmayr, S., Gross, J., Klimesch, W., & Shapiro, K. L. (2011). The role of alpha oscillations in temporal attention. *Brain Research Reviews, 67*, 331–343. http://dx.doi.org/10.1016/j.brainresrev.2011.04.002

Herman, J. (1992). *Trauma and recovery*. New York, NY: Basic Books.

Houran, J., Lange, R., & Crist-Houran, M. (1997). An assessment of contextual mediation in trance states of Shamanic journeys. *Perceptual and Motor Skills, 85*, 59–65. http://dx.doi.org/10.2466/pms.1997.85.1.59

Hove, M. J., Stelzer, J., Nierhaus, T., Thiel, S. D., Gundlach, C., Margulies, D. S., ... Merker, B. (2015). Brain network reconfiguration and perceptual decoupling during an absorptive state of consciousness. *Cerebral Cortex, 26*, 3116–3124. http://dx.doi.org/10.1093/cercor/bhv137

ICD-10, W.H.O. (1992). *International statistical classification of diseases and related health problems*. Geneva: World Health Organization.

Ives-Deliperi, V. L., Solms, M., & Meintjes, E. M. (2011). The neural substrates of mindfulness: An fMRI investigation. *Social Neurosceince, 6*, 231–242. http://dx.doi.org/10.1080/17470919.2010.513495

Jilek, W. G. (2005). Transforming the shaman: Changing Western views of shamanism and altered states of consciousness. *Investigación en Salud, 7*, 8–15.

Kandel, E. (1998). Biology and the future of psychoanalysis: A new intellectual framework for psychiatry. *American Journal of Psychiatry, 155*, 457–469. http://dx.doi.org/10.1176/ajp.155.4.457

Kirenskaya, A. V., Novototsky-Vlasov, V. Y., & Zvonikov, V. M. (2011). Waking EEG spectral power and coherence differences between high and low hypnotizable subjects. *International Journal of Clinical and Experimental Hypnosis, 59*, 441–453. http://dx.doi.org/10.1080/00207144.2011.594744

Klimesch, W. (1999). EEG alpha and theta oscillations reflect cognitive and memory performance: A review and analysis. *Brain Research Reviews, 29*, 169–195. http://dx.doi.org/10.1016/S0165-0173(98)00056-3

Knox, J. (2009). The analytic relationship: Integrating Jungian, attachment theory and developmental perspectives. *British Journal of Psychotherapy, 25*, 5–23. http://dx.doi.org/10.1111/bjp.2009.25.issue-1

Kok, B. E., & Singer, T. (2017). Phenomenological fingerprints of four meditations: Differential state changes in affect, mind wandering, meta-cognition, and interoception before and after daily practice across 9 months of training. *Mindfulness, 8*, 218–231. http://dx.doi.org/10.1007/s12671-016-0594-9

Koles, Z. J., Lind, J. C., & Flor-Henry, P. (2004). A source-imaging (low-resolution electromagnetic tomography) study of the EEGs from unmedicated men with schizophrenia. *Psychiatry Research: Neuroimaging, 130*, 171–190. http://dx.doi.org/10.1016/j.pscychresns.2003.08.005

Krippner, S. C. (2000). The epistemology and technologies of shamanic states of consciousness. *Journal of Consciousness Studies, 7*, 93–118.

Krippner, S. C. (2002). Conflicting perspectives on shamans and shamanism: Points and counterpoints. *American Psychologist, 57*, 962–977. http://dx.doi.org/10.1037/0003-066X.57.11.962

Krippner, S. C., & Combs, A. (2002). The Neurophenomenology of Shamanism: An essay review. *Journal of Consciousness Studies, 9*, 77–82.

Lehmann, D., Faber, P. L., Achermann, P., Jeanmonod, D., Gianotti, L. R., & Pizzagalli, D. (2001). Brain sources of EEG gamma frequency during volitionally meditation-induced, altered states of consciousness, and experience of the self. *Psychiatry Research: Neuroimaging, 108*, 111–121. http://dx.doi.org/10.1016/S0925-4927(01)00116-0

Lieberman, M. D. (2007). Social cognitive neuroscience: A review of core processes. *Annual Review of Psychology, 58*, 259–289. http://dx.doi.org/10.1146/annurev.psych.58.110405.085654

Lutz, J., Brühl, A. B., Scheerer, H., Jäncke, L., & Herwig, U. (2016). Neural correlates of mindful self-awareness in mindfulness meditators and meditation-naïve subjects revisited. *Biological Psychology, 119*, 21–30. http://dx.doi.org/10.1016/j.biopsycho.2016.06.010

Lyons-Ruth, K. (2001). The emergence of new experiences: Relational improvisation, recognition process, and non-linear change in psychoanalytic theory. *Psychologist-Psychoanalyst, 21*, 13–17.

Masson, J., & Bernoussi, A. (2014). Shamanic healing and psychotherapy. In Parish, A. (Ed.), *Rituals: Practices, ethnic and cultural aspects and role in emotional healing* (Ch. 3, pp. 115–136). New York, NY: Nova.

Michel, C. M., Lehmann, D., Henggeler, B., & Brandeis, D. (1992). Localization of the sources of EEG delta, theta, alpha and beta frequency bands using the FFT dipole approximation. *Electroencephalography and Clinical Neurophysiology, 82*, 38–44. http://dx.doi.org/10.1016/0013-4694(92)90180-P

Money, M. (2000). Shamanism and complementary therapy. *Complementary Therapies in Nursing and Midwifery, 6*, 207–212. http://dx.doi.org/10.1054/ctnm.2000.0507

Newberg, A. B., & d'Aquili, E. G. (2000). The neuropsychology of religious and spiritual experience. *Journal of Consciousness Studies, 7*, 251–266.

Nishimura, K. (1987). Shamanism and medical cures. *Current Anthropology, 28*, S59–S64. http://dx.doi.org/10.1086/203589

Noll, R. (1983). Shamanism and schizophrenia: A state-specific approach to the "schizophrenia metaphor" of shamanic states. *American Ethnologist, 10*, 443–459. http://dx.doi.org/10.1525/ae.1983.10.3.02a00030

Northoff, G. (2010, March 25). Humans, brains, and their environment: Marriage between neuroscience and anthropology? *Neuron, 65*, 748–751. http://dx.doi.org/10.1016/j.neuron.2010.02.024

Northoff, G., & Heinzel, A. (2006a). First-person neuroscience: A new methodological approach for linking mental and neuronal states. *Philosophy, Ethics, and Humanities in Medicine, 1*(1), 1.

Northoff, G., Heinzel, A., de Greck, M., Bermpohl, F., Dobrowolny, H., & Panksepp, J. (2006b). Self-referential processing in our brain: A meta-analysis of imaging studies on the self. *NeuroImage, 31*, 440–457. http://dx.doi.org/10.1016/j.neuroimage.2005.12.002

Ogden, T., Minton, K., & Pain, C. (2006). *Trauma and the body: A sensorimotor approach to psychotherapy*. New York, NY: Norton.

Oohashi, T., Kawai, N., Honda, M., Nakamura, S., Morimoto, M., Nishina, E., & Maekawa, T. (2002). Electroencephalographic measurement of possession trance in the field. *Clinical Neurophysiology, 113*, 435–445. http://dx.doi.org/10.1016/S1388-2457(02)00002-0

Pagnoni, G., Cekic, M., & Guo, Y. (2008). "Thinking about not-thinking": Neral correlates of conceptual processing during Zen meditation. *PLoS One, 3*(9), 1–10.

Pathania, R. (2015). Therapeutic potential of psychedelic agents. *The British Journal of Psychiatry, 206*, 433–433.

Pechey, R., & Halligan, P. (2012). Prevalence and correlates of anomalous experiences in a large non-clinical sample. *Psychology and Psychotherapy: Theory, Research and Practice, 85*, 150–162. http://dx.doi.org/10.1111/papt.2012.85.issue-2

Persinger, M. A. (1993). Vectorial cerebral hemisphericity as differential sources for the sensed presence, mystical experiences and religious conversions. *Perceptual and Motor Skills, 76*, 915–930. http://dx.doi.org/10.2466/pms.1993.76.3.915

Peters, L. G. (1989). Shamanism: Phenomenology of a spiritual discipline. *The Journal of Transpersonal Psychology, 21*, 115.

Sabourin, M. E., Cutcomb, S. D., Crawford, H. J., & Pribram, K. (1990). EEG correlates of hypnotic susceptibility and hypnotic trance: Spectral analysis and coherence. *International Journal of Psychophysiology, 10*, 125–142. http://dx.doi.org/10.1016/0167-8760(90)90027-B

Schore, A. N. (2011). The right brain implicit self lies at the core of psychoanalysis. *Psychoanalytic Dialogues, 21*, 75–100. http://dx.doi.org/10.1080/10481885.2011.545329

Seligman, R., & Kirmayer, L. J. (2008). Dissociative experience and cultural neuroscience: Narrative, metaphor and mechanism. *Culture, Medicine and Psychiatry, 32*, 31–64. http://dx.doi.org/10.1007/s11013-007-9077-8

Shapiro, Y. (2015). Dynamical systems therapy (DST): Theory and practical applications. *Psychoanalytic Dialogues, 25*, 83–107. http://dx.doi.org/10.1080/10481885.2015.991245

Shapiro, Y., John, N., Scott, R., & Tomy, N. (2016a). Psychotherapy and its role in psychiatric practice: A position paper. I. Psychiatry as a psychobiological discipline. *Journal of Psychiatric Practice, 22*, 221–231. http://dx.doi.org/10.1097/PRA.0000000000000159

Shapiro, Y., John, N., Scott, J. R., & Tomy, N. (2016b). Psychotherapy and its role in psychiatric practice: A position paper. II. Objective, subjective, and intersubjective science. *Journal of Psychiatric Practice*, 22, 221–232.

Shapiro, Y., & Scott, J. R. (in press). Dynamical systems therapy (DST): Complex adaptive systems in psychiatry and psychotherapy. Chapter 26. In Prof. E. Mitleton-Kelly, Prof. A. Paraskevas, C. Day (Eds.), *Handbook of research methods in complexity science: Theory & application*. London: Edward Elgar Publishing.

Sombrun, C. (2004). *Mon initiation chez les chamanes*. Paris: Albin Michel.

Stephen, M., & Suryani, L. K. (2000). Shamanism, psychosis and autonomous imagination. *Culture, Medicine and Psychiatry, 24*, 5–38. http://dx.doi.org/10.1023/A:1005528028869

Stuckey, D. E., Lawson, R., & Luna, L. E. (2005). EEG gamma coherence and other correlates of subjective reports during ayahuasca experiences. *Journal of Psychoactive Drugs, 37*, 163–178. http://dx.doi.org/10.1080/02791072.2005.10399798

Tei, S., Faber, P. L., Lehmann, D., Tsujiuchi, T., Kumano, H., Pascual-Marqui, R. D., Gianotti, L. R. R., & Kochi, K. (2009). Meditators and non-meditators: EEG source imaging during resting. *Brain Topography, 22*, 158–165. http://dx.doi.org/10.1007/s10548-009-0107-4

Tsakiris, M., Costantini, M., & Haggard, P. (2008). The role of the right temporo-parietal junction in maintaining a coherent sense of one's body. *Neuropsychologia, 46*, 3014–3018. http://dx.doi.org/10.1016/j.neuropsychologia.2008.06.004

Vaitl, D., Birbaumer, N., Gruzelier, J., Jamieson, G. A., Kotchoubey, B., Kübler, A., ... Lehmann, D. (2005). Psychobiology of altered states of consciousness. *Psychological Bulletin, 131*, 98. http://dx.doi.org/10.1037/0033-2909.131.1.98

VanPool, C. S. (2009). The signs of the sacred: Identifying shamans using archaeological evidence. *Journal of Anthropological Archaeology, 28*, 177–190. http://dx.doi.org/10.1016/j.jaa.2009.02.003

Walsh, R. (1989). What is a shaman? Definition, origin and distribution. *The Journal of Transpersonal Psychology, 21*(1), 1.

Wang, S., Lewis, Jr., C. M., Jakobsson, M., Ramachandran, S., Ray, N., Bedoya, G., ... Mazzotti, G. (2007). Genetic variation and population structure in Native Americans. *PloS Genetics, 3*, 2049–2067.

Winkelman, M. (2010). The shamanic paradigm: Evidence from ethnology, neuropsychology and ethology. *Time and Mind, 3*, 159–182. http://dx.doi.org/10.2752/17516961 0X12632240392758

Wright, P. A. (1989). The nature of the shamanic state of consciousness: A review. *Journal of Psychoactive Drugs, 21*, 25–33. http://dx.doi.org/10.1080/02791072.1989.10472140

7

Conducting neuromarketing studies ethically-practitioner perspectives

David Hensel[1*], Ana Iorga[2], Lisa Wolter[3] and Judith Znanewitz[1]

*Corresponding author: David Hensel, Institute of Marketing, Helmut Schmidt University/University of the Federal Armed Forces Hamburg, Hamburg, Germany
E-mail: hensel@hsu-hh.de
Reviewing editor: Benny Briesemeister, Neurospective GmbH, Germany

Abstract: Understanding consumer behavior has always been a marketer's goal. No wonder that, with the emergence of consumer neuroscience, which promised to shed light into what made consumers tick, companies were attracted to this new field. A major downside of this promising field is that especially commercial studies have struggled in the past with ethical issues. This may be the effect of less transparent ethical standards in the business world compared to academia. The potential of neuromarketing can only be exploited effectively, if trust in the industry rises and this correlates strongly with ethical behavior. Therefore, guidelines for conducting ethical neuromarketing studies have already emerged, but have not been evaluated from a practitioner perspective so far. Hence, the aim of this study is first to check the validity of additionally developed ethical aspects that are supplementary to the NMSBA (Neuromarketing Science & Business Association) code of ethics, contained in the EGNM (Ethical Guideline In Neuromarketing) guideline by determining whether there is a consensus with the answers provided by neuromarketing practitioners. The second objective is to refine the ethical guideline with additional aspects which are relevant for practitioners. Interview data, collected from 10 neuromarketing practitioners, showed that all seven aspects are important when conducting neuromarketing studies. Furthermore, the results indicate five additional ethical aspects that should be considered.

ABOUT THE AUTHORS

David Hensel, Ana Iorga, Lisa Wolter, and Judith Znanewitz are (neuro)marketing specialists with a passion for applying science to marketing.

David Hensel has over 7 years of experience in both implicit and explicit market research. He is responsible for the advertising research of the employer brand Bundeswehr.

Ana Iorga has over 10 years of experience as an advertising professional and entrepreneur, and leads a full-service advertising agency. In 2012, she founded Buyer Brain, a consumer neuroscience research lab.

Lisa Wolter has over 10 years of experience in the field of media and brand management. She consults to companies in media strategy issues and is a founder of the Hamburg Media School.

Judith Znanewitz has over 5 years of experience in implicit and explicit market research. She is responsible for research and consulting for the internal and external employer branding strategy of the Bundeswehr.

PUBLIC INTEREST STATEMENT

Understanding consumer behavior has always been a marketing objective. No wonder that, with the emergence of consumer neuroscience, which promises to shed light into what made consumers tick, companies are attracted to this new field. The current paper looks at several ethical issues raised by neuromarketing research and analyzes the Ethics Guidelines available to date. It then proposes some potential improvements, based on original research presented in the paper and on previous findings. Among the issues discussed are the need to restrict stealth marketing, protect vulnerable respondent groups (like children or people with mental diseases) and the appropriateness of applying neuromarketing research to help industries that promote unhealthy behaviors and products, like tobacco and alcohol. Another aspect addressed in the paper refers to the varied approaches of different stakeholders in the neuromarketing industry (e.g. neuromarketing vendors or beneficiary companies), regarding ethical issues that have emerged in this field.

Subjects: Ethics of Research; Consumer Psychology; Cognitive Neuropsychology; Cognitive Neuroscience; Business Ethics; Marketing; Marketing Research; Consumer Behaviour

Keywords: consumer neuroscience; ethics; practical guidelines; neuromarketing code; NMSBA; business ethics; consumer neuroscience and neuromarketing

1. Introduction

In the last few years, most of the debates concerning neuromarketing and ethics have focused on the commercial use of neuromarketing. The main issues were consumer manipulation and the lack of transparency in this field (Fisher, Chin, & Klitzman, 2010). Another important ethical issue refers to shortfalls in consumer autonomy (Murphy, Illes, & Reiner, 2008). Ramsøy (2014) states "while academic researchers are, or should be well versed in ethics codes of conduct, this is often not the case for commercial uses of neuroscience" (p. 498). Because of the commercial nature of the studies, some people fear that the data collected could be used unethically (Satel & Lilienfeld, 2013). According to Satel and Lilienfeld (2013), "in 2011, a consortium of consumer protection groups filed a complaint with the Federal Trade Commission against Frito-Lay for allegedly using neuromarketing" in order to determine emotional and subconscious reactions that would help "promote high-fat snack food to teens" (p. 43). This demonstrates that conducting neuromarketing research poses several ethical issues that marketers need to take into account.

Therefore, academics and practitioners have called for the development of a regulatory ethical guideline in neuromarketing (Briesemeister, 2015; Ulman, Cakar, & Yildiz, 2015). Most of the existing ethics codes are rather general, which can be useful, but does not clarify certain issues that are important for marketers (Hensel, Wolter, & Znanewitz, 2016). Accordingly, Hensel et al. (2016) created an extended guideline, the "EGNM" (Ethical Guideline in Neuromarketing) of a common piece, the NMSBA (Neuromarketing Science & Business Association) Code of Ethics, which provides guidelines on conducting neuromarketing studies ethically. Based on both a literature and a market analysis, they identified and incorporated seven additional aspects concerning the implementation of neuromarketing studies in general.

Since neuromarketing is a very practical field, it is important to integrate the practitioners' point of view regarding the supplementary codes. Hence, the aim of this study is to refine and improve the EGNM guideline from Hensel et al. (2016) by looking for consensus with the answers provided by neuromarketing practitioners. Expert interviews helped the researchers to gather direct feedback and new directions at the same time. To this end, we held 10 semi-structured interviews with neuromarketing practitioners, discussing what is important from a business perspective when conducting neuromarketing studies.

The paper is structured as follows: First, we provide the conceptual background to the study, briefly analyzing the ethics of neuroscience in marketing research and practice. Next, we evaluate the consensus between EGNM guideline (Hensel et al., 2016) and expert answers from neuromarketing practitioners, furthermore refining the ethical guidelines with the findings from the expert interviews. We then provide a final discussion, draw some conclusions and outline avenues for future research in the field of neuromarketing ethics for business practice.

2. Code of ethics status quo in neuromarketing research

Both marketing professionals and academics highlight the importance of developing a regulatory framework that applies specifically to neuromarketing (Briesemeister, 2015; Ulman et al., 2015). Yet, few researchers have addressed this topic so far. Some of those who have done so, like Kimberly Clark, have argued that it is unlikely that potentially unethical practices will be deployed by scientists who call themselves neuromarketers. The ethical issues would most probably stem from the *commercial application* of established neuromarketing findings (Clark, 2016). A recent ethical guideline for conducting neuromarketing studies, the EGNM is provided by Hensel et al. (2016). The focus is on practitioners and not the scientific perspective, because, according to Ramsøy (2014) most ethical problems occur in business usage. This does not, however, inevitably exclude its use for (academic) neuroscientists. Hensel et al.'s (2016) EGNM is grounded in Roskies (2005) considerations on the ethics of neuroscience and extends the NMSBA Code of Ethics (2013) by integrating, *inter alia*, the five-star code of ethics from Murphy et al. (2008). Since neuromarketing technologies and tools are continually evolving, an ethical guideline in this field also needs ongoing improvements from both academics and practitioners. A regular update and discussion with hands-on neuromarketers, researchers, and organizations like the NMSBA is surely necessary in this dynamic environment. In this study, we focus on practitioners' improvements of the abovementioned guideline. Thus, this paper sheds light on the business perspective of using ethical guidelines in neuromarketing and closes with suggestions for further enhancing the current framework.

Several parties are involved in the neuromarketing research process—the beneficiary companies that commission the studies, the research agencies that carry them out, the participants involved and the general public. All of these stakeholders have different views on the ethical issues raised by neuromarketing research and it is therefore important to integrate the "big picture." Their various views are shaped according to their direct interests in the field (applicable for the first two categories) or to the image conveyed by mass media, which is valid for the participants and general public).

Pop, Dabija, and Iorga (2016) published a comparative analysis, looking at the results of several studies that they performed on different categories of stakeholders. The first study was conducted on companies from all over the world, working in the neuromarketing field (Pop, Dabija, & Iorga, 2014). The second study was of advertising agencies that use findings from neuromarketing research to create better and more efficient communication campaigns. The third study looked at the approach of beneficiary companies regarding the ethical issues raised by neuromarketing research.

Based on a literature review, De Oliveira, De Moura Engracia Giralid, Jabbour, Netto, and Betti (2015) discussed ethical issues within the field of neuromarketing research and developed a framework of ethical mapping. Furthermore, Olteanu (2015) focused on neuroimaging studies in particular and examined the issues for several involved parties, i.e. study participants and researchers. In this context, the Olteanu (2015) offers a guideline of 10 principles that neuromarketing practitioners should implement in neuroimaging research.

It is worth mentioning that none of the stakeholder groups considered neuromarketing to be an inherently unethical practice. However, the first study revealed that neuromarketing practitioners were concerned about their companies' reputation and the way media reported on the industry as a whole. The concern with media stemmed from the fact that journalists were often poorly informed about the scope or procedures of neuromarketing research and were focusing excessively on the manipulative side of the story (Pop et al., 2014). In their daily activities, the surveyed companies took into account the Ethical code issued by NMSBA and some of them had implemented internal conduct codes that were even more strict than external ones. They made sure that participants were fully informed, by providing them with a detailed description of the tools and procedures that were going to be used, and by requesting signed consent. Furthermore, collected data were anonymized and the databases containing raw data or results were not shared with third parties.

The second study performed by Pop et al. (2016) asked CEOs and managers of advertising agencies to compare neuromarketing to traditional research, in terms of efficiency and ethicality. Not surprisingly, twice as many advertisers thought of neuromarketing as more efficient than traditional research, whereas traditional research was seen as the more ethical of the two. An interesting finding is that some of the neuro tools are considered to raise fewer ethical issues than others. For example, people are more comfortable with the use of biometric recordings, facial coding, eye tracking, or implicit association, than with electroencephalography, galvanic skin response, or fMRI.

Advertisers were asked specifically what they think about the manipulative aspect of neuromarketing research. The unanimous attitude was that the ethical issues arise not from data collection, such as the tools and methodologies used when conducting research, but from the way that data are used. For example, they believed that it would be unethical to use neuromarketing to influence a political election.

The third category of stakeholders, which was studied by Pop et al. (2016) was represented by beneficiary companies—those buying neuromarketing research. It should first be mentioned that most companies have limited exposure to or experience with neuromarketing research. Therefore, their opinion is based heavily on the information acquired through different media channels, specialty books or websites. One interesting finding is that the research scope (be it academic or commercial) influences respondent perceptions of research ethicality. Scientific research is considered to be more ethical than its commercial counterpart. On the same note, respondents were more positive about the ethics of research aimed at solving social issues, like curing compulsive shopping or pathological addictions.

The conclusion emerging from the comparative analysis was that all commercial stakeholders bear a responsibility for making sure that their conduct complies with the ethical codes and that respondent rights and privacy are protected.

3. Theoretical framework

Neuroethics has evolved as a new and independent field, due to the ethical issues raised by brain research (Fuchs, 2006). The term was first used in 2002 by William Safire (Sebastian, 2014), and subsequently, different authors describe neuroethics in different ways. Illes and Bird (2006), for example, believe that neuroethics should deal with the social, legal, and ethical issues raised by neuroscience research. A different view is that of Gazzaniga (2006), for whom neuroethics should be concerned with the way society deals with issues like the philosophy of life and lifestyle, or fatality and illness, based on prior knowledge about how the brain works.

Ethical issues are classified by Murphy et al. (2008) into two groups: (1) protection of various parties who may be harmed or exploited by the research, marketing, and deployment of neuromarketing and (2) protection of consumer autonomy if neuromarketing reaches a critical level of effectiveness. Hensel et al. (2016) go further and identify five angles within the two groups: (1) *protection of research subjects*, (2) *protection of vulnerable populations from marketing exploitation*, (3) *full disclosure of goals, risks, and benefits*, (4) *accurate media and marketing representation*, and (5) *internal and external scientific validity*. This code builds the basis for the expert interview guideline in this study and is summarized in the following section.

3.1. Protection of research subjects

Several aspects are taken into consideration when looking at the protection of test participants. One of them deals with the management of incidental results or clinical findings that are not directly related to the objective of the research. Other aspects look at the impact of high incentives on respondents, at the procedures in place to ensure informed consent and respondents' rights (e.g. the right to unilaterally terminate a study) (Murphy et al., 2008).

3.2. Protection of vulnerable niche populations from marketing exploitation

Another sensitive ethical issue raised by neuromarketing research deals with communicating with and protecting niche populations, such as young children or teenagers that may not be able to protect themselves when faced with advertising messages perfected using neuroscience (Murphy et al., 2008). Pop et al. (2016) argue that targeting these groups with messages that promote unhealthy habits (like smoking or eating sweets), is less ethical than prompting adults with the same messages, as the former in particular, lack the power to resist persuasive messages and to refrain from acting on them.

Table 1. Seven additional codes by Hensel et al. (2016)

Additional ethical codes	Neuromarketing code of ethics from Murphy et al. (2008)				
	1. Research subjects	2. Vulnerable populations	3. Full disclosure	4. Accurate representation	5. Scientific validity
Incentives should be appropriate to avoid distortions of participants' behavior	x				
Prevent manipulation of consumer behavior ("stealth marketing")		x			
Protect vulnerable groups (e.g. elderly, infants, disabled) from marketing exploitation		x			
Participation of vulnerable groups (e.g. disabled, adolescents, elderly) should be subject to particular care	x				
Debriefing in case of covert data collection/incomplete disclosure			x		
Disclosure of tools and measurement scales when possible				x	
Ensure detailed rules for acting ethically with respect to communication of neuromarketing results				x	

3.3. Full disclosure of goals, risks, and benefits
When conducting a neuromarketing project, researchers should transparently communicate the procedures they have in place, including written materials and verbal commands, which ensure that they comply with the ethical standards adopted by the industry (Murphy et al., 2008).

3.4. Accurate media and marketing representation
Disclosing the methodology and measurements used in a neuromarketing research is of considerable importance (Murphy et al., 2008), especially in the business environment, where methodological transparency and metrics' validity are truly essential. Transparency and validity are important not only for business interactions, but also for building trust among the general public and to "promote the development of effective technologies" (p. 299).

3.5. Internal and external scientific validity
Validity becomes extremely important when using neuroscience research in industries that do not have a formal watchdog, like the Food and Drug Administration (FDA) (Eaton & Illes, 2007). "There are challenges in initial and sustained product validity in the commercialization of any marketing product influenced by neuromarketing research" (Murphy et al., 2008, p. 299).

The EGNM delivers, *inter alia*, an overview of ethical challenges for practitioners. This is achieved by expanding the NMSBA Code of Ethics (2013) with seven additional aspects and a systematization based on the five star code of ethics (see Table 1).

Hensel et al. (2016) stated *inter alia* that the identified seven codes should be additionally reflected on by practitioners. Therefore, these findings were checked by means of expert interviews and investigated by the authors, the results of which are presented in the following section. The EGNM will be further developed with the interview findings.

4. Methodological framework
Due to the lack of research in the field of neuromarketing on ethical guidelines, we conducted an exploratory, qualitative study. The approach is useful for further developing existing theory on ethical aspects in the field of neuromarketing and to generate new theoretical insights in this research

area, by gathering data and information on unexpected aspects. Qualitative data allows for an open-ended approach, which is needed to answer exploratory questions like those of our research (Graebner, Martin, & Roundy, 2012; Pratt, 2009). We interviewed 10 experts who have in-depth knowledge of neuromarketing practices through their daily work, in order to explore the general dynamics and characteristics of ethical aspects in conducting neuromarketing studies. Their varying experiences with different neuromarketing studies allow generalizations to be made, as well as the identification of differences and similarities between individual experiences. A close examination of interviewees' personal interpretations and experiences is enabled by the qualitative approach of using interviews (Denzin & Lincoln, 2011), which yields a rich and nuanced description (Weick, 2007). Consequently, a qualitative approach helps to focus on additional ethical aspects that should be considered in neuromarketing studies and that entail a new ethical code for such studies.

5. Research context and sample

To provide substantial insight into ethical aspects of conducting neuromarketing studies, we interviewed 10 practitioners, assuming that they had a certain level of expertise due to their work and experience, and with very different backgrounds, in order to maximize the diversity of opinions. They comprise founders, directors, and research officers of international (neuro)marketing companies conducting neuromarketing studies (see Table 2).

These representatives are selected in order to ensure the replicability of the findings and to extend our theoretical framework (Eisenhardt & Graebner, 2007). Their experience with and knowledge of neuromarketing studies gives them the capacity to provide detailed insights into ethical aspects in practice, and to make meaningful generalizations. We thus attempt to minimize bias caused by impression management or retrospective sense-making by "using numerous and highly knowledgeable informants who view the focal phenomena from diverse perspectives" (Eisenhardt & Graebner, 2007, p. 28), The insights of the different interviewees allow us to compare their experiences, in order to find similarities and differences between them (Yin, 2014). According to a theoretical sampling strategy, we chose the interviewees for "theoretical" reasons, instead of sampling interviewees from a chosen population (Eisenhardt, 1989a). They were selected according to working experience and position within their companies and the possibility of carrying out a personal interview. We preferred personal interviews in order to create a trustful atmosphere, in which interviewees are usually more willing to give insights into a sensitive issue such as ethics (Jehn & Jonsen, 2010).

Table 2. Overview of position and experience of our interview partners

Position	Academic degree	Experience
Founder and Joint Managing Director	PhD in Psychology	Active in the field of neuromarketing for 10 years
Co-Founder and Chief Research Officer	PhD Psychological & Brain Sciences	Active in the field of neuromarketing for 16 years
Chief Operating Officer and CEO	Master of Business Administration	Active in the field of marketing for 25 years and in the field of neuromarketing for 6 years
Founder and joint Managing Director	PhD in Psychology	Active in the field of neuromarketing for 10 years
Founder and Managing Director	PhD in Computer Science	Active in the field of neuromarketing for 14 years
Founder and Owner	PhD in Psychology	Active in the field of neuromarketing for 5 years
Scientific/Academic Director and CEO	PhD in Germanic Philology	Active in the field of marketing for 30 years
Marketing consultant	MS in International Business and Management Development	Active in the field of marketing for 15 years
Head of Consumer Research	PhD in Economics	Active in the field of neuromarketing since 6 years
Head of Strategy	Master of Science in Management	Active in the field of neuromarketing for 7 years

6. Data collection and analysis

The qualitative study was based on data gathered from semi-structured interviews with neuromarketing practitioners. The interviews took 30–60 min and were conducted over a period of three months. Semi-structured interviews enabled us to ask a standard set of questions, but also allow to reactions according to the responses of the interviewees. The questionnaire was drawn up by the authors, referring to their earlier analysis of ethical challenges in neuromarketing (Hensel et al., 2016). There were 17 questions in total and the interviewees were instructed to answer the questions according to their experiences and views. The first phase of the interviews included four open-ended questions, in order to obtain background information about the interviewees and their professional experience in the field of neuromarketing. Thirteen more open-ended questions were posed in the second phase of the interviews, so as to explore general ethical aspects in conducting neuromarketing studies, the practical relevance of the five-star code of ethics by Murphy et al. (2008) and the neuromarketing tool-based view of ethical aspects.

The interviews were transcribed and anonymized. Data analysis followed procedures recommended by Corbin and Strauss (2015) and Miles, Huberman, and Saldana (2014). According to the structure of the interview questions, interviews and documents were coded with both *in*ductively and *de*ductively developed codes. If an interview passage could not be assigned under one of the codes, a new code was created. All interviews were coded by following the scheme that resulted from an inductively and deductively code construction. The analysis focused on structuring and summarizing the interview material. At the beginning, we analyzed each interview separately. Afterward we compared the interviews across the categories to identify differences and similarities (Eisenhardt, 1989b). This resulted, firstly, in the identification of the seven ethical aspects of the EGNM by Hensel et al. (2016) and, secondly, in the identification of additional ethical aspects. In sum, the data were analyzed iteratively, switching between the qualitative data and an emerging structure of theoretical arguments (Corbin & Strauss, 2015; Miles et al., 2014).

Our research context was selected as a theoretically relevant case for the following reasons (Eisenhardt, 1989a):

- Academics and practitioners call for regulatory ethical guidelines in neuromarketing (Briesemeister, 2015; Ulman et al., 2015).
- Hensel et al. (2016) stated that, *inter alia*, the seven identified ethical codes should be additionally investigated by practitioners.
- Neuromarketing Ethical Codes are still in their infancy.

7. Results

7.1. Confirmation of the seven additional codes by Hensel et al. (2016)

Hensel et al. (2016) identified seven additional ethical codes (see Table 1). All additional ethical codes were identified in the interviews with the practitioners. Table 3 provides an overview of the additional codes, with selected illustrative quotes, extracted from the interview data.

7.2. Five additional codes evaluated in interviews

Furthermore, five additional ethical aspects were extracted from the interview data. The following Table 4 provides an overview.

8. Discussion

8.1. Discussion of the seven additional codes from Hensel et al. (2016)

Hensel et al. (2016) developed seven additional ethical codes for conducting neuromarketing studies for practitioners. The relevance of these additional codes is supported by their presence in the expert interviews. The first additional code is about determining the correct number of incentives for

Table 3. Additional codes and selected verification interview quotes

Seven additional codes by Hensel et al. (2016)	Illustrative quotes
Code 1: Incentives should be appropriate to avoid distortions of participants' behavior	According to their participation, participants are [...] given fair compensation for their time
Code 2: Prevent manipulation of consumer behavior ("stealth marketing")	I would say that an ethical problem is that one could probably implicitly push underneath something or that the study could be used to develop advertisements, which is so tricky, it will seduce us into buying something that we usually wouldn't
Code 3: Protect vulnerable groups (e.g. elderly, infants, disabled) from marketing exploitation	In cases that involve minors, we only take on projects that foster the betterment of their mental or physical well-being
Code 4: Participation of vulnerable groups (e.g. disabled, adolescents, elderly) should be subject to particular care	When children are involved, we obtain consent by parental proxy
Code 5: Debriefing in case of covert data collection/incomplete disclosure	Given the nature of the data we collect, it is a pleasure to personally debrief participants on our studies
	Generally stated, we debrief all participants in lay terms and answer all questions to the best of our ability
	Following their participation, participants are debriefed on the nature of the research question [...]
Code 6: Disclosure of tools and measurement scales when possible	Even the algorithms we use are public available information, because we obtain these algorithms from reputable scientific sources. We only utilize neuromarketing tools when we are absolutely convinced that they are scientifically based and have been proven by independent parties. As such, everything we do has already been completely documented and is from published sources
	We only use equipment and protocols that have been validated by the scientific community
Code 7: Ensure detailed rules for acting ethically with respect to communication of neuromarketing results	The real ethical problems in our business are the overpromises (and even lies) of companies and/or "neuro TV evangelists," who cause great harm to our industry. [...] Many people without experience in marketing and with no neurology knowledge are conducting research and doing business consulting

Table 4. Five additional codes from neuromarketing practitioners' interviews

Additional aspects	Illustrative quotes
Sufficient sample size for neuromarketing studies	This is a way to ensure validity and in general, to conduct data collection correctly for the target group and a sufficient number of cases
	We need at least 20 data points to draw a valid conclusion. This is the minimum amount of data points for scientific studies
Specific quality check of neuromarketing data	We actually go through each individual data-set manually and look at the data quality, correct for artifacts, etc., in order to reach the highest possible level of data quality
No NM for optimization of "unhealthy" products (e.g. tobacco or alcohol industry) (especially with respect to youth customers)	We would never run studies that could endanger the health of people. For example, we have never managed studies for the tobacco Industry
	Cigarettes, by which people harm themselves, or alcohol. Where it would help the tobacco companies to influence even more young people, so that more start smoking and harm themselves or even die younger. This is all highly ethically problematic
No use of non-scientific methods	From our point of view, the use of Toy Tools and this associated nonprofessional issue are the real ethical problem in our business
	First and foremost, we only work with equipment that meets scientific standards. We do not use any toy EEGs, no cheap eye trackers or things which you can somehow have huge accuracy drifts from
	Only use the ones validated by the scientific field of neuroscience
Conducted by neuroscientists for studies with complex methods (e.g. fMRI)	[...] EEG, Eye tracking and fMRI with neuroscientist's guide
	All our studies are conducted by neuroscientists and can be checked by any neurologist or marketing expert

participating in a study. The level of incentives should be appropriate to avoid distortions of participant response behavior. The undue influence of (excessively high) incentives for participating on the validity of the study is also mentioned by Murphy et al. (2008) and Ulman et al. (2015); it could, for example, result in indirect coercion of the research subject. Several experts mentioned this issue in their interview.

The second additional code concerns the prevention of consumer behavior manipulation ("stealth marketing"). Nowadays, such stealth neuromarketing is not really possible with current neuroscience technology (*despite speculation along these lines in the media*) (Loiacono, 2009). But someday, advanced technology in neuroscience might enable corporations to influence consumer behavior without their awareness of the manipulation (Murphy et al., 2008). If this scenario does arise in the future, the application of "stealth marketing" should be restricted, especially with respect to specific advanced neuroscience tools. Concerns about an (excessively) effective technological advance of neuroscience tools in neuromarketing practice, is also reflected in the interviews with practitioners and should be regulated by an ethical code as early as possible.

The next two additional codes apply to protection from marketing exploitation (code No. 3) and particular care in participation (code No. 4) of vulnerable groups (e.g. elderly, disabled, infants, and adolescents[1]). The participation of children and physically or mentally disabled persons in neuromarketing studies should be regulated, at least through requiring informed consent from their legal guardian. Especially the participation and protection of children is mentioned in most of the interviews. Children represent a sensitive population that can be easily manipulated. Their neural inhibitory mechanisms are not yet mature, so that they find it extremely difficult to refrain from using products that appeal to them, the moment they want them. Therefore, neuromarketing companies are not encouraged to perform research on young children, as they would be helping advertisers take advantage of their lack of sophisticated reasoning and self-control. Some practitioners generally refuse to have anything do with neuromarketing studies with children. Other interview partners demand informed consent from their legal guardian when doing research on children. One interview partner only, conducts neuromarketing studies with children and only in presence of their legal guardian.

Additional code No. 5 is about debriefing the participants when research design does not allow fully informing the participants in advance. A proper debriefing informs the participants about the purpose of the research and why deception was necessary and legitimate. The American Psychological Association (APA) recommends leaving the participant with a positive attitude (American Psychological Association, 2010, code 8.03). The interviewed practitioners confirmed the issue with research designs which often do not allow the briefing of participants in advance (e.g. for unaffected brand knowledge). But *de*briefing the participants after a study was conducted by nearly all of the interviewed practitioners.

The sixth and seventh additional codes are related to the disclosure of tools and measurement scales, and the communication of the neuromarketing results. The companies' fear of making premature claims about the predictive power of neuroscience for consumer behavior, is reported by Fisher et al. (2010). They analyzed 16 neuromarketing companies and only 13 of them described their methodology. In many cases, the descriptions were insufficient to determine what was being done. Therefore, Fisher et al. (2010) did not find much evidence that neuromarketing works or is effective on the basis of the studies included. This could be prevented, if private companies were to publish their methodology and results. This was a controversial issue in the interviews with the practitioners. On the one hand, they confirm that their methodology and measures are fully published and validated by the scientific community. But on the other hand, also confirmed in the interviews, their unique, specialist knowledge about the methodology and measures gives the companies a competitive advantage on the market and, therefore, will not be fully disclosed. Accordingly, the disclosure of tools and measurement scales refers to a controversial ethical code for neuromarketing practice. Neuromarketing should strike a balance between the scientific way of fully disclosing the tools used in the studies and the need for competitive advantage through (proprietary) company knowledge. But too little transparency does not support the overall neuromarketing industry, and prevents a rapid adoption of probably helpful knowledge.

Further on, one expert noted that he does not see an ethical problem in neuromarketing and that he could not make up his mind about the topic until now. This shows the importance of integrating practitioners into the discussion to stimulate their ethical thinking.

8.2. Discussion of the five additional codes evaluated in interviews

8.2.1. Sufficient sample size for neuromarketing studies

The sample size used in neuromarketing studies has been subject to ongoing debate, with supporters of traditional research complaining that neuromarketers use small sample sizes which are insufficiently large to draw valid conclusions. One of the main sampling differences between neuromarketing and traditional research is that the former does not require a representative sample for the whole population. This is the case because, in neuromarketing research, the subgroups to be studied are defined prior to starting the actual study, based on demographic or behavioral criteria that are relevant for the objectives of the study. According to Genco, Pohlmann, and Steidl (2013), neuromarketing studies that record brain activity can be run within smaller sample sizes, as the random noise in brain measurements is not as high as in survey responses. This is consistent with the findings of Sands (2009), that the optimum sample size for EEG research is around 30–40 people.

The sample size depends on the tools or techniques employed—brain measurements require fewer respondents, while studies performed with facial coding or implicit association would benefit from a larger sample size. When designing a neuromarketing study, it is advisable to plan for some extra respondents, just in case some of the data needs to be discarded, or some of the respondents quit during the process. Also, there needs to be a balance between the costs of recruitment and data collection and the incremental benefit of increasing the sample size. Last but not least, how the sample is chosen is equally important, as a large sample from a biased population will be as worthless as a sample that is simply too small.

8.2.2. Specific quality check of neuromarketing data

GIGO is a widely used concept in computing and mathematics—it stands for “garbage in, garbage out.” This couldn’t be more true, as far as neuromarketing research is concerned—if the data used as input is not appropriately cleaned and processed, the results cannot be trusted.

Another challenge regarding the quality of the recorded data derives from the fact that in neuromarketing research, one works with small samples (see above discussion). Therefore, researchers need to check the quality of the recordings during the data collection phase—pay attention to the sensors, in order to notice any potential malfunction, instruct respondents to follow the instructions and not engage in a behavior that could jeopardize the process (move or speak during the recording), as that will reduce the accuracy of data available for analysis.

This aspect ties in nicely with the issue discussed above about the sample size, where one needs to make sure that there are enough respondents to allow for discarding collected data, if required.

8.2.3. No neuromarketing studies for optimizating “unhealthy” products (e.g. tobacco or alcohol industry) (especially with respect to youth customers)

The NMSBA Code of Ethics does not explicitly ban neuromarketing vendors from working for potentially controversial industries, like tobacco, alcohol, or politics. Therefore, it is up to the industry players to impose self-regulating policies that prevent the use of consumer insights gained through neuromarketing research on those potentially harmful groups. In the last few years, NMSBA community members have expressed their interest in updating the Ethical Code, so as to better reflect the industry values and establish a balance between their economic interests and external ethical pressures (Clark, 2016).

8.2.4. No use of non-scientific methods

There is a lot of hype around neuromarketing research and the rapid advancement of technology plays an important role in maintaining that hype. That occurs because technology vendors are eager to be the first to get their tools on the market and increase their market share, sometimes at the expense of sound scientific principles and practices. Therefore, when choosing between different tools or technologies, one needs to take into consideration publications and third-party assessments of those particular tools.

8.2.5. Conducted by neuroscientists for studies with complex methods (e.g. fMRI)

Neuromarketing companies initially developed around neuroscientists who were working in universities and had access to medical equipment and data analysis software. As the field attracted more attention, and decision-makers from the business world started to understood its commercial potential, more and more companies jumped on the bandwagon. Nowadays, most neuromarketing vendors employ neuroscientists either as full time staff or consultants. One of their roles is to ensure that the claims and findings extrapolated from brain recordings are grounded in science and that salespeople do not get carried away in promising clients that they can solve all manner of problems with neuromarketing research.

9. Conclusion and outlook

The aim of our study was to check recent codes, especially that from Hensel et al. (2016) for consensus with the answers of neuromarketing practitioners, with the aim of refining them with additional relevant aspects. The paper was based on a qualitative study, interviewing 10 experts about their experiences with ethical aspects of neuromarketing studies.

We consider the recent aspects raised by Hensel et al. (2016) as relevant for marketing practitioners, as all experts mentioned the additional codes from Hensel et al. (2016): *fair level of incentives, restriction of stealth marketing, protection and participation of vulnerable groups, debriefing of participants, disclosure of tools/measurement scales and accurate communication of the results*. This conformity validates the relevance to these ethical aspects, also from a neuromarketing practitioner perspective. Furthermore, we extracted five additional ethical aspects: *A sufficient sample size for neuromarketing studies*, the *need for a specific quality check of neuroscientific data, no neuromarketing studies for optimizing "unhealthy" products*, e.g. tobacco or alcohol industry, especially with respect to youth customers), and particularly *the problem of using non-scientific tools and methods in neuromarketing*.

Such a study is not without limitations. First of all, we only interviewed neuromarketing practitioner experts on this topic. Interviews with academic researchers about ethical aspects would also be useful, because of the close relationship between neuromarketing and neuroeconomics. There is, thus, also potential for interdisciplinary research. This again leads to a future study path, which should shed light on the academic perspective in the field. Another limitation is the sample size, which is caused by the qualitative nature of the given expert interview approach. After the qualitative identification of the five new codes as next, a quantitative approach would be necessary to confirm these findings (Graebner et al., 2012). Besides the perspective of users, be they academic or practical, the view of participants also needs to be taken into account when developing an integrated guideline.

Funding
The authors received no direct funding for this research.

Competing Interests
The authors declare no competing interest.

Author details

David Hensel[1]
E-mail: hensel@hsu-hh.de
Ana Iorga[2]
E-mail: ana@buyerbrain.com
Lisa Wolter[3]
E-mail: l.wolter@hamburgmediaschool.com
Judith Znanewitz[1]
E-mail: znanewitz@hsu-hh.de
[1] Institute of Marketing, Helmut Schmidt University/University of the Federal Armed Forces Hamburg, Hamburg, Germany.
[2] Buyer Brain, Bucharest, Romania.
[3] Hamburg Media School, Hamburg, Germany.

Note

1. Adolescence extends into the early 20s (Steinberg, 2002) and their participation should be regulated, because of their biological vulnerability (Pechmann, Levine, Loughlin, & Leslie, 2005). Adolescents are fundamentally different from adults in terms of impulsivity, "planfulness," and sensitivity to peer influence (Johnson & Giedd, 2015). The brain system of adolescents underlies different conditions to those of adults. Their frontal lobe and amygdala are still under construction (Durston et al., 2001). Furthermore, some researchers believe that adolescents' reward system (limbic system) is more reactive than adults' (Galvan et al., 2006). Furthermore, the connection between frontal lobe and amygdala is incomplete. Thus, the frontal lobe exerts less control over the amygdala, and exerts less influence over emotions and behavior than a fully mature frontal lobe of adults. In most cases, adolescents have less influence over emotions and behavior than fully mature adults (American Medical Association, 2005).

References

American Medical Association. (2005). *Brief of the American medical association, American psychiatric association, American society for adolescent psychiatry, American academy of child and adolescent psychiatry, American academy of psychiatry and the law, national association of social workers, Missouri chapter of the national association of social workers, and national mental health association as Amici Curiae in support of respondent.* Retrieved from https://www.aacap.org/App_Themes/AACAP/docs/Advocacy/amicus_curiae/Roper_v_Simmons.pdf

American Psychological Association. (2010). *Ethical principles of psychologists and code of conduct.* Retrieved from http://www.apa.org/ethics/code/principles.pdf

Briesemeister, B. (2015). *Discover-neuro.de.* Retrieved from http://discover-neuro.de/

Clark, K. R. (2016). Dealing with the devils. The responsibility of neuromarketing practitioners in conducting research for ethically bubious client agendas in neuromarketing research. In A. R. Thomas, N. A. Pop, A. M. Iorga, & C. Ducu (Eds.), *Ethics and neuromarketing - implications for market research and business practice* (pp. 147–156). Switzerland: Springer. doi: 10.1007/978-3-319-45609-6_9

Corbin, J., & Strauss, A. (2015). *Basics of qualitative research: Techniques and procedures for developing grounded theory* (4th ed.). Thousand Oaks, CA: Sage.

De Oliveira, J. H. C., De Moura Engracia Giralid, J., Jabbour, C. J. C., Netto, C. F., & Betti, K. C. M. (2015). Improving business innovation and research through the application of neuromarketing with ethics: A framework. *International Journal of Business Innovation and Research, 9*, 52–64. doi:10.1504/IJBIR.2015.065953

Denzin, N. K., & Lincoln, Y. S. (2011). Introduction. The discipline and practice of qualitative research. In N. Denzin & Y. Lincoln (Eds.), *The Sage handbook of qualitative research* (pp. 1–15). Thousand Oaks, CA: Sage.

Durston, S., Hulshoff Pol, H. E., Casey, B. J., Giedd, J. N., Buitelaar, J. K., & Van Engeland, H. (2001). Anatomical MRI of the developing human brain: What have we learned? *Journal of the American Academy of Child and Adolescent Psychiatry, 40*, 1012–1020. doi:10.1097/00004583-200109000-00009.

Eaton, M. L., & Illes, J. (2007). Commercializing cognitive neurotechnology - the ethical terrain. *Nature Biotechnology, 25*, 393–397. doi:10.1038/nbt0407-393

Eisenhardt, K. M. (1989a). Building theories from case study research. *Academy of Management Review, 14*, 532–550. doi:10.5465/AMR.1989.4308385

Eisenhardt, K. M. (1989b). Making fast strategic decisions in high-velocity environments. *Academy of Management Journal, 32*, 543–576. doi:10.2307/256434.

Eisenhardt, K. M., & Graebner, M. E. (2007). Theory building from cases: Opportunities and challenges. *Academy of Management Journal, 50*, 25–32. doi:10.5465/AMJ.2007.24160888

Fisher, C. E., Chin, L., & Klitzman, R. (2010). Defining neuromarketing: Practices and professional challenges. *Harvard Review of Psychiatry, 18*, 230–237. doi:10.3109/10673229.2010.496623

Fuchs, T. (2006). Ethical issues in neuroscience. *Current opinion in psychiatry, 19*, 600–607. doi:10.1097/01.yco.0000245752.75879.26

Galvan, A., Hare, T. A., Parra, C. E., Penn, J., Voss, H., Glover, G., & Casey, B. J. (2006). Earlier development of the accumbens relative to orbitofrontal cortex might underlie risk-taking behavior in adolescents. *Journal of Neuroscience, 26*, 6885–6892. doi:10.1523/JNEUROSCI.1062-06.2006

Gazzaniga, M. S. (2006). *The ethical brain: The science of our moral dilemmas.* New York, NY: Harper Perennial.

Graebner, M. E., Martin, J. A., & Roundy, P. T. (2012). Qualitative data: Cooking without a recipe. *Strategic Organization, 10*, 276–284. doi:10.1177/1476127012452821

Genco, S. J., Pohlmann, A. P., & Steidl, P. (2013). *Neuromarketing for dummies.* Canada: John Wiley & Sons.

Hensel, D., Wolter, L., & Znanewitz, J. (2016). A guideline for ethical aspects in conducting neuromarketing studies. In A. R. Thomas, N. A. Pop, A. M. Iorga, & C. Ducu (Eds.), *Ethics and neuromarketing - implications for market research and business practice* (pp. 65–87). Switzerland: Springer. doi:10.1007/978-3-319-45609-6_4

Illes, J., & Bird, S. J. (2006). Neuroethics: a modern context for ethics in neuroscience. *Trends in Neurosciences, 29*, 511–517. doi:10.1016/j.tins.2006.07.002

Jehn, K. A., & Jonsen, K. (2010). A multimethod approach to the study of sensitive organizational issues. *Journal of Mixed Methods Research, 4*, 313–341. doi:10.1177/1558689810380920

Johnson, S. B., & Giedd, J. N. (2015). Normal brain development and child/adolescent policy. In J. Clausen & N. Levy (Eds.), *Handbook of neuroethics* (pp. 1721–1735). New York, NY: Springer. doi:10.1007/978-94-007-4707-4_148

Loiacono, C. (2009). *Can brain science manipulate consumers?* Retrieved from http://news.ubc.ca/2009/04/02/archive-ubcreports-2009-09apr02-manipulate/

Miles, M. B., Huberman, A. M., & Saldana, J. (2014). *Qualitative data analsyis. A methods sourcebook* (3rd ed.). Thousand Oaks, CA: Sage.

Murphy, E. R., Illes, J., & Reiner, P. B. (2008). Neuroethics of neuromarketing. *Journal of Consumer Behaviour, 7*, 293–302. doi:10.1002/cb.252

NMSBA. (2013). *NMSBA code of ethics.* Retrieved from http://www.neuromarketing-association.com/ethics

Olteanu, M. D. B. (2015). Neuroethics and responsibility in conducting neuromarketing research. *Neuroethics, 8*, 191–202. doi:10.1007/s12152-014-9227-y

Pechmann, C., Levine, L., Loughlin, S., & Leslie, F. (2005). Impulsive and self-conscious: adolescents' vulnerability to advertising and promotion. *Journal of Public Policy & Marketing, 24*, 202–221. doi:10.1509/jppm.2005.24.2.202

Pop, N. A., Dabija, D.-C., & Iorga, A. M. (2014). Ethical responsibility of neuromarketing companies in harnessing the market research - a global exploratory approach. *Amfiteatru Economic, 16*, 26–40. Retrieved from https://ssrn.com/abstract=2579933

Pop, N. A., Dabija, D.-C., & Iorga, A. M. (2016). Ethical considerations regarding stakeholders in neuromarketing research. In A. R. Thomas, N. A. Pop, A. M. Iorga, & C. Ducu (Eds.), *Ethics and Neuromarketing: Implications for Market Research and Business* (pp. 123–146). Switzerland: Springer. https://doi.org/10.1007/978-3-319-45609-6_8

Pratt, M. G. (2009). From the editors: For the lack of a boilerplate: Tips on writing up (and reviewing) qualitative research. *Academy of Management Journal, 52*, 856–862. doi:10.5465/AMJ.2009.44632557

Ramsøy, T. Z. (Ed.). (2014). *Selected Readings in Consumer Neuroscience & Neuromarketing* (2nd ed.). Rørvig: Neurons Inc.

Roskies, A. L. (2005). A case study of neuroethics: The nature of moral judgment. In J. Illes (Ed.), *Neuroethics: Defining the issues in theory, practice, and policy* (pp. 17–32). Oxford: Oxford University Press. doi:10.1093/acprof:oso/9780198567219.003.0002

Sands, S. (2009). *Sample size analysis for brainwave collection (EEG) methodologies*. Retrieved from http://www.sandsresearch.com/assets/white-paper.pdf

Satel, S., & Lilienfeld, S. (2013). *Brainwashed - the seductive appeal of mindless neuroscience*. Retrieved from http://reports-archive.adm.cs.cmu.edu/anon/2005/CMU-CS-05-151.pdf

Sebastian, V. (2014). Neuromarketing and neuroethics. *Procedia - Social and Behavioral Sciences, 127*, 763–768. doi:10.1016/j.sbspro.2014.03.351

Steinberg, L. D. (2002). *Adolescence*. Boston, MA: McGrawHill.

Ulman, Y. I., Cakar, T., & Yildiz, G. (2015). Ethical issues in neuromarketing: "I Consume, Therefore I am!". *Science and Engineering Ethics, 21*, 1271–1284. doi:10.1007/s11948-014-9581-5

Weick, K. E. (2007). The generative properties of richness. *Academy of Management Journal, 50*, 14–19. doi:10.5465/AMJ.2007.24160637

Yin, R. K. (2014). *Case study research: Design and methods* (5th ed.). Thousand Oaks, CA: Sage.

8

Preventing falls in older adults: Can improving cognitive capacity help?

Joseph E. Robinson[1]* and John Kiely[1]

*Corresponding author: Joseph E. Robinson, School of Sport and Wellbeing, Institute of Coaching and Performance, University of Central Lancashire, Preston, Lancashire PR1 2HE, UK

E-mail: jrobinson5@uclan.ac.uk

Reviewing editor: Peter Walla, University of Newcastle, Australia

Abstract: Evidence linking physical health with beneficial cognitive outcomes is well established. However, the potential bi-directional nature of this relationship is far less explored. Falls-related injuries are frequently caused by age-related deterioration of walking gait, and cost the NHS in Britain ~£1 billion per annum. Interventions capable of reducing falls risk are significantly beneficial from both health and economical perspectives. In recent years, evidence has emerged suggesting that the cognitive capacity required for executive function and motor stabilisation share a fundamentally limited pool of neural resources. In tandem, research suggesting that computer-based cognitive training can—via neuro-plastic mechanisms—stimulate executive function enhancements. Subsequently, this suggests the possibility that cognitive training can positively impact motor control functions, such as walking gait. Thereby raising the potential that movement coordination may be enhanced through cognitive training interventions. This novel perspective is just beginning to be explored within the literature, and some intriguing evidence already exists. Accordingly, the objective of this discussion is to review the rationale and evidence underpinning the suggested linkage between cognitive resources and walking gait and to suggest how such interventions could provide novel, impactful and financially efficient practical applications for reducing the fall risk in older adults.

Subjects: Motor Control and Development; Physical Activity and Health; Motor Skills; Cognitive Science; Cognitive Development

Keywords: cognitive training; cognitive capacity; walking gait; falls

ABOUT THE AUTHOR

Joseph E. Robinson is a doctoral student at University of Central Lancashire, following completion of BSc (Hons) and MSc degrees on Sport and Exercise Science. He works for a family business promoting healthy and active lifestyles for the over 60s. He works on a day-to-day basis to develop the company and has created eLearning courses for CPD of exercise instructors. His interest in cognitive and physical function of older adults stemmed from his professional work. Hence, he is keen to ensure his research has a practical application to enhance the quality of life of this demographic. He aims to complete his PhD in 2017 and continue to research this area of science.

PUBLIC INTEREST STATEMENT

Physical activity and exercise has been widely accepted as beneficial for both physical and cognitive function. Interestingly, recent research has shown that this link could potentially work reciprocally. Certain cognitive functions, called executive functions have been linked to physical actions such as one's walking gait. This suggests that interventions to improve cognition could also improve associated physical functions. Clearly, this holds significant potential to benefit quality of life for those whose cognitive and physical abilities are in decline, such as older adults. Furthermore, falls-related injuries cost the UK NHS in excess £1 billion per annum hence any intervention able to reduce the risk of falling holds significant economic benefit. This article will investigate this premise further and present evidence to discuss the potential of such interventions.

1. Introduction

It is well known that in order to achieve and maintain physical health, one must partake in regular physical activity. With regard to promoting health and preventing disease in older adults (65 years and over) The American College of Sports Medicine (ACSM) and American Heart Association (AHA) recommends 30 min of moderate-intensity aerobic activity five times a week, or 20 min of vigorous-intensity aerobic activity three times a week, in addition to muscle-strengthening exercises at least twice a week (Nelson et al., 2007). In addition to this a meta-analysis of studies published between 1966 and 2001 revealed a significant positive effect of physical exercise on cognitive function in older adults (Colcombe & Kramer, 2003). Psychosocial benefits of physical exercise have also been reported in the literature (Taylor et al., 2004).

However, whether a bi-directional relationship exists is less clear as the potential consequences of cognitive training on physical function, such as walking, are far less prevalent within the literature. However, there is emerging evidence of a link between executive brain functions and walking gait, which holds potential for a novel approach to enhancing physical function through cognitive training. Accordingly, the aims of this article are to:

(1) Present current knowledge on physical and cognitive exercise and the functional interaction between them.
(2) Review emerging evidence surrounding cognition, cognitive training and walking gait, specifically in older adults.
(3) Suggest a logical conceptual framework explaining why cognitive training might improve walking gait.

2. Current knowledge: Physical exercise for physical and cognitive function

Adults over 50 years of age represent the most sedentary segment of the adult population, with 88% of over 65s living with at least one chronic health condition (King, Rejeski, & Buchner, 1998). Both low- (40–60% VO_{2max}) and high-intensity aerobic exercise (75% VO_{2max}) have been demonstrated to increase endurance capacity, by 12 and 20–30%, respectively (Lakatta, 1993). Further, studies have demonstrated that aerobic endurance training can lead to reduced body fat, fat mass and waist-to hip ratios in 60–70-year-old men and women (Kohrt, Obert, & Holloszy, 1992). Moreover, resistance training in older adults has been shown to increase muscle strength and bone density, therefore, potentially reducing falls risk and the subsequent risk of fracture following a fall (Taylor et al., 2004).

As well as improving physical function, physical exercise has also been shown to positively affect cognitive function. This has been demonstrated in both children (Sibley & Etnier, 2003) and adults (Moonen, van Boxtel, de Groot, & Jolles, 2008), as well as across the human lifespan (6–90 years) (Etnier et al., 1997). In a recent study, cognitive function in older adults aged 50 years and over was reported to improve, after aerobic and resistance-based exercise programmes of at least moderate intensity (Northey, Cherbuin, Pumpa, Smee, & Rattray, 2017). Thus, illustrating the importance of physical exercise for the development and maintenance of cognitive function in childhood and adult life. Importantly for older adults, regular participation in physical exercise has been shown to attenuate cognitive decline (Fox, 1999), and has repeatedly been reported to reduce risk of cognitive impairment such as dementia (Barha, Galea, Nagamatsu, Erickson, & Liu-Ambrose, 2017). One potential reason is through aerobic exercise promoting the secretion of brain-derived neurotropic factor (BDNF), a protein that encourages the growth of new neurons termed *neurogenesis* and formation of new synapses termed *synaptogenesis*. Lower concentrations of BDNF are associated with Alzheimer's disease, Parkinson's disease, depression, anorexia and many other diseases (Adlard, Perreau, Pop, & Cotman, 2005). However, not all studies investigating the influence of BDNF on cognition have been positive. It is thought this may be due to the form of BDNF being tested, as the precursor molecule, pro-BDNF is neurotoxic, which is later converted into the neuroprotector, mature BDNF (Barha et al., 2017). Nonetheless, whether BDNF is the primary driver for morphological and structural changes to cognitive function in response to exercise or not, the benefits of physical exercise in the prevention of cognitive morbidities is clear (Taylor et al., 2004).

Strength, or resistance training (RT) seems to promote different responses to aerobic training, resulting in greater increases in levels of insulin-like growth factor 1 (IGF-1) (Kramer, Colcombe, McAuley, Scalf, & Erickson, 2005). Together, IGF-1 and BDNF interact to fulfil a neuro-protective function, preserving neuronal micro-architectures from progressive structural deterioration, thereby facilitating the preservation of higher order cognitive processes (Cassilhas et al., 2007; Kramer et al., 2005). Following aerobic training, such changes are less pronounced, thereby proposing different mechanisms through which aerobic and RT mediate cognitive enhancements (Barha et al., 2017). This, therefore, suggests the importance of both aerobic and resistance training to elucidate the cognitive enhancing effects of physical exercise, as previously reported (Northey et al., 2017). This is one potential explanation for the positive effects of physical exercise on cognitive function, as it stimulates biochemical and neurological processes, and thus influences change to cognitive capacity.

It is also evident that physical exercises promote psychosocial benefits such as reduced levels of depression (Kritz-Silverstein, Barrett-Connor, & Corbeau, 2001), enhanced mood (Arent, Landers, & Etnier, 2000) and reduced feelings of loneliness (McAuley et al., 2000). It is thought that the increased neurotropic factor expression and the increased opportunities for social interaction presented, for example, by attending an exercise class, are potential reasons for these psychosocial benefits (For further review see Duman, 2005; Taylor et al., 2004).

2.1. Current knowledge: Cognitive exercise for cognitive function

Just as the body adapts in response to regular physical stimuli, the brain adapts to regular cognitive stimuli through robust neuroplasticity (Anguera et al., 2013; Fernandez & Goldberg, 2009). Such stimulation can be applied through adequately challenging, structured and focussed cognitive training (Fernandez & Goldberg, 2009; Gates & Valenzuela, 2010). As such, cognitive training demands that the participant attempts to solve novel cognitive challenges, specifically targeted to dimensions of cognitive function such as attention, working memory and processing speed. Thus, it requires the participant to stimulate specific functional brain networks on multiple occasions, promoting neurogenesis and synaptogenesis (Perrey, 2013).

Previous research has illustrated that cognitive training for older adults can drive the maintenance and enhancement of cognitive function (Anguera et al., 2013; Gates & Valenzuela, 2010). A systematic review by Keuider and colleagues (2012) examined 38 studies of computerised cognitive training methods with older adults between 1984 and 2011. The studies were split into three categories: classic cognitive training; to train specific aspects of cognition individually, neuropsychological software; designed to enhance multiple cognitive domains with a variety of tasks, and video games; involving manipulating "on-screen" images to achieve a goal (Kueider et al., 2012). All three types of training provided improvements to cognitive abilities with the authors concluding that computer-based interventions are less labour intensive than paper-and-pencil methods, and being technology savvy is not a requirement in order to benefit (Kueider et al., 2012).

These findings are of importance as cognitive decline is a common feature of ageing, particularly with regard to processing speed, working memory and inductive reasoning (Singer, Verhaeghen, Ghisletta, Lindenberger, & Baltes, 2003). Cognitive training of such functions has been shown to improve self-efficacy, and preserve independence in older adults (Wolinsky et al., 2009). Openness to experience—thinking creatively and enjoying intellectual pursuits—also declines with age, but can be increased following a period of cognitive training (Jackson, Hill, Payne, Roberts, & Stine-Morrow, 2012). Similar to physical exercise, it appears that participating in cognitive training has an indirect benefit of improving psychosocial health in older adults, as well as improving functional cognitive abilities.

3. Emerging evidence: Cognitive training for cognitive and physical function

Motor stabilisation is central to proficient movement execution (Skoyles, 2008). Uniquely within the animal kingdom, human's predominant locomotive gait is bipedal in nature which poses unique stabilisation challenges requiring continuous skeletomuscular adjustments and multi-level neural control to maintain posture and on-going gait stability (Hausdorff, 2007; Skoyles, 2008). These adjustments require cognitive processing and demand uptake of neural resources, (Melzer, Benjuya, & Kaplanski, 2001) using sensory systems to anticipate destabilising perturbations and initiate remediating limb movements in advance of destabilisation occurring (Hausdorff, 2007; Skoyles, 2006). Therefore, it is clear that walking not only requires muscular activation, but also demands higher order neural processing capacity, dependant on the integration of input from cortical and sensory systems to coordinate locomotion (Hausdorff, 2007). As such cerebral cortical processing abilities and balance are closely linked (Skoyles, 2006) in which emerging evidence is beginning to explain and broaden the understanding of how it can be utilised to enhance cognitive and physical function.

3.1. Executive function

Executive function refers to high-order cognitive processes that control, integrate and organise cognitive abilities to enable goal-orientated tasks such as decision-making and problem solving (Fernandez & Goldberg, 2009; Segev-Jacubovski et al., 2011). Recent evidence has suggested a close relationship exists between executive function and walking gait (Ijmker & Lamoth, 2012).

Walking is often thought of as an automatic task in young adults, requiring no cognitive effort (Smith-Ray et al., 2013), whereas in the early and late phases of life it is visibly less automated requiring greater conscious effort. The complex processing essential to anticipatory movement control to maintain a stable gait demands dedication of an inevitably limited reservoir of higher level cortical resources, not fully developed in the young, and in a state of decline in the old (Lacquaniti, Ivanenko, & Zago, 2012). Under normal walking conditions, gait pattern is relatively rhythmical due to the natural bilateral coordination of α-motoneurons, controlled by spinal neuronal networks activating on both sides of the body in synchronisation (Ivanenko, Poppele, & Lacquaniti, 2006; Lacquaniti et al., 2012). When task constraints become unpredictable, and the consequence of error is high—for example, when traversing icy or broken surfaces—additional attentional capacity is required to effectively process sensorimotor information. The autonomous motor programme is, therefore, competing with high-level cortical capacity, or executive functions, to safely navigate the demanding environmental conditions. As individual safety is instinctively paramount, gait stability is prioritised to maintain an upright posture (Schabrun, van den Hoorn, Moorcroft, Greenland, & Hodges, 2014), and so the timing of muscle activation is altered to counteract perturbations and thus gait pattern becomes less rhythmical (Ivanenko et al., 2006; Skoyles, 2008).

Additionally, in persons with cognitive impairments such as, for example, Alzheimer's disease, deterioration of physical abilities such as walking decline in tandem with cognitive capacity (Wittwer, Webster and Menz, 2010). Many community-dwelling activities such as walking through a crowd of people depend on the successful execution of executive functions. Problem solving and decision-making ensure a safe route through the crowd, working memory ensures information can be manipulated in real-time, inhibition allows distractions to be withstood and mental flexibility allows the brain to quickly switch between functions (Fernandez & Goldberg, 2009; Smith-Ray et al., 2013). All this needs to take place along with the execution of motor function to allow the person to walk, regulate gait fluctuations (Decker, Cignetti, & Stergiou, 2013) and reduce the risk of falling through maintaining stability (Mirelman et al., 2012).

3.2. Linking executive function and physical function

In the ageing brain, neural connections begin to deteriorate from 40 years of age (Fernandez & Goldberg, 2009). Authors have demonstrated an age-related decline in executive functions such as working memory (Buckner, 2004) and processing speed (Park, 2000). Multi-tasking performance also declines with age (Anguera et al., 2013), which requires executive functions such as mental flexibility and attention—a specific type of executive function (Segev-Jacubovski et al., 2011). Although age-related cognitive decline is an inevitability, its consequences can be offset through regular stimulation. Research has demonstrated that being cognitively active delays the onset of cognitive morbidities such as mild cognitive impairment, dementia and Alzheimer's disease (Wilson et al., 2010). It is thought the stimulation of different brain regions builds a resilience to decline likely to be due to its promotion of neurogenesis and synaptogenesis (Fernandez & Goldberg, 2009). Moreover, such declines in executive function have been demonstrated to present more than just reductions in cognitive function. For example, older adult fallers perform more poorly in computerised tests of executive function than their non-faller counterparts (Hausdorff et al., 2006). Similarly, older adult fallers with poor working memory overestimate their reach capacity by 16% compared to only 2% in older adult fallers with good working memory (Liu-Ambrose, Ahamed, Graf, Feldman, & Robinovitch, 2008). Further, in persons with dementia a reduction in walking gait velocity has been reported (Ijmker & Lamoth, 2012). Such findings support the aforementioned high-level cortical capacity demands of bipedal gait mastery and motor stabilisation. This capacity naturally declines with age, and is worsened with disease, but if stimulated regularly it can be maintained (Fernandez & Goldberg, 2009), benefiting both cognitive and physical function.

3.3. Dual-tasking

An implication of cognitive deterioration within the older adult population is increased falls risk. One key contributing factor to falls risk appears to be the decline of attention. This impacts on the ability to maintain focus on a stimulus to complete one or more tasks simultaneously (Segev-Jacubovski et al., 2011). This is known as dual-tasking which often occurs in community-dwelling daily living (Muir et al., 2012; Segev-Jacubovski et al., 2011). Should an individual be required to walk and complete a second attention-demanding task, the competition for resources within the cerebello-cerebral circuitry would lead to a deterioration of concurrent performance, posing a risk to safety by increasing the risk of falling (Schabrun et al., 2014; Skoyles, 2008). Furthermore, age-related deteriorations to the brain regions—primarily, but not exclusively, located in the prefrontal cortical areas—facilitating executive function, are reported to influence the risk of falling (Herman, Mirelman, Giladi, Schweiger, & Hausdorff, 2010).

In a novel study, walking while reading and typing text on a mobile phone slowed walking gait, incurred postural changes and caused deviation from walking in a straight line (Schabrun et al., 2014). The cognitive task (reading or typing text) was prioritised over walking, as it is a more complex task, hence the walking gait was affected. The two tasks were unable to be executed simultaneously as they draw upon the same high-order cortical resources, forcing task prioritisation of the more cognitively complex task leading to a deterioration in performance (Segev-Jacubovski et al., 2011). The authors suggest that these changes to walking gait impact on the safety of the individual (Schabrun et al., 2014).

This affect has been further demonstrated in the literature by researchers who have asked participants to walk while performing cognitively stimulating tasks, such as counting backwards from 100 in ones or sevens (Muir et al., 2012). Inevitably this dual-task resulted in reduced gait velocity and increased stride time gait variability, indicating the gait pattern became unstable increasing the likelihood of a fall (Muir et al., 2012). In older adults with mild cognitive impairment or Alzheimer's disease, there is a much greater reduction to gait velocity than those with normal cognitive function (35% and 39% vs. 15%, respectively), and increases in stride time gait variability exceed the fall-risk threshold (Muir et al., 2012). Such findings highlight the increased risk of falling when cognition is in a state of decline, and completing more than one cognitively stimulating task simultaneously is required.

However, it is important to acknowledge that a deterioration of gait in the aged may be due to physical reasons such as arthritis, joint pain and diminished range of motion, leading to gait and balance disorders which influence gait variability and stride length (Salzman, 2010). The authors do not intend to suggest that changes to executive function will bring about transformations to structures such as joints and musculature. The intention here is to present the emerging evidence of a link between cognitive capacity—in particular executive function—and walking gait and how cognitive training may provide a novel solution to enhancing ones walking competence through potential hierarchical pathways (Figure 1).

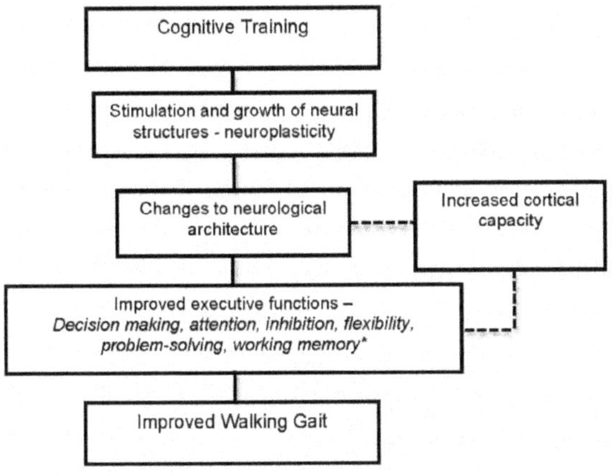

Figure 1. Hierarchical pathway to improve walking gait following a cognitive training programme.

Source: *Fernandez and Goldberg (2009), Segev-Jacubovski et al. (2011).

4. Can executive function be improved?

Despite age-related cognitive decline often proving detrimental to health, studies have demonstrated that older adults can improve cognitive capacity, through specific training. A recent study by Saposnik and colleagues (2011) has shown how virtual reality gaming, which taxed decision-making and processing speed, enhanced motor function in stroke patients. It is thought that the games drive neurological change in the participants' brains, due to neuroplasticity, which leads to improvements in motor function (Saposnik et al., 2011). Essentially, the game works as a form of cognitive training stimulating neurogenesis and synaptogenesis as the brain "remodels" its neural network. In further support of this, playing a custom-designed video game improved the multi-tasking abilities of older adults (65–80 years old) to greater levels than those found in "untrained" 20-year-olds (Anguera et al., 2013). One hour per day, three times a week for one month playing the multi-tasking game enhanced cognitive abilities, which the authors claim is due to the robust plasticity of the ageing brain (Anguera et al., 2013).

Intriguingly, recent research suggests that dimensions of walking performance (specifically gait velocity and balance), can be improved in older adults, consequent to computerised cognitive training programmes (Smith-Ray et al., 2013; Verghese, Mahoney, Ambrose, Wang, & Holtzer, 2010). Ten weeks of computerised visual, spatial memory and decision-making games slowed the decline of walking speed and balance in a cohort of older adults on average 83 years of age (Smith-Ray et al., 2013). The authors attributed the results to the nature of the training, which focused on elements of executive function. Similarly, Verghese and colleagues (2010) reported a statistically significant improvement in walking speed (0.68 ± 0.20 vs. 0.77 ± 0.18 ms^{-1}) in 10 sedentary older adults following an eight-week computerised cognitive training intervention. These findings hold even greater significance when considered alongside the increased likelihood of mortality at walking speeds less than 0.82 ms^{-1} (Stanaway et al., 2011). Furthermore, the Advanced Cognitive Training for Independent and Vital Elderly (ACTIVE) study—the largest cognitive intervention study to date ($N = 2802$)—has demonstrated that training induced improvements to cognitive abilities such as memory, reasoning and processing speed are maintained for 24 months (Ball et al., 2002). Such findings demonstrate the robustness of the ageing brain and highlight the important role cognitive training can play in maintaining cognitive and physical function in the ageing population and it should be applied in a structured and specific manner.

5. Conclusions

Studies have outlined the importance of physical exercise for physical, cognitive and psychosocial function (Colcombe and Kramer, 2003; Duman, 2005; Nelson et al., 2007). Similarly, cognitive training has also been shown to be beneficial to cognitive and psychosocial health (Anguera et al., 2013; Gates & Valenzuela, 2010). These outcomes are advantageous in terms of attenuating age-related declines to biopsychosocial well-being. However, approximately 50% of community-dwelling older adults aged 85 and over will fall each year. Crucially, those with a cognitive impairment are twice as likely to suffer a fall (Iinattiniemi, Jokelainen, & Luukinen, 2009). This not only impacts individuals, but also has huge economical implications with fall-related treatment costing the UK NHS ~£1 billion per annum (Davis et al., 2010).

The uniqueness of human bipedal gait demands high-level cognitive processing to enable motor stabilisation and an erect posture suggesting that cognition and gait mastery share cerebello-cerebral circuitry (Skoyles, 2008). Recent evidence has emerged within the literature suggesting such a link between executive function and walking gait (Ijmker & Lamoth, 2012) and its impact on fall risk. It has, therefore, been suggested that improving executive function would reduce falls risk (Segev-Jacubovski et al., 2011).

One method of doing this is via computerised cognitive training and measuring the impact on characteristics of walking gait, such as stride length, stride time and stride time variability in single and dual-task environments. Studies such as Verghese and colleagues (2010) and Smith-Ray and colleagues (2013), have shown the power of cognitive training to reduce the effects of cognitive decline and how this impacts on walking gait velocity and balance. The neuroplasticity and robustness of the ageing brain to rejuvenate has also been demonstrated (Anguera et al., 2013; Bherer et al., 2005, 2008; Saposnik et al., 2011). Importantly, however, further research is needed to broaden understanding of the relationship between this type of cognitive function and walking gait. Furthermore, the utility of computerised training to augment cognitive capacity may, following the rationale and evidence presented here, prove a novel intervention capable of indirectly reducing falls risk in the ageing population.

Funding
The authors received no direct funding for this research.

Competing Interests
The authors declare no competing interest.

Author details
Joseph E. Robinson[1]
E-mail: jrobinson5@uclan.ac.uk
ORCID ID: http://orcid.org/0000-0001-7968-4537
John Kiely[1]
E-mail: jkiely@uclan.ac.uk
[1] School of Sport and Wellbeing, Institute of Coaching and Performance, University of Central Lancashire, Preston, Lancashire PR1 2HE, UK.

References

Adlard, P. A., Perreau, V. M., Pop, V., & Cotman, C. W. (2005). Voluntary exercise decreases amyloid load in a transgenic model of Alzheimer's disease. *Journal of Neuroscience, 25*, 4217–4221. https://doi.org/10.1523/JNEUROSCI.0496-05.2005

Anguera, J. A., Boccanfuso, J., Rintoul, J. L., Al-Hashimi, O., Faraji, F., Janowich, J., ... Gazzaley, A. (2013). Video game training enhances cognitive control in older adults. *Nature, 501*, 97–101. doi:10.1038/nature12486

Arent, A. M., Landers, D. M., & Etnier, J. L. (2000). The effects of exercise on mood in older adults: A meta-analytic review. *Journal of Aging and Physical Activity, 8*, 407–430. https://doi.org/10.1123/japa.8.4.407

Ball, K., Berch, D. B., Helmers, K. F., Jobe, J. B., Leveck, M. D., ... Willis, S. L. (2002). Effects of cognitive training interventions with older adults: A randomized controlled trial. *The Journal of the American Medical Association, 288*(18), 2271–2281. https://doi.org/10.1001/jama.288.18.2271

Barha, C. K., Galea, L. A., Nagamatsu, L. S., Erickson, K. I., & Liu-Ambrose, T. (2017). Personalising exercise recommendations for brain health: Considerations and future directions. *British Journal of Sports Medicine, 51*, 636–639. https://doi.org/10.1136/bjsports-2016-096710

Bherer, L., Kramer, A. F., Peterson, M. S., Colcombe, S., Erickson, K., & Becic, E. (2005). Training effects on dual-task performance: Are there age-related differences in plasticity of attentional control? *Psychology and Aging, 20*(4), 695–709. https://doi.org/10.1037/0882-7974.20.4.695

Bherer, L., Kramer, A. F., Peterson, M. S., Colcombe, S., Erickson, K., & Becic, E. (2008). Transfer effects in task-set cost and dual-task cost after dual-task training in older and younger adults: Further evidence for cognitive plasticity in attentional control in late adulthood. *Experimental Aging Research, 34*(3), 188–219. https://doi.org/10.1080/03610730802070068

Buckner, R. L. (2004). Memory and executive function in aging and AD: Multiple factors that cause decline and reserve factors that compensate. *Neuron, 44*(1), 195–208. https://doi.org/10.1016/j.neuron.2004.09.006

Cassilhas, R. C., Viana, V. A. R., Grassman, V., Santos, R. T., Santos, R. F., Tufik, S., & Mello, M. T. (2007). The impact of resistance exercise on the cognitive function of the elderly. *Medicine & Science in Sports & Exercise, 39*(8), 1401–1407. https://doi.org/10.1249/mss.0b013e318060111f

Colcombe, S., & Kramer, A. F. (2003). Fitness effects on the cognitive function of older adults: A meta-analytic study. *Psychological Science, 14*(2), 125–130.

Davis, J. C., Robertson, M. C., Ashe, M. C., Liu-Ambrose, T., Khan, K. M., & Marra, C. A. (2010). International comparison of cost of falls in older adults living in the community: A systematic review. *Osteoporosis International, 21*(8), 1295–1306. https://doi.org/10.1007/s00198-009-1162-0

Decker, L. M., Cignetti, F., & Stergiou, N. (2013). Executive function orchestrates regulation of task relevant gait fluctuations. *Gait & Posture*. In Press. doi:10.1016/j.gaitpost.2012.12.018

Duman, R. S. (2005). Neurotropic factors and regulations of mood: Role of exercise, diet and metabolism. *Neurobiology of Aging, 26*(1), 88–93. https://doi.org/10.1016/j.neurobiolaging.2005.08.018

Etnier, J. L., Salazar, W., Landers, D. M., Petruzzello, S. J., Han, M., & Nowell, P. (1997). The influence of physical fitness and exercise upon cognitive functioning: A meta-analysis. *Journal of Sport and Exercise Psychology, 19*(3), 249–277. https://doi.org/10.1123/jsep.19.3.249

Fernandez, A., & Goldberg, E. (2009). *The sharpbrains guide to brain fitness. 18 interviews with scientists, practical advice and product reviews, to keep your brain sharp.* doi:0-9823629-0-0

Fox, K. R. (1999). The influence of physical activity on mental well-being. *Public Health Nutrition, 2*(3a), 411–418.

Gates and Valenzuela. (2010). Cognitive exercise and its role in cognitive function in older adults. *Current Psychiatry Reports, 12*(1), 20–27.

Hausdorff, J. M. (2007). Gait dynamics, fractals and falls: Finding meaning in the stride-to-stride fluctuations of human walking. *Human Movement Science, 26*(4), 555–589. https://doi.org/10.1016/j.humov.2007.05.003

Hausdorff, J. M., Doniger, G. M., Springer, S., Yogev, G., Giladi, N., & Simon, E. S. (2006). A common cognitive profile in elderly fallers and in patients with Parkinson's disease: The prominence of impaired executive function and attention. *Experimental Aging Research, 32*, 411–429. https://doi.org/10.1080/03610730600875817

Herman, T., Mirelman, A., Giladi, N., Schweiger, A., & Hausdorff, J. M. (2010). Executive control deficits as a prodrome to falls in healthy older adults: A prospective study linking thinking, walking, and falling. *Journal of Gerontology, 65A*(10), 1086–1092.

Iinattiniemi, S., Jokelainen, J., & Luukinen, H. (2009). Falls risk among a very old home-dwelling population. *Scandinavian Journal of Primary Health Care, 27*, 25–30. https://doi.org/10.1080/02813430802588683

Ijmker, T., & Lamoth, C. J. C. (2012). Gait and cognition: The relationship between gait stability and variability with executive function in persons with and without dementia. *Gait & Posture, 35*, 126–130. doi:10.1016/j.gaitpost.2011.08.022

Ivanenko, Y. P., Poppele, R. E., & Lacquaniti, F. (2006). Motor control programs and walking. *The Neuroscientist, 12*(4), 339–348. https://doi.org/10.1177/1073858406287987

Jackson, J. J., Hill, P. L., Payne, B. R., Roberts, B. W., & Stine-Morrow, E. A. L. (2012). Can an old dog learn (and want to experience) new tricks? Cognitive training increases openness to experience in older adults. *Psychology and Aging, 27*(2), 286–292. doi:10.1037/a0025918

King, A. C., Rejeski, W. J., & Buchner, D. M. (1998). Physical activity interventions targeting older adults: A critical review and recommendations. *American Journal of Preventative Medicine, 15*, 316–333. https://doi.org/10.1016/S0749-3797(98)00085-3

Kohrt, W., Obert, A. K., & Holloszy, J. (1992). Exercise training improves fat distribution patterns in 60-to 70-year-old men and women. *Journal of Gerontology, 47*, M99–M105. https://doi.org/10.1093/geronj/47.4.M99

Kramer, A. F., Colcombe, S. J., McAuley, E., Scalf, P. E., & Erickson, K. I. (2005). Fitness, aging and neurocognitive function. *Neurobiology of Aging, 26*, 124–127. https://doi.org/10.1016/j.neurobiolaging.2005.09.009

Kritz-Silverstein, D., Barrett-Connor, E., & Corbeau, C. (2001). Cross-sectional and prospective study of exercise and depressed mood in the elderly: The Rancho Bernardo study. *American Journal of Epidemiology, 153*, 596–603. https://doi.org/10.1093/aje/153.6.596

Kueider, A. M., Parisi, J. M., Gross, A. L., & Rebok, G. W. (2012). Computerized cognitive training with older adults: A systematic review. *PLoS One, 7*(7), e40588.

Lacquaniti, F., Ivanenko, Y. P., & Zago, M. (2012). Patterned control of human locomotion. *The Journal of Physiology, 590*(10), 2189–2199. doi:10.1113/jphysiol.2011.215137

Lakatta, E. G. (1993). Cardiovascular regulatory mechanisms in advanced age. *Physiological Reviews, 73*, 413–469.

Liu-Ambrose, T., Ahamed, Y., Graf, P., Feldman, F., & Robinovitch, S. N. (2008). Older fallers with poor working memory overestimate their postural limits. *Archives of Physical and Medical Rehabilitation, 89*, 1335–1340. https://doi.org/10.1016/j.apmr.2007.11.052

McAuley, E., Blissmer, B., Marquez, D. X., Jerome, G. J., Kramer, A. F., & Katula, J. (2000). Social relations, physical activity, and well-being in older adults. *Preventive Medicine, 31*, 608–617. https://doi.org/10.1006/pmed.2000.0740

Melzer, I., Benjuya, N., & Kaplanski, J. (2001). Age-related changes of postural control: Effect of cognitive tasks. *Gerontology, 47*(4), 189–194. https://doi.org/10.1159/000052797

Mirelman, A., Herman, T., Brozgol, M., Dorfman, M., Specher, E., Schweiger, A., ... Hausdorff, J. M. (2012). Executive function and falls in older adults: New findings from a five-year prospective study link fall risk to cognition. *PLoS One, 7*(6), e40297.

Moonen, H. M. R., van Boxtel, M. P. J., de Groot, R. H. M., & Jolles, J. (2008). Improvement in physical functioning protects against physical decline: A 6-year follow-up in the Maastricht Aging Study. *Mental Health and Physical Activity, 1*, 62–68. https://doi.org/10.1016/j.mhpa.2008.09.001

Muir, S. W., Speechley, M., Wells, J., Borrie, M., Gopaul, K., & Montero-Odasso, M. (2012). Gait assessment in mild cognitive impairment and Alzheimer's disease: The effect of dual-task challenges across the cognitive spectrum. *Gait & Posture, 35*, 96–100. https://doi.org/10.1016/j.gaitpost.2011.08.014

Nelson, M. E., Rejeski, W. J., Blair, S. N., Duncan, P. W., Judge, J. O., King, A. C., ... Castaneda-Sceppa, C. (2007). Physical activity and public health in older adults: Recommendation from the American College of Sports Medicine and the American Heart Association. *Medicine & Science in Sport & Exercise, 116*, 1435–1445. doi:10.1249/mss.0b013e3180616aa2

Northey, J. M., Cherbuin, N., Pumpa, K. L., Smee D. J., & Rattray, B. (2017). Exercise interventions for cognitive function in adults older than 50: A systematic review with meta-analysis. *British Journal of Sports Medicine*. Published Online First: 24 April 2017. doi:10.1136/bjsports-2016-096587

Park, D. C. (2000). The basic mechanisms accounting for age-related decline in cognitive function. In D. Park & N. Schwartz (Eds.), *Cognitive aging: A primer* (pp. 3–21). Philadelphia, PA: Psychology Press.

Perrey, S. (2013). Promoting motor function by exercising the brain. *Brain Sciences, 3*, 101–122. https://doi.org/10.3390/brainsci3010101

Salzman, B. (2010). Gait and balance disorders in older adults. *American Family Physician, 82*(1), 61–68.

Saposnik, G., Barinagarrementeria, F., Brown, R. D., Bushnell, C. D., Cucchiara, B., Cushman, M. ... Tsai, F. Y. (2011). Diagnosis and management of cerebral venous thrombosis: A statement for healthcare professionals from the American Heart Association/American Stroke Association. *Stroke, 42* (4), 1158–1192. doi:10.1161/STR.0b013e31820a8364

Schabrun, S. M., van den Hoorn, W., Moorcroft, A., Greenland, C., & Hodges, P. (2014). Texting and walking: Strategies for postural control and implications for safety. *PLoS One, 9*(1), e84312. doi:10.1371/journal.pone.0084312

Segev-Jacubovski, O., Herman, T., Yogev-Seligmann, G., Mirelman, A., Giladi, N., & Hausdorff, J. M. (2011). The interplay between gait, falls and cognition: Can cognitive therapy reduce fall risk? *Expert Review of Neurotherapeutics, 11*(7), 1057–1075. https://doi.org/10.1586/ern.11.69

Sibley, B. A., & Etnier, J. L. (2003). The relationship between physical activity and cognition in children: A meta-analysis. *Pediatric Exercise Science, 15*, 243–256. https://doi.org/10.1123/pes.15.3.243

Singer, T., Verhaeghen, P., Ghisletta, P., Lindenberger, U., & Baltes, P. (2003). The fate of cognition in very old age: Six-year longitudinal findings in the Berlin Aging Study (BASE). *Psychology and Aging, 18*, 318–331. https://doi.org/10.1037/0882-7974.18.2.318

Skoyles, J. R. (2006). Human balance, the evolution of bipedalism and dysequilibrium syndrome. *Medical Hypotheses, 66*, 1060–1068. https://doi.org/10.1016/j.mehy.2006.01.042

Skoyles, J. R. (2008). Respiratory, postural and spatio-kinetic motor stabilization, internal models, top-down timed motor coordination and expanded cerebello-cerebral circuitry: A review. *Nature Precedings*. doi:10.1038/npre.2008.2092.1

Smith-Ray, R. L., Hughes, S. L., Prohaska, T. R., Little, D. M., Jurivich, D. A., & Hedeker, D. (2013). Impact of cognitive training on balance and gait in older adults. *Journal of Gerontology Series B: Psychological Sciences*. doi: https://doi.org/10.1093/geronb/gbt097

Stanaway, F. F., Gnjidic, D., Blyth, F. M., Couteur, D. G., Naganathan, V., Waite, L., ... Cumming, R. G. (2011). How fast does the Grim Reaper walk? Receiver operating characteristics curve analysis in healthy men aged 70 and over. *British Medical Journal, 343*, d7679. https://doi.org/10.1136/bmj.d7679

Taylor, A. H., Cable, N. T., Faulkner, G., Hillsdon, M., Narici, M., & Van Der Bij, A. K. (2004). Physical activity and older adults: A review of health benefits and the effectiveness of interventions. *Journal of Sports Sciences, 22*, 703–725. https://doi.org/10.1080/02640410410001712421

Verghese, J., Mahoney, J., Ambrose, A. F., Wang, C., & Holtzer, R. (2010). Effect of cognitive remediation on gait in sedentary seniors. *The Journals of Gerontology. Series A, Biological Sciences and Medical Sciences, 65A*(12), 1338–1343. https://doi.org/10.1093/gerona/glq127

Wilson, R. S., Barnes, L. L., Aggarwal, N. T., Boyle, P. A., Hebert, L. E., Mendes de Leon, C. F., & Evans, D. A. (2010). Cognitive activity and the cognitive morbidity of Alzheimer disease. *Neurology, 75*(11), 990–996. https://doi.org/10.1212/WNL.0b013e3181f25b5e

Wittwer, J. E., Webster, K. E., & Menz, H. B. (2010). A longitudinal study of measures of walking in people with Alzheimer's Disease. *Gait & Posture, 32*, 113–117. doi:10.1016/j.gaitpost.2010.04.001.

Wolinsky, F. D., Vander Weg, M. W., Martin, R., Unverzagt, F. W., Willis, S. L., Marsiske, M., ... Tennstedt, S. L. (2009). Does cognitive training improve internal locus of control among older adults? *Journal of Gerontology: Social Sciences, 65B*(5), 591–598. doi:10.1093/geronb/gbp117

9

A posterior variant of corticobasal syndrome: Evidence from a longitudinal study of cognitive and functional status in a single case

Carlo Abbate[1*], Pietro Davide Trimarchi[2], Laura Manzoni[3], Anna Maria Quarenghi[3], Gian Pietro Salvi[3], Silvia Inglese[1], Fabrizio Giunco[2], Renzo Bagarolo[2], Daniela Mari[4] and Beatrice Arosio[1,4]

*Corresponding author: Carlo Abbate, Geriatric Unit, Fondazione IRCCS Ca' Granda, Ospedale Maggiore Policlinico, via Pace 9, 20122 Milan, Italy.

E-mail: carlo.abbate@guest.unimi.it

Reviewing editor: Peter Walla, University of Newcastle, Australia

Abstract: We describe a patient (CG) suffering from early onset dementia who presented with corticobasal syndrome (CBS). The aims of the study were as follows: (i) a detailed description of the cognitive phenotype; (ii) a comprehensive, longitudinal evaluation of apraxia; (iii) an appraisal of the impact of apraxia and other cognitive impairments on patient functional status; and (iv) an indirect mapping of degeneration spreading. A three-year longitudinal, observational follow-up study of cognitive and functional status was performed. Four main results emerged. First, an unusual CBS phenotype appeared that was characterized by symmetrical presentation, asymmetrical course, and prominent posterior (bi-parietal) cognitive and motor cortical manifestations. Second, some findings of limb apraxia in CBS were replicated and substantiated; moreover, some novel findings of other cognitive impairments emerged. Third, an early, significant functional decline, probably related to apraxia and to visuospatial attention impairments, became apparent. Fourth, CG's clinical picture was compatible with an underlying dysfunction of the large-scale, dorsal sensory-motor association network, as already suggested in previous CBS cases.

ABOUT THE AUTHORS

Carlo Abbate and Pietro Davide Trimarchi are neuropsychologists and clinical researchers, who specialize in dementia diagnosis. Carlo Abbate has a PhD in Physiopathology of Aging at the University of Milan and works at the Fondazione Ca' Granda, Ospedale Maggiore Policlinico in Milan. Pietro Davide Trimarchi has a PhD in Experimental Psychology and Cognitive Neuroscience at the University of Milano-Bicocca and works at Fondazione Don Carlo Gnocchi, in Milan. They have been working together for years in many research areas: early cognitive markers of dementia, Mild Cognitive Impairment, clinical syndromes of dementia, qualitative neuropsychological examination, and variants of Alzheimer's disease. The firm belief that neuropsychology can be a helpful tool both to understand and to diagnose dementia has guided their work. The detailed longitudinal study of the cognitive and behavioral status of a young adult patient with degenerative dementia presented here well exemplifies the method adopted by the authors.

PUBLIC INTEREST STATEMENT

Our research group studies the dramatic mind's decline resulting from the progressive brain damage caused by Alzheimer's disease and other dementias. Specifically, we aim to precisely report all the impairments that dementia causes in mental abilities as well as in feelings and behavior of the patients, and how these disorders change over time. This scientific knowledge may help detect the early features of dementia to diagnose it as soon as possible. Moreover, we are interested in forecast what difficulties patients will have in their daily lives, as well as how they will behave in some circumstances and what emotions they will feel. The ultimate aim of this long-lasting and demanding study is to know better how to help patients and make them feel well. Also, we want to make patients' mind stronger and to promote social engagement for them.

This case report confirms the heterogeneity of CBS and suggests the emergence of a possible less common variant, i.e. the posterior CBS (P-CBS).

Subjects; Aphasia; Apraxia; Clinical Neuropsychology

Keywords; corticobasal; limb-apraxia; limb-kinetic; alien hand syndrome; brain network

1. Introduction

Corticobasal syndrome (CBS) is a variable but recognizable neurological disorder with an insidious onset and a progressive course. It is characterized by an asymmetric, akinetic, and rigid syndrome, with prominent apraxia and other symptoms suggesting cortical (i.e. myoclonus, cortical sensory loss, alien limb phenomenon) and basal ganglionic dysfunction (e.g. dystonia, tremor) (Boeve, Lang, & Litvan, 2003; Burrell, Hodges, & Rowe, 2014; Graham, Bak, & Hodges, 2003; Mathew, Bak, & Hodges, 2011). Cognitive impairments and/or behavioral features are often associated with motor symptoms early on in the disease course (Burrell et al., 2014; Graham et al., 2003).

Apraxia is one of the core features in the current diagnostic criteria of CBS (Armstrong et al., 2013). In particular, limb apraxia is very frequent, with estimates between 70 and 80% of cases, and it is often a presenting feature (Stamenova, Roy, & Black, 2009). Many patients suffering from CBS also present with limb-kinetic apraxia; conversely, oro-facial apraxia may be absent or develop later in the disease progression (Ozsancak, Auzou, Dujardin, & Hannequin, 2000; Ozsancak, Auzou, & Hannequin, 2004; Stamenova et al., 2009). Finally, apraxia affecting other body parts (e.g. trunk, eyelid, gaze) has been reported less frequently (Okuda, Tanaka, Kawabata, Tachibana, & Sugita, 2001; Rajagopal, Bateman, & Van Stavern, 2011). Taking into account the type of apraxia, it was found that ideomotor apraxia is the most common type in CBS, whereas ideational apraxia could be present in an advanced stage (Grijalvo-Perez & Litvan, 2014). Considering the distinction between conceptual and production systems in praxis functions (Roy, Square, Adams, & Friesen, 1985), apraxia in CBS seems to affect the production system. In contrast, no severe impairments of the conceptual system (i.e. semantic memory of gestures) are typically found (Jacobs et al., 1999; Salter, Roy, Black, Joshi, & Almeida, 2004; Soliveri, Piacentini, & Girotti, 2005; Stamenova, Roy, & Black, 2011). Concerning gesture modalities, CBS patients usually obtain worse results when tested by imitation rather than by pantomime (Jacobs et al., 1999; Peigneux et al., 2001; Spatt, Bak, Bozeat, Patterson, & Hodges, 2002; Stamenova et al., 2011). Moreover, difficulties in gesture execution usually improved when CBS patients could use concrete tools (Graham, Zeman, Young, Patterson, & Hodges, 1999; Jacobs et al., 1999; Leiguarda et al., 2003; Spatt et al., 2002; Stamenova et al., 2009). Finally, as for the type of gestures, no clear differences in the amount of apraxia between transitive and intransitive gestures (Buxbaum, Kyle, Grossman, & Coslett, 2007; Jacobs et al., 1999; Leiguarda et al., 2003; Peigneux et al., 2001) as well as between representational and non-representational gestures (Buxbaum et al., 2007; Leiguarda et al., 2003; Merians et al., 1999; Salter et al., 2004; Spatt et al., 2002; Stamenova et al., 2009) were found.

Visuospatial impairment is another distinctive cognitive feature of CBS (Burrell et al., 2014), and it is included in the current diagnostic criteria, i.e. the Mayo Clinic criteria (Boeve et al., 2003) and the modified Cambridge criteria (Mathew et al., 2011). In particular, CBS patients show difficulties in performing visuospatial tasks, such as Benton's judgment of line orientation (Soliveri et al., 1999) or the spatial tasks of the Visual Objects Spatial Performance (VOSP) battery (Bak, Caine, Hearn, & Hodges, 2006). Moreover, constructional apraxia and hemineglect are frequently reported (Boeve et al., 2003; Tang-Wai et al., 2003). Finally, there are some case reports of CBS patients who showed partial or complete Gerstmann's syndrome (i.e. digit agnosia, left-right disorientation, agraphia, and acalculia) (Di Stefano et al., 2016; Tang-Wai et al., 2003) and/or Balint-Holmes syndrome (i.e. oculomotor apraxia, optic ataxia, simultanagnosia, and deficits on estimating depth and distances) (Mendez, 2000; Rajagopal et al., 2011), which include some visuospatial impairments together with impairment of other abilities (Vallar, 2007).

Alien limb syndrome, which is characterized by the sensation that a limb is foreign or has a will of its own and/or by complex unintentional limb movements interfering with normal tasks (Armstrong et al., 2013) is another typical disorder in CBS (Armstrong et al., 2013; Grijalvo-Perez & Litvan, 2014; Murray et al., 2007). Several additional phenomena have been described in CBS that are likewise regarded as manifestations of alien hand syndrome (e.g. magnetic apraxia, intermanual conflict, grasping, impulsive hand groping, and purposeless wandering of the limb) (Grijalvo-Perez & Litvan, 2014). Interestingly, while CBS patients with frontal dysfunction may show alien limb movements characterized by continuous tactile pursuits of the examiner's hand ("tactile mitgehen"), the alien limb of patients with more parietal damage is more likely to drift or levitate and assume odd postures (Delrieu et al., 2010; Grijalvo-Perez & Litvan, 2014; Semenza, 2003).

Aphasia is a very common impairment in CBS (Di Stefano et al., 2016; Frattali, Grafman, Patronas, Makhlouf, & Litvan, 2000; Graham et al., 2003; Mahapatra, Edwards, Schott, & Bhatia, 2004; McMonagle, Blair, & Kertesz, 2006; Murray et al., 2007), and typically it is of the non-fluent type (Graham et al., 2003; Mahapatra et al., 2004; McMonagle et al., 2006; Tree & Kay, 2008). Moreover, longitudinal studies on aphasia in CBS suggested that patients either show non-fluent speech production from the first presentation (Tree & Kay, 2008) or are initially anomic and then develop disorders of expressive language resembling a progressive non-fluent aphasia (McMonagle et al., 2006). In contrast, receptive language and single word comprehension are relatively preserved, except in few cases (Di Stefano et al., 2016; Graham et al., 2003; McMonagle et al., 2006).

Regarding the remaining cognitive domains, even though some executive and memory impairments can be found in CBS, many studies have failed to find a specific pattern of prefrontal dysfunction and amnesia. Therefore, the evaluation of these cognitive functions is regarded as being worthless to the differential diagnosis of CBS and other diseases (Burrell et al., 2014). Finally, modifications of behavior and personality, similar to those reported in frontotemporal dementia (FTD), are common in CBS (Burrell et al., 2014).

Taking into account the brain pathology underlying CBS, it appears with great heterogeneity (Boeve, 2011; Boeve et al., 2003; Lee et al., 2011; Ouchi et al., 2014). Specifically, corticobasal degeneration (CBD)—a neurodegenerative condition characterized by atrophy, gliosis, and tau-immunoreactive pathology in the gray and white matter of the neocortex, basal ganglia, and substantia nigra (Murray et al., 2007)—is the most frequent underlying pathology. However, other neuropathologies have been reported, including Alzheimer's disease (AD), frontotemporal lobar degeneration (FTLD), progressive supra-nuclear palsy (PSP), and Creutzfeldt-Jakob disease (CJD) (Boeve, 2011; Boeve et al., 2003; Lee et al., 2011; Ouchi et al., 2014).

Bearing in mind the pathological heterogeneity underlying CBS and in hopes that disease-modifying drugs for neurodegenerative dementias will be soon available, detailed clinic-pathological correlation studies are promoted for the purpose of recognizing an early clinical/cognitive marker of a specific pathology. In-depth investigations of CBS clinical and/or cognitive phenotypes are also important for many other reasons. First, few detailed descriptions of CBS have been reported to date. Second, CBS has often been regarded as clinically heterogeneous (Burrell et al., 2014; Di Stefano et al., 2016), but definite variants of the syndrome have rarely been acknowledged (e.g. symmetric CBS, Dopper et al., 2011). Third, many features of the syndrome (e.g. alien hand syndrome, left-right disorientation) have been described exclusively by clinical-observational exams and lack a quantitative validation. Fourth, there are few studies including longitudinal, quantitative assessments of apraxia (Stamenova et al., 2009) and other cognitive impairments in CBS (Huang, Hornberger, Hodges, & Burrell, 2014). Fifth, an in-depth syndrome description is important because the pattern of cognitive and motor impairments could determine how and to what level the patient fails in performing her/his everyday activities (see, for example, Shakespeare, Yong, Foxe, Hodges, & Crutch, 2015 in the realm of Posterior Cortical Atrophy syndrome). In this regard, few data are available of the functional impact of CBS on everyday skills (Stamenova et al., 2009). Finally, since the clinical phenotype of dementia is most likely dictated by the topographical distribution of degeneration in the brain (Ouchi et al., 2014; Weintraub & Mesulam, 2009), an accurate report of the clinical syndrome and its progression over time could identify which core regions are targeted by degeneration and in which directions it spreads along in the brain.

Therefore, the overall aim of this study was to fill the gaps reported above with an in-depth, longitudinal investigation of a clinical and cognitive phenotype of an early onset dementia patient presenting with CBS. The more specific aims of the study were as follows: (i) a detailed evaluation of the cognitive impairments by adopting quantitative tests whenever possible; (ii) an in-depth, longitudinal, and quantitative evaluation of apraxia; (iii) an appraisal of the impact of apraxia and other cognitive impairments on patient functional status; (iv) an indirect mapping of the degeneration spreading in a case of CBS, starting from data on symptom progression as well as clinic-anatomical correlations reported in the literature.

2. Case description

Patient CG came to our attention at approximately 18 months post-disease onset (T1). She was a 53-year-old woman with 8 years of education. Her past medical history was unremarkable. In particular, there was no history of stroke, traumatic brain injury, or alcohol or drug abuse. Moreover, family history was negative for dementia. Only a brief minor depressive episode occurred more than 20 years before. At the first visit, CG reported some difficulties in performing complex actions that all seemed to involve arms movements (e.g. problems in opening the clotheshorse, errors in setting the table, difficulties folding clothes, and slight indecisions in dressing and ironing as well as writing). These reports were confirmed by her relatives, who specified that the symptoms had an insidious onset when CG was approximately 51 years old (approximately 18 months earlier) and showed a progressive course. On the other hand, no fluctuations of cognition and attention were reported. CG was fully aware of her difficulties and consequently very agitated and worried. A neurological examination showed bilateral limb apraxia and upper-limb plastic hypertonia and hyperreflexia. The Mini-Mental State Examination (MMSE) showed a mild cognitive decline (MMSE = 22/30). A neuropsychological evaluation confirmed bilateral ideomotor apraxia and preserved insight (Table 1). Moreover, the evaluation showed some deficits in visuospatial abilities and very mild prefrontal executive impairments. Conversely, no clear signs of amnesia, aphasia, visual agnosia and topographical disorientation emerged. Finally, all the aspects of orientation (i.e. temporal, spatial, contextual, and personal) were preserved. A behavioral examination showed mild anxiety and depression but was negative for psychotic symptoms and behavioral disturbances (Neuropsychiatric Inventory, NPI = 10). Functional status was reduced slightly, especially in some activities of daily living (Table 2). A brain MRI-scan showed initial focal atrophy of bilateral parietal cortices (Figures 1 and 2). An electroencephalogram (EEG) highlighted a diffuse and moderate slowing of the brain activity. A preliminary diagnosis of neurodegenerative dementia not otherwise specified was formulated, and therapies with donepezil, paroxetine and alprazolam were initiated.

A follow-up visit was performed approximately one year later at 32 months post-disease onset (T2). Difficulties in performing complex motor actions were increased (e.g. CG had fallen while catching the bus, had difficulties opening the car door and fastening her seatbelt, had burned her fingers by ironing, had grasped the receiver upside down and wrapped herself in telephone wire), and involuntary, brief muscle contractions of both her arms, closely resembling myoclonus, had been noticed for the first time. Rare odorous misperceptions (e.g. bad smells from fresh-cooked foods made her sick) and simple odorous hallucinations (i.e. unreal bad smells in her home) had also appeared. A neurological examination highlighted extra-pyramidal hypertonia, especially in the left upper limb, hyperreflexia more severe on the left side, deficits in discriminating tactile stimuli applied to symmetrical parts of the body, agraphesthesia, limb apraxia more severe in the left upper limb, and dysdiadochokinesia. The MMSE score was slightly decreased (19/30). A follow-up neuropsychological examination showed that ideomotor apraxia, visuospatial impairments, and prefrontal executive impairments had all worsened (Table 1). Moreover, the examination confirmed that apraxia had become asymmetric, with the left arm more affected. Also, mild aphasia emerged for the first time. On the other hand, orientation and insight were still preserved, and no signs of amnesia, visual agnosia, and topographical disorientation emerged. A follow-up behavioral assessment showed that

Table 1. Longitudinal neuropsychological assessment

	First evaluation T1	Second evaluation T2	Third evaluation T3	Maximum score	Cut-off score
Global					
MMSE	22*	19*	21*	/30	24
Raven '47	10*	6*	NA	/36	18
Attention					
Digit cancellation test	16*	NA	NA	/60	31
Bell's test	-	25*	17*	/35	30
Bell's test omissions (L/R)	-	3/7	15/3*	17/17	5
Raven '47 pp (right–left)	9*	21*	NA	/36	8
Pre-frontal functions					
Digit span backwards	2*	2*	0*		
CET total	12	19*	18*	/42	18
CET bizarre errors	3	7*	8*	/21	4
Category fluency	13.5	8.5	4.3*		7.25
Letter fluency	23	27	9*		17
Memory					
Prose recall	5.3	10	7	/16	4.75
Digit span forwards	4	4	3*		3.75
Language					
Picture naming	73	69	59*	/80	61
AAT battery					
Token test	-	19*	35*	/0	8
Repetition	-	137*	124*	/150	142
Written language	-	53*	17*	/90	81
Picture naming	-	106	93*	/120	104
Comprehen-sion	-	91*	62*	/120	108
Praxis function					
De Renzi test (right)	53*	42*	24*	/72	53
De Renzi test (left)	53*	25*	6*	/72	53
Visuospatial functions					
Geometrical figures copy	0*	2*	0*	/14	8

Notes: NA = not administrable; MMSE = Mini Mental State Examination; CET = Cognitive Estimates Test; AAT = Achener Aphasia Test; L/R = left/right; (Raven '47) pp = position preference.

*Impaired scores (< 5th percentile); NA = not administrable; MMSE = Mini Mental State Examination; CET = Cognitive Estimates Test; AAT = Achener Aphasia Test; L/R = left/right; (Raven '47) pp = position preference.

Table 2. Evaluation of functional status

18 months	MMSE:	22/30
Post onset	ADL:	5/6
	IADL:	7/8
	Test*:	Mild to moderate apraxia
	Report:	(Apraxia) The Patient was no longer able to open the drying rack. It was difficult to her to fold laundry. Several errors in setting the table and hesitation in arranging food on the plate were present. Minor impairments in putting her clothes on, ironing and writing were reported
22 months	ADL:	4.5/6
Post onset	IADL:	5/8
	Report:	(Apraxia) She needed help in getting in a car (open the car door for her) and in belting up. Major impairments in putting her clothes on (totally dependent from her caregiver). Worsening of manual tasks as to peel a potato or an apple, and to cut up a steak
32 months	MMSE:	19/30
Post onset	ADL:	5/6
	IADL:	2/8
	Test:	Moderate ideomotor apraxia
	Report:	(Apraxia) The patient was able to hand-launder small clothes but was no longer able to use the washing machine. In several occasions the patient burnt her fingers while she was ironing clothes. Major impairments in the use of cuttlery during the meal (i.e. cut up the steak or roll up the spaghetti on the fork) and in putting her clothes on (i.e. Put on a t-shirt or button up a blouse). (executive functions) The patient was less focused during housework and she lost the thread of ongoing tasks. She forgot to add ingredients in simple dishes and she made mistakes in the choice of ingredients doses. (visual-spatial attention) When she was cooking she stirred the food in a single spot of the pot. Episodes in which CG remain fixed at the roadside staring at a point for a while before to cross the street. (language) Difficulties in formulate phrases, to find words was a time-consuming task, sometimes sound errors were present in the pronounced words
38 months	ADL:	4.5/6
Post onset	IADL:	2/8
	Report:	(Apraxia) She pushed the pot laterally when she stired some food. Major impairment in opening the umbrella and keeping it on the head. Major errors were present when she tried to pour the water into the glass or to open small packets. (executive functions) CG was no more able to coordinate the several activities involved in the preparation of food; she fixated on the idea that she has to clean the bathroom tiles or the doors edge often, she does it in a perseverative way losing the sense of time. (visual-spatial attention) CG was absent-minded and her attention has to be drawn when you are talking to her; apparently CG has not been able to read a daily; she is not able to read the clock; while she is talking to a person she looks at another person and she becomes aware of it just after a while; when she is in a place she does not notice the presence of somebody who is there. (language) More difficulties in word finding, in particular for person names and common names of objects. More pronounced use of passepartout words. Difficulties in sentence construction
49 months	MMSE:	21/30
Post onset	ADL:	4.5/6

(Continued)

Table 2. (*Continued*)

	IADL:	1/8
	Test:	Severe ideomotor apraxia
	Report:	(Apraxia) Marked difficulties in getting in the front seat of a car (impossible to get in the rear seat). Difficulties in picking up the food with the fork. (visual-spatial attention) Getting in the car, instead of waiting in front of the passenger car door CG follow her daughter toward the pilot car door; sometimes getting in the car CG stand fast in front of the passenger car door; CG talks to a person looking at another person; suspected motor neglect for left arm (she almost does not use her left arm...she does not help herself with that arm doing things; it seems that her left arm does not exist for her). (language) It is difficult that she can say a complete and correct sentence, she does not find the words and they are usually warped; verbal comprehension is preserved. (insight) Insight for cognitive deficit is just partial even if sometimes a complete insight is present ("she is not aware of her condition...sometimes she'd like to go out by herself and she is not aware that she can't, sometimes she is aware of her cognitive deficits and says: when I was not ill yet ...)

Notes: MMSE = mini mental state examination. ADL = activities of daily living scale. IADL = instrumental activities of daily living scale. The caregiver's report of CG's cognitive impairment in everyday life as well as the results of functional status scales are shown. The results from longitudinal assessment of global cognitive functioning (i.e. MMSE) and apraxia (i.e. De Renzi test) were reported as frames of reference.

*De Renzi test of limb and limb-kinetic apraxia.

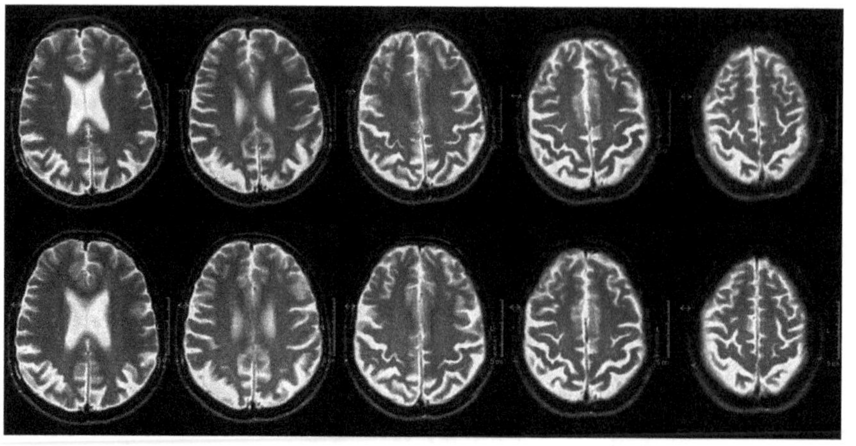

Figure 1. CG's brain imaging. A selection of axial slices from brain MRI scan performed at the first assessment (top) and follow-up visit about one year later (bottom), where focal and increasing bi-parietal cortex atrophy is clearly visible.

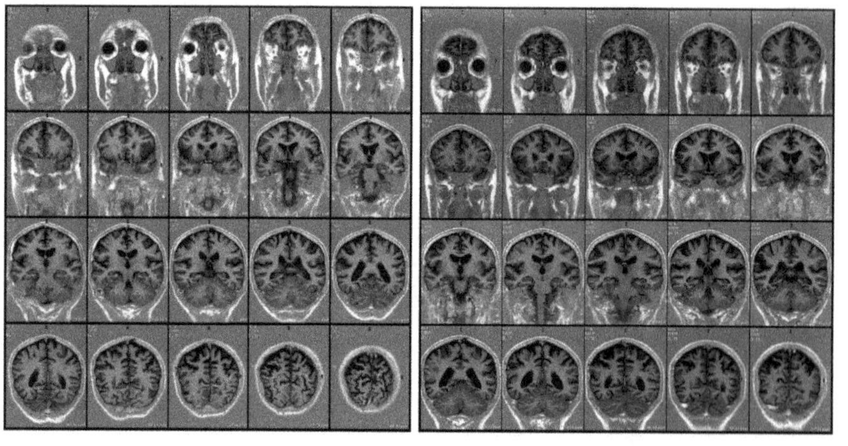

Figure 2. Coronal slices from the first (left) and follow-up (right) MRI examinations further showing posterior bi-parietal atrophy and demonstrating relative sparing of medial temporal and frontal cortices.

anxiety and depression had improved, but moderate apathy emerged (NPI = 8). Functional status had worsened, especially in the IADL scale (Table 2). A control brain MRI scan highlighted mild atrophy to bilateral parietal cortices (Figures 1 and 2). FP-CIT (dopamine transporter) SPECT brain imaging showed normal tracer uptake in basal nuclei. A diagnosis of CBS according to all the current diagnostic criteria (Mathew et al., 2011), i.e. Toronto criteria (Lang, Riley, & Bergeron, 1994), Mayo Clinic criteria (Boeve et al., 2003) and modified Cambridge criteria (Bak, Hodges, & Thomas, 2008; Mathew et al., 2011), was formulated. Finally, levetiracetam was prescribed to treat myoclonus.

A third evaluation was performed approximately one year later, at 49 months post-disease onset (T3). The errors in performing complex motor activities had further increased (e.g. the patient was no longer able to sit in the back seat of her car and showed some difficulties in sitting in the front seat as well; she had difficulties picking up foods with a fork). Moreover, CG's relatives reported that she sometimes postured with her trunk tilted leftwards, both while on her feet and walking. The brief occurrence of this abnormal posture closely resembled a short-lived episode of trunk dystonia known as Pisa tower syndrome. Besides, CG's relatives noticed that her left arm sometimes was quite inactive (i.e. a probable sign of motor neglect) and other times stayed somewhat raised (i.e. a probable sign of levitation). Furthermore, they reported that myoclonus of the upper limbs had improved slightly with levetiracetam therapy and that it was more severe in the left limb than in the right limb at this time. Finally, they noticed that odorous misperceptions and simple odorous hallucinations had completely disappeared. A follow-up neurological examination showed hypomimia, fixed gaze, dysarthria, camptocormia, extrapyramidal hypertonia of the four limbs (more severe on the left side), hyperreflexia, at-rest myoclonus of the upper limbs (more severe on the left side), and limb apraxia. The MMSE score was unchanged (21/30). A follow-up neuropsychological assessment showed that many of CG's cognitive impairments had worsened (Table 1). In particular, both ideomotor apraxia and visuospatial impairments reached a severe grade, and aphasia reached a moderate grade. Moreover, insight was slightly impaired for the first time. To the contrary, executive prefrontal impairments were unvaried and still mild, and both visual agnosia and topographical disorientation were still absent. Finally, because of aphasia, it was difficult to test both amnesia and orientation at this time. However, no signs of severe amnesia emerged at the clinical-observational examination (e.g. no perseverations in discourse, no oblivion to recalling autobiographical information). Moreover, orientation was tested by using an ad hoc recognition version of the spatiotemporal orientation test (i.e. a multiple-choice task), instead of the standard free recall version, and CG tested as being unimpaired. A behavioral examination was still negative for behavior disturbances and psychiatric symptoms (NPI = 1). Functional status was severely reduced on the IADL scale (Table 2). A brain CT scan confirmed moderate cortical atrophy, especially to bilateral frontal-parietal cortices. A brain HMPAO SPECT scan showed a severely decreased blood flow to bilateral temporal cortices, especially to the right superior temporal gyrus and to bilateral parietal-occipital cortices. A very mild decreased blood flow also emerged in the cuneus, precuneus and bilateral posterior cingulate gyri. Homozygosity of the epsilon-3 allele of the APOE gene resulted from the genetic testing. A globally slow and unstructured brain activity emerged at a follow-up EEG. A levodopa challenge test was negative.

At successive follow-up visits, both motor and cognitive impairments had progressively and rapidly worsened. In particular, three years after the first visit, at approximately 60 months post-disease onset (56 years of age), the MMSE score was 9/30, and a neuropsychological examination was not administrable because of severe dementia. At that time, by GC's relatives' wishes, no further examinations were performed.

3. Cognitive assessment

CG underwent the first neuropsychological evaluation at approximately 20 months post-disease onset. Two follow-up evaluations were carried out at 32 and 49 months post-disease onset. A supplementary neuropsychological evaluation was performed to refine the pattern of cognitive impairments at the same time as the second evaluation. Table 1 shows the results of the longitudinal neuropsychological assessment, and Table 3 shows the results of the supplementary neuropsychological examination. CG and her daughter gave their written consent to participate in the study. The study was approved by the Ethical Committee of the Casa di Cura Quarenghi and was done in accord with The Code of Ethics of the World Medical Association (Declaration of Helsinki) for experiments involving humans.

3.1. Global cognitive functioning

Global cognitive functioning was assessed using the Mini-Mental State Examination (MMSE) (Folstein, Folstein, & McHugh, 1975). The results showed a mild global cognitive decline at the first evaluation that remained relatively unvaried at the successive follow-ups up to the third evaluation at 49 months post-disease onset (Table 1). Then, one year later, at approximately 60 months post-disease onset, a more remarkable cognitive decline emerged that reached the stage of severe dementia (MMSE = 9/30). Interestingly, despite the cognitive decline being mild during the first 49 months of the disease course, severe selective neuropsychological syndromes (i.e. apraxia and visuospatial attention disorders) were already present at 18–20 months post-disease onset and subsequently showed a relatively rapid worsening over time.

3.2. Praxis processing

3.2.1. Limb and limb-kinetic apraxia

Limb (ideomotor) and limb-kinetic apraxia were examined employing the De Renzi test (De Renzi, 1985; De Renzi, Motti, & Nichelli, 1980). It is a test of concurrent or immediately delayed imitation of

Table 3. Supplementary neuropsychological assessment

	Raw score	Maximum score	Cut-off score
Calculus			
(arithmetical section of ENPA)			
Repetition	10	/10	8,8
Reading	7*	/10	7,6
Dictate	3*	/8	6,3
Transcoding	0*	/8	4,2
Addiction	1*	/3	2,2
Subtraction	1*	/3	1,0
Moltiplication	1*	/4	1,4
Visual perception			
Discrimination of scribbles	29	/36	21
Object decision task (hard) (BORB)	21*	/32	23
Object decision task (easy) (BORB)	28	/32	28
Visual-spatial functions			
Dot-Counting (VOSP)	3*	/10	8
Hand-eye coordination			
Reaching task (left hand)	12	/12	
Reaching task (right hand)	12	/12	
Awareness of body parts			
Finger gnosis			
Finger localization (left/right)	9* (3/6)	/24	13.75
Somatognosis (Bisiach battery)			
Naming body parts (of patient)	10	/12	
Naming body parts (of examiner)	12	/12	
Pointing body parts (of patient)	11	/12	
Pointing body parts (of examiner)	12	/12	
Pointing body parts (crossed)	7	/8	
Left-right orientation (Bisiach battery)			
Naming body parts (of patient)	8*	/16	
Pointing body parts (of patient)	6*	/16	
Pointing body parts (of examiner)	3*	/8	
Pointing body parts (crossed)	1*	/8	

Notes: ENPA = esame neuropsicologico per l'Afasia; BORB = Birmingham Object Recognition Battery; VOSP = Visual Object and Spatial Perception Battery. The emergence of acalculia, finger agnosia and left-right disorientation, together with agraphia, resulted on the AAT battery, leading us to diagnose a complete Gerstmann syndrome. In contrast, only a partial Balint's-Holmes syndrome was present. In fact, some signs of simultanagnosia resulted on the object decision task and a narrowing of attentive focus emerged, but the reaching task was negative for optic ataxia.

*Impaired scores (<5th percentile).

intransitive gestures that comprises two sections: one involving gestures by arms-and-hands (limb-apraxia) and the second involving gestures by fingers (limb-kinetic apraxia). Moreover, both the presentation and execution gestures are unilateral, e.g. the examiner moves her/his right (or left) arm to probe the movements of the right (or left) arm of the patient. Thus, the De Renzi test returns four partial scores, two of them relating to left and right arm-and-hand movements (limb-apraxia), and the other two scores relating to left and right finger movements (limb-kinetic apraxia). Two total scores, each corresponding to the sum of the partial scores obtained at the two sections of gestures for each body side, are calculated.

A more comprehensive assessment of ideomotor apraxia was accomplished by also administering the task of Pantomimes tool use to verbal command (De Renzi, Faglioni, Scarpa, & Crisi, 1986; De Renzi et al., 1980). Fifteen tools (e.g. a knife, toothbrush, hammer, comb) were included, and two attempts for the execution of each pantomime were offered to the patient. CG's performance was scored as 3 points (correct pantomime), 2 points (correct but imprecise pantomime), 1 point (vaguely similar pantomime) or 0 points (wrong pantomime). The total score of each tool was the sum of the scores obtained with the two attempts. The single-item score range was 0–6, and the total test score range was 0–90.

Also, a longitudinal study of limb and limb-kinetic apraxia was carried out by considering CG's results of three successive administrations of the De Renzi test and the task of Pantomimes tool use to verbal command over a period of three years. A statistical analysis of the longitudinal scores of the De Renzi test and pantomime task was performed by applying Friedman's ANOVA. Post hoc tests were computed using a Wilcoxon signed-rank test applying the Bonferroni correction.

The results showed that CG's performance of the De Renzi test of imitation of intransitive gestures was impaired at the first evaluation (Tables 1 and 4), supporting an early diagnosis of limb and limb-kinetic apraxia. Then, starting from the second evaluation, a diagnosis of ideomotor apraxia was also confirmed by CG's impaired performance on the pantomime task (Table 4). The longitudinal study showed a significant worsening of limb apraxia as well as limb-kinetic apraxia over time, both considering the results of the imitation test (De Renzi test total score, $\chi^2 = 43.145$, $df = 5$, $p < 0.001$; De Renzi test limb apraxia score, $\chi^2 = 31.649$, $df = 5$, $p < 0.001$; De Renzi test limb-kinetic apraxia score, $\chi^2 = 20.837$, $df = 5$, $p = 0.001$) and the pantomime task (pantomime task, $\chi^2 = 20.844$, $df = 2$, $p < 0.001$) (Table 4).

Moreover, CG's total score on the De Renzi test significantly worsened on the second evaluation of the left side of the body (T2–T1 score difference = 53–25, $z = -2.751$, $p = 0.006$, two-tailed). No statistical difference was found on the right side (T2–T1 score difference = 53–42, $z = -1.580$, $p = 0.114$, two-tailed). Moreover, both left and right limb apraxia significantly worsened on the second evaluation (left arm T2–T1 score difference = 24–1, $z = -2.772$, $p = 0.006$, two-tailed; right arm T2–T1 score difference = 27–15, $z = -2.058$, $p = 0.040$, two-tailed), but limb-kinetic apraxia remained relatively unchanged (left hand T2–T1 score difference = 29–24, $z = -0.850$, $p = 0.395$, two-tailed; right hand T2-T1 score difference = 26–27, $z = -0.368$, $p = 0.713$, two-tailed). At the third visit, CG's total score on the De Renzi test further worsened both for the left and right sides of the body (left side T3–T2 score difference = 25–6, $z = -2.565$, $p = 0.010$, two-tailed; right side T3–T2 score difference = 42–24, $z = -2.456$, $p = 0.014$, two-tailed). Moreover, limb apraxia results were relatively unchanged (left arm T3–T2 score difference = 1–0, $z = -1.000$, $p = 0.317$; right arm T3-T2 score difference = 15–10, $z = -1.342$, $p = 0.180$), whereas limb-kinetic apraxia had worsened (left hand T3–T2 score difference = 24–6, $z = -2.428$, $p = 0.015$, two-tailed; right hand T3–T2 score difference = 27–14, $z = -2.121$, $p = 0.034$, two-tailed).

3.2.2. Other types of apraxia

Oral apraxia was evaluated using a test by De Renzi, Pieczuro, and Vignolo (1966), and gaze apraxia was evaluated through an *ad hoc* task requiring bi-ocular movements along the horizontal and vertical axes to verbal commands. In detail, four directions of gaze were tested (i.e. upward, downward, rightward and leftward), and CG had to repeat each movement three times. Every single correct movement was scored as one point, and the total range score was 0–12. Regarding other remaining apraxia, truncal, dressing and eyelid apraxia were examined both by observing the patient's behavior at the visits and by interviewing the caregiver. Moreover, the copy of geometrical figures test (Spinnler & Tognoni, 1987) was used to test for constructional apraxia. Finally, ideational apraxia was investigated by means of some items involving multi-step actions taken from the pantomime tool use task as well as the object use task (see below) (De Renzi, 1985; De Renzi, Pieczuro, & Vignolo, 1968) (e.g. CG had to light a candle with matches, pour a glass of water from a bottle).

Table 4. Apraxia longitudinal assessment

	T1 First exam	T2 Second exam	T3 Third exam	Max score	Longitudinal analysis (*p*-value)			Left/right difference (*p*-value)			Meaningful/not meaningful difference		
					T3–T2–T1	T2–T1	T3–T2	T1	T2	T3	T1	T2	T3
De Renzi test													
Total score left	53	25	6	72	<0.001	0.006	0.010	ns	0.036	0.040			
Total score right	53	42	24	72		ns	0.014						
Limb apraxia left	24	1	0	36	<0.001	0.006	ns	ns	0.034	ns			
Limb apraxia right	27	15	10	36		0.040	ns						
Limb-kinetic apraxia left	29	24	6	36	<0.001	ns	0.015	ns	ns	ns			
Limb-kinetic apraxia right	26	27	14	36		ns	0.034						
Meaningful gestures left	24	13	3	36							ns	ns	ns
Not meaning-ful gestures left	29	12	3	36									
Meaningful gestures right	28	27	13	36							ns	ns	ns
Not meaning-ful gestures right	25	15	12	36									
Pantomime tool use (15 items)	88	66	26	/90	<0.001	0.015	0.005						
Pantomime tool use (10 items) (a)	-	46	-	/60									
Object use (b)	-	51	-	/60					(a–b) ns				
Pantomime intransitive (c)	-	28	-	/30					(a–c) 0.025				
Imitation intransitive (d)	-	24	-	/30					(c–d) ns				
Recognition of gestures	-	30	-	/30									

(*Continued*)

Table 4. *(Continued)*

	T1 First exam	T2 Second exam	T3 Third exam	Max score	Longitudinal analysis (p-value)			Left/right difference (p-value)			Meaningful/not meaningful difference		
					T3–T2–T1	T2–T1	T3–T2	T1	T2	T3	T1	T2	T3
Tool naming task	18	17	15	/20	ns								
Oro-facial apraxia	20	20	18	/20	ns								
Gaze apraxia	12	6	–	/12									
Constructional apraxia	0	2	0	/14									

Notes: A statistically significant decline of longitudinal assessment emerged in the following tests: De Renzi test, limb apraxia subtest, limb-kinetic subtest, and 15 items version of pantomime tool use task. In contrast, no significant decline emerged in the tool naming task as well as in the oro-facial apraxia test. Moreover, note the quantitative confirmation that limb and limb-kinetic apraxia were both symmetric at the first exam and that limb-apraxia, but not limb-kinetic apraxia, became asymmetric at the second exam, with the left upper limb more impaired. Furthermore, both limb and limb-kinetic apraxia were asymmetric at the third exam, but the score difference (left–right) did not reach statistical significance. In addition, a statistically significant difference resulted between transitive and intransitive gestures, with transitive gestures more impaired at pantomime (a–c). Finally, no differences emerged between meaningful and not meaningful gestures on the De Renzi test pantomime and object use (a–b) as well as pantomime and imitation (c–d).

Results showed that oral, eyelid, gaze, dressing and truncal apraxia were all absent on the first evaluation. Moreover, ideational apraxia was ruled out because CG had no difficulties on items involving multi-step actions taken from both the pantomime tool use task and the objects use task (see the section Modality of gesture performance: pantomime, imitation and tool use). On the other hand, severe constructional apraxia resulted from the copy of geometrical figure test (Tables 1 and 4). On the second evaluation, oral, eyelid and ideational apraxia were still absent, whereas mild gaze dyspraxia emerged (Table 4). Moreover, the emergence of dressing apraxia was suggested by CG's caregiver reports (Table 2). Also, some suspicion for truncal apraxia emerged for the first time, especially by noticing some marked hesitations by CG in sitting in the chair in the evaluation room. Finally, constructional apraxia was still severe. On the third evaluation, the total score of the oral praxis test was still in the normal range; nonetheless, some errors emerged for the first time (Table 4). Moreover, truncal and dressing apraxia had worsened, and constructional apraxia was of extreme severity. Furthermore, some rare errors in performing multistep actions suggesting a very mild ideational apraxia emerged for the first time with the pantomime tool use task. In contrast, eyelid apraxia was still absent. Finally, gaze praxis was not further evaluated.

3.2.3. Left–right differences

The De Renzi test is a useful tool also for studying left–right differences in limb and limb-kinetic apraxia. In fact, it invites the patient to imitate the same set of intransitive gestures successively with her/his right upper limb and then with her/his left upper limb, and the test accordingly provides separate scores for the performance of the limb of each side of the body. Left–right differences with the De Renzi test were first examined by applying Friedman's ANOVA. Post hoc tests were computed with the Wilcoxon signed-rank test applying the Bonferroni correction.

Results showed that limb and limb-kinetic apraxia were clearly symmetric on the first examination; in fact, no differences between the left and right sides of the body emerged on the De Renzi test (i.e. left-right total score = 53–53, $z = 0.000$, $p = 1.000$, two-tailed; limb-apraxia score = 24–27, $z = -0.604$, $p = 0.546$, two-tailed; limb-kinetic apraxia score = 29–26, $z = -0.816$, $p = 0.414$, two-tailed) (Table 4). However, a significant difference between the right and left body sides, with the left side more impaired, emerged on the De Renzi test total score at the second evaluation (left-right difference = 25–42, $z = -2.092$, $p = 0.036$, two-tailed) (Table 4). In particular, an asymmetric limb-apraxia emerged with the left upper limb more severely affected than the right limb (left–right difference = 1–15, $z = -2.121$, $p = 0.034$, two-tailed), whereas limb-kinetic apraxia was still symmetric (left-right difference = 24–27, $z = -828$, $p = 0.408$, two-tailed) (Table 4). At the third visit, the left body side was still more impaired than the right side on the total score of the De Renzi test (left-right difference = 6–24, $z = -2.058$, $p = .040$) (Table 4), but this time both limb apraxia (left-right difference = 0–10) and limb-kinetic apraxia (left–right difference = 6–14) seemed to be asymmetric, even if the amount of the left-right difference did not reach statistical significance both for limb apraxia ($z = -1.890$, $p = 0.059$, two-tailed) and limb-kinetic apraxia ($z = -1.131$, $p = 0.258$, two-tailed).

3.2.4. Modality of gesture performance: pantomime, imitation and tool use

To advance the study of CG's apraxia, different modalities of gesture performance were tested (i.e. pantomime, object use, and imitation). The task of pantomimes tool use to verbal command and the parallel task of object use were administered to CG. The first task has been already described in the previous section Limb and limb-kinetic apraxia. The object use task involved 10 concrete tools similar to a subset of those utilized in the pantomime tool use task. In particular, the concrete objects were placed successively on the table in front of CG, and she had to grasp them and show to the examiner how they should be used. The same scoring procedure as the pantomime task was adopted. In particular, two attempts for each object use demonstration were given to the patient. CG's performance was scored as 3 points (correct demonstration), 2 points (correct but imprecise demonstration), 1 point (vaguely similar demonstration) or 0 points (wrong demonstration). The total score of each tool was the sum of the scores obtained from the two attempts. The single item score range was 0–6, and the total test score range was 0–60.

A comparison between the pantomime and object use tasks was performed on the second visit. A Wilcoxon signed-rank test was applied to test for differences in the patient's performance.

To compare imitation and pantomime, CG's ability to pantomime to verbal command 10 meaningful intransitive gestures, taken from the De Renzi test, was examined first (e.g. "please, do the sign of the cross"). Then, we compared CG's performance on the pantomime of these ten intransitive gestures with her performance on the imitation of the same gestures that had resulted from the standard De Renzi test. Differences were computed as the mean of the Wilcoxon signed-rank test.

Results showed that CG's performance on the object use task seemed to be slightly better than that on the pantomime tool use task (i.e. 51/60 vs. 46/60) (Table 4), but even so, this difference did not reach the statistical significance ($z = -1.512$, $p = 0.131$, two-tailed). Similarly, the comparison between pantomime and imitation performed at the time of the second evaluation did not return any statistically significant difference ($z = -1.342$, $p = 0.180$, two-tailed) (Table 4). However, a clear difference in favor of pantomime emerged at an early stage of disease. In fact, the extended version of the pantomime task (i.e. 15 items) resulted as unimpaired at the first evaluation; conversely, the imitation task (i.e. De Renzi test) resulted as impaired at the same evaluation.

3.2.5. Type of gestures: Transitive vs. intransitive, meaningful vs. non-meaningful

The type of gesture was included as a variable in the evaluation of CG's apraxia. In particular, a comparison between transitive gestures taken from the test of pantomime tool use to verbal command and intransitive gestures taken from the test of pantomime meaningful gestures to verbal command (see the preceding section) was performed at the second evaluation. A Wilcoxon signed-rank test was used to test for differences.

In addition, since the De Renzi test (De Renzi, 1985; De Renzi et al., 1980) involves an equal number (i.e. 12) of meaningful (e.g. the sign of victory) and non-meaningful gestures (e.g. put the thumb between the index and middle fingers), a comparison between the two types of gestures was performed. A Wilcoxon signed-rank test was adopted.

The results showed that CG's performance of transitive gestures on the pantomime tool use task was slightly worse than the performance on the intransitive gestures of the pantomime meaningful gestures task (respectively, 46/60, equivalent to 76.6%, and 28/30, equivalent to 93.3%) (Table 4). Moreover, this last difference was statistically significant ($z = -2.235$, $p = 0.025$, two-tailed). Regarding the comparison between meaningful and non-meaningful gestures, results did not show any significant differences. In particular, although both types of gestures were slightly impaired on the first examination (Table 4), no differences emerged between them when considering both the right and the left upper limbs (right side, $z = -0.212$, $p = 0.832$, two-tailed; left side, $z = -637$, $p = 0.524$, two-tailed). At the second evaluation, an advantage in the meaningful gestures seemed to emerge exclusively for the right arm (i.e. 27/36 vs. 15/36) (Table 4), but this difference did not reach statistical significance ($z = -1.000$, $p = 0.317$, two-tailed). At the third evaluation, both types of gestures were severely impaired, but no differences emerged between them (right side, $z = -0.137$, $p = 0.891$, two-tailed; left side, $z = -1.000$, $p = 0.317$, two-tailed) (Table 4).

3.2.6. Input: Recognition of gestures

Recognition of gestures was studied using a task of gesture naming by action at the second evaluation. In particular, the task called for CG to name 10 meaningful intransitive gestures (e.g. military greeting, stop gesture, the sign of the cross) taken from the De Renzi test that were pantomimed by the examiner. In addition, we took into account the results by CG in naming 20 pictures belonging to the categories of tools (e.g. hammer, saw, pliers) as well as musical instruments (e.g. violin, piano, trumpet) (tool naming task) taken from the picture naming test (Laiacona, Barbarotto, Trivelli, & Capitani, 1993) at all three successive examinations.

The results showed that CG had no difficulties in recognizing all of the 10 intransitive meaningful gestures taken from the De Renzi test (score = 30/30) at time of the second evaluation. Interestingly, at the same time, CG's performance on imitation of the same 10 intransitive meaningful gestures on the standard version of the De Renzi test was impaired, especially for the left upper limb (i.e. left upper limb score = 12/30, right upper limb score = 24/30). Regarding the results from the tool naming task, GC's performance on the 20 items belonging to the categories of tools and musical instruments was relatively unimpaired at both the first (score = 18/20) and the second examinations (score = 17/20). In contrast, mild deficits on the tool naming task suggest a possible initial impairment of the conceptual system of praxis at the third examination (score = 15/20). However, the language impairment found in naming at this time could better explain this result.

3.2.7. Functional impact

The impact of apraxia on CG's functional status was studied by interviewing the caregiver and using the basic and instrumental activities of daily living scales (ADL, Katz, Downs, Cash, & Grotz, 1970; IADL, Lawton & Brody, 1969).

The results showed that an early mild decline in CG's functional status was evident since the first evaluation (Table 2). Moreover, CG's performance resulted as impaired, especially on those activities of her daily life that mainly involved arm movements (e.g. problems in opening the clotheshorse, errors in setting the table, difficulties in folding clothes, slight indecisions in dressing and ironing, difficulty writing) (Table 2). This fact suggests that CG's functional decline was probably strictly related to limb apraxia. Then, at successive visits, a progressive decline in CG's functional status was documented, probably due to a concurrent worsening of apraxia. However, starting from 32 months post-disease onset, CG's caregiver frequently reported errors suggesting not only apraxia but also impairment of other cognitive functions, especially visuospatial functions (Table 2). Therefore, it is probable that the reduction in CG's competence in performing activities of her daily life was related not only to apraxia but also to other multiple cognitive impairments starting from an intermediate stage of disease onset.

3.3. Visuospatial processing

3.3.1. Spatial abilities as a whole

Several tests were used to evaluate CG's visuospatial abilities (Tables 1 and 3). In particular, tests of constructional apraxia, visuospatial attention impairments, unilateral neglect, (dorsal) simultanagnosia, and optic ataxia were administered. Moreover, the possible emergence of complex syndromes (i.e. Balint–Holmes' syndrome and Gerstmann's syndrome) was checked by using tests of both visuospatial impairments and other different cognitive impairments (e.g. left–right disorientation, acalculia). Finally, data concerning CG's abilities of topographical orientation were obtained by interviewing the caregiver.

The results showed that visuospatial function disorders were the second more important impairment in CG's cognitive profile. In fact, several different spatial ability impairments emerged (e.g. constructional impairments, visuospatial attention disorders, unilateral neglect, simultanagnosia). However, it should be noted that some spatial abilities were unimpaired (i.e. hand–eye coordination and topographical orientation).

3.3.2. Constructional functions impairments

A test of drawing geometrical figures was used to test for constructional apraxia (i.e. Copy of geometrical figures test, Spinnler & Tognoni, 1987). The results showed severe impairment in the visuoconstructional functions starting from the first evaluation (Table 1). Noteworthy, closing-in was one of the most frequent errors. In particular, CG had a strong tendency to draw lines inside the models as if her hand was captured by them (magnetism).

3.3.3. Visuospatial attention disorders

Two tests of visual search were administered to CG for assessing selective attention as well as visuospatial attention (i.e. digit cancellation test, Spinnler & Tognoni, 1987; Bell's test, Gauthier, Dehaut, & Joanette, 1989). Moreover, further data about CG's visuospatial attention impairments were reported by the caregiver and were collected by observing her behavior at the visits.

The results showed that CG's performance on the two visual search tests was moderately impaired (Table 1) at the first examination and then worsened over time. In particular, CG seemed not to be able to efficiently explore the visual space, such that many omissions of targets resulted in the visual search tests. Moreover, a severe difficulty to follow printed stimuli from line-to-line emerged. Furthermore, distractibility was another relevant feature of CG's attention disorders: in fact, her attention was often captured by task-irrelevant events during the visits. Interestingly, distractibility was not associated with a more general environmental dependency; in fact, utilization and imitation behaviors (Iaccarino, Chieffi, & Iavarone, 2014; Lhermitte, 1983) never appeared. Another aspect of CG's attention disorders was a difficulty in disengaging her attention from stimuli (sticky fixation) (e.g. when she has to cross a street, she stares at a point at the far side of the street for a long time before starting to move). Finally, a pathological narrowing of the visuoattentional focus (tubular vision) also seemed to emerge.

3.3.4. Unilateral neglect

Unilateral neglect was assessed through a visual search test (i.e. Bell's test, Gauthier et al., 1989) and by considering possible position-preference effects on the Raven progressive colored matrices test (Basso, Capitani, & Laiacona, 1987). In detail, "position-preference effect" refers to the tendency of a patient with left (or right) unilateral neglect to pick drawings especially on the right (or left) side of a page on the Raven test. To further evaluate unilateral neglect, CG's performance on writing and reading tasks used in the assessing of aphasia was considered. Conversely, CG's performance in drawing was not usable because of severe constructional apraxia.

Regarding the results, a mild left unilateral neglect emerged on Raven's test that showed a significant position-preference effect on right-sided items at the first evaluation (Table 1). Then, at the second evaluation, left visuospatial neglect was confirmed, with both a more pronounced position-preference effect with right-sided items on the Raven test and the occurrence of some errors with neglect point on a reading task (AAT battery). At the third evaluation, Bell's test was positive for left unilateral neglect for the first time, and further errors with neglect point emerged on the reading task. Moreover, signs of motor neglect exclusively affecting the left arm were reported by the caregiver and confirmed on the observational examination (e.g. CG's left arm assumed a quite passive posture and remained inactive during the visit).

3.3.5. Simultanagnosia

Simultanagnosia was evaluated using an object decision task (i.e. chimerical figures) taken from the Birmingham Object Recognition Battery (BORB, Riddoch & Humphreys, 1993). Moreover, the dot counting task taken from the Visual Object and Space Perception Battery (VOSP, Warrington & James, 1991) was administered to examine the spatial abilities further.

Results showed that a mild impairment emerged with the object decision task (Table 3) as well as with the Dot counting task at the second evaluation (Table 3). Such results were suggestive of simultanagnosia, especially considering that CG's performances on concurrent tasks of visual processing, both at a pre-associative (i.e. discrimination of Scribble test) and associative stage (i.e. picture-naming task) (see the section Visual-perceptual processing), were all unimpaired. Moreover, since CG suffered from marked visuospatial impairments more than visual perception impairments and had never read letter-by-letter, as is usually done by ventral simultagnosics (Riddoch et al., 2010), we hypothesized that her simultanagnosia was of the dorsal type.

3.3.6. *Optic ataxia*

A simple reaching task was devised and administered to CG for assessing optic ataxia. In particular, CG had to reach and grasp an object (e.g. a little bottle of water) with her hand that was placed alternatively at one of three different locations (i.e. in high, middle, and low positions) in both her left and right visual hemifields. Moreover, CG had to execute the test under both the conditions of central (foveal) and peripheral vision and alternatively by using her right arm and her left arm. One point was scored for any appropriate grasping. The total score for each hand was 12 points (6 locations × 2 conditions). The results showed that CG's performance on the reaching task was fully unimpaired (Table 3). Thus, optic ataxia was ruled out.

3.3.7. *Balint–Holmes' syndrome*

A complete Balint–Holmes' syndrome (see Vallar, 2007) never appeared; nonetheless, some features of the syndrome emerged. In particular, some signs of gaze apraxia and a suspected narrowing of the visuospatial attentional focus was noticed in the observational examination at the second visit. Moreover, simultanagnosia resulted in the object decision task being taken from BORB. Nonetheless, both optic ataxia and a defective ability in estimating distances and in-depth perception never emerged.

3.3.8. *Gerstmann's syndrome*

A complete Gerstmann syndrome (for a review see Rusconi, Pinel, Dehaene, & Kleinschmidt, 2010) emerged starting at the second evaluation. The emergence of the four impairments of the syndrome (i.e. finger agnosia, left–right disorientation, dysgraphia, and acalculia) was supported by the results of quantitative testing (see the sections Finger agnosia, left–right disorientation, Written language processing, and Number processing).

3.4. Body awareness processing

3.4.1. *Finger agnosia*

Finger gnosis was tested using a modified version of the task for finger localization by Spinnler and Tognoni (1987). In the standard version of the task, the patient's hand is covered, and the examiner touches simultaneously two of her/his out-of-sight fingers. The patient's task is to point to the fingers on a drawing of her/his hand that she/he feels touched by the examiner. However, since CG showed severe difficulties in pointing, probably because of apraxia, we had to modify the standard procedure of the task and train CG to name the out-of-sight fingers that she felt was touched by the examiner instead of pointing them on a drawing of the hand as in the standard version.

Results showed that CG's performance was severely impaired in the modified version of the finger localization task, especially, but not exclusively, for the left hand (Table 3). These results were suggestive for finger agnosia. An alternative explanation based on CG's difficulty in naming related to aphasia seemed less convincing. In fact, CG suffered from mild aphasia at that time, whereas her performance on the finger gnosis task was severely impaired. Moreover, omissions and other signs of word-finding problems (e.g. circumlocutions, verbal and semantic paraphasias, semantic conduite d'approche) were rare (i.e. 2 omissions out of 12 items). Finally, CG was able to retrieve the names of no less than four different fingers (i.e. the thumb, forefinger, middle finger, and little finger) without any word-finding hesitations during the visit.

3.4.2. *Autotopagnosia*

Body schema abilities were examined using a shortened version of Semenza and Goodglass (1985) battery, which included some tests of naming as well as of pointing to body parts. More details are that two tasks of naming body parts (respectively on patient's body and on examiner's body) and two tasks of pointing to body parts (respectively, on patient's body and on examiner's body) were administered (Table 3). Both the tasks of naming and pointing to body parts on the patient's body had to be executed with eyes open in the first section and with eyes closed in the second section. A crossed-pointing task was also administered in which CG had to use her right hand to point to some parts on her left hemi-body and her left hand to point to some parts on her right hemi-body (Table 3).

Results showed that both tasks of naming body parts were relatively unimpaired (Table 3). Also, the three pointing tasks of the Bisiach battery (i.e. the two tasks of pointing to body parts and the crossed-pointing task) all resulted in being relatively unimpaired (Table 3). Therefore, a diagnosis of autotopagnosia was excluded. Moreover, no differences emerged between the conditions of open and closed eyes in the task of pointing to body parts on the patient's body.

3.4.3. Left–right disorientation

Left–right disorientation was assessed using the same tasks utilized for assessing autotopagnosia. The pointing tasks included in the Bisiach battery called for the patient to point to alternating right or left body parts. In the same way, the patient had to declare the parts of the left vs. right side of the body pointed to by the examiner in the naming tasks of the battery. Therefore, the results from these tests were also used to identify possible left–right disorientation. Moreover, the crossed-pointing task from the same battery was also an appropriate tool for the assessing of left–right discrimination.

The results showed that CG had severe left–right disorientation. In fact, the tasks from the Bisiach battery requiring left–right discrimination were all impaired (Table 3). On the whole, CG made 30 errors out of the 48 left–right discriminations requested (62.5%).

3.4.4. Agonistic dyspraxia

Awareness and representation of body parts were studied only in a preliminary way overall by observing CG's behaviors and reactions while she was performing tests involving limbs and hands movements, especially the De Renzi test of limb and limb-kinetic apraxia (De Renzi, 1985; De Renzi et al., 1980).

The results were somewhat unexpected. In fact, a phenomenon similar, but not coincident, to what other authors previously described and named as agonistic dyspraxia (Aboitiz et al., 2003) emerged. In particular, when a request of executing a movement of a forelimb (for example, the right one) is made, the patient suffering from agonistic dyspraxia correctly executes that movement but does it by using her/his contralateral forelimb (the left one in the example) instead of the correct forelimb that remains immobilized. Moreover, this contralateral movement is experienced as involuntary by the patient, who has serious difficulties in controlling it. Finally, agonistic dyspraxia occurs only when unilateral movements are requested by a verbal command and not under imitation or spontaneous execution. Similar to the descriptions of agonistic dyspraxia, when CG had to perform a movement with her left or right hand, the other hand (the right or the left, respectively) replaced it and automatically or compulsively executed that movement, performing the same purposeful action in its place (i.e. the agonistic hand). CG had difficulties counteracting these substitutions, and after she corrected herself, a new replacement occurred. As a consequence, her behavior appeared as being hesitant. This phenomenon of replacing was evident both under imitation and verbal command and only occasionally presented also in spontaneous movement. However, in a quite different way from patients with agonistic dyspraxia (Aboitiz et al., 2003), the substitutions managed by the agonistic arm and hand of CG seemed to start exclusively after that the correct arm had begun its movement, just like in mirror movement (see Boeve et al., 2003). It seemed that the agonistic arm of CG was called to action in a mirroring way, but as soon as it started to imitate what the other arm was doing, this last arm stopped moving. Therefore, simultaneous concurrent movements of both arms, as it occurs in the classical mirror phenomenon (see Boeve et al., 2003), never appeared. Interestingly, there emerged no differences in agonistic dyspraxia between the left and right arm and hand up to the second visit (i.e. the left hand replaced the right one and vice versa with the same frequency). In contrast, at a more advanced stage of disease, CG's right hand replaced the left one more often.

3.4.5. Other phenomena

The possible occurrences of intermanual conflict, as well as of the anarchic and alien hand syndromes, were studied by interviewing CG's caregiver and by observing her spontaneous behavior at the visits and during her performance on the De Renzi test.

The results showed that, even if CG experienced involuntary movements like those described above (i.e. agonistic dyspraxia), an experience of estrangement from and personification of the limbs never appeared (i.e. alien hand). Moreover, CG sometimes experienced hand and arm movements as being slightly unwilled but never as being strange and uncooperative (i.e. anarchic hand). Furthermore, no feelings of having additional fingers or limbs emerged (i.e. supernumerary hand). In addition, bimanual coordination was preserved, and CG had no problems performing actions requiring simultaneous cooperation of both hands (e.g. opening a bottle of water, closing her pencil case, putting on and off a pen's cap, cutting a sheet of paper with a scissors, opening a padlock with a key). Additionally, we never observed one of CG's hands performing actions to the contrary and in an opposite way to (i.e. diagonistic dyspraxia), or interfering with (i.e. intermanual conflict), the actions performed by the other hand. Also, although clear signs of somatic personal neglect (i.e. hemisomatoagnosia) never appeared, some signs of motor neglect affecting the left upper limb were noticeable at the observational examination starting at the second evaluation. Furthermore, at the time of the second evaluation, CG's caregiver reported that CG's left forearm remained frequently raised to approximately 45 degrees when she was holding her bag (i.e. levitating hand). Finally, magnetic errors (i.e. magnetic apraxia) frequently emerged on the De Renzi test, without differences between the left and right body side, at all the three evaluations, and a more general magnetism was confirmed in CG from many occurrences of the closing-in phenomenon when drawing (see Ambron & Della Sala, 2017; Conson, Salzano, Manzo, Grossi, & Trojano, 2009). On the whole, all the symptoms collected (i.e. bilateral agonistic dyspraxia, left arm levitation and bilateral magnetic apraxia) resembled a mild corticobasal or posterior variant of alien hand syndrome (Semenza, 2003).

3.5. Language processing

3.5.1. Oral language processing

The language was examined using the picture-naming test (Laiacona et al., 1993) and by the Achener Aphasia Test (Luzzatti, Willmes, & De Bleser, 1996).

Results showed overall that aphasia was a salient aspect of the CG's cognitive profile, even if less prominent and early when compared to impairments of other cognitive domains. In fact, aphasia started only from the second evaluation and was never severe. Specifically, no signs of aphasia appeared in the conversational speech during the first evaluation; only rare hesitations of articulation and infrequent and brief word-finding latencies were noticeable. Auditory comprehension was preserved. No difficulties emerged with the repetition item of the MMSE, and the picture naming test was unimpaired (Table 1).

At the second visit, speech was fluent with normal utterance length, but its rate was slowed by word-finding difficulties. Moreover, frequent use of imprecise words was evident, and negligible impairments of articulation, as well as minimal signs of paragrammatism, were also noticeable. Furthermore, some suspects for auditory comprehension impairment emerged with conversation. Regarding the results of the AAT, repetition was globally preserved with some minor difficulties exclusively emerging with the longest sentences. Moreover, no significant deficits emerged in the naming task (Table 1). In contrast, moderate impairments of both auditory and written comprehension were confirmed in the Token test as well as in the comprehension task of the AAT. On the whole, a profile resuming transcortical sensory aphasia of mild gravity resulted from the data collected.

At the third evaluation, aphasia had worsened, and its profile had changed to mixed transcortical aphasia of moderate gravity. The conversational speech appeared globally fluent; nonetheless, brief, stereotyped and often interrupted utterances, together with mild articulatory problems, were evident. Moreover, mild echolalia and more clear signs of paragrammatism, as well as some phonological paraphasias, were present. Furthermore, both word-finding difficulties and auditory comprehension impairments had worsened in conversation. Regarding the results of testing, the deficits in both the picture naming test (Laiacona et al., 1993) and the naming task of the AAT had worsened (Table 1). Moreover, the impairment in the Token test as well as in the comprehension tests of the AAT became severe. Finally, repetition was still minimally impaired, with some slight difficulties emerging exclusively with the longest sentences.

3.5.2. Written language processing

Written language processing was assessed only in a preliminary way. In particular, three tasks of written language included in the AAT battery were administered: a task of reading of words (both regular and irregular) as well as of brief sentences, a task of writing with tokens (the tokens representing single letters in a first section of the task and words in a second section), and finally a task of handwriting to dictate. Moreover, spontaneous handwriting was also examined.

No difficulties emerged on the reading of simple sentences, like those included on the MMSE, at the first evaluation. At the second evaluation, the reading abilities resulted as minimally impaired, especially in the task of reading brief sentences on the AAT (score = 26/30). Moreover, some errors containing the neglect point (Ellis, Flude, & Young, 1987) emerged, suggesting very mild neglect dyslexia. At the third evaluation, the performance on the reading task of the AAT was more clearly impaired (score = 17/30). In particular, there were many errors, especially in the reading of sentences as well as of irregular words (i.e. reading irregular words scored 1/3 compared to a score of 3/3 in reading regular words). Moreover, errors in neglect point were also frequent. Consequently, a diagnosis of peripheral dyslexia, probably neglect dyslexia, was confirmed, and a preliminary diagnosis of surface dyslexia was suggested for the first time by considering the selective errors in the reading of irregular words. Unfortunately, the reading task included a limited number of items (i.e. only 3 regular and 3 irregular words) and did not include non-words; therefore, a more accurate diagnosis of dyslexia cannot be made.

Regarding the results of writing abilities, CG's performance resulted as being severely impaired (score = 3/30) in the task of writing words and brief phrases under dictation, starting from the second evaluation. In contrast, only a minimal impairment in the task of writing with tokens under dictation (score = 24/30) emerged at the same evaluation. Concomitantly, severe difficulties emerged in the spontaneous handwriting of single words, and the handwriting of sentences was unfeasible. At the third evaluation, CG's dysgraphia had notably worsened, and any further examination was not possible. Taking into account a qualitative analysis of CG's errors in writing, as a whole, CG's handwriting was almost completely illegible. Specifically, most of her errors involved letter morphology and suggested allographic impairments (e.g. the use of upper- and lower case letters in the same word). Moreover, frequent scrawls emerged in CG's writing because either the letters in a word often overlapped and/or the lines of a single letter were perseverated (i.e. motor, continuous perseverations). Furthermore, spatial errors characterized especially by misalignment also emerged. In contrast, micrography was absent. In sum, taking into account the characteristics of CG's spontaneous handwriting, as well as the dissociation that resulted between the two dictation tasks, with a severe impairment on handwriting and a relative preservation in writing with tokens, a diagnosis of peripheral dysgraphia (i.e. apraxic agraphia) was formulated (Passov, Gavrilova, Strand, Cerhan, & Josephs, 2011). Unfortunately, because of the severity of peripheral distortions, a study of possible forms of central dysgraphia was unfeasible.

3.5.3. Number processing

CG's arithmetical abilities were examined using a brief test battery for acalculia included in the Esame Neuropsicologico per l'Afasia (Capasso & Miceli, 2001). It involves some different tasks of number processing (i.e. repetition, reading, dictating and transcoding tasks) as well as some common arithmetical operations (i.e. addition, subtraction and multiplication).

Results were strongly indicative of acalculia: among the seven tasks included in the ENPA battery, only the task of repetition resulted in being unimpaired (Table 3). In particular, a diagnosis of acalculia, including impairment of both number-processing and calculation, was formulated.

Regarding number-processing, both number production (i.e. writing of numbers from dictation) and comprehension (i.e. reading of numbers) were impaired. Moreover, selective impairment of graphemic processing, both of Arabic numerals and verbal numerals, seemed to emerge. Furthermore, a qualitative analysis of the errors showed that both syntactic and lexical errors were evident, both in the reading and writing of numbers. Besides, severe difficulties emerged also in the transcoding task. In contrast, no impairment of phonological processing emerged (i.e. repetition was preserved). Regarding impairments of calculation, they seemed to involve the retrieval of both arithmetical facts and calculation procedures. In contrast, no disorder in processing arithmetical symbols emerged.

3.5.4. Pre-frontal executive processing

Executive pre-frontal functions were evaluated by means of a task of working memory (digit span backward; Orsini et al., 1987), the phonological fluency test (Novelli et al., 1986), a verbal semantic fluency task (Spinnler & Tognoni, 1987) and the Cognitive Estimate Test (CET; Della Sala, MacPherson, Phillips, Sacco, & Spinnler, 2003). Moreover, logical deductive visual reasoning was investigated using Raven's colored progressive matrices test (Basso et al., 1987).

The results showed that some pre-frontal functions were slightly impaired, starting at the second evaluation. However, executive impairments were very mild, and a complete dysexecutive syndrome never appeared; therefore, these impairments should be considered as a secondary aspect of CG's cognitive profile. In particular, a selective mild deficit of working memory resulted in digit span backward at the first evaluation. Conversely, the other tests of executive functioning were unimpaired (Table 1). Moreover, CG preserved good insight. Finally, the results of Raven's colored progressive matrices test were at all times disputable because of the emergence of a preference effect for right-side items, probably due to unilateral neglect.

At the second evaluation, executive impairments were slightly more evident. In particular, some deficits emerged both in the working memory task and the cognitive estimates test. Noteworthy is that CG's performance on the verbal fluency tasks was still in the normal range; moreover, she still preserved full insight. At the third evaluation, executive impairments had worsened slightly (Table 1); moreover, CG showed partial insight for the first time.

As described above, CG's pre-frontal function impairments involved the executive functions exclusively, and apart from a mild bradyphrenia, compelling signs of akinetic and disinhibited pre-frontal syndromes never appeared.

3.5.5. Memory processing and orientation

Anterograde long-term memory was assessed using the prose recall test (Spinnler & Tognoni, 1987), and verbal short-term memory was assessed using the forward digit span test (Orsini et al., 1987). Results showed that long-term memory was one of the best preserved cognitive domains. In fact, the anterograde verbal memory test (prose recall) resulted as unimpaired. Moreover, memory problems were never reported by CG's caregiver, and perseverations in the discourse or other signs of episodic amnesia never emerged from the observational examinations at the successive visits. Furthermore, signs of retrograde amnesia never emerged by interviewing CG. Also, the unimpaired performance on the picture naming test supported the preservation of semantic memory. However, a slight impairment in short-term memory emerged on the digit span test at the third visit (Table 1). Regarding orientation, it emerged that personal, familial, temporal, spatial and contextual orientations were all preserved at the first and second evaluations. At the third visit, it was difficult to test orientation because of aphasia. Nevertheless, orientation was tested by recognition instead of free recall, and CG did not make any errors.

3.5.6. Visual-perceptual processing
Visual perception was studied using the discrimination of Scribbles test (Spinnler & Tognoni, 1987) and by analyzing CG's object recognition performance on the picture-naming task (Laiacona et al., 1993).

Results showed that visual perception was one of the best preserved cognitive domains. The caregiver never reported difficulties of CG at recognizing and identifying familiar faces as well as known objects or places. Moreover, the task of apperceptive agnosia (Scribble discrimination test, Table 3) resulted in the normal range at the time of the second evaluation, supporting the preservation of an early stage of visual processing. Furthermore, CG's performance on object recognition on the picture naming task was unimpaired; thus, the emergence of associative agnosia was ruled out (Table 1). A mild deficit in the picture naming task emerged at the third visit; nevertheless, the errors were attributable to aphasia and not to agnosia.

4. Discussion

4.1. The cognitive phenotype of CBS

4.1.1. General
This single case study supports the notion that cognitive impairments are a very relevant feature of CBS. In fact, the longitudinal neuropsychological assessment showed a significant cognitive dysfunction, with some cognitive impairments starting at an early stage of disease. Moreover, the complex pattern of cognitive impairments demonstrated by CG overlapped the pattern usually described in CBS (Graham et al., 2003; Murray et al., 2007). In particular, CG's cognitive profile was dominated by limb apraxia, which was associated with limb-kinetic as well as constructional apraxia from an early stage of disease. Moreover, gaze, truncal and dressing apraxia were present starting from a later stage of disease. In contrast, oral, eyelid, ideational and conceptual apraxia were relatively absent. Visuospatial skills disorder, especially involving visuospatial attention impairments, constructional apraxia, mild unilateral neglect and simultanagnosia, was the second most important impairment of CG's cognitive profile. In contrast, topographical disorientation never appeared. Aphasia was another salient impairment, even if it was not a prominent aspect at an early stage. It first was diagnosed with mild transcortical sensory aphasia and then changed into mixed transcortical aphasia of moderate severity. Moreover, early and severe agraphia, probably of the peripheral type, together with very mild neglect dyslexia, was associated with aphasia. Another relevant syndrome of the CG's cognitive phenotype was a posterior variant of alien hand syndrome (Semenza, 2003). It comprised different phenomena, including (left) levitating hand, magnetic apraxia and an impairment similar to what some authors named agonistic dyspraxia (Lavados et al., 2002). Furthermore, a complete Gerstmann syndrome emerged, characterized by acalculia, finger agnosia without autotopagnosia, left-right disorientation and agraphia, and a partial Balint's syndrome, including gaze dyspraxia, simultanagnosia and a narrowing of the visual attention focus but without manifest optic ataxia and no apparent deficits in estimating distances and in depth perception. Considering the secondary aspects of CG's cognitive phenotype, some executive impairments emerged, starting at the second visit. However, insight was preserved, and compelling signs of the akinetic or disinhibited pre-frontal syndromes never appeared. The remaining cognitive domains appeared well preserved. In particular, signs of amnesia (i.e. anterograde, retrograde and semantic amnesia), disorientation (i.e. spatial, temporal, personal, familial and contextual disorientation), and visual agnosia (both apperceptive and associative) never emerged.

4.1.2. Apraxia
To the best of our knowledge, there are few studies in which limb apraxia has been assessed longitudinally using a standardized test in CBS patients as made in this study (Stamenova et al., 2009). In doing so, not only the relevance and severity of limb apraxia in CBS was confirmed by precise quantitative data, but also its pejorative and relatively rapid course over time was adequately traced. Moreover, quantitative measures of apraxia allowed us to make accurate comparisons between the

left and the right upper limb performance. Thus, robust data about the issue of symmetry vs. asymmetry of apraxia along the disease course were obtained (see Section 5).

Regarding the results about limb-kinetic apraxia in CG's case, it should be noted that since the De Renzi test includes items also investigating finger movements, it was considered an adequate tool for evaluating not only limb but also limb-kinetic apraxia (Borroni et al., 2008a; Soliveri et al., 2005). In this respect, data from this study confirmed the relevance of limb-kinetic apraxia in CBS and its association with limb apraxia (Borroni et al., 2008a; FitzGerald et al., 2007; Leiguarda et al., 2003; Soliveri et al., 2003, 2005). Moreover, CG's case highlighted that limb-kinetic apraxia could have an early onset in CBS and that it could also be bilateral instead of unilateral as usually reported (Stamenova et al., 2009). Furthermore, the different drop in time traced between limb and limb-kinetic apraxia supported the distinction between these two forms of apraxia as well as the notion of limb-kinetic apraxia as a separate clinical entity.

As for other apraxias in CG's case, on the whole, this study suggested a relative heterogeneity. First, apraxia also affected movements of body parts different from the arms (limb-apraxia) and the fingers (limb-kinetic apraxia). For example, clear signs of gaze and truncal apraxia emerged in CG's case, as similarly reported in other CBS cases (Okuda et al., 2001; Rajagopal et al., 2011). Second, apraxia seemed to strongly contribute to an impairment of complex functions, such as handwriting (apraxic agraphia), drawing (constructional apraxia) and dressing (dressing apraxia) in CG's case. However, relative preservation of orofacial praxis was confirmed (Stamenova et al., 2009). Regarding the analysis of type as well as mode of gestures, CG's case study seems to confirm previous data showing that imitation was more affected than pantomime in CBS (Jacobs et al., 1999; Peigneux et al., 2001; Spatt et al., 2002; Stamenova et al., 2011). In fact, even though the comparison between pantomime and imitation tasks was not statistically significant at the time of the second evaluation, a clear difference emerged between them early on at the first evaluation, when the pantomime task resulted as unimpaired and the imitation task was clearly impaired and suggestive of limb apraxia (De Renzi test). The fact that imitation was exclusively impaired constitutes an original finding in a CBS patient, considering that usually both pantomime and imitation are reported as impaired in CBS (Stamenova et al., 2009). Moreover, this finding suggests that an imitation task could be the most sensitive to detect limb apraxia in an early stage of CBS. Taking into account the comparison between pantomime and object use, no statistically significant difference emerged; nonetheless, a small advantage of object use seemed to emerge, in agreement with many previous data (Graham et al., 1999; Jacobs et al., 1999; Leiguarda et al., 2003; Spatt et al., 2002; Stamenova et al., 2009). Regarding the comparison between transitive and intransitive gestures (with pantomime), it emerged that both types of gestures were affected, but transitive gestures were more affected, as already found in previous CBS cases (Chainay & Humphreys, 2003; Pharr et al., 2001; Salter et al., 2004). As to the distinction between meaningful (representational) and meaningless (non-representational) gestures, the results showed that both types of gestures were equally affected, just as reported in other CBS patients (Buxbaum et al., 2007; Leiguarda et al., 2003; Merians et al., 1999; Salter et al., 2004; Spatt et al., 2002; Stamenova et al., 2009).

Regarding the possible accounts of apraxia, some further conclusions seemed to emerge from the CG's case study. First, following the apraxia information-processing model proposed by Roy (1996), CG's case study further confirms the view that apraxia in CBS was characterized by an impairment in the production system overall in an early and/or intermediate stage of disease with a concurrent preservation of the conceptual system (Stamenova et al., 2009). Forthcoming damage to the conceptual system seemed to emerge in a late stage of disease in CG's case, as signaled by the errors in the tool naming task. Moreover, the study of the different task modalities and gesture types shows that overall CBS affects the direct route to imitation at an early stage of disease with relative preservation of the indirect route. CG concurrently showed, in fact, impaired imitation of meaningless gestures (direct route) and relative preservation of pantomimes (indirect route). The concurrent impairment of the imitation of meaningful gestures found in CG's case could be explained, as suggested by other authors (Stamenova et al., 2011), either from the patient being in some way forced to use the direct route to imitation or from a disconnection between hypothetical input and output semantic systems (input and output praxicon) in gesture processing (Gonzalez Rothi, Ochipa, & Heilman, 1991). Finally, a definite impairment of the pantomimes, also signaling disruption of the indirect route of gesture production, was evident starting at an intermediate stage of the disease.

4.1.3. Visuospatial functions impairment

CG's case study confirms the relevance of visuospatial skill disorders in CBS; in fact, CG showed many significant visuospatial impairments, including visuoconstructional impairments, visuospatial attention disorders, unilateral neglect, and probably simultanagnosia. Considering that visual agnosia and severe dyslexia were absent, CG's case supports the view that CBS is a "where" stream disorder that is against the preservation of the "what" stream (Bak et al., 2006; Possin, 2010). Moreover, CG's case draws attention to visual-spatial attention impairments, a feature less frequently reported in CBS. Actually, some previous descriptions of CBS patients included features that could suggest visual spatial attention impairments, such as being unable to follow printed material from line-to-line (Tang-Wai et al., 2003), correctly cancel a target in a field of letters (FitzGerald et al., 2007) or find objects within visual space (Rajagopal et al., 2011). However, CG had striking and primary visuospatial attention disorders characterized by an inefficient exploration of the visual space, distractibility, problems in disengaging attention (i.e. sticky fixation) and a suspected narrowing of the visual attentional focus. These elements strongly suggest a dysfunction of the posterior attentional system (PAS, Posner & Petersen, 1990), the complex system comprising cortical and sub-cortical centers (i.e. posterior parietal cortex, especially lateral parietal cortex, thalamic nuclei connected with the pulvinar and the reticular nucleus, and superior colliculus) that manage the spatial components of visual attention.

4.1.4. Posterior alien hand syndrome

What the mild form of alien hand syndrome showed by CG is known as a corticobasal or posterior variant of alien hand syndrome (Kloesel, Czarnecki, Muir, & Scott Keller, 2010; Semenza, 2003), and it has already been reported in other CBS cases (Delrieu et al., 2010). The posterior alien hand syndrome of CG included left arm levitation, magnetic apraxia (Denny-Brown, 1958) and an impairment similar to a condition that some authors have named agonistic dyspraxia (Aboitiz et al., 2003). However, magnetic apraxia, which is a well-known form of the alien limb phenomenon (FitzGerald et al., 2007), was very mild in CG's case and only consisted of some involuntary reaching behaviors with her hands in some tests and some occurrences of the closing-in phenomenon in the drawing. Agonistic dyspraxia in CG consisted in "substitutions of movements" for which, as soon as one of her forelimbs and/or hands (left or right) started to perform a requested movement (invariably on verbal command, imitation, and sometimes also in spontaneous execution), the other limb (right or left, respectively), probably after being activated in a mirrored way, replaced it and automatically or compulsively performed the same action in its place.

Regarding other manifestations of alien hand syndrome, CG never exhibited phenomena pertaining to frontal magnetic apraxia, like a compulsive tactile exploration of objects, grasping and groping behaviors, and imitation and utilization behaviors (Lhermitte, 1983; Lhermitte, Pillon, & Serdaru, 1986). Moreover, other features of the classical alien hand syndrome (e.g. alien and anarchic hand, intermanual conflict) were absent. Finally, the emergence of a posterior variant of alien hand syndrome in CG's case was consistent with her primary bi-parietal neuropsychological dysfunction and the mild impairment of more anterior functions, like pre-frontal executive functions.

4.1.5. Aphasia

As reported in the introduction section, aphasia is a very common impairment in CBS (Frattali et al., 2000; Graham et al., 2003; Mahapatra et al., 2004; McMonagle et al., 2006; Murray et al., 2007) and is typically of the non-fluent type (Graham et al., 2003; Mahapatra et al., 2004; McMonagle et al., 2006; Tree & Kay, 2008). Despite this apparent general agreement about the pattern of language impairments in CBS, a relative heterogeneity emerged among aphasic syndrome diagnoses in the studies in which an accurate classification of aphasia was possible. Actually, all the main classic aphasic syndromes seemed to be reported, in at least some CBS cases (i.e. global, Broca, transcortical motor, conduction, anomic, Wernicke, and transcortical sensory aphasias) (Frattali et al., 2000; Graham et al., 2003; Kimura et al., 2008; McMonagle et al., 2006). CG's case seems to confirm this heterogeneity of the aphasic presentations in CBS. In fact, although the transcortical sensory aphasia shown by CG at an early stage of disease has already been reported in some previous CBS cases (Graham et al., 2003; McMonagle et al., 2006), to the best of our knowledge, there are no preceding reports of mixed transcortical aphasia in CBS at an intermediate or a more advanced stage. Specifically, aphasia in CG's case was fluent, with prominent word-finding difficulties and comprehension deficits. Nonetheless, it showed a progressive conversion from a posterior (e.g. anomic aphasia) to a more anterior aphasia, with some features of non-fluent aphasia added at an intermediate stage (e.g. brief, stereotyped and often interrupted utterances; mild articulatory problems; signs for paragrammatism), similar to what is recorded in the course of aphasia in other CBS cases (McMonagle et al., 2006).

Therefore, CG's case report supports the view that aphasic syndrome in CBS could strictly depend on the time of evaluation, and there might be a tendency to find the non-fluent type at an intermediate or a more advanced stage of disease. Vice versa, the fluent type could be present at an earlier stage of the disease, as shown in CG's case. In conclusion, caution is required when assessing a typical aphasic syndrome in CBS, irrespective of the evaluation time along the disease course. Interestingly, according to Catani et al.'s hypothesis (Catani, 2005; Catani, Jones, & Ffytche, 2005), mixed transcortical aphasia could be provoked by damage to the posterior segment of the indirect pathway of the arcuate fasciculus linking Wernicke's area to the inferior parietal lobule and concurrently to the anterior segment (in CG's case probably partially) linking the inferior parietal lobule to Broca's area. This model aligns with the possible origin of mixed transcortical aphasia in CG. In fact, damage to left inferior parietal lobule in CG's case probably extended to deep white matter and thus possibly intercepted the posterior segment of the indirect pathway of the arcuate fasciculus.

4.2. CBS clinical heterogeneity: A posterior variant

4.2.1. Diagnostic criteria for CBS

CG exhibited a complex syndrome characterized by an insidious onset and a progressive course that involved motor (i.e. rigidity, myoclonus, and truncal dystonia), cortical motor-sensory (i.e. apraxia, number processing deficits, cortical sensory loss, and posterior alien hand syndrome), and cognitive features (i.e. language impairment, visuospatial deficits and mild pre-frontal dysfunction) that are levodopa-resistant and associated with early focal parietal and later parietal-frontal atrophy on brain imaging. Moreover, albeit initially symmetric, the motor (i.e. rigidity and myoclonus) and cortical motor-sensory features (i.e. limb apraxia and posterior alien hand syndrome) became asymmetric, with the left side more affected than right one, starting at the second evaluation at 32 months post-disease onset. From this stage on, CG's clinical picture assumed an asymmetrical course. The whole clinical phenotype described at 32 months post-onset fully resembles a diagnosis of CBS according to all the current accepted diagnostic criteria (Mathew et al., 2011) (i.e. Toronto criteria (Lang et al., 1994), Mayo Clinic criteria (Boeve et al., 2003) and modified Cambridge criteria (Bak et al., 2008; Mathew et al., 2011)). Moreover, CG's syndrome resembles the clinical phenotype of possible corticobasal syndrome recently outlined by some authors (Armstrong et al., 2013) in their proposal of new criteria for the diagnosis of CBD.

4.2.2. Symmetry vs. asymmetry

Interestingly, CG could be viewed as an unusual case of CBS because her motor symptoms had a bilateral and symmetric onset. In fact, parkinsonism and myoclonus affected both her arms equally at CBS presentation. Also, limb and limb-kinetic apraxia (Table 4), as well as the mild posterior alien hand syndrome, were first bilateral, affecting both upper limbs with the same gravity. In full agreement, a strongly symmetrical parietal atrophy appeared on neuroimaging. The CBS-defining feature of marked asymmetry of the motor symptoms (Mahapatra et al., 2004), together with asymmetry of limb apraxia (Table 4) as well as of posterior alien hand syndrome, emerged only at the second visit, approximately 30 months post-disease onset. Then, CBS assumed the usual progressive asymmetric course with both motor and motor sensory-cortical features affecting the left limb more than the right one. At this time, an initial mild asymmetric hypometabolism (right hemisphere > left hemisphere) was found on the brain SPECT scan. The symmetrical onset as well as the asymmetrical course of disease in this study was supported by quantitative data from the De Renzi test of apraxia that did not show any left-right difference at the first evaluation and did show more severe apraxia to the left limb at all the subsequent assessments (Table 4). Interestingly, Dopper et al. (2011) described the case of a 61-year-old male patient with an atypical CBS presentation, including symmetrical rigidity, ideational and ideomotor apraxia and later dystonia in his left leg, without alien hand phenomenon and myoclonus. This clinical presentation paralleled mild symmetrical cerebral atrophy, especially frontoparietal and perisylvian, on MRI and symmetrical frontoparietal hypometabolism on SPECT. Moreover, the patient was found to be a sporadic case of FTLD-TDP type 3 pathology due to a novel progranulin mutation. The authors named this case as symmetrical CBS. CG's case study replicates the finding by these authors (Dopper et al., 2011) of a symmetrical CBS (S-CBS), even when considering the first part of the disease course. Moreover, this replication extends this finding to a more classic CBS. A patient studied by (Dopper et al., 2011) in fact exhibited some unusual features in respect to a classical CBS (e.g. marked behavioral changes, memory impairment, and preserved visuospatial functions) but lacked other typical CBS signs and symptoms (e.g. myoclonus and alien hand syndrome). Another finding from CG's case study suggests that cases of S-CBS might not be so rare and atypical if patients were studied at a very early stage of disease. In fact, the time interval between disease onset and the first visit in both CG's case and the case described by Dopper and co-authors (i.e. respectively 18 and 24 months post-disease onset) was relatively briefer than those in other CBS case series (e.g. 32 months post-disease onset, Murray et al., 2007; 36 months post-disease onset, Borroni et al., 2008b; 48 months post-disease onset, Stamenova et al., 2009; 84 months post-disease onset, Stamenova et al., 2011). Therefore, in agreement with the symptoms progression in CG's case, which was first symmetric and became asymmetric at approximately 30 months post-onset, it cannot be excluded that typical asymmetric CBS reported at a middle stage of disease course, when patients are usually studied, actually would have been preceded by an atypical symmetric CBS presentation. This hypothesis seems to be plausible for those patients whose motor and motor-sensory cortical symptoms were bilateral but more severe on a defined body-side at a middle disease stage (relative asymmetry). In contrast, it obviously appears to be less plausible for those patients who presented with focal symptoms at a middle disease stage (absolute asymmetry).

Regarding another previous study that is relevant to the issue of symmetry/asymmetry, some authors retrospectively selected five patients with symmetrical clinical presentations from an autopsy-proven CBD case series and compared them with other classical asymmetric CBD patients of the same series (Hassan et al., 2010). All symmetric CBD cases had symmetric brain atrophy on MRI scans and an absence of asymmetric frontoparietal hypometabolism and/or hypoperfusion on PET and/or SPECT scans. Age of onset of symmetric CBD was more praecox (i.e. mean age of 61 years, with a range of 40–69 years vs. a mean age of 66 years with a range of 61–73 years); moreover, it had a similar duration but a more frequent family history of dementia. Phenotypes of symmetric CBD cases were: atypical AD (one case), bvFTD (three cases) and FTDP (one case). Behavioral changes were prominent in symmetric CBD cases and core features of CBS, such as myoclonus, dystonia, limb apraxia and alien limb phenomenon, were all absent. Based on these findings, the authors suggested that symmetric CBD (S-CBD) may be different from the more typical asymmetric variant presenting as CBS.

No pathological data were available in CG's case, and this was a limitation of the study. However, irrespective of the brain pathology, this study demonstrates that the attribute of symmetry can be associated with an otherwise classical CBS over a reliable period of the disease course, and more generally, that symmetric and asymmetric phenotypes can be associated with the same syndrome/disease at different moments of its course. Thus, CG's case study suggests that caution should be used in using symmetry or asymmetry as a defining feature of CBS and/or CBD. In other words, the evidence of an S-CBS suggests not stressing asymmetry in the diagnostic criteria of CBS overall at onset or at an early stage of the disease, which are the most important times for diagnosing dementia. On the other hand, this study confirms the association between an asymmetric course and CBS starting at an intermediate stage of the disease.

4.2.3. CBS and PCA

CBS and PCA are two distinct clinical entities, each one with its current diagnostic criteria (for PCA see Crutch et al., 2017). Nonetheless, as previously reported by some authors (Alladi et al., 2007), there is an overlap of cognitive features between CBS and PCA, with both syndromes being characterized by apraxia and prominent visuospatial features (e.g. visual neglect, Gerstmann's syndrome). Moreover, the possible involvement of parietal cortex asymmetry in both clinical variants makes it difficult to clinically distinguish CBS from PCA in certain cases (Alladi et al., 2007). Furthermore, clinically diagnosed CBS patients have been reported who show marked visuospatial dysfunction (Bak et al., 2006), including signs of Balint's syndrome (Mendez, 2000; Rajagopal et al., 2011), which is considered one of the core features of the PCA syndrome (Crutch et al., 2017). In addition, at least three pathologically diagnosed CBD patients and one patient without pathologic diagnosis have been reported with a PCA syndrome as a presenting symptom followed by signs of CBS (i.e. asymmetric apraxia and parkinsonism) later in the course of the illness (two patients studied by Tang-Wai et al., 2003; one patient by Lee et al., 2011; one patient by Giorelli, Losignore, Bagnoli, Difazio, & Zimatore, 2014). Finally, a subgroup of PCA patients has been found to show motor features commonly associated with CBS (i.e. limb rigidity and apraxia, myoclonus, tremor and alien limb phenomenon) (Ryan et al., 2014).

In this regard, CG's case study further confirms that there is a close overlap between CBS and PCA syndrome. In fact, CG's clinical picture comprised many features in agreement with the diagnostic criteria of CBS; nonetheless, it also included some of the core diagnostic features of PCA. Moreover, CG showed many cognitive features of a PCA variant known as the bi-parietal syndrome (i.e. apraxia, visuospatial impairments, agraphia, preserved basic perceptual abilities, and preserved object recognition and reading) (Alladi et al., 2007; Crutch et al., 2017). As recently noted by some authors (Crutch et al., 2017), further studies are necessary to better disentangle PCA syndrome from related syndromes, such as CBS. CG's case study highlights that a detailed study of the bi-parietal syndrome may play an important role to this aim because it may pertain to both PCA syndrome and CBS.

4.2.4. Posterior variant of CBS (P-CBS)

In sum, CBS in CG's case showed some atypical features characterized overall by a clear symmetrical presentation and an early posterior global aspect of cognitive and motor cortical impairments (e.g. initial fluent aphasia, posterior alien hand syndrome), included many features of the PCA bi-parietal syndrome, and lacked more anterior CBS-typical features (e.g. alien hand, early non-fluent aphasia, behavioral disturbances, personality changes). Moreover, basal ganglia were apparently not involved, which was found in previous CBS cases (Ceravolo et al., 2013; Cilia et al., 2011; Hammesfahr et al., 2016; Homma et al., 2014). Thus, CG's case study further supports the clinical heterogeneity of CBS's presentation. Moreover, it suggests the emergence of a specific clinical variant of CBS with pronounced posterior involvement (posterior-CBS), as recently found by some authors who proposed to label it as a Gerstmann variant of CBS (Di Stefano et al., 2016). Considering the underlying brain pathology, despite the absence of an e4 allele from the apolipoprotein E (APOE) genotyping, Alzheimer's disease could be the main disease in CG's case, as it is frequently found in many previously described CBS patients (from 23 to 50%, Hu et al., 2009), In fact, CG showed many of the clinical features suggestive of AD pathology vs. CBD pathology (e.g. young age of onset, occurrence of myoclonus, absence of tremors, severe visuospatial deficits, lack of orofacial apraxia, presence of dysgraphia, and important functional decline) (Burrell, Hornberger, Villemagne, Rowe, & Hodges, 2013; Hu et al., 2009). Moreover, some studies found that widespread atrophy extending to involve the posterior parietal and temporal lobes, as found in CG's case, may indicate an underlying AD pathology (Burrell et al., 2013; Burrell et al., 2014; Di Stefano et al., 2016; Josephs et al., 2010; Lee et al., 2011; McMillan et al., 2016; Whitwell et al., 2010).

4.2.5. *Functional impact of CBS*

Few studies have examined the impact of limb and limb-kinetic apraxia on competence and autonomy in performing activities of daily living in CBS patients (Stamenova et al., 2009). To this purpose, successive semi-structured interviews, as well as basic (and instrumental) Activities of Daily Living scales (ADL and iADL), were administered to the caregiver. On the whole, the results showed that CBS was associated with a significant reduction of competence in performing activities of daily living at a very early stage of disease (i.e. before 18 months post-disease onset) in CG's case. Regarding the question of what cognitive impairments were responsible for the functional reduction, some authors underlined that it is difficult to distinguish the impact of apraxia from that of other motor and cognitive impairments that probably contribute to disrupting the performance on ADL in brain-damaged patients (Sunderland & Shinner, 2007). With regards to this point, the analysis of CG's errors in performing activities of daily living strongly suggests impairment of praxis abilities rather than of other cognitive functions, at least for up to 32 months post disease onset (Table 4). Moreover, starting from 32 months post onset, CG's caregiver frequently reported errors highly suggestive of a motor and/or other cognitive impairments and especially of visuospatial functions impairments (Table 2). Thus, it is probable that the reduction of CG's autonomy in her daily life recorded from an intermediate stage and onward would be related not only to apraxia but also to other multiple cognitive impairments. In particular, we believe that the visual-spatial attention impairments played the main role in limiting CG's functional ability. In fact, they probably forced CG to perform actions in a warped visual spatial attention space and/or upon the wrong objects, toward which her attention focus was automatically engaged and from which she could not disengage her attention. As a consequence, visual spatial attention impairments probably neutralized the advantages offered by affordances to guide action and invite the use of objects (Norman, 1988). Therefore, a concurrent disruption of both top-down (praxis) and bottom-up (affordance and invitation to use) processes, which are guides for action, inevitably caused important failures in performing activities of daily living in this CBS case. However, other different explanations cannot be excluded. For example, some authors proposed an interesting account based on the "technical reasoning hypothesis" that postulates that the ability to use tools and objects in daily life depends not only on semantic knowledge about tool function and context of use but also on technical reasoning of mechanical properties of tools and objects (Baumard et al., 2016; Goldenberg & Spatt, 2009). In particular, they suggested and preliminarily verified that the difficulties in tool use showed by CBS patients can be due to technical reasoning deficits following parietal lobe damage (Baumard et al., 2016).

4.3. From symptoms progression to degeneration spreading

4.3.1. *Neuroanatomical substrate of CG's cognitive impairments*

The in-depth study of CG's cognitive impairments let us recognize some specific symptoms and syndromes that were well-known in the clinical literature. At this point, starting from data about known anatomo-clinical correlations, we tried to retrace the map of CG brain regions involved as neuroanatomical substrates of her symptoms and syndromes (Figure 3). Moreover, taking into account the data from the longitudinal cognitive assessment over three years, a brain map of the possible spreading of neurodegeneration in this case of CBS was reconstructed (Figure 3). We are aware both that the method used in this section was quite unconventional and that data showed (Figure 3 included) were highly speculative. Indeed, no advanced imaging study was performed to support our conclusions, and this is a limitation of this section of the study.

Regarding the results of the first evaluation, at approximately 18–20 months post-disease onset, the core cognitive impairments were bilateral limb and limb-kinetic apraxia and visuospatial disorders, including visuoconstructional and visuospatial attention deficits. Minimal working memory deficits, suspected elements of an incoming Gerstmann syndrome (writing difficulties and dyscalculia noticed by GC's relatives) and a suspected mild left visuospatial neglect, were all associated with the core impairments at this time. Therefore, following data about anatomo-clinical correlations, early and preferential damage to the bilateral dorsolateral parietal cortices (Goldenberg, 2009), including both the superior and the inferior parietal lobules (probably the more anterior parts) as well

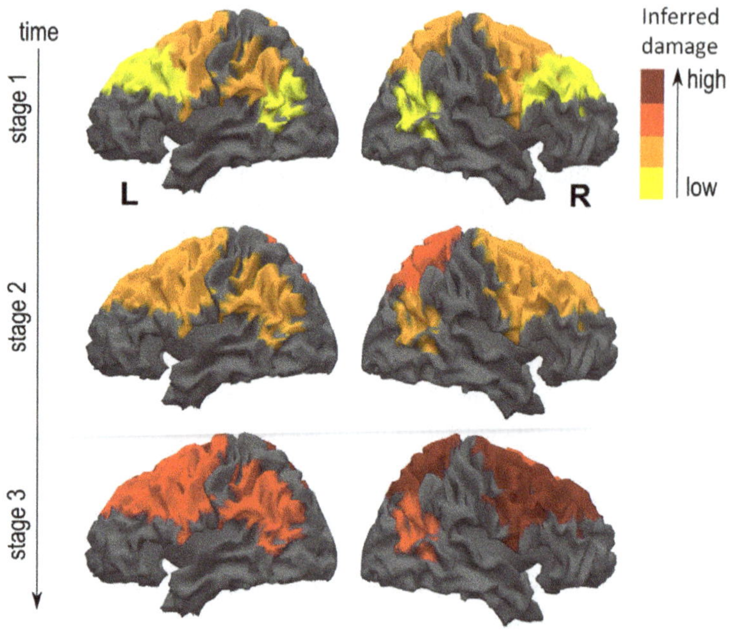

Figure 3. Longitudinal mapping of degeneration spreading in patient CG. Colored areas represent the brain loci of degeneration that were inferred from CG's cognitive phenotype and by considering well-known brain anatomical-functional correlations found in the literature. The reported stages refer to the successive evaluations performed in the study.

as to the bilateral premotor cortices, could be hypothesized. In particular, the left inferior parietal lobule, especially the supramarginal gyrus (BA 40) (ideomotor apraxia) (Clark, Boutros, & Mendez, 2005, chapter 4) and the right superior parietal lobule (BA 5 and 7) (visuoconstructional impairment and visuospatial attention impairment) (Clark et al., 2005, chapter 4), were surely involved. In contrast, more posterior parts of the parietal cortex (i.e. the left angular gyrus (BA 39)) (Gerstmann syndrome, Clark et al., 2005, chapter 4) and the more inferior parts of the inferior parietal lobule (i.e. the right temporoparietal junction) (visuospatial neglect, Bisiach & Vallar, 2000) were only minimally involved at the time of the first assessment. Moreover, apart from an early preferential damage targeting the bilateral frontal premotor cortices (BA 6) (limb-kinetic apraxia, Binkofski & Reetz, 2008), and a probable involvement also of the frontal eyes fields (BA 8) (visual search deficits, Malloy, Cohen, & Jenkins, 1998), the prefrontal dorsolateral cortex (probably BA 8, 9) (working memory impairment) (Clark et al., 2005, chapter 6) was only minimally damaged. The analysis of the neural substrate of CBS in CG's case was supported enough by morphological brain imaging (MRI) data at the time of the first evaluation, which showed mild focal atrophy in bilateral parietal cortices (Figures 1 and 2).

At the second visit, 32 months post-disease onset, all core (i.e. limb apraxia and visuospatial impairments) and associated mild or incoming deficits (i.e. dysexecutive syndrome, unilateral neglect, and Gerstmann's syndrome with dysgraphia, acalculia, left-right disorientation, and digital agnosia) emerged before they had worsened except for limb-apraxia, which appeared as unvaried. Moreover, novel cognitive impairments emerged for the first time: agraphesthesia, truncal apraxia, dressing apraxia, some signs of the Balint's syndrome (i.e. gaze dyspraxia, simultanagnosia, and narrowing of the field of spatial attention, with the exclusion of optic ataxia), some elements of the posterior alien hand syndrome (i.e. agonistic dyspraxia and magnetic apraxia), and a mild transcortical sensory aphasia. Finally, limb but not limb-kinetic apraxia started to be asymmetric, with the left arm more impaired than the right one. Therefore, regarding the neural substrate, we could hypothesize that damage to the earliest foci of neurodegeneration in dorsolateral parietal cortex (e.g. right superior parietal lobule for dressing apraxia and agraphesthesia) (Clark et al., 2005, chapter 4) had increased and that some regions in the right hemisphere were slightly more affected than their left counterparts at the time of the second evaluation. Moreover, the posterior and inferior parts of the parietal cortices, which were partially affected at the first evaluation, i.e. the left angular gyrus (BA 39, Gerstmann syndrome) (Clark et al., 2005, chapter 4) and the right temporoparietal junction (visuospatial neglect, Bisiach & Vallar, 2000), were probably more diffusely damaged at this time. Furthermore, the amount of neurodegeneration of the bilateral frontal premotor cortices (BA 6) (limb-kinetic apraxia, Binkofski & Reetz, 2008) seemed to be equivalent, while the damage to the prefrontal dorsolateral cortex (probably BA 8, 9) (working memory impairment and executive functions) (Clark et al., 2005; chapter 6) was slightly increased. Finally, it seemed that degeneration had spread from the earliest core foci on dorsolateral parietal cortices to more posterior and inferior parietal regions, following a direction toward the adjacent occipital and temporal lobes. In fact, multiple sites of damage to the right parietal-occipital cortex (posterior form of alien hand syndrome with agonistic dyspraxia) (Semenza, 2003), bilateral parietal-occipital cortices (partial Balint's syndrome, Clark et al., 2005, chapter 4), posterior temporoparietal junction (mild truncal apraxia, Okuda et al., 2001) and finally to the left temporal-parietal–occipital carrefour (mild transcortical sensory aphasia, Catani et al., 2005) could be hypothesized at the time of the second evaluation. Unfortunately, follow-up brain imaging data were not available at this stage of the disease course.

At the third evaluation, 49 months post-disease onset, limb and limb-kinetic apraxia, as well as visuospatial disorders and prefrontal functions impairments, had all worsened. Moreover, limb apraxia continued to be asymmetric, and limb-kinetic apraxia started to be asymmetric for the first time, with the left side of the body side more affected than the right, just as had occurred before for limb apraxia. Furthermore, other relevant changes emerged at this time: aphasia worsened, and its profile converted into mixed transcortical aphasia of moderate gravity, impairment of verbal short-term memory started to be associated with aphasia, and minimal signs of ideational apraxia appeared for the first time. In addition, the posterior alien hand syndrome worsened, and signs of left levitating hand were also evident at that time. Finally, clear signs of motor neglect affecting the left arm emerged, and a minimal hesitation without significant apraxia resulted in the orofacial praxis test. Regarding the neural substrate underlying these further changes in the clinical phenotype, we first could hypothesize increased damage to the brain regions already targeted by the degeneration. Moreover, our analysis seemed to suggest that degeneration had spread to posterior and inferior regions of the parietal cortex near to the occipital lobe, such as the right parietal-occipital cortex (i.e. more complete posterior alien hand syndrome including left levitating hand, Delrieu et al., 2010) and to the temporal lobe, such as left temporoparietal regions (ideational apraxia, Binkofski & Reetz, 2008; and short-term memory impairment, Lheman & Schnider, 2008). Furthermore, according to Catani et al.'s hypothesis (Catani, 2005; Catani et al., 2005), mixed transcortical aphasia could be provoked by damage to the posterior segment of the indirect pathway of the arcuate fasciculus linking Wernicke's area to the inferior parietal lobule and to the anterior segment linking the inferior parietal lobule to Broca's area. Also, damage to anterior regions, such as premotor cortex (more severe limb-kinetic apraxia, Binkofski & Reetz, 2008) or dorsolateral prefrontal cortex (worsening of executive function impairments) (Clark et al., 2005, chapter 6), had probably increased at the third evaluation. Finally, the probable symmetry in the amount of degeneration affecting posterior regions at the second evaluation, which caused a more severe left limb apraxia, extended forward to right frontal deep regions (left motor neglect, Goldenberg, 2003) and to the right premotor cortex (asymmetric limb-kinetic apraxia, Binkofski & Reetz, 2008) at the third evaluation. Interestingly, the severe hypoperfusion in the bilateral temporal cortices, especially the right superior temporal gyrus and in the bilateral parietal-occipital cortices, emerged on SPECT scan at the third evaluation, supporting the hypothesis of a degeneration spreading to more posterior and inferior parietal regions along directions toward the occipital and the temporal lobe, respectively.

Moreover, the results seemed to confirm that the brain damage had become asymmetric, with some regions of the right brain hemisphere more affected than their left counterparts. Finally, bilateral frontoparietal atrophy emerged on the follow-up CT scan, compared to the previous focal bilateral parietal atrophy that had emerged on the MRI scan, supporting that degeneration spreads from posterior parietal regions to anterior frontal regions.

4.3.2. Large-scale brain network hypothesis in CBS

The performed analysis suggests that the bilateral dorsolateral parietal and predominantly lateral frontal cortices, as well as the bilateral prefrontal cortices, are the possible underlying neuroanatomic substrates of the clinical syndrome of CG. Moreover, longitudinal data seemed to suggest that degeneration had started in hubs of the parietal and frontal cortices and then spread toward adjacent regions in the brain. However, a long-distance spreading of degeneration from parietal to frontal (and prefrontal) regions cannot be excluded. In fact, a gradient of disease propagation from posterior (i.e. parietal cortex) to more anterior regions (i.e. premotor cortex) was suggested by the fact that limb apraxia started to worsen and become asymmetric, with the left side more impaired than the right one, about one year before limb-kinetic apraxia. Similarly, the modification of aphasia over time from transcortical sensory aphasia to mixed transcortical aphasia seemed to suggest a gradient of disease propagation from posterior to more anterior regions in the left hemisphere. Therefore, the anatomical substrates underlying the disease propagation in CG's case were probably not only the short association fibers (i.e. arcuate or U-fibers) connecting neighboring gyri inside the parietal lobe or between the parietal gyri and the adjacent occipital and temporal gyri but also the long association fibers connecting the parietal lobules with frontal and prefrontal cortex, including the frontal eye field (i.e. the superior longitudinal fasciculus) (Bartolomeo, Thiebaut de Schotten, & Chica, 2012; Catani, 2005; Catani et al., 2005; Clark et al., 2005, chapter 4; de Schotten et al., 2011) as well as the indirect route of the arcuate fasciculus (Catani, 2005; Catani et al., 2005).

Interestingly, CG's case study seems to support the hypothesis that neurodegenerative diseases selectively target distinct large-scale intrinsic brain networks (Seeley, Crawford, Zhou, Miller, & Greicius, 2009). In fact, the multiple brain regions assumed to be the neuroanatomic substrates in CG's case (i.e. bilateral dorsolateral parietal and predominantly lateral frontal cortices as well as bilateral prefrontal cortices) matched well with the large-scale intrinsic network involving the dorsal parietal and predominantly lateral prefrontal cortices (i.e. dorsal sensorimotor association network) (De Luca, Beckmann, De Stefano, Matthews, & Smith, 2006; Seeley et al., 2009) already identified as the best candidate for CBS. Moreover, the longitudinal study seems to suggest that degeneration remained confined to this large primary network for over three years without involving other large-scale networks (e.g. default mode network (Buckner et al., 2005; Seeley et al., 2009), salience network (Seeley et al., 2007)) usually implicated in other diseases (Alzheimer's disease, AD, and behavioral variant frontotemporal dementia, bvFTD). A proof of this fact is that the precuneus, which is considered one core region in the AD default network, was unimpaired at an early stage of disease and/or only minimally impaired at an advanced stage (see the results from SPECT imaging), despite the fact that it was confined to a core and an early focus of degeneration in CG's case (i.e. the dorsolateral region of the superior parietal lobule (BA 5 and 7)). Moreover, the fact that degeneration seemed to start and spread inside a unique large-scale functional network gives some clues of a disease propagation mode along trans-synaptic connections, mimicking a prion-protein domino effect in which just (or mainly) neurons functionally connected with dysfunctional neurons become impaired (for a review, see Guo & Lee, 2014).

Considering a higher level of detail, the large-scale parieto-frontal network found as the underlying functional network of CBS includes or is associated with more local and specific networks. In particular, a dorsal attentional network (DAN) as well as a ventral attentional network (VAN) (Bartolomeo et al., 2012; Corbetta & Shulman, 2002; de Schotten et al., 2011), an executive-control network (Seeley et al., 2007), a medial frontal-prefrontal network (Wolpe et al., 2014) and a basal ganglia network (Rittman, Ghosh, & Rowe, 2013; Südmeyer et al., 2012) have been documented. In this respect, bearing in mind CG's cognitive phenotype, we think that some of these sub-networks were surely involved in CG's case, especially a dorsal attentional network (DAN) as well as a ventral attentional network (VAN) (Bartolomeo et al., 2012; Corbetta & Shulman, 2002; de Schotten et al., 2011) and an executive-control network (Seeley et al., 2007). However, another local network (i.e. a medial frontal-prefrontal network Wolpe et al., 2014) was probably not involved. Moreover, although bilateral extra-pyramidal symptoms were present from the first evaluation, FP-CIT SPECT imaging of CG showed normal tracer uptake in basal nuclei. Thus, data suggested that the basal ganglia network (Rittman et al., 2013; Südmeyer et al., 2012) was not involved in CG's case. This finding supports the current hypothesis that suggests extrapyramidal motor symptoms in CBS are not invariably associated with SNc neuronal degeneration and that supra-nigral factors may play a major role in several cases (Ceravolo et al., 2013; Cilia et al., 2011; Homma et al., 2014).

5. Conclusions

CG's case study confirms that CBS is a heterogeneous syndrome and suggests that a less common variant could emerge (i.e. a posterior CBS (P-CBS)). This somewhat atypical CBS phenotype would be characterized by a symmetrical presentation, an asymmetrical course, and prominent posterior (bi-parietal) cognitive and cortical motor manifestations, including many features of the PCA bi-parietal syndrome and lacking more anterior CBS typical features. Moreover, it seems to lack basal ganglia involvement. Thus, this study demonstrates that the attribute of symmetry can be associated with an otherwise classical CBS for a reliable period of its course and more generally that the attributes of symmetry and asymmetry can be associated with the same syndrome/disease in different moments of its course. Furthermore, the evidence of early (temporary) symmetrical manifestations in the CBS phenotype suggests not stressing "asymmetry" in CBS diagnostic criteria at an early stage of disease, as current clinical criteria do for diagnosing dementia.

The present study offers a further detailed outline of the cognitive phenotype in CBS and its progression over time. Many findings of limb apraxia in CBS have been replicated and substantiated, and some novel findings have emerged, such as distinct trajectories of worsening between the limb and limb-kinetic apraxia, relevant visuospatial attention disorders, the emergence of a posterior alien hand syndrome and mixed transcortical aphasia.

Data collected seem to suggest that apraxia and visuospatial attention disorders have an early and relevant functional impact on the patient performance of activities in daily life. In particular, we made the hypothesis that visuospatial attention impairments could neutralize the advantages of guide for action offered by affordances and invitations to use the objects. Therefore, a concurrent disruption of both top-down (i.e. praxis) and bottom-up (i.e. ineffective affordances and invitations to use the objects due to visuospatial attention impairment) processes that guide the action inevitably caused an early and severe decline in the functional status of CG.

Finally, the present study seems to support the hypothesis that neurodegenerative diseases selectively target distinct large-scale intrinsic brain networks. In particular, clinical data were compatible with an overall dysfunction of the underlying large-scale intrinsic network (i.e. dorsal sensory-motor association network) already identified as a proper candidate of CBS. Moreover, longitudinal data suggested that degeneration might remain confined within this network without involving other neighboring networks and that it spread not only along short association fibers connecting neighboring gyri inside the parietal lobe or between parietal and adjacent occipital and temporal gyri but also through long association fibers connecting the parietal lobules with the frontal and prefrontal cortex, including the frontal eye field (i.e. superior longitudinal fasciculus) and the indirect route of the fasciculus arcuatus.

Acknowledgments
Special thanks are due both to patient CG and her daughter for their longstanding cooperation with interviews, examinations and testing. Moreover, many thanks are due to Luigi Ghilardini for editing digital Figures 1 and 2 and to Silvia Casarotto for her help in editing Figure 3.

Funding
The authors received no direct funding for this research.

Competing interests
The authors declare no competing interest.

Author details
Carlo Abbate[1]
E-mail: carlo.abbate@guest.unimi.it
ORCID ID: http://orcid.org/0000-0002-0368-3834
Pietro Davide Trimarchi[2]
E-mail: pd.trimarchi@gmail.com
Laura Manzoni[3]
E-mail: lauramanzoni1969@hotmail.it
Anna Maria Quarenghi[3]
E-mail: annamariaquarenghi@gmail.com
Gian Pietro Salvi[3]
E-mail: segreteriasan@clinicaquarenghi.it

Silvia Inglese[1]
E-mail: inglesesilvia@gmail.com
Fabrizio Giunco[2]
E-mail: fgiunco@dongnocchi.it
Renzo Bagarolo[2]
E-mail: rbagarolo@dongnocchi.it
Daniela Mari[4]
E-mail: daniela.mari@unimi.it
Beatrice Arosio[1,4]
E-mail: beatrice.arosio@unimi.it

[1] Geriatric Unit, Fondazione IRCCS Ca' Granda, Ospedale Maggiore Policlinico, via Pace 9, 20122 Milan, Italy.

[2] Alzheimer's Assessment Unit, S. Maria Nascente, Fondazione IRCCS Don Carlo Gnocchi, via Alfonso Capecelatro 66, 20148 Milan, Italy.

[3] Istituto Clinico Quarenghi, via San Carlo 70, 24016 San Pellegrino Terme, Italy.

[4] Department of Medical Sciences and Community Health, University of Milan, via Francesco Sforza 35, 20122 Milan, Italy.

References

Aboitiz, F., Carrasco, X., Schröter, C., Zaidel, D., Zaidel, E., & Lavados, M. (2003). The alien hand syndrome: Classification of forms reported and discussion of a new condition. *Neurological Sciences, 24*, 252–257. doi:10.1007/s10072-003-0149-4

Alladi, S., Xuereb, J., Bak, T., Nestor, P., Knibb, J., Patterson, K., & Hodges, J. R. (2007). Focal cortical presentations of Alzheimer's disease. *Brain, 130*(10), 2636–2645. doi:10.1093/brain/awm213

Ambron, E., & Della Sala, S. (2017). A critical review of closing-in. *Neuropsychology, 31*(1), 105. doi:10.1037/neu0000295

Armstrong, M., Litvan, I., Lang, A. E., Bak, T. H., Bhatia, K. P., Borroni, B., ... Weiner, W. J. (2013). Criteria for the diagnosis of corticobasal degeneration. *Neurology, 80*, 496–503. doi:10.1212/WNL.0b013e31827f0fd103

Bak, T. H., Caine, D., Hearn, V. C., & Hodges, J. R. (2006). Visuospatial functions in atypical parkinsonian syndromes. *Journal of Neurology, Neurosurgery, and Psychiatry, 77*, 454–456. doi:10.1136/jnnp.2005.068239

Bak, T. H., Hodges, J. R., & Thomas, H. B. (2008). Corticobasal degeneration: Clinical aspects. In C. Duyckaerts & I. Litvan (Eds.), *Handbook of clinical neurology* (pp. 509–521). Amsterdam: Elsevier.

Bartolomeo, P., Thiebaut de Schotten, M., & Chica, A. B. (2012, May 4). Brain networks of visuospatial attention and their disruption in visual neglect. *Frontiers in Human Neuroscience*. doi:10.3389/fnhum.2012.00110.

Basso, A., Capitani, E., & Laiacona, M. (1987). Raven's coloured progressive matrices: Normative values on 305 adult normal controls. *Functional Neurology, 2*(2), 189–194.

Baumard, J., Lesourd, M., Jarry, C., Merck, C., Etcharry-Bouyx, F., Chauviré, V., ... Le Gall, D. (2016). Tool use disorders in neurodegenerative disease: Roles of semantic memory and technical reasoning. *Cortex, 82*, 119–132. doi:10.1016/j.cortex.2016.06.007

Binkofski, F., & Reetz, K. (2008). Apraxia. In S. F. Cappa (Ed.), *Cognitive neurology: A clinical textbook* (pp. 67–88). USA: Oxford University Press. https://doi.org/10.1093/acprof:oso/9780198569275.001.0001

Bisiach, E., & Vallar, G. (2000). Unilateral neglect in humans. In F. Boller, J. Grafman, & G. Rizzolatti (Eds.), *Handbook of neuropsychology* (2nd ed., Vol. 1, Chapter 16, pp 459–502). Amsterdam: Elsevier Science B.V.

Boeve, B. F. (2011). The multiple phenotypes of corticobasal syndrome and corticobasal degeneration: Implications for further study. *Journal of Molecular Neuroscience, 45*, 350. doi:10.1007/S12031-011-9624-1

Boeve, B. F., Lang, A. E., & Litvan, I. (2003). Corticobasal degeneration and its relationship to progressive supranuclear palsy and frontotemporal dementia. *Annals of Neurology, 54*(S5), S15–S19. doi:10.1002/ana.10570

Borroni, B., Gabirotto, V., Agosti, C., Brambati, S. M., Bellelli, G., Gasparotti, R., ... Perani, D. (2008). White matter changes in corticobasal degeneration syndrome and correlation with limb apraxia. *Archives of Neurology, 65*(6), 796–801. doi:10.1001/archneur.65.6.796

Borroni, B., Turla, M., Bertasi, V., Agosti, C., Gilberti, N., & Padovani, A. (2008). Cognitive and behavioral assessment in the early stages of neurodegenerative extrapyramidal syndromes. *Archives of Gerontology and Geriatrics, 47*, 53–61. doi:10.1016/j.archger.2007.07.005

Buckner, R. L., Snyder, A. Z., Shannon, B. J., LaRossa, G., Sachs, R., Fotenos, A. F., & Mintun, M. A. (2005). Molecular, structural, and functional characterization of alzheimer's disease: Evidence for a relationship between default activity, amyloid, and memory. *Journal of Neuroscience, 25*(34), 7709–7717. doi:10.1523/JNEUROSCI.2177-05.2005

Burrell, J. R., Hodges, J. R., & Rowe, J. B. (2014). Cognition in corticobasal syndrome and progressive supranuclear palsy. A review. *Movement Disorders, 29*(5), 684–693. doi:10.1002/mds.25872

Burrell, J. R., Hornberger, M., Villemagne, V. L., Rowe, C. C., & Hodges, J. R. (2013). Clinical profile of PiB-positive corticobasal syndrome. *PLoS ONE, 8*(4), e61025. doi:10.1371/journal.pone.0061025

Buxbaum, L. J., Kyle, K., Grossman, M., & Coslett, B. (2007). Left inferior parietal representations for skilled hand-object interactions: Evidence from stroke and corticobasal degeneration. *Cortex, 43*, 411–423. doi:10.1016/S0010-9452(08)70466-0

Capasso, R., & Miceli, G. (2001). *Esame neuropsicologico per l'Afasia: ENPA* (Vol. 4). Springer Science & Business Media.

Catani, M. (2005). The rises and falls of disconnection syndromes. *Brain, 128*(10), 2224–2239. doi:10.1093/brain/awh622

Catani, M., Jones, D. K., & Ffytche, D. H. (2005). Perisylvian language networks of the human brain. *Annals of Neurology, 57*(1), 8–16. doi:10.1002/ana.20319

Ceravolo, R., Rossi, C., Cilia, R., Tognoni, G., Antonini, A., Volterrani, D., & Bonuccelli, U. (2013). Evidence of delayed nigrostriatal dysfunction in corticobasal syndrome: A SPECT follow-up study. *Parkinsonism & Related Disorders, 19*(5), 557–559. doi:10.1016/j.parkreldis.2013.01.013

Chainay, H., & Humphreys, G. W. (2003). Ideomotor and ideational apraxia in corticobasal degeneration: A case study. *Neurocase, 9*(2), 177–186. doi:10.1076/neur.9.2.177.15073

Cilia, R., Rossi, C., Frosini, D., Volterrani, D., Siri, C., Pagni, C., ... Ceravolo, R. (2011). Dopamine transporter SPECT imaging in corticobasal syndrome. *PLoS ONE, 6*(5), e18301. doi:10.1371/journal.pone.0018301

Clark, D. L., Boutros, N. N., & Mendez, M. F. (2005). *The brain and behavior: An introduction to behavioral neuroanatomy*. New York, NY: Cambridge University Press. https://doi.org/10.1017/CBO9780511543661

Conson, M., Salzano, S., Manzo, V., Grossi, D., & Trojano, L. (2009). Closing-in without severe drawing disorders: The "fatal" consequences of pathological attraction. *Cortex, 45*(3), 285–292. doi:10.1016/j.cortex.2007.11.013

Corbetta, M., & Shulman, G. (2002). Control of goal-directed and stimulus-driven attention in the brain. *Nature Reviews Neuroscience, 3*, 201–215. doi:10.1038/nrn755

Crutch, S. J., Schott, J. M., Rabinovici, G. D., Murray, M., Snowden, J. S., van der Flier, W. M., ... Boeve, B. F. (2017). Consensus classification of posterior cortical atrophy. *Alzheimer's & Dementia*. doi:10.1016/j.jalz.2017.01.014

Della Sala, S., MacPherson, S. E., Phillips, L. H., Sacco, L., & Spinnler, H. (2003). How many camels are there in Italy? Cognitive estimates standardised on the Italian population. *Neurological Sciences, 24*(1), 10–15. doi:10.1007/s100720300015

De Luca, M., Beckmann, C. F., De Stefano, N., Matthews, P. M., & Smith, S. M. (2006). fMRI resting state networks define distinct modes of long-distance interactions in the human brain. *NeuroImage, 29*(4), 1359–1367. doi:10.1016/j.neuroimage.2005.08.035

De Renzi, E. (1985). Methods of limb apraxia examination and their bearing on the interpretation of the disorder. In E. A. Roy (Ed.), *Neuropsychological studies of apraxia and related disorders* (pp. 45–64). Amsterdam: The Netherlands.

De Renzi, E., Faglioni, P., Scarpa, M., & Crisi, G. (1986). Limb apraxia in patients with damage confined to the left basal ganglia and thalamus. *Journal of Neurology, Neurosurgery and Psychiatry, 49*, 1030–1038. doi:10.1136/jnnp.49.9.1030

De Renzi, E., Motti, F., & Nichelli, P. (1980). Imitating gestures. A quantitative approach to ideomotor apraxia. *Archives of Neurology, 37*, 6–10. doi:10.1001/archneur.1980.00500500036003

De Renzi, E., Pieczuro, A., & Vignolo, L. A. (1966). Oral apraxia and aphasia. *Cortex, 2*, 50–73. doi:10.1016/S0010-9452(66)80028-X

De Renzi, E., Pieczuro, A., & Vignolo, L. A. (1968). Ideational apraxia: A quantitative study. *Neuropsychologia, 6*(1), 41–52. doi:10.1016/0028-3932(68)90037-7

Delrieu, J., Payoux, P., Toulza, O., Esquerre, J.-P., Vellas, B., & Voisin, T. (2010). Sensory alien hand syndrome in corticobasal degeneration: A cerebral blood flow study. *Movement Disorders, 25*, 1288–1291. doi:10.1002/mds.23064

Denny-Brown, D. (1958). The nature of apraxia. *The Journal of Nervous and Mental Disease, 126*(1), 9–32. Retrieved from http://journals.lww.com/jonmd/Citation/1958/01000/the_Nature_of_Apraxia.3.aspx https://doi.org/10.1097/00005053-195801000-00003

Di Stefano, F., Kas, A., Habert, M. O., Decazes, P., Lamari, F., Lista, S., ... Teichmann, M. (2016). The phenotypical core of Alzheimer's disease-related and nonrelated variants of the corticobasal syndrome: A systematic clinical, neuropsychological, imaging, and biomarker study. *Alzheimer's & Dementia, 12*(7), 786–795. doi:10.1016/j.jalz.2016.02.005

Dopper, E. G., Seelaar, H., Chiu, W. Z., de Koning, I., van Minkelen, R., Baker, M. C., & Van Swieten, J. C. (2011). Symmetrical corticobasal syndrome caused by a novel c.314dup progranulin mutation. *Journal of Molecular Neuroscience, 45*(3), 354. doi:10.1007/s12031-011-9626-z

Ellis, A. W., Flude, B. M., & Young, A. W. (1987). "Neglect dyslexia" and the early visual processing of letters in words and nonwords. *Cognitive Neuropsychology, 4*(4), 439–464. doi:10.1080/02643298708252047

FitzGerald, D. B., Drago, V., Jeong, Y., Chang, Y.-L., White, K. D., & Heilman, K. M. (2007). Asymmetrical alien hands in corticobasal degeneration. *Movement Disorders, 22*(4), 581–584. doi:10.1002/mds.21337

Folstein, M. F., Folstein, S. E., & McHugh, P. R. (1975). "Mini-mental state": A practical method for grading the cognitive state of patients for the clinician. *Journal of Psychiatric Research, 12*(3), 189–198. doi:10.1016/0022-3956(75)90026-6

Frattali, C. M., Grafman, J., Patronas, N., Makhlouf, F., & Litvan, I. (2000). Language disturbances in corticobasal degeneration. *Neurology, 54*(4), 990–992. doi:10.1212/WNL.54.4.990

Gauthier, L., Dehaut, F., & Joanette, Y. (1989). The Bells Test: A quantitative and qualitative test for visual neglect. *International Journal of Clinical Neuropsychology, 11*(2), 49–54. Retrieved from http://psycnet.apa.org/psycinfo/1989-31545-001

Giorelli, M., Losignore, N. A., Bagnoli, J., Difazio, P., & Zimatore, G. B. (2014). The progression of posterior cortical atrophy to corticobasal syndrome: Lumping or splitting neurodegenerative diseases? *Tremor and Other Hyperkinetic Movements*. doi:10.7916/D81G0JCQ

Goldenberg, G. (2003). Neuropsychological assessment and treatment of disorders of voluntary movements. In P. Halligan, U. Kischka, & J. C. Marshall (Eds.), *Handbook of clinical neuropsychology* (pp. 340–352). New York: Oxford University Press.

Goldenberg, G. (2009). Apraxia and the parietal lobes. *Neuropsychologia, 47*, 1449–1459. doi:10.1016/j.neuropsychologia.2008.07.014

Goldenberg, G., & Spatt, J. (2009). The neural basis of tool use. *Brain, 132*, 1645–1655. doi:10.1093/brain/awp080

Gonzalez Rothi, L. J., Ochipa, C., & Heilman, K. M. (1991). A cognitive neuropsychological model of limb praxis. *Cognitive Neuropsychology, 8*(6), 443–458. doi:10.1080/02643299108253382

Graham, N. L., Bak, T. H., & Hodges, J. R. (2003). Corticobasal degeneration as a cognitive disorder. *Movement Disorders, 18*(11), 1224–1232. doi:10.1002/mds.10536

Graham, N. L., Zeman, A., Young, A. W., Patterson, K., & Hodges, J. R. (1999). Dyspraxia in a patient with corticobasal degeneration: The role of visual and tactile inputs to action. *Journal of Neurology, Neurosurgery and Psychiatry, 67*, 334–344. doi:10.1136/jnnp.67.3.334

Grijalvo-Perez, A. M., & Litvan, I. (2014). Corticobasal degeneration. *Seminars in Neurology, 34*, 160–173. doi:10.1055/s-0034-1381734

Guo, J. L., & Lee, V. M. (2014). Cell-to-cell transmission of pathogenic proteins in neurodegenerative diseases. *Nature Medicine, 20*(2), 130–138. doi:10.1038/nm.3457

Hammesfahr, S., Antke, C., Mamlins, E., Beu, M., Wojtecki, L., Ferrea, S., ... Südmeye, M. (2016). FP-CIT- and IBZM-SPECT in corticobasal syndrome: Results from a clinical follow-up study. *Neurodegenerative Diseases, 16*(5–6), 342–347. doi:10.1159/000443667

Hassan, A., Whitwell, J. L., Boeve, B. F., Jack, C. R., Parisi, J. E., Dickson, D. W., & Josephs, K. A. (2010). Symmetric corticobasal degeneration (S-CBD). *Parkinsonism & Related Disorders, 16*(3), 208–214. doi:10.1016/j.parkreldis.2009.11.013

Homma, T., Takubo, H., Takahashi, K., Matsubara, S., Takahashi, M., Funata, N., ... Uchihara, T. (2014). Lateralized cortical involvement and contralateral parkinsonism without basal ganglia involvement in two autopsy cases of corticobasal syndrome-Alzheimer's disease. *Journal of Alzheimer's Disease, 40*(1), 51–55. doi:10.3233/JAD-131676

Huang, N., Hornberger, M., Hodges, J. R., & Burrell, J. R. (2014). Measuring disease progression in corticobasal syndrome. *Journal of Neurology, 261*(8), 1598–1605. doi:10.1007/s00415-014-7389-5

Hu, W. T., Rippon, G. W., Boeve, B. F., Knopman, D. S., Petersen, R. C., Parisi, J. E., & Josephs, K. A. (2009). Alzheimer's disease and corticobasal degeneration presenting as corticobasal syndrome. *Movement Disorders, 24*(9), 1375–1379. doi:10.1002/mds.22574

Iaccarino, L., Chieffi, S., & Iavarone, A. (2014). Utilization behavior: What is known and what has to be known? *Behavioural Neurology, 2014*, 1599, Article ID 297128. doi:10.1155/2014/29712

Jacobs, D. H., Adair, J. C., Macauley, B., Gold, M., Gonzalez Rothi, L. J., & Heilman, K. M. (1999). Apraxia in corticobasal degeneration. *Brain and Cognition, 40*, 336–354. doi:10.1006/brcg.1999.1085

Josephs, K. A., Whitwell, J. L., Boeve, B. F., Knopman, D. S., Petersen, R. C., Hu, W. T., ... Jack, C. R. (2010). Anatomical differences between CBS-corticobasal degeneration and CBS-Alzheimer's disease. *Movement Disorders, 25*(9), 1246–1252. doi:10.1002/mds.23062

Katz, S., Downs, T. D., Cash, H. R., & Grotz, R. C. (1970). Progress in development of the index of ADL. *The Gerontologist, 10*(1 Part 1), 20–30. doi:10.1093/geront/10.1_Part_1.20

Kimura, N., Kumamoto, T., Hanaoka, T., Hazama, Y., Nakamura, K., & Arakawa, R. (2008). Corticobasal de generation presentino with progressive conduction aphasia. *Journal of the Neurological Sciences, 269*, 163–168. doi:10.1016/j.jns.2007.12.017

Kloesel, B., Czarnecki, K., Muir, J. J., & Scott Keller, A. (2010). Sequellae of a left-sided parietal stroke: posterior alien hand syndrome. *Neurocase, 16*(6), 488–493. doi:10.1080/13554794.2010.497154

Laiacona, M., Barbarotto, R., Trivelli, C., & Capitani, E. (1993). Dissociazioni semantiche intercategoriali: Descrizione di una batteria standardizzata e dati normativi. *Archivio di Psicologia, Neurologia e Psichiatria, 54*, 209–248. Retrieved from http://hdl.handle.net/2434/194743

Lang, A. E., Riley, D. E., & Bergeron, C. (1994). Cortico-basal ganglionic degeneration. In D. B. Calne (Ed.), *Neurodegenerative diseases*. (pp. 877–894). Philadelphia, PA: WB Saunders.

Lavados, M., Carrasco, X., Pena, M., Zaidel, E., Zaidel, D., & Aboitiz, F. (2002). A new sign of callosal disconnection syndrome: Agonistic dyspraxia. *A case study. Neurocase, 8*(6), 480–483. doi:10.1076/neur.8.5.480.16178

Lawton, M. P., & Brody, E. M. (1969). Assessment of older people: Self-maintaining and instrumental activities of daily living. *The Gerontologist, 9*, 179–186. https://doi.org/10.1093/geront/9.3_Part_1.179

Lee, S. E., Rabinovici, G. D., Mayo, M. C., Wilson, S. M., Seeley, W. W., DeArmond, S. J., ... Sidhu, M. (2011). Clinicopathological correlations in corticobasal degeneration. *Annals of Neurology, 70*(2), 327–340. doi:10.1002/ana.22424

Leiguarda, R. C., Merello, M., Nouzeilles, M. I., Balej, J., Rivero, A., & Nogués, M. (2003). Limb-kinetic apraxia in corticobasal de generation: clinical and kinematic features. *Movement Disorders, 18*(1), 49–59. doi:10.1002/mds.10303

Lheman, S., & Schnider, A. (2008). Memory disorders. In S. F. Cappa (Ed.), *Cognitive neurology: A clinical textbook* (pp. 119–141). USA: Oxford University Press. https://doi.org/10.1093/acprof:oso/9780198569275.001.0001

Lhermitte, F. (1983). Utilization behaviour and its relation to lesions of the frontal lobes. *Brain, 106*, 237–255. doi:10.1093/brain/106.2.237

Lhermitte, F., Pillon, B., & Serdaru, M. (1986). Human autonomy and the frontal lobes. Part I: Imitation and utilization behavior: A neuropsychological study of 75 patients. *Annals of Neurology, 19*(4), 326–334. doi:10.1002/ana.410190404

Luzzatti, C., Willmes, K., & De Bleser, R. (1996). *Aachener aphasie test: Versione Italiana*. Firenze: Organizzazioni Speciali.

Mahapatra, R. K., Edwards, M. J., Schott, J. M., & Bhatia, K. P. (2004). Corticobasal degeneration. *The Lancet Neurology, 3*, 736–743. doi:10.1016/S1474-4422(04)00936-6

Malloy, P. F., Cohen, R. A., & Jenkins, M. A. (1998). Frontal lobe function and dysfunction. In P. J. Snyder, P. D. Nussbaum, & D. L. Robins (Eds.), *Clinical neuropsychology: A pocket handbook for assessment* (pp. 573–590). Washington, DC: American Psychological Association.

Mathew, R., Bak, T. H., & Hodges, J. R. (2011). Diagnostic criteria for corticobasal syndrome: A comparative study. *Journal of Neurology, Neurosurgery, and Psychiatry*. doi:10.1136/jnnp-2011-300875

McMillan, C. T., Boyd, C., Gross, R. G., Weinstein, J., Firn, K., Toledo, J. B., ... Lee, E. B. (2016). Multimodal imaging evidence of pathology-mediated disease distribution in corticobasal syndrome. *Neurology, 87*(12), 1227–1234. doi:10.1212/WNL.0000000000003119

McMonagle, P., Blair, M., & Kertesz, A. (2006). Corticobasal degeneration and progressive aphasia. *Neurology, 67*, 1444–1451. doi:10.1212/01.wnl.0000240215.43492.01

Mendez, M. F. (2000). Corticobasal ganglionic degeneration with Balint's syndrome. *The Journal of Neuropsychiatry and Clinical Neurosciences, 12*, 273–275. doi:10.1176/jnp.12.2.273

Merians, A. S., Clark, M., Poizner, H., Jacobs, D. H., Adair, J. C., Macauley, B., ... Heilman, K. M. (1999). Apraxia differs in corticobasal degeneration and left-parietal stroke: A case study. *Brain and Cognition, 40*(2), 314–335. doi:10.1006/brcg.1999.1084

Murray, R., Neumann, M., Forman, M. S., Farmer, J., Massimo, L., Rice, A., ... Gorno-Tempini, M. L. (2007). Cognitive and motor assessment in autopsy-proven corticobasal degeneration. *Neurology, 68*(16), 1274–1283. doi:10.1212/01.wnl.0000259519.78480.c3

Norman, D. A. (1988). *The psychology of everyday things*. New York, NY: Basic books.

Novelli, G., Papagno, C., Capitani, E., Laiacona, M., Vallar, G., & Cappa, S. F. (1986). Three clinical tests for the assessment of lexical retrieval and production: Norms from 320 normal subjects. *Archivio di Psicologia, Neurologia e Psichiatria, 47*, 477–506.

Okuda, B., Tanaka, H., Kawabata, K., Tachibana, H., & Sugita, M. (2001). Truncal and limb apraxia in corticobasal degeneration. *Movement Disorders, 16*, 760–762. doi:10.1002/mds.1150

Orsini, A., Grossi, D., Capitani, E., Laiacona, M., Papagno, C., & Vallar, G. (1987). Verbal and spatial immediate memory span: Normative data from 1355 adults and 1112 children. *The Italian Journal of Neurological Sciences, 8*(6), 537–548. doi:10.1007/BF02333660

Ouchi, H., Toyoshima, Y., Tada, M., Oyake, M., Aida, I., Tomita, I., ... M. L., T. (2014). Pathology and sensitivity of current clinical criteria in corticobasal syndrome. *Movement Disorders, 29*(2), 238–244. doi:10.1002/mds.25746

Ozsancak, C., Auzou, P., & Dujardin & Hannequin, D. (2000). Dysarthria and orofacial apraxia in corticobasal degeneration. *Movement Disorders, 15*(5), 905–910. doi:10.1002/1531-8257(200009)15:5<905::AID-MDS1022>3.0.CO;2-D

Ozsancak, C., Auzou, P., & Hannequin, D. (2004). Orofacial apraxia in corticobasal de generation, progressive supranuclear palsy, multiple system atrophy and Parkinson's disease. *Journal of Neurology, 251*(11), 1317–1323. doi:10.1007/s00415-004-0530-0

Passov, V., Gavrilova, R. H., Strand, E., Cerhan, J. H., & Josephs, K. A. (2011). Sporadic corticobasal syndrome with progranulin mutation presenting as progressive apraxic agraphia. *Archives of Neurology, 68*(3), 376–380. doi:10.1001/archneurol.2011.26

Peigneux, P., Salmon, E., Garraux, G., Laureys, S., Willems, S., Dujardin, K., ... Franck, G. (2001). Neural and cognitive

bases of upper limb apraxia in corticobasal degeneration. *Neurology, 57*(7), 1259–1268. doi:10.1212/WNL.57.7.1259
Pharr, V., Uttl, B., Stark, M., Litvan, I., Fantie, B., & Grafman, J. (2001). Comparison of apraxia in corticobasal degeneration and progressive supranuclear palsy. *Neurology, 56*, 957–963. doi:10.1212/WNL.56.7.957
Posner, M. I., & Petersen, S. E. (1990). The attention system of the human brain. *Annual Review of Neuroscience, 13*(1), 25–42. doi:10.1146/annurev.ne.13.030190.000325
Possin, K. L. (2010). Visual spatial cognition in neurodegenerative disease. *Neurocase, 16*(6), 466–487. doi:10.1080/13554791003730600
Rajagopal, R., Bateman, R., & Van Stavern, G. P. (2011). Visual involvement in corticobasal syndrome. *Journal of Neuro-Ophthalmology*, 1–3. doi:10.1097/WNO.0b013e3182305162
Riddoch, M. J., Chechlacz, M., Mevorach, C., Mavritsaki, E., Allen, H., & Humphreys, G. W. (2010). The neural mechanisms of visual selection: The view from neuropsychology. *Annals of the New York Academy of Sciences, 1191*, 156–181. doi:10.1111/j.1749-6632.2010.05448.x
Riddoch, M. J., & Humphreys, G. W. (1993). *BORB: Birmingham object recognition battery*. Hove: Lawrence Erlbaum Associates.
Rittman, T., Ghosh, B., & Rowe, J. (2013). Exploration of functional brain networks in neurodegenerative disease. *The Lancet, 381*, S92. doi:10.1016/S0140-6736(13)60532-2
Roy, E. A. (1996). Hand preference, manual asymmetries, and limb apraxia. In D. Elliot (Ed.), *Manual asymmetries in motor control* (pp. 215–236). Boca Raton, FL: CRC Press.
Roy, E. A., Square, P. A., Adams, S., & Friesen, H. (1985). Error/movement notation systems in apraxia. *Recherches Semitiques/Semiotic Inquiry, 5*, 402.
Rusconi, E., Pinel, P., Dehaene, S., & Kleinschmidt, A. (2010). The enigma of Gerstmann's syndrome revisited: A telling tale of the vicissitudes of neuropsychology. *Brain, 133*, 320–332. doi:10.1093/brain/awp281
Ryan, N. S., Shakespeare, T. J., Lehmann, M., Keihaninejad, S., Nicholas, J. M., Leung, K. K., ... Crutch, S. J. (2014). Motor features in posterior cortical atrophy and their imaging correlates. *Neurobiology of Aging, 35*(12), 2845–2857. doi:10.1016/j.neurobiolaging.2014.05.028
Salter, J. E., Roy, E. A., Black, S. E., Joshi, A., & Almeida, Q. (2004). Gestural imitation and limb apraxia in corticobasal degeneration. *Brain and Cognition, 55*, 400–402. doi:10.1016/j.bandc.2004.02.058
de Schotten, M. T., Dell'Acqua, F., Forkel, S. J., Simmons, A., Vergani, F., Murphy, D. G., & Catani, M. (2011). A lateralized brain network for visuospatial attention. *Nature Neuroscience, 14*(10), 1245–1246. doi:10.1038/nn.2905
Seeley, W. W., Crawford, R. K., Zhou, J., Miller, B. L., & Greicius, M. D. (2009). Neurodegenerative diseases target large-scale human brain networks. *Neuron, 62*, 42–52. doi:10.1016/j.neuron.2009.03.024
Seeley, W. W., Menon, V., Schatzberg, A. F., Keller, J., Glover, G. H., Kenna, H., ... Greicius, M. D. (2007). Dissociable intrinsic connectivity networks for salience processing and executive control. *Journal of Neuroscience, 27*(9), 2349–2356. doi:10.1523/JNEUROSCI.5587-06.2007
Semenza, C. (2003). Assessing disorders of awareness and representation of body parts. In P. W. Halligan, U. Kischka, & J. Marshall (Eds.), *Handbook of clinical neuropsychology* (Chapter 12, pp. 195–213). New York, NY: Oxford University Press.
Semenza, C., & Goodglass, H. (1985). Localization of body parts in brain injured subjects. *Neuropsychologia, 23*(2), 161–175. doi:10.1016/0028-3932(85)90101-0
Shakespeare, T. J., Yong, K. X., Foxe, D., Hodges, J., & Crutch, S. J. (2015). Pronounced impairment of everyday skills and self-care in posterior cortical atrophy. *Journal of Alzheimer, 43*(2), 381–384. doi:10.3233/JAD-141071
Soliveri, P., Monza, D., Paridi, D., Radice, D., Grisoli, M., Testa, D., ... Girotti, F. (1999). Cognitive and magnetic resonance imaging aspects of corticobasal degeneration and progressive supranuclear palsy. *Neurology, 53*(3), 502–502. doi:10.1212/WNL.53.3.502
Soliveri, P., Piacentini, S., & Girotti, F. (2005). Limb apraxia in corticobasal degeneration and progressive supranuclear palsy. *Neurology, 64*, 448–453. doi:10.1212/01.WNL.0000150732.92567.BA
Soliveri, P., Piacentini, S., Paridi, D., Testa, D., Carella, F., & Girotti, F. (2003). Distal-proximal differences in limb apraxia in corticobasal degeneration but not progressive supranuclear palsy. *Neurological Sciences, 24*, 213–214. doi:10.1007/s10072-003-0136-9
Spatt, J., Bak, T., Bozeat, S., Patterson, K., & Hodges, J. R. (2002). Apraxia, mechanical problem solving and semantic knowledge. *Journal of Neurology, 249*, 601–608. doi:10.1007/s004150200070
Spinnler, H., & Tognoni, G. (1987). Standardizzazione e taratura italiana di test neuropsicologici. *Italian Journal of Neurological Sciences, 8*(Supplement 8), 1–120.
Stamenova, V., Roy, E. A., & Black, S. (2009). A model-based approach to understanding apraxia in corticobasal syndrome. *Neuropsychology Review, 19*, 47–63. doi:10.1007/s11065-008-9079-5
Stamenova, V., Roy, E. A., & Black, S. E. (2011). Limb apraxia in corticobasal syndrome. *Cortex, 47*, 460–472. doi:10.1016/j.cortex.2010.04.010
Südmeyer, M., Pieperhoff, P., Ferrea, S., Krause, H., Groiss, S. J., Elben, S., ... Schnitzler, A. (2012). Longitudinal deformation-based morphometry reveals spatio-temporal dynamics of brain volume changes in patients with corticobasal syndrome. *PLoS ONE, 7*(7), e41873. doi:10.1371/journal.pone.0041873
Sunderland, A., & Shinner, C. (2007). Ideomotor apraxia and functional ability. *Cortex, 43*, 359–367. doi:10.1016/S0010-9452(08)70461-1
Tang-Wai, D. F., Josephs, K. A., Boeve, B. F., Dickson, D. W., Parisi, J. E., & Petersen, R. C. (2003). Pathologically confirmed corticobasal degeneration presenting with visuospatial dysfunction. *Neurology, 61*, 1134–1135. doi:10.1212/01.WNL.0000086814.35352.B3
Tree, J., & Kay, J. (2008). Longitudinal assessment of language and memory impairments in pathologically confirmed cortico-basal ganglionic degeneration. *Cortex, 44*, 1234–1247. doi:10.1016/j.cortex.2007.08.017
Vallar, G. (2007). Spatial neglect, Balint-Holmes' and Gerstmann's syndromes, and other spatial disorders. *CNS Spectrums, 12*(7), 527–536. doi:10.1017/S1092852900021271
Warrington, E. K., & James, M. (1991). *The VISUAL object and space perception battery*. Bury St. Edmunds: Thames Valley Test Company.
Weintraub, S., & Mesulam, M. (2009). Scientific commentary. With or without FUS, it is the anatomy that dictates the dementia phenotype. *Brain, 132*, 2906–2908. doi:10.1093/brain/awp286
Whitwell, J. L., Jack, C. R., Boeve, B. F., Parisi, J. E., Ahlskog, J. E., Drubach, D. A., ... Josephs, K. A. (2010). Imaging correlates of pathology in corticobasal syndrome. *Neurology, 75*(21), 1879–1887. doi:10.1212/WNL.0b013e3181feb2e8
Wolpe, N., Moore, J. W., Rae, C. L., Rittman, T., Altena, E., Haggard, P., & Rowe, J. B. (2014). The medial frontal-prefrontal network for altered awareness and control of action in corticobasal syndrome. *Brain, 137*, 208–220. doi:10.1093/brain/awt302

10

Cognitive processes across anxiety disorders related to intolerance of uncertainty

Marie Vander Haegen[1]* and Anne-Marie Etienne[1]

*Corresponding author: Marie Vander Haegen, Unit of Health Psychology, Université de Liège, Quartier Village 2, Rue de l'Aunaie 30, Liège 4000, Belgium

E-mail: mvanderhaegen@doct.ulg.ac.be

Reviewing editor: Cornelia Duregger, Neuroconsult, Austria

Abstract: *Objective*: Being a relatively recent concept, the intolerance of uncertainty (IU) suffers from inconsistent definitions and conceptual overlap. The core objective of the study is to clarify its clinical manifestations and its involved cognitive processes. *Method*: The procedure is based on algorithms (equations of keywords) encoded simultaneously in databases (Scopus, PubMed, and PsycArticles). Results are filtered by the year (range of 10 years [2005–2015] because it is a recent concept) and the relevance of abstracts. Once the studies are appraised, results are categorized in two groups: studies which examine the IU in a clinical perspective (relations with one or several anxiety disorders) (cluster A) and those which measure the IU through a cognitive perspective (cognition, metacognition) (cluster B). *Results:* 66 results are retrieved: 50 results concern the cluster A and 16 examine the cluster B. The state of the IU varies between studies (e.g. predictor and mediator), which make comparisons difficult. Notwithstanding, the IU construct seems to be a broad transdiagnostic maintaining risk factor involved in a range of psychological disorders. *Conclusion*: This clustering supported that researchers and clinicians may benefit from incorporating IU within cognitive and computational research design and as a specific treatment target.

ABOUT THE AUTHORS

Our laboratory participates in psychologists' formation in the field of the health psychology and its specificities. Our researchers and clinicians develop research projects and clinical activities in the field of the emergencies, the quality of life, the chronic diseases, the anxiety and the psycho-oncology in children and adults.

This study integrates the psychology-oncology axis and takes root in other related themes of the laboratory such as the anxiety (related with intolerance of uncertainty and its components) and the quality of life in parents of child cancer survivor. This project is approved by all of Ethics Committees and is led in Belgian hospitals.

PUBLIC INTEREST STATEMENT

Who was not ever worried about a situation or event of the everyday life? When we are worried about a situation, we feel hesitating, uncomfortable or anxious. Nevertheless, worries and uncertainties are normal phenomena of the individual (the life is full of uncertainties).

For some individuals, they tend to be extremely "allergic" to uncertain events. Those individuals are called "intolerant of uncertainty". This phenomenon is observed as a personality's characteristic that may leads to distress for the individual (anxiety, depression ...) and impacts her/his quality of life.

The study aims to investigate the state of the literature on the intolerance of uncertainty and especially their relation with psychological distress (the anxiety and the depression). Results show evidence that the intolerance of uncertainty could give rise to several psychological distresses and may impair diverse individual's skills such as the resolution of daily problem or still mental strategies to cope with uncertain event. Note that Marie Vander Haegen has been set as corresponding author, since she is the first author.

Subjects: Behavioral Medicine; Behavioral Neuroscience; Health and Social Care; Mental Health; Psychological Disorders; Psychological Science; Trauma Studies

Keywords: intolerance of uncertainty; cognitive processes; anxiety disorders; metacognition

1. Review outline and aims

The current study sought to advance understanding of IU through a review of its relations to symptoms of anxiety disorders; namely generalized anxiety disorder (GAD), obsessive-compulsive disorder (OCD) and its cognitive processes. The originality of this review lies in considering the psychopathological and cognitive perspectives of IU. Indeed, previous studies examined either the pathological links with the UI, or the cognitive processes involved in the UI.

The aim of the study is the examination of the relations between IU and anxiety disorders and also its involved cognitive components. Two gradual steps are proposed in order to achieve the aim. The first step is to estimate the association of IU with GAD and OCD and its clinical aspects. The second step is to examine the cognitive components of IU. Methodological strengths and weaknesses of empirical studies in the IU's area are argued in the "discussion section".

Increasing interest for IU in understanding psychopathology has boomed in recent decades. In spite of a flourishing literature of anxiety disorders, few have examined the cognitive state of the IU across anxiety disorders. The organization of the clinical review is divided into two major theme parts as follows: *IU and Anxiety Disorders Perspective* (cluster A) and *IU and Cognitive Processes Perspective* (cluster B). It is mentioned that each cluster brings together research involving either clinical variables (i.e. solely an advanced clinical hypothesis) or cognitive variables (i.e. solely an advanced cognitive hypothesis).

The outline of this review is as follows: first, we provide background material delineating IU and its correlates but also, the core cognitive elements in anxiety disorders; we review the algorithmic method and its statistical outcomes. Based on this, we provide a critical review of the current state of research led in the domain and how IU activates through clinical and cognitive perspectives. Future research avenues about IU construct are proposed in the "discussion section".

2. Theoretical framework

2.1. Uncertainty until a certain acceptable point

The state of uncertainty is seen as a realization that our beliefs and representations of the world are unable to accurately predict future events in our environment. Despite the normal state of uncertainty (i.e. life is full of uncertainties), empirical evidence supports that uncertainty is a significant stressor involving physiological and psychological consequences for the individual (Rosen, Ivanova, & Knäuper, 2013; Zlomke & Jeter, 2014).

In contrast, IU refers to a trait of the individual (dispositional risk factor developed during childhood) rather than a perceived characteristic of the event (Zentner & Bates, 2008). IU is observed as a set of negative cognitive, emotional and behavioural reactions to situational uncertainty. Researchers have defined IU as a single construct made up of four dimensions: (1) individual perceives that uncertainty upsetting and stressful, (2) attributes it is an intolerable situation and should be avoided, (3) conceives that uncertainty is unfair and (4) lead to an inability to act (Robichaud, 2013).

In other words, for the same situational uncertainty, two individuals with identical perceptions of occurrence and consequences may differ in their threshold of tolerance of uncertainty towards the situation (Freeston, Rhéaume, Letarte, Dugas, & Ladouceur, 1994). For example, an individual who is intolerant of uncertainty would evaluate the situation as being more disturbing, and tend to view uncertainty as threatening, and overwhelming whereas an individual who is not intolerant of uncertainty would evaluate the situation less disturbing and may view uncertainty as solvable and acceptable.

Empirical studies observed that individuals who are intolerant of uncertainty will perceive more many sources of danger in their daily life and have more reactions of hypervigilance when they are faced with uncertain or ambiguous situations (Dugas, Burh, & Ladouceur, 2004; Nelson & Shankman, 2011).

2.2. Anxiety disorders: cognitive perspective

Anxiety disorders form a category (DSM V code: 300.00; American Psychiatric Association, 2013) of mental pathologies that are characterized by overwhelming feelings of panic and fear, uncontrollable intrusive thoughts, painful and intrusive memories, excessive worries, sleep disturbance and somatic symptoms (e.g. muscle tension, stomach disorders, heart pounding ...). Anxiety disorders share a continuum of symptoms (comorbid pathology) with other pathologies, especially major depressive disorders (MDD). Moreover, they are often recurring in nature and impaired quality of life (e.g. personal distress, substance abuse, greater mortality, suicide risk factor) (Garner, Möhler, Stein, Mueggler, & Baldwin, 2009).

Cognitive theorists (e.g. Hallion & Ruscio, 2011) propose that biases and dysfunctions are frequently reported in anxiety disorders. Distorted thoughts about the dangerousness of certain situations/events or sensations are the most preponderant outcomes. The observations of these biases have been highlighted in several cognitive tasks (e.g. the modified Stroop task, the spatial cueing task, the dot probe task) suggesting that the phenomenon is not an artefact of the particular situation procedures (for a review see MacLeod & Mathews, 2012). Some explanations of these attentional biases have put forward.

Two types of processes or systems typically one more automatic (affective/motivational) and one more controlled (calculating/deliberative) are recognized in cognitive models. The so-called dual-process model differentiates the "cold" from the "hot" cognition. The "cold cognition" concerns the self-control; encompasses automatic processes, and is more slow, reflective and complex. Conversely, the "hot cognition" refers to a system encompassing affective and motivational processes that are affect-charged (affective processes themselves as well as a phenomenon such as emotional appraisal) (David & Szentagotai, 2006; Prencipe et al., 2011). Several cognitive domains of dysfunction in anxiety disorders are reported in the literature; mainly cold and hot cognition deficits.

2.2.1. Cold cognition deficits in anxiety disorders

2.2.1.1. Executive functions and attentional process. The former category concerns disproportionate attention allocation to threatening stimuli in anxious disorders (Eysenck, Derakshan, Santos, & Calvo, 2007). Cisler and Koster (2010) located three core elements of attentional bias: (1) *facilitated attentional deployment*, (2) *the attentional disengagement* and (3) *the attentional avoidance*.

Significant results for facilitated attention among anxious individuals were found in studies (e.g. Fox, Russo, Bowles, & Dutton, 2001; Yiend & Mathews, 2001). Data suggest that facilitated attention towards threat is moderated by the threat intensity and its duration during task performance (i.e. highly threatening and presented 100 ms or less). Studies have therefore demonstrated that selective attention detects faster threat cues than unrelated stimuli (Williams, Watts, MacLeod, & Mathews, 1997). The second element of attentional bias concerned the attentional disengagement. In anxiety disorders, it appears that the disengagement component is not performed accurately. Studies evidenced a significant difficulty to disengage selective attention towards threat cues (automatic biases for threatening information advanced and inhibition deficit) (Amir, Elias, Klumpp, &

Przeworski, 2003; Eysenck et al., 2007) leading to increased emotional reactivity. The maladaptive attentional disengagement is considered as the core factor of preservation of the anxiety state.

Lastly, cognitive-motivational designs (e.g. Mogg & Bradley, 1998) demonstrated that hypervigilance and avoidance co-occur in a temporally ordered manner in anxiety disorders. Anxious individuals initially direct their attention towards threat (facilitated attention deployment for threat-cueing stimulus) but afterwards, avoid detailed processing of such stimulus in an attempt to decrease their anxious state. In other words, anxious individuals are preoccupied to vigilantly scan the environment for threats (Williams et al., 1997).

2.2.1.2. Memory. The second category involves the memory and especially the episodic and the autobiographical memory. It has been proposed that one factor that may contribute to the maintenance of negative beliefs and avoidance behaviour is the dysfunctional retrieval of past mental events from autobiographical and episodic memory (Mathews & MacLeod, 2005; Mitte, 2008). Researchers proposed that clinical anxious individuals tend to explicitly re-experienced past fear experiences (episodic memory process) when confronted with aversive stimulus, which in turn, potential fear responses. Moreover, studies observed impaired episodic memory for neutral, emotionally irrelevant information (de Quervain & Margraf, 2008).

2.2.2. Hot cognition deficits in anxiety disorders

Cognition could be defined as all mental processes and skills in which individuals engage on a daily basis (e.g. memory, problem solving, decision-making). The cognition allows generating new knowledge through mental processes and helping to use the acquired knowledge in a certain situation. The metacognition is usually conceptualized as "thinking about thinking". Metacognition refers to beliefs and appraisals held about cognition. Metacognition is made up of two components: knowledge and regulation (Friedenberg & Silverman, 2006).

Metacognition of knowledge includes explicit beliefs (declarative/verbally expressed) (e.g. worrying can cause distress) and implicit beliefs (procedural/not directly verbally penetrable) (e.g. use of heuristics in forming social judgements) (Robinson, Vytal, Cornwell, & Grillon, 2013).

These metacognitive beliefs could be positive (i.e. advantages of engaging in cognitive activities) or negative (i.e. beliefs concerning the meaning and dangerousness of thoughts and cognitive experiences) (Wells, 2007). Conversely, metacognition of regulation is the monitoring of one's cognition including planning activities, awareness of comprehension and evaluation of the efficacy of monitoring processes and strategies. Metacognition is then conceptualized as a dynamic and multi-level information processing (Wells, 2000).

2.2.2.1. Contain of cognitions in anxiety disorders. In anxiety disorders, combined maladaptive knowledge, experiences and strategies gave rise to a toxic pattern of thinking that lead to psychological vulnerability and disturbance (e.g. fear of negative evaluation, negative evaluation of positive event, and overestimation of threat, rumination but also inflated responsibility) (Cisler & Koster, 2010; Robinson et al., 2013).

2.2.2.2. Metacognition in anxiety disorders. In anxiety disorders, the central roles of worry and IU as general factors contributing to emotional disorders have been highlighted. According to researchers, certain types of metacognition (especially metacognitive knowledge/positive and negative beliefs) are impaired in anxiety disorders (Wells, 2007).

The influential "Self-Regulatory Executive Function Model" (S-REF; Figure 1) is widely used to understand the development and maintenance of anxiety disorder across a cognitive psychopathology perspective. The S-REF model (S-REF; Wells & Matthews, 1994) is based upon a multi-level architecture integrating three interacting cognitive levels: (1) the level of automatic and reflexive-driven processing (the "on-line" level), (2) the level of voluntary (controlled processing demanding

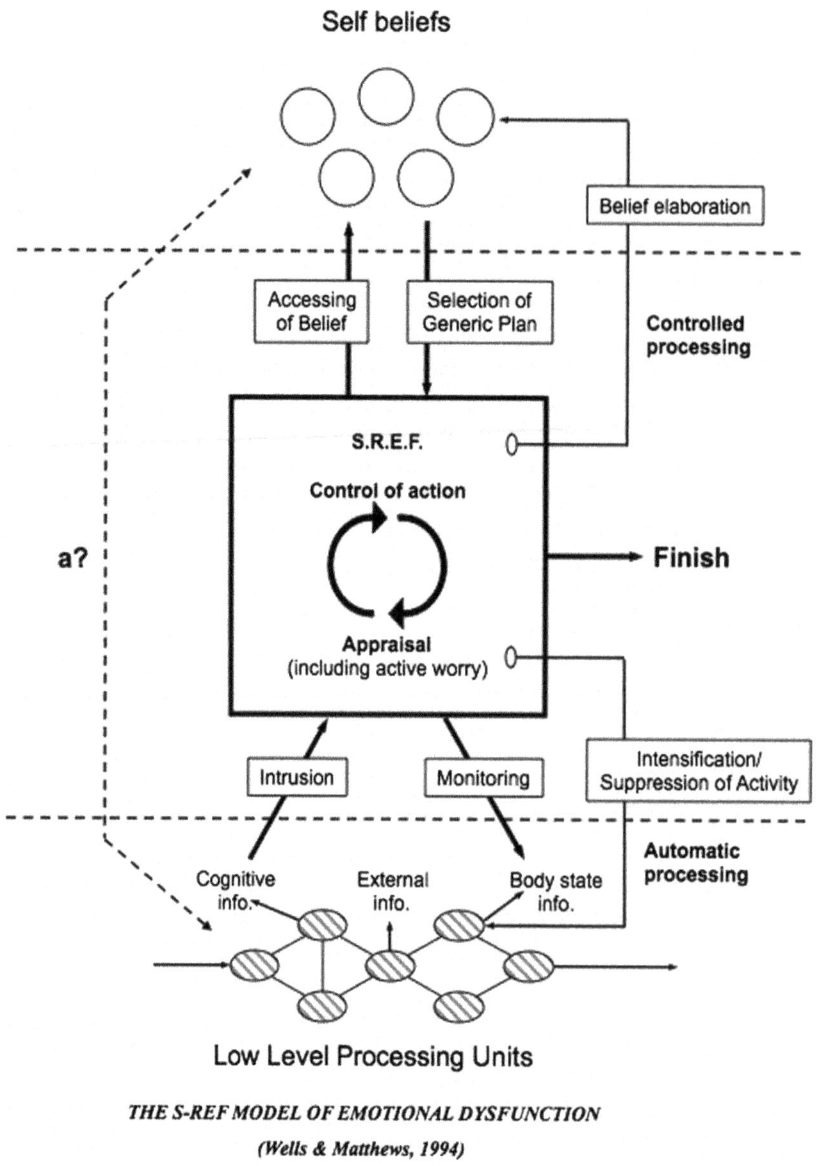

Figure 1. The S-REF Model.

attentional resources) and (3) the level of stored self-beliefs and strategies for self-regulation stored in long-term memory.

The first automatic and reflexive level comprises stimulus-driven information, which is proceeded outside of the conscious mental state. However, stimulus-driven information may pervade into consciousness, which induces adverse negative automatic thoughts (or intrusions) and activates the S-REF (the middle level).

The second level of the model includes a voluntary and a conscious appraisal of events (i.e. control of action and thought). The execution of on-line level of processing requires attentional resources, which by nature are restricted.

The third level involves self-beliefs and strategies for regulation stored in the long-term memory. Two types of self-beliefs are described: (1) declarative and (2) procedural self-beliefs. Declarative self-beliefs consist of explicit statements (self-knowledge about the meaning of thoughts) such as: "I am a worrier". Conversely, procedural self-beliefs are plans that guide the execution of the controlled processes and have a metacognitive status. Two modes (processing configurations) can be executed and are involved in modifying beliefs: (1) object mode and (2) metacognitive mode.

> When in object mode, thoughts (i.e. appraisals) and perceptions are taken as unevaluated and accurate representations of events; this is the default mode of cognitive operation that usually runs in daily circumstances. When in metacognitive mode, the individual is distanced from thoughts, and thoughts and perceptions can be evaluated and not necessarily accepted as direct representations of reality. (Wells, 2000, p. 16)

The S-REF model hypotheses that in the case of emotional disturbances, this metacognitive system becomes dysfunctional, resulting in a toxic pattern: the "Cognitive Attentional Syndrome" (CAS). This toxic pattern is characterized by recurrent styles of thinking in response to negative thoughts (worry and rumination), intensified self-focused attention to threat, decreased cognitive functioning, activated dysfunctional self-beliefs and increased maladaptive coping strategies.

Lastly, the metacognitive model (Wells & Matthews, 1994) argues that the psychological disturbance is maintained by a combination of perseverative thinking styles, maladaptive attentional routines (sustained attention to threatening cued-stimuli) and dysfunctional behaviours (coping strategies) that constitutes the CAS (Wells, 2000).

3. Method

3.1. Search strategy for identification studies

It is noteworthy that none ethical approval for this type of study is needed.

Sources in the current review have been drawn from several databases: *Scopus*, *PubMed* and *PsycArticles*. The following inclusion criteria were established: (1) *year of publication*: studies published between 1 January 2005 and 1 January 2015; (2) *language*: only English publications; (3) *method*: quantitative and qualitative experimental studies (cross-sectional, longitudinal, randomized controlled study); (4) *article design*: only peer-reviewed articles and (5) *target population*: clinical adult sample.

Please note that the search procedure was done on a range of 10 years (studies led between 2005 and 2015). This choice is argued by the fact that the IU is a relatively recent concept (early 2000s).

There were restrictions (exclusion criteria) according to: (1) *type of source*: book chapters, guidelines, commentaries and dissertations and (2) *target population*: children, adolescents, students and the elderly and non-clinical sample.

It is noteworthy that studies about children, adolescents or elderly were not taken into account because most of the literature considers these issues and would require an additional clinical review. So excluded studies did not focus on the intolerance of uncertainty (IU) assessed in a clinical adult sample.

3.2. Algorithmic procedures

Figure 2 shows the Prisma diagram of trial identification and selection. An initial algorithm (*Algorithm A = intolerance of uncertainty + anxiety disorders*) was encoded through databases. Three hundred and thirty-two results listed by date (2005–2015) were obtained.

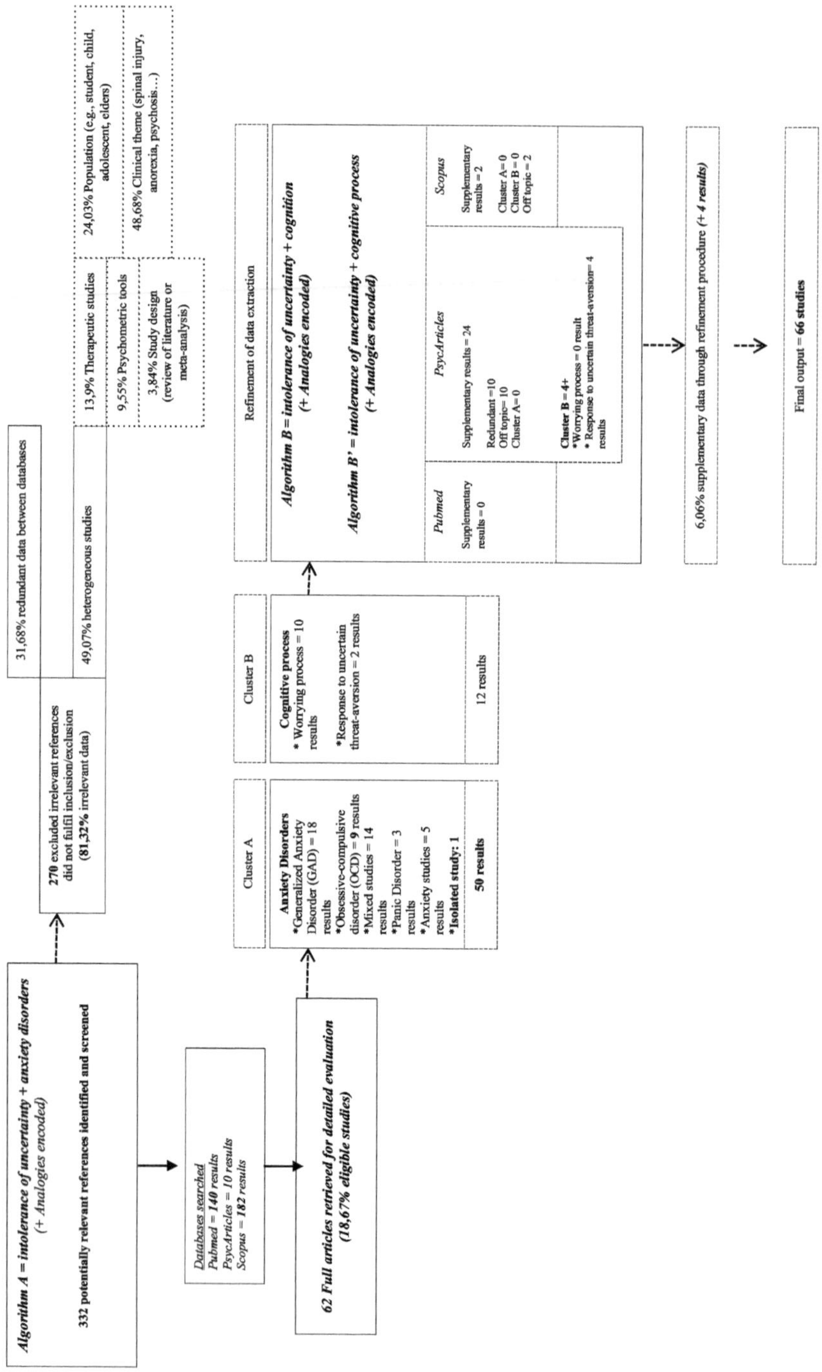

Figure 2. Algorithmic diagram of study identification and selection.

The following process was to pigeonhole the relevant studies within the research cluster. These were identified as following: anxiety disorders perspective (cluster A) and cognitive processes perspective (cluster B).

Fifty studies involved anxiety disorders studies (*cluster A*) of which eighteen investigated the GAD (36%), nine concerned the OCD (18%), fourteen gathered mixed clinical studies (28%), five were about anxiety studies (10%), three related to the panic disorder (PD) (6%) and one was a qualitative study (2%).

Studies not deemed eligible had no decisive criteria (heterogeneous studies (49.07%). Through these heterogeneous studies, 48.68% included clinical off topic themes (e.g. psychosis, spinal injury, breast cancer, Meniere's syndrome), 31.68% were already found through databases (redundant data), 24.03% incorporated non-eligible population (e.g. child, adolescent), 13.9% of the studies were therapeutic researches, 9.55% included psychometric tools validation and 3.84% concerned the study design (i.e. review of the literature or meta-analysis).

3.3. Refinement data extraction

Further algorithms were encoded through databases in order to highlight the cognitive processes (and its components) implied in the IU. A second algorithm was encoded: *Algorithm B = intolerance of uncertainty + cognition* and a third algorithm was encoded: Algorithm B′ = *intolerance of uncertainty + cognitive process.* This second step of refinement data extraction enabled the addition of twenty-six new results of which were redundant data ($K = 10$), were off topic ($K = 12$) and four were integrated into the cluster B (cognitive processes).

It is noteworthy that analogies were also considered such as uncertainty (*concern, scepticism, unpredictability, doubtfulness, hesitancy and wonder*), anxiety disorders (apprehension, *doubt, psychopathology, panic, depression, GAD, distress, restlessness*), cognition (*perception, awareness, insight, evaluation*) and cognitive process (attention, *biases, memory, controlled, mental*). Several spreadsheets were created in order to organize the relevant data. Two tables are included in the appendices section.

4. Results

4.1. Cluster A: IU and anxiety disorders perspective

4.1.1. Core clinical issues in GAD

Generalized Anxiety Disorder [DSM V code: 300.02; American Psychiatric Association, 2013] is characterized by excessive anxiety and worry, occurring more days than not for at least 6 months, about various activities or events. The focus of the anxiety and the worry is not confined to features of Axis I disorders (e.g. linked for instance of a panic attack) and it is difficult for the individual to control the worry. The anxiety, the worry or somatic disturbance cause clinically significant distress or, impairment in social or other areas of functioning. Lastly, the disturbance is not due to substance abuse (American Psychiatric Association, 2013).

Eighteen studies have investigated the GAD issue according to the IU since the early 2005s. Seventeen studies used cross-sectional design and one was a case study. The gathering procedure of results was led according to overriding models established on GAD: the Emotion Dysregulation Model (EDM; Mennin, Heimberg, Turk, & Fresco, 2005) (1), the Avoidance Model of Worry (AMW; Borkovec, Alcaine, & Behar, 2004) (2) and the Intolerance of Uncertainty Model (IUM; Dugas, Gagnon, Ladouceur, & Freeston, 1998) (3). These models can be classified into three fields: cognitive models (i.e. IUM), emotional/behavioural (i.e. EDM) and an integrated field (i.e. AMW).

The EDM demonstrated that individual with GAD experience emotional hyperarousal, poor understanding of emotions, negative cognitive reactions to emotions and maladaptive emotion management and regulation. Studies postulating an emotion dysregulation in GAD observed that the combination of the emotional hyperarousal with a poor understanding of emotions leads to the perception that emotions are threatening. These results stipulate that GAD patients become overwhelmed, anxious, or uncomfortable when emotions occur, thereby creating a toxic feedback loop (e.g. Andreescu et al., 2011; Palm, Elliott, McKie, Deakin, & Anderson, 2011). Other results have demonstrated the extreme hypervigilance for threatening information and increased selective attention either towards or away from emotions, relevant negative beliefs (Nitschke et al., 2009) and impulsivity (Whalen et al., 2008).

Other studies using the EDM suggested that emotion dysregulation is the core predictor to GAD diagnosis. Indeed, individual with GAD have emotional reactions that occur more easily and intensely than non-anxious people and they have significant difficulties in their ability to identify and clarify their emotional experience (Andreescu et al., 2011). Further, GAD patients also display negative cognitive control, as demonstrated a greater endorsement of catastrophic beliefs concerning the issue of emotions (comprising positive emotions) (Greenberg, Carlson, Cha, Hajcak, & Mujica-Parodi, 2013). The ability to soothe one's self when experiencing negative emotions was observed to be distorted in GAD compared to non-anxious (Palm et al., 2011).

Lastly, some neural underpinnings in emotion dysregulation in GAD patients have been advanced. The most impressive findings have focused on the role of brain deficits into the anterior cingulate and dorsal medial prefrontal cortex (Paulesu et al., 2010). Other studies (e.g. Whalen et al., 2008) have observed activation during uncertainty and ambiguous situation of the dorsal anterior cingulate cortex (dACC), the rostral anterior cingulate cortex (rACC) and the amygdala. Results suggest the dACC detects conflict, while the rACC evaluates emotional information and is potentially involved in emotion regulation. Moreover, some studies have observed hyperactivity in the dACC, the amygdala and the insula cortex and hypo activation of the rACC (e.g. Hölzel et al., 2013).

The AMW postulated the central function of worry in the development and the maintenance of GAD. The forerunners of the AMW defined the worry as "chain of thoughts and images, negatively affect-laden and relatively uncontrollable" (Borkovec, Robinson, Pruzinsky, & DePree, 1983, p. 10). The AMW advocates that worry emphasizes the commitment in the field of catastrophizing (i.e. a succession of "what if" questions to each thought generated), which in turn results in an increased discomfort, an emotional distress and hyperarousal.

Other studies evidenced that worry is seen as a positive coping factor in GAD. Worry is reinforced by positive beliefs about worrying (i.e. worry is helpful for problem-solving, motivating but also avoiding future negative topics) (Dugas et al., 2007; Robichaud, 2013). Conversely, some studies evidenced that the function of worry is a cognitive avoidance response to perceiving future threats (Crittendon & Hopko, 2006; Lee, Orsillo, Roemer, & Allen, 2010). Moreover, two types of avoidant functions posited for worry are proposed: (1) worry is a cognitive attempt to generate cognitive patterns to anticipate threatening topics and (2) worry is a verbal-linguistic thought that inhibit mental imagery and associated with somatic and emotion arousal (Khawaja, McMahon, & Strodl, 2011; Ruggiero et al., 2012).

Finally, studies based on IUM argued the dynamic process between the IU and GAD. Four factors distinguish GAD patients from healthy individuals: (1) to be intolerant of uncertainty, (2) to have positive beliefs about worry, (3) to use cognitive avoidance and (4) to present negative problem orientation.

Results retrieved from algorithmic procedure demonstrated that GAD patients do not tolerate uncertain or ambiguous situations, interpret them as potential threats and worry would serve to either help them to cope or to prevent those events from occurring at all (i.e. positive beliefs about worry) (Boelen & Reijntjes, 2009; Koerner & Dugas, 2008). Results suggested that misinterpretation of events leads to (1) negative problem orientation, (2) cognitive avoidance (e.g. thought suppression or replacement), both of which allow exacerbating the worry and the anxiety (van der Heiden et al., 2010).

Lastly, IUM posits that IU is the core transdiagnostic factor across anxiety disorders such as anxiety, OCD or panic disorder (PD) (van der Heiden et al., 2010).

In a nutshell, results found through databases emphasize the importance of the avoidance process of emotional events in IU. The AMW observes that worry is seen as a strategy for avoiding emotional stimuli (e.g. vivid images) whereas the IUM asserts worry as a toxic strategy for avoiding uncertainty and the EDM identifies worry as an ineffective coping strategy to regulate internal emotions.

4.1.2. Core clinical issues in OCD

The Obsessive-Compulsive Disorder [DSM V code: 300.3; American Psychiatric Association, 2013] is characterized by the presence of obsessions (i.e. obsessive preoccupations) and compulsions (i.e. repetitive behaviours) or both. Obsessions and compulsions are very time-consuming (i.e. take more than 1 h per day) and cause clinically distress or impairment in social, occupational or other areas of functioning. The obsessive-compulsive symptom are not due to substance or chemical abuse (e.g. drug or a medication) and is not better explained by the symptoms of another mental disorder (e.g. excessive worries in GAD, body dysmorphic disorder, hoarding disorder, trichotillomania [hair-pulling disorder], excoriation disorder [skin-picking] or ritualized eating behaviour) (American Psychiatric Association, 2013).

Nine results have studied the OCD issue according to the IU since the early 2005s. Eight of these nine studies are quantitative studies and one was a qualitative study (Kobori, Salkovskis, Read, Lounes, & Wong, 2012). Quantitative results showed that patients with OCD, present more intrusive thoughts (Kaiser, Bouvard, & Milliery, 2010), produce high negative affects (Taylor, McKay, & Abramowitz, 2005) and perceive as difficult to control (Taylor et al., 2005; Williams & Grisham, 2013).

Studies also revealed the significant link between IU and perfectionism in this clinical population (Calleo, Hart, Björgvinsson, & Stanley, 2010). Consistent results of the link between worry and obsession were found. Beliefs in perfectionism were similarly increased in clinical OCD patients (e.g. Belloch et al., 2010; Calamari et al., 2006).

Certain cognitive impairment was found through databases outcomes. Impaired performance on the Object Alternation Task was observed. Indeed, OCD patients committed more perseveration errors following prior correct response from controls (Williams & Grisham, 2013). Studies evinced also an attentional bias towards threatening words but also a significant cognitive inhibition deficit (Calamari et al., 2006).

Lastly, qualitative study (Kobori et al., 2012) highlighted four main themes in terms of reassurance seeking: (1) interpersonal concern and worry, (2) revulsion to seek reassurance, (3) difficulties to understand the uncertainty and its normal state (difficult position to make sense) and (4) extreme effort of vigilance. All of these themes maintain in the long run the worry and the IU (vicious circle).

4.1.3. Others core clinical issues

This section of results highlights "heterogeneous studies" which either combined anxious disorders in accordance with the processes in the IU or isolated psychopathological disorders. Twenty three studies among which 14 were mixed studies (combined psychological pathologies), 5 were studies led among clinical anxious population and 3 investigated the PD and one was a qualitative study.

As regards combined psychopathological studies, IU has been observed to be higher in the clinical sample than in controls (Agheli, Hasanzadeh, & Ghasemian, 2013; Jacoby, Abramowitz, Buck, & Fabricant, 2014; Nelson, Shankman, & Proudfit, 2014).

McEvoy and Mahoney (2012) found that IU explained unique variance in all symptoms after controlling for neuroticism and major depressive disorder. Results showed that neuroticism was highly correlated with IU ($r = .55$) and interestingly extraversion was negatively correlated with IU ($r = .18$).

As regards social anxiety disorders (Carleton, Fetzner, Hackl, & McEvoy, 2013; Carleton et al., 2014), analysis of variance revealed one statistically significant difference in IU Scale-12 scores across diagnostic groups in the clinical sample ($p < .01$; η (2) = .03) than people with PD (Carleton et al., 2012).

Study led on eating disorders highlighted that the IU score appears to be higher than controls with more distress (García-Soriano, Roncero, Perpiñá, & Belloch, 2014). The qualitative study (Sternheim, Konstantellou, Startup, & Schmidt, 2011) demonstrated that patients with anorexia nervosa perceive uncertainty as a stressor and use more avoidance strategies.

Concerning, clinical anxious group present more intrusive thoughts (Gutierrez, Hershey, & Douglas, 2013; Mahoney & McEvoy, 2011), worry, cognitive avoidance (Dupuy & Ladouceur, 2008) and distress (Jacoby et al., 2014) compared to controls.

Lastly, neurological studies evinced that IU was associated with reduced frontal EEG asymmetry (Nelson et al., 2014) but also evidence of emotion-related disorder-specificity emerged in medial prefrontal cortex and amygdala (Blair et al., 2012).

Evidence that IU does not share the unique link with GAD pattern raises the question of its status. Studies propose that IU is a broad transdiagnostic maintaining risk factor but also IU is always found in disorders characterized by negative affects. Past studies have found already this link (e.g. Dugas, Gosselin, & Ladouceur, 2001).

Outcomes retrieved from databases revealed the potential role of IU as a correlate of emotional disorders and allow also to understand in which way it may play a role on cognitive mechanisms or processes by which it is related to these disorders (Table 1). This question would be investigated in the next section (Cluster B).

4.2. Cluster B: IU and cognitive perspective

4.2.1. IU and worry

Research on worry has burgeoned since the early 1990s. The worry is observed at first as an adaptive factor but can become pathological if it is excessive at the individual's. The present section investigates the link between excessive worries and IU. Worry is considered as an effort to problem-solve in an uncertain situation, where ultimate issues may be aversive. In line with this definition, Mathews (1990) conceptualized worry as "thwarted" attempts to problem-solve, during danger, which is constantly rehearsed, but no issues found. This evidence suggested that pathological worriers (individuals with excessive and uncontrollable worries) have a lower threshold for uncertainty and ambiguous situations.

Ten studies have examined the relationship between worry and IU independently of anxiety disorders. Worry is observed to be a process allowing the avoidance of vivid images and intense negative emotions in the short-run (Zlomke & Jeter, 2014). Consequently, the worry is likely to prevent access to fear structures in memory and allows inhibition of negative emotional stimuli (Buhr & Dugas, 2009; Dash & Davey, 2012). Indeed, IU triggers worry as a result of experiencing uncertainty (IU is a filter through which individuals scan their environment). IU seems to share the unique

Table 1. Summary of included studies on clinical comorbidities related to IU, in chronological order

ID study	Design of study	Syndrome	Sample (*N*)	Main results
Generalized anxiety disorders (GAD)				
Emotion dysregulation hypothesis (EDM)				
Greenberg et al. (2013)	CR	GAD	32 GAD 25 HC	There is a link between deficits in fear regulation and the prevalence of GAD
Hölzel et al. (2013)	CR	GAD	26 GAD	Higher amygdala activation is observed in GAD with emotion dysregulation
Andreescu et al. (2011)	CR	GAD	7 GAD (elderly patients)	GAD patients tend to use not effective thoughts strategies namely though suppression that is involved in the maintenance of worries
Palm et al. (2011)	CR	GAD	15 GAD	There is a link between the hypo-responsivity to external emotional stimuli and GAD
			16 HC	These decreases impact internally and externally directed attentional processes (encoding and retrieving)
Paulesu et al. (2010)	CR	GAD	8 GAD 12 HC	Deficits in anterior cingulate and dorsal medial prefrontal cortex were found in GAD patients with severe emotion dysregulation
Nitschke et al. (2009)	CR	GAD	14 GAD 12 HC	GAD patients showed more anticipatory activity (emotion dysregulation) than controls in the bilateral dorsal amygdala preceding aversive and neutral pictures
Whalen et al. (2008)	CR	GAD	15 GAD	GAD patients showed more reactivity in the Rostral Anterior Cingulate Cortex (rACC) and hypo activity in the amygdala. Emotion dysregulation is observed in GAD patients
The avoidance of Worry Hypothesis (AMW)				
Robichaud (2013)	Case study	GAD	1 (clinical case)	IU and its components (positive beliefs about the usefulness of worry, negative problem orientation and cognitive avoidance) are intractably linked to GAD
Ruggiero et al. (2012)	CR	GAD	118 GAD 54 controls	Deficits in metacognition and control beliefs in the cognitive process reinforced the development of worry
Lee et al. (2010)	CR	GAD	50 GAD 41 HC	GAD patients experiment more experiential avoidance, distress and angry compared with control group
Dugas et al. (2007)	CR	GAD	84 GAD	GAD severity depends on the magnitude of positive beliefs about worry but also the development of maladjusted cognitive avoidance strategies. Intolerance of uncertainty and the negative problem orientation have a significant link with GAD prevalence
Pawluk and Koerner (2013)	CR	GAD	63 GAD 77 HC	Negative affects and lower functional impulsivity were predictors of GAD severity
Khawaja et al. (2011)	CR	GAD	107 GAD 91 HC	The levels of IU are implied in the severity of GAD. Moreover, meta-worry (positive beliefs about the usefulness of worry) distinguishes these three groups (more meta-worry in the high GAD group compared to middle or low GAD group)
Crittendon and Hopko (2006) (Study 1)	CR	GAD	115 sample of older 183 young adults	GAD patients tend to have more worries but also suffer from more distress and anxiety than controls
The intolerance of uncertainty hypothesis (IUM)				
van der Heiden et al. (2010)	CR	GAD	137 GAD	Neuroticism and symptoms of GAD were mediated by the factors of IU and negative metacognitions
Boelen and Reijntjes (2009)	CR	GAD	126 GAD	IU is linked to symptom levels of GAD, OCD and social anxiety, but not depression, when controlling the shared variance among these symptoms

(Continued)

Table 1. *(Continued)*

ID study	Design of study	Syndrome	Sample (*N*)	Main results
Koerner and Dugas (2008)	CR	GAD	199 GAD (110 low in IU and 89 high in IU)	Individuals who are intolerant of uncertainty (high scores) appraised all situations (neutral or ambiguous) as more threatening. Results showed that ambiguous situations partly mediate the relationship of IU to worry
González, Ibáñez and Cubas (2008)	CR	GAD	503 GAD	GAD patients tend to be more intolerant of uncertainty but also use more belief suppression strategies
Obsessive-compulsive disorders				
Jacoby, Fabricant, Leonard, Riemann and Abramowitz (2013)	CR	OCD	205 OCD	Inhibitory intolerance of uncertainty (unacceptable thoughts of worry) is linked with obsessive-compulsive symptoms. Patients with compulsions and obsessions tend to use more mental neutralizing strategies (e.g. suppression and avoidance)
Williams and Grisham (2013)	CR	OCD	89 OCD	OCD patients tend to present anxiety and more non-adaptive physiological responses
Kobori et al. (2012)	QL	OCD	10 OCD	Four main themes in terms of reassurance seeking: (1) interpersonal concern and worry, (2) revulsion to seek reassurance, (3) difficulties to understand the uncertainty and its normal state (difficult position to make sense) and (4) extreme effort of vigilance
Belloch et al. (2010)	CR	OCD	Study 1: 573 non-clinical subjects Study 2: 75 OCD (+comorbid sample)	Study 1/Study 2: OCD patients use dysfunctional beliefs (e.g. negative thoughts overestimated, cognitive control, overestimation of threat, intolerance of uncertainty, perfectionism)
Calleo et al. (2010)		OCD	70 OCD	Perfectionism and intolerance of uncertainty are linked with worry. Beliefs and cognitive control of thoughts and thought-action fusion are linked with obsession severity
Kaiser et al. (2010)	CR	OCD	96 OCD 53 non-clinical subjects	Washers, ruminators and checkers tend to present more impaired thought control strategies than controls
Radomsky, Ashbaugh and Gelfand (2007)	CR	OCD	33 OCD 143 HC	Checkers have greater trait anger than controls. Moreover, beliefs about perfectionism and intolerance of uncertainty are positively correlated with trait anger
Calamari et al. (2006)	CR	OCD	367 OCD	Both OCD groups (low and high obsessive beliefs) present an overestimating of threat, perfectionism thoughts and are intolerant of uncertainty
Taylor et al. (2005)	CR	OCD	202 OCD	Hierarchical results showed 3 core factors/processes in OCD: (i) responsibility and overestimation of threat, (ii) perfectionism and intolerance of uncertainty and (iii) importance and control of thoughts
Mixed studies (Combined psychopathological disorders as regards IU)				
Laposa, Collimore, Hawley and Rector (2015)	CR	OCD + ANX	Not reported	OCD and anxious patients tend to present more distress of tolerance. Moreover distress of tolerance predicted not the severity of OCD
García-Soriano et al. (2014)	CR	OCD + ED	79 OCD	In the OCD group, intolerance of uncertainty and thought importance predicted emotional distress
			177 ED	Both OCD and ED present cognitive intrusions
Nelson et al. (2014)	CR	MDD + PD	156 MDD (+PD) + HC	Experimental group (MDD+PD) present high scores for intolerance of uncertainty compared to control group. IU is seen as a mediator between MDD and reduced reward anticipation
Agheli et al. (2013)	CR	GAD + OCD	50 GAD 50 OCD Controls	GAD and OCD patients reported greater intolerance of uncertainty than controls

(Continued)

Table 1. *(Continued)*

ID study	Design of study	Syndrome	Sample (*N*)	Main results
Manber Ball, Ramsawh, CampbellSills, Paulus and Stein (2013)	CR	GAD + PD + HC	28 GAD patients 18 PD patients 23 HC	GAD and PD patients showed less dorsolateral and dorsomedial prefrontal cortex activation than controls. It is mentioned that these areas are implied in emotion regulation and are impaired in GAD and PD
Boswell, Thompson-Hollands, Farchione and Barlow (2013)	L	MDD + ANX	Not reported	Intolerance of uncertainty is positively correlated with depressive symptoms and the severity of worry
Anderson et al. (2012)	CR	GAD + ANX	GAD group and anxious group	Results observed no differences between GAD and anxious patients in their interpretations of negative or positive appraisals
Blair et al. (2012)	CR	GAD + SAD	34 GAD 37 SAD 36 HC	Experimental group (GAD + SAD) reported hypo activity in the medial prefrontal cortex and amygdala compared to controls. Moreover, these areas are implied in emotion-regulation. Evidence of emotion-regulation impairments is advanced in GAD or SAD
Carleton et al. (2012)	CR	ANX + GAD + OCD + MDD	376 clinical sample 428 HC 571 community sample	Intolerance of uncertainty is seen as a transdiagnostic factor across anxiety disorders provoking distress and leading to the preservation of symptoms
Mahoney and McEvoy (2012)	CR	ANX + MDD	218 comorbid sample	Intolerance of uncertainty is a maintaining factor for anxious and depressed patients. The degree of comorbidity plays a pivotal role in the prediction of prospective IU
McEvoy and Mahoney (2012)	CR	ANX + MDD	328 comorbid sample	Intolerance of uncertainty is linked with neuroticism, SAD, PD, OCD, GAD and MDD Results reported that intolerance of uncertainty was a significant partial mediator between neuroticism and all symptom measures
Yook, Kim, Suh and Lee (2010)	CR	GAD + MDD	28 GAD 27 MDD 16 GAD/MDD	Worry, rumination, intolerance of uncertainty, anxiety and depressive symptoms correlated significantly with each other. Worry partially mediated the relationship between intolerance of uncertainty and anxiety whereas rumination completely mediated the relationship between intolerance of uncertainty and depressive symptoms
Blair et al. (2008)	CR	GAD	17 GAD + 17 SAD 17HC	SAD patients reported hyperactivation to fearful and neutral expressions in several neurological areas (namely the amygdala) whereas GAD patients present hypo-activation in these areas
Dupuy and Ladouceur (2008)	CR	GAD + MDD	32 GAD /MDD	Comorbid group (GAD + MDD) reported high symptoms of intolerance of uncertainty, presented poorer problem orientation and more cognitive avoidance compared to clinical group (either GAD or either MDD)
Anxiety disorders				
Jacoby et al. (2014)	CR	ANX	69 ANX 26 HC	During the Beads Task, anxious participants reported greater distress than controls Intolerance of uncertainty is positively correlated with draws to decision and distress during the task
Bertrams, Englert, Dickhäuser and Baumeister (2013)	CR	ANX	Study 1: 67 ANX Study 2: 96 ANX Study 3: 99 ANX	In study 1 and study 2: the state of anxiety is negatively correlated with performance of verbal learning. In study 3: worry is linked with cognitive distraction strategies
Gutierrez et al. (2013)	CR	ANX	87 ANX (related to retirement anxiety)	Participants with retirement anxiety experienced impairments in information processing that ensue from the negative emotional content linked to retirement concepts in long-term memory

Table 1. *(Continued)*

ID study	Design of study	Syndrome	Sample (*N*)	Main results
McEvoy and Mahoney (2013)	CR	ANX	99 ANX	Intolerance of uncertainty partially mediated the relationship between neuroticism and worry
Gerolimatos and Edelstein (2012)	CR	ANX	86 older anxious adults 117 young anxious adults	Anxiety and intolerance of uncertainty partially mediated the relation between age and health anxiety. Moreover, perceived anxiety control, reappraisal, and suppression did not mediate the relation between age and health anxiety
Panic disorders				
Carleton et al. (2014)	CR	PD	132 PD	Results indicated direct and indirect effects of IU on panic symptoms. None interaction between IU and PD is observed
Gorka, Lieberman, Nelson, Sarapas and Shankman (2014)	CR	PD	172 adults (74 of which had current diagnoses of PD)	PD is linked with significant startle potentiation during safety when IU is high whereas, at low levels of IU, PD is not linked with startle potentiation during safety. PD patients with high levels of IU fail to inhibit aversive response during safety task due to an impairment to interpret distal threat as disturbing
Carleton et al. (2013)	CR	PD	122 PD	Correlation and regression showed a significant relationship between inhibitory IU and PD
Isolated qualitative study				
Sternheim et al. (2011)	QL	ED	9	Patients with anorexia nervosa perceive uncertainty as a stressor and use more avoidance strategies

Notes: ANX: anxiety disorder; CR: cross-sectional design (quantitative study), ED: eating disorders; GAD: generalized anxiety disorder; HC: healthy control; IU: intolerance of uncertainty; MDD: major depressive disorder; OCD: obsessive compulsive disorder; PD: panic disorder; QL: qualitative study; SAD: social anxiety disorder.

relationship with worry gathering cognitive avoidance, metaworry and negative problem orientation (Fergus & Wu, 2013; Kertz, Stevens, McHugh, & Björgvinsson, 2015).

In addition, some studies have observed that worriers who are intolerant of uncertainty tend to perceive ambiguous situations as a threat and interpret the situation more negatively (i.e. catastrophizing scenario) than control group (e.g. Davey, Eldridge, Drost, & MacDonald, 2007). As already mentioned, the worry is significantly linked to IU. In the face of uncertainty, individuals who are high in IU seem to be more prone to worry. Studies concluded to the central role of IU in the development and the maintenance of worry itself. IU leads to "What if" thinking that in turns lead to more excessive and uncontrollable worry (i.e. IU is seen as the most salient predictor of worry) (Ottaviani et al., 2014; Zlomke & Jeter, 2014).

In a nutshell, individuals who are high in IU present more positive beliefs about worry (e.g. Davey et al., 2007), tend to a negative problem orientation (Zlomke & Jeter, 2014) and use more cognitive avoidance (e.g. Kertz et al., 2015).

4.2.2. IU and response to uncertain threat aversion

Individual is bombarded with uncertainty and potential threats throughout their everyday life (e.g. personal uncertainty, perceptual surprises or cognitive goal conflicts). These aversive situations amplify negative impacts of event and motivate individuals to resolve them.

The resolution of uncertainty occurs through the identification by the individual of the relationship between environmental cues and subsequent outcomes of the situation (Britton & Davey, 2014).

Cognitive paradigms have shown the link between certain types of cognition and emotions. For instance, negative beliefs about personal skills (e.g. "I am a loser") lead to depression. As also mentioned in section A (IU and Anxiety disorders) a large body of literature indicates that anxiety disorders are associated with negative beliefs or perceptions, automatic thoughts concerning threatening stimuli and the inability to resolve them (e.g. Cisler & Koster, 2010).

Since the early 2005s until today, we retrieved six studies investigating IU related to the threat construct. All of these studies advanced an overestimation of threat stimulus when intolerant of uncertainty individual is confronted with an ambiguous situation (e.g. Grupe & Nitschke, 2011; Nelson & Shankman, 2011). Indeed, individual with high IU associated the ambiguity with a higher occurring probability of negative events (Dugas et al., 2005).

Moreover, cognitive studies have already mentioned the intrinsic link between selective attention and threat cues (e.g. Amir et al., 2003). Studies demonstrated that this sensitivity to threat impaired its management (Britton & Davey, 2014), the efficiency of decision-making (Luhmann, Ishida, & Hajcak, 2011), the cognitive control of threat (Nelson & Shankman, 2011) and created information processing biases (Dugas et al., 2005) (Table 2).

5. Discussion

The current review aimed to probe the relations between IU and the anxiety disorders and its cognitive components. The first step concerns the estimation of IU with GAD and OCD and its clinical aspects. The algorithmic procedure has allowed the retrieving of fifty empirical studies of 66 studies (covering approximately 75% of the results for the review). IU is observed to share a unique relationship with anxiety disorders (namely GAD, OCD, MDD) and is seen as a predictor (transdiagnostic risk factor).

Researchers emphasized significant perception of threat and more reactions of hypervigilance when anxiety is combined with IU. Certain neural dysfunctions are advanced namely the insula cortex, dACC and the amygdala when IU individuals are confronted with ambiguous stimuli.

Paradigms in anxiety disorders have already demonstrated impairments in hot and cold cognition. As regards cold cognition studies evidenced impairments in attentional and memory processes. Anxious individuals seem to have a facilitated attentional deployment, a difficulty to disengage allocated resources on specific stimuli (especially threatening stimuli) and they used more easily an attentional avoidance. The memory process has revealed a cognitive dysfunction in the episodic and the autobiographical memory (impairments in retrieval process). Concerning the hot cognition studies demonstrated several dysregulation of thought and maladaptive knowledge in anxiety disorders given rise to a defective pattern of thinking and leading to diverse psychological vulnerabilities (e.g. poor orientation problem, avoidance, metaworry).

Studies investigating GAD and IU demonstrated the central role of IU in the development and the maintenance of symptoms (high rate of comorbidity). Other features have been advanced such as positive beliefs about worry moderating negatively the outcome, a poor problem orientation (i.e. impairments in problem perception, problem attribution, problem appraisal and personal control of these beliefs), and cognitive avoidance of threatening mental images (i.e. semantic cognitive activity has the effect of decreasing somatic activity resulting from vivid or fearful imagery).

Researchers studied OCD and IU evidenced intrusive thoughts producing emotional dysregulation and impairments in cognitive control. It has been advanced that rituals and compulsions serve to decrease the distress resulting from uncertainty about a potential threat stimulus. These results have been also observed in other clinical populations (e.g. depression). All of these studies have highlighted the central mechanism of negative repetitive thoughts (i.e. worry) through GAD, OCD and MDD. It has been advanced that worry mediates the relationship of IU to symptoms of these psychopathological disorders when the IU is seen as the predictor.

Table 2. Summary of included studies on cognitive processes related to IU, in chronological order

Cognitive hypothese

ID study	Design of study	Syndrome	N	Outcome(s)
**A/Worrying process*				
Byrne, Hunt and Chang (2015)	CR	IU	*N* = 104	Ambiguity and unpredictability are core components in IU that stem from different types of responses
Kertz et al. (2015)	CR	IU	*N* 1(XP) = 281	Worry is linked with high levels of IU, cognitive avoidance, negative beliefs of worry (metaworry) and negative problem orientation
			N 2(HC) = 123	In the experimental group (XP), negative problem orientation and negative beliefs about worry partially mediated the association between distress and worry
Ottaviani et al. (2014)	CR	IU	*N*1 = 31	Worriers showed hyper-activation into sympathetic and hypo-activation into parasympathetic during the worry condition compared to non-worriers. Worry is seen as a default/automatic and pathological response
			*N*2 = 36	
Zlomke and Jeter (2014)	CR	IU	*N* = 1,092	IU partially moderated the relationship between daily stress and worry. Results showed also the contribution of IU in the development of anxiety disorders
Fergus and Wu (2013)	CR	IU	*N*1 (IU white population) = 1,185	Both groups, correlations between IU and worry are observed
			*N*2 (IU black population) = 301	
Norr et al. (2013)	CR	IU	*N*1 = 217	IU is seen as a transdiagnostic factor associated with anxiety symptoms and obsessive-compulsive symptoms
			*N*2 = 241	
Reuther et al. (2013)	CR	IU	*N* = 475	IU substantially mediates the relationship between perfectionism and the severity of distress
Dash and Davey (2012)	CR	IU	Not reported	High worry levels is linked with negative mood. Induced negative mood allowed the endorsement of cognitive appraisals known to increase systematic as opposed to heuristic information processing
Buhr and Dugas (2009)	CR	IU	/	Fear of anxiety symptoms are correlated with significant levels of worry
				The combination of IU with fear anxiety lead to the highest level of worry (additive effect observed)
Davey et al. (2007)	CR	IU	Study 1	Study 1/Study 2: pathological worriers tended to be sensitive in negative mood and unresponsive in positive mood over the course of catastrophizing
			Study 2	
			Sample not reported	
**B/A response to uncertain threat aversion*				
Britton and Davey (2014)	CR	IU	Study 1 = 59	Study 1, 2 & 3: Indirect effects of IU on inflated responsibility through negative mood are highlighted. Indirect effects of negative mood on IU through inflated responsibility are also revealed. Moreover, anxiety is seen as a motivational system implied to manage threat
			Study 2 = 63	
			Study 3 = 61	
Grupe and Nitschke (2011)	CR	IU	Not reported	IU is related with biased expectancies of aversion and heightened responses to aversion (anticipatory dysfunction)
Luhmann et al. (2011)	CR	IU	Not reported	IU is correlated with the tendency to select the immediately available, but less valuable and less probable rewards. Moreover, IU predicted decision-makers' sensitivity to outcomes
Mahoney and McEvoy (2011)	CR	IU	*N* = 218	IU is seen as a transdiagnostic factor, is associated with neuroticism and GAD symptoms but also leading to impairments in emotion regulation
Nelson and Shankman (2011)	CR	IU	*N* = 69	IU is negatively correlated with startle during the uncertain threat condition in that those with higher IU had a smaller startle response. Perceived control over anxiety-related events partially mediated the relation between IU and startle to uncertain threat. IU is correlated with mitigated aversive responding to uncertain threat
Dugas et al. (2005)	CR	IU	Not reported	High levels of IU are significant correlated with ambiguous situation. Results observed more cognitive biases (impairments in information process) in participants with high levels of IU when they are confronted with ambiguous situations

Notes: CR: cross-sectional design (quantitative study); IU: intolerance of uncertainty.

The second step in the study was to examine the cognitive state of IU. Sixteen results were retrieved (covering approximately 25% of the results for the review). The majority of studies investigated the link between IU and worry (10 of 16 studies). Studies demonstrated the intrinsic link where worry is seen as a mediator between the predictor (IU) and the issues (symptoms of anxiety, depression or OCD). Therefore, IU, worry and anxiety disorders are inseparable components. Researchers have demonstrated that excessive worries are related to positive beliefs about the function of worry (e.g. worrying help to avoid negative events and protect me against future threat), with poor or negative problem orientation, with cognitive avoidance of vivid mental imagery and IU. It seems that excessive and uncontrollable worry reinforced the vicious circle. Findings observed also that pathological worriers have a lower threshold for uncertainty and ambiguous situations but also tend to perceive more sources of threat in the environment compared to control. Lastly, certain results suggested that personality traits (mainly perfectionism) provoke more excessive worries and IU by the individual.

A last remark concerns more particularly the methodology of all eligible studies. In general, it exists a lack of consensus of the definition of IU. Through the data extraction and refinement procedures, others synonyms for IU are proposed (e.g. intolerance of ambiguity, need for predictability), which make scientific position difficult and do not allow generalization. Moreover, the high level of comorbidity between IU and anxiety disorders may have complicated the status of IU. It would be appropriate to systematically target the statistical status of IU (e.g. predictor, mediator ...). Eligible studies were predominately quantitative. It would be useful to examine the IU through more qualitative design, allowing the understanding of certain interpersonal themes in anxiety disorders.

Nevertheless, the present clinical review of IU reveals potential areas of improvement in future research. It would be interesting to extend the range of the year of published studies, to increase the number of databases and to examine other variables such as health behaviours (obesity, drug addiction, alcoholism ...); some personality's factors (neuroticism, attachment or alexithymia) or to include this issue in the field of medical chronic disease (where the phenomenon of uncertainty is already activated).

6. Clinical implication

Few studies have investigated the cognitive process in IU across anxiety disorders. Some runways were cleared but it would be extremely interesting to measure (e.g. time reaction) the degree of the cognitive bias (attention and memory) by a computational task where intolerant of uncertainty individuals should activate some cognitive patterns (e.g. emotional Stroop, dot probe task ...). Effective interventions will need to balance theoretically grounded models, careful clinical observations and empirical evidences. There are many opportunities for developing interventions across the spectrum of IU. It would be advantageous to include more "computational studies" in order to accurately understand the toxic pattern of thoughts (cognition) and psychopathological behaviours in IU across anxiety disorders.

Abbreviations

IU	Intolerance of uncertainty.
GAD	Generalized anxiety disorder.
MDD	Major depressive disorder.
OCD	Obsessive-compulsive disorder.
PD	Panic Disorder.

Funding
The authors received no direct funding for this research.

Competing Interests
The authors declare no competing interests.

Author details
Marie Vander Haegen[1]
E-mail: mvanderhaegen@doct.ulg.ac.be
Anne-Marie Etienne[1]
E-mail: am.etienne@ulg.ac.be
[1] Unit of Health Psychology, Université de Liège, Quartier Village 2, Rue de l'Aunaie 30, Liège 4000, Belgium.

References

Agheli, F., Hasanzadeh, R., & Ghasemian, D. (2013). Compare of intolerance of uncertainty among obsessive-compulsive disorder, generalized anxiety disorder and healthy subjects. *Journal of Novel Applied Sciences, 2*, 896–899.

American Psychiatric Association. (2013). *Diagnostic and statistical manual of mental disorders* (5th ed.). Arlington, VA: American Psychiatric Publishing.

Amir, N., Elias, J., Klumpp, H., & Przeworski, A. (2003). Attentional bias to threat in social phobia: Facilitated processing of threat or difficulty disengaging attention from threat? *Behaviour Research and Therapy, 41*, 1325–1335. http://dx.doi.org/10.1016/S0005-7967(03)00039-1

Anderson, K. G., Dugas, M. J., Koerner, N., Radomsky, A. S., Savard, P., & Turcotte, J. (2012). Interpretive style and intolerance of uncertainty in individuals with anxiety disorders: A focus on generalized anxiety disorder. *Journal of Anxiety Disorders, 26*, 823–832. doi:10.1016/j.janxdis.2012.08.003

Andreescu, C., Gross, J. J., Lenze, E., Edelman, K. D., Snyder, S., Tanase, C., & Aizenstein, H. (2011). Altered cerebral blood flow patterns associated with pathologic worry in the elderly. *Depression and Anxiety, 28*, 202–209. http://dx.doi.org/10.1002/da.v28.3

Belloch, A., Morillo, C., Luciano, J. V., García-Soriano, G., Cabedo, E., & Carrió, C. (2010). Dysfunctional belief domains related to obsessive-compulsive disorder: A further examination of their dimensionality and specificity. *The Spanish Journal of Psychology, 13*, 369–381.

Bertrams, A., Englert, C., Dickhäuser, O., & Baumeister, R. F. (2013). Role of self-control strength in the relation between anxiety and cognitive performance. *Emotion, 13*, 668–680. http://dx.doi.org/10.1037/a0031921

Blair, K. S., Geraci, M., Smith, B., Hollon, N., DeVido, J., Otero, M., ... Pine, D. S. (2012). Reduced dorsal anterior cingulate cortical activity during emotional regulation and top-down attentional control in Generalized Social Phobia (GSP), Generalized Anxiety Disorder (GAD) and comorbid GSP/GAD. *Biological Psychiatry, 72*, 476–482. doi:10.1016/j.biopsych.2012.04.013

Blair, K., Shaywitz, J., Smith, B. W., Rhodes, R., Geraci, M., Jones, M., ... Pine, D. S. (2008). Response to emotional expressions in generalized social phobia and generalized anxiety disorder: Evidence for separate disorders. *American Journal of Psychiatry, 165*, 1193–1202. http://dx.doi.org/10.1176/appi.ajp.2008.07071060

Boelen, P. A., & Reijntjes, A. (2009). Intolerance of uncertainty and social anxiety. *Journal of Anxiety Disorders, 23*, 130–135. http://dx.doi.org/10.1016/j.janxdis.2008.04.007

Borkovec, T. D., Alcaine, O., & Behar, E. S. (2004). Avoidance theory of worry and generalized anxiety disorder. In: R. Heimberg, D. Mennin, & C. Turk (Eds.), *Generalized anxiety disorder: Advances in research and practice* (pp. 77–108). New York, NY: Guilford Press.

Borkovec, T. D., Robinson, E., Pruzinsky, T., & DePree, J. A. (1983). Preliminary exploration of worry: Some characteristics and processes. *Behaviour Research and Therapy, 21*, 9–16. http://dx.doi.org/10.1016/0005-7967(83)90121-3

Boswell, J. F., Thompson-Hollands, J., Farchione, T. J., & Barlow, D. H. (2013). Intolerance of uncertainty: A common change factor in the treatment of emotional disorders. *Journal of Clinical Psychology, 69*, 630–645. http://dx.doi.org/10.1002/jclp.21965

Britton, G. I., & Davey, G. C. (2014). Interrelationships between negative mood and clinical constructs: a motivational systems approach. *Frontiers in Psychopathology, 5*, 1–11. doi:10.3389/fpsyg.2014.00393

Buhr, K., & Dugas, M. J. (2009). The role of fear of anxiety and intolerance of uncertainty in worry: An experimental manipulation. *Behaviour Research Therapy, 47*, 215–223. doi:10.1016/j.brat.2008.12.004

Byrne, S. P., Hunt, C. J., & Chang, B. P. L. (2015). Comparing the roles of ambiguity and unpredictability in intolerance of uncertainty. *Behaviour Change, 32*, 26–34. http://dx.doi.org/10.1017/bec.2014.27

Calamari, J. E., Cohen, R. J., Rector, N. A., Szacun-Shimizu, K., Riemann, B. C., & Norberg, M. M. (2006). Dysfunctional belief-based obsessive-compulsive disorder subgroups. *Behaviour Research and Therapy, 44*, 1347–1360. http://dx.doi.org/10.1016/j.brat.2005.10.005

Calleo, J. S., Hart, J., Björgvinsson, T., & Stanley, M. A. (2010). Obsessions and worry beliefs in an inpatient OCD population. *Journal of Anxiety Disorders, 24*, 903–908. http://dx.doi.org/10.1016/j.janxdis.2010.06.015

Carleton, R. N., Duranceau, S., Freeston, M. H., Boelen, P. A., McCabe, R. E., & Antony, M. M. (2014). "But it might be a heart attack": Intolerance of uncertainty and panic disorder symptoms. *Journal of Anxiety Disorders, 28*, 463–470. http://dx.doi.org/10.1016/j.janxdis.2014.04.006

Carleton, R. N., Fetzner, M. G., Hackl, J. L., & McEvoy, P. (2013). Intolerance of uncertainty as a contributor to fear and avoidance symptoms of panic attacks. *Cognitive Behaviour Therapy, 42*, 328–341. http://dx.doi.org/10.1080/16506073.2013.792100

Carleton, R. N., Mulvogue, M. K., Thibodeau, M. A., McCabe, R. E., Antony, M. M., & Asmundson, G. J. G. (2012). Increasingly certain about uncertainty: Intolerance of uncertainty across anxiety and depression. *Journal of Anxiety Disorders, 26*, 468–479. http://dx.doi.org/10.1016/j.janxdis.2012.01.011

Cisler, J. M., & Koster, E. H. (2010). Mechanisms of attentional biases towards threat in anxiety disorders: An integrative review. *Clinical Psychology Review, 30*, 203–216. doi:10.1016/j.cpr.2009.11.003

Crittendon, J., & Hopko, D. R. (2006). Assessing worry in older and younger adults: Psychometric properties of an abbreviated Penn State Worry Questionnaire (PSWQ-A). *Journal of Anxiety Disorders, 20*, 1036–1054. http://dx.doi.org/10.1016/j.janxdis.2005.11.006

Dash, S. R., & Davey, G. C. L. (2012). An experimental investigation of the role of negative mood in worry: The role of appraisals that facilitate systematic information processing. *Journal of Behavior Therapy and Experimental Psychiatry, 43*, 823–831. doi:10.1016/j.jbtep.2011.12.002

Davey, G. C. L., Eldridge, F., Drost, J., & MacDonald, B. A. (2007). What ends a worry bout? An analysis of changes in mood and stop rule use during a catastrophizing task. *Behaviour Research & Therapy, 45*, 1231–1243.

David, D., & Szentagotai, A. (2006). Cognitions in cognitive-behavioral psychotherapies; toward an integrative model. *Clinical Psychology Review, 26*, 284–298. doi:10.1016/j.cpr.2005.09.003

de Quervain, D. J., & Margraf, J. (2008). Glucocorticoids for the treatment of post-traumatic stress disorder and phobias: A novel therapeutic approach. *European Journal of Pharmacology, 583*, 365–371. doi:10.1016/j.ejphar.2007.11.068

Dugas, M. J., Burh, K., & Ladouceur, R. (2004). The role of intolerance of uncertainty in etiology and maintenance. In R. H. Heimberg, C. L. Turk, & D. S. Mennin (Eds.), *Generalized anxiety disorder: Advances in research and practice* (pp. 143–163). New York, NY: Guilford Press.

Dugas, M. J., Gagnon, F., Ladouceur, R., & Freeston, M. H. (1998). Generalized anxiety disorder: A preliminary test of a conceptual model. *Behaviour Research and Therapy, 36*, 215–226. http://dx.doi.org/10.1016/S0005-7967(97)00070-3

Dugas, M. J., Gosselin, P., & Ladouceur, R. (2001). Intolerance of uncertainty and worry: Investigating specificity in a nonclinical sample. *Cognitive Therapy and Research, 25*, 551–558. http://dx.doi.org/10.1023/A:1005553414688

Dugas, M. J., Hedayati, M., Karavidas, A., Buhr, K., Francis, K., & Phillips, N. A. (2005). Intolerance of uncertainty and information processing: Evidence of biased recall and interpretations. *Cognitive Therapy and Research, 29*, 57–70. http://dx.doi.org/10.1007/s10608-005-1648-9

Dugas, M. J., Savard, P., Gaudet, A., Turcotte, J., Laugesen, N., Robichaud, M., ... Koerner, N. (2007). Can the components of a cognitive model predict the severity of generalized anxiety disorder? Behavior Therapy, *38*, 169–178. http://dx.doi.org/10.1016/j.beth.2006.07.002

Dupuy, J. B., & Ladouceur, R. (2008). Cognitive processes of generalized anxiety disorder in comorbid generalized anxiety disorder and major depressive disorder. *Journal of Anxiety Disorders, 22*, 505–514. http://dx.doi.org/10.1016/j.janxdis.2007.05.010

Eysenck, M. W., Derakshan, N., Santos, R., & Calvo, M. G. (2007). Anxiety and cognitive performance: Attentional control theory. *Emotion, 7*, 336–353. doi:10.1037/1528-3542.7.2.336

Fergus, T. A., & Wu, K. D. (2013). The intolerance of uncertainty scale: Measurement invariance, population heterogeneity, and its relation with worry among self-identifying white and black respondents. *Assessment, 20*, 555–564. doi:10.1177/1073191112460272

Fox, E., Russo, R., Bowles, R., & Dutton, K. (2001). Do threatening stimuli draw or hold visual attention in subclinical anxiety? *Journal of Experimental Psychology: General, 130*, 681–700. http://dx.doi.org/10.1037/0096-3445.130.4.681

Freeston, M. H., Rhéaume, J., Letarte, H., Dugas, M. J., & Ladouceur, R. (1994). Why do people worry? *Personality and Individual Differences, 17*, 791–802. http://dx.doi.org/10.1016/0191-8869(94)90048-5

Friedenberg, J., & Silverman, G. (2006). *Cognitive science: An introduction to the study of mind*. Thousand Oaks, CA: Sage.

García-Soriano, G., Roncero, M., Perpiñá, C., & Belloch, A. (2014). Intrusive thoughts in obsessive-compulsive disorder and eating disorder patients: A differential analysis. *European Eating Disorders Review, 22*, 191–199. http://dx.doi.org/10.1002/erv.v22.3

Garner, M., Möhler, H., Stein, D. J., Mueggler, T., & Baldwin, D. S. (2009). Research in anxiety disorders: From the bench to the bedside. *European Neuropsychopharmacology, 19*, 381–390. http://dx.doi.org/10.1016/j.euroneuro.2009.01.011

Gerolimatos, L. A., & Edelstein, B. A. (2012). Anxiety-related constructs mediate the relation between age and health anxiety. *Aging Mental Health, 16*, 975–982. doi:10.1080/13607863.2012.688192

González, M., Ibáñez, I., Cubas, R., (2006). Variables de proceso en la determinación de la ansiedad generalizada y su generalización a otras medidas de ansiedad y depresión. International journal of clinical and health psychology, 6, 23–39.

Gorka, S. M., Lieberman, L., Nelson, B. D., Sarapas, C., & Shankman, S. A. (2014). Aversive responding to safety signals in panic disorder: The moderating role of intolerance of uncertainty. *Journal of Anxiety Disorders, 28*, 731–736. http://dx.doi.org/10.1016/j.janxdis.2014.06.004

Greenberg, T., Carlson, J. M., Cha, J., Hajcak, G., & Mujica-Parodi, L. R. (2013). Ventromedial prefrontal cortex reactivity is altered in generalized anxiety disorder during fear generalization. *Depression and Anxiety, 30*, 242–250. doi:10.1002/da.22016

Grupe, D. W., & Nitschke, J. B. (2011). Uncertainty is associated with biased expectancies and heightened responses to aversion. *Emotion, 11*, 413–424. doi:10.1037/a0022583

Gutierrez, H. C., Hershey, D. A., & Douglas, A. (2013). Impact of retirement worry on information processing. *Journal of Neuroscience, Psychology and Economics, 6*, 264–277. doi:10.1037/npe0000013

Hallion, L. S., & Ruscio, A. (2011). A meta-analysis of the effect of cognitive bias modification on anxiety and depression. *Psychological Bulletin, 137*, 940–958. doi:10.1037/a0024355

Hölzel, B. K., Hoge, E. A., Greve, D. N., Gard, T., Creswell, J. D., Brown, K. W., ... Lazar, S. W. (2013). Neural mechanisms of symptom improvements in generalized anxiety disorder following mindfulness training. *NeuroImage: Clinical, 2*, 448–458. doi:10.1016/j.nicl.2013.03.011

Jacoby, R. J., Abramowitz, J. S., Buck, B. E., & Fabricant, L. E. (2014). How is the beads task related to intolerance of uncertainty in anxiety disorders? *Journal of Anxiety Disorders, 28*, 495–503. http://dx.doi.org/10.1016/j.janxdis.2014.05.005

Jacoby, R. J., Fabricant, L. E., Leonard, R. C., Riemann, B. C., & Abramowitz, J. S. (2013). Just to be certain: Confirming the factor structure of the intolerance of uncertainty scale in patients with obsessive-compulsive disorder. *Journal of Anxiety Disorders, 27*, 535–542. http://dx.doi.org/10.1016/j.janxdis.2013.07.008

Kaiser, B., Bouvard, M., & Milliery, M. (2010). Washing, checking, and rumination: Are the belief domains, obsessions and compulsions specific to OCD subtypes? *Encephale, 36*, 54–61. http://dx.doi.org/10.1016/j.encep.2008.09.003

Kertz, S. J., Stevens, K. T., McHugh, R. K., & Björgvinsson, T. (2015). Distress intolerance and worry: the mediating role of cognitive variables. *Anxiety, Stress & Coping: An International Journal, 28*, 408–424. doi:10.1080/10615806.2014.974571

Khawaja, N. G., McMahon, J., & Strodl, E. (2011). Intolerance of uncertainty and meta-worry: Relative importance in discriminating GAD. *Behaviour Change, 28*, 181–194. doi:10.1375/bech.28.4.181

Kobori, A., Salkovskis, P. M., Read, J., Lounes, N., & Wong, V. (2012). A qualitative study of the investigation of reassurance seeking in obsessive—Compulsive disorder. *Journal of Obsessive Compulsive and Related Disorders, 1*, 25–32. doi:10.1016/j.jocrd.2011.09.001

Koerner, N., & Dugas, M. J. (2008). An investigation of appraisals in individuals vulnerable to excessive worry: The role of intolerance of uncertainty. *Cognitive Therapy and Research, 32*, 619–638. http://dx.doi.org/10.1007/s10608-007-9125-2

Laposa, J. M., Collimore, K. C., Hawley, L. L., & Rector, N. A. (2015). Distress tolerance in OCD and anxiety disorders, and its relationship with anxiety sensitivity and intolerance of uncertainty. *Journal of Anxiety Disorders, 33*, 8–14. doi:10.1016/j.janxdis.2015.04.003

Lee, J. K., Orsillo, S. M., Roemer, L., & Allen, L. B. (2010). Distress and avoidance in generalized anxiety disorder: Exploring the relationships with intolerance of uncertainty and worry. *Cognitive Behaviour Therapy, 39*, 126–136. doi:10.1080/16506070902966918

Luhmann, C. C., Ishida, K., & Hajcak, G. (2011). Intolerance of uncertainty and decisions about delayed, probabilistic rewards. *Behaviour Therapy, 42*, 378–386. doi:10.1016/j.beth.2010.09.002

MacLeod, C., & Mathews, A. (2012). Cognitive bias modification approaches to anxiety. *Annual Review of Clinical Psychology, 8*, 189–217. doi:10.1146/annurev-clinpsy-032511-143052

Mahoney, A. E. J., & McEvoy, P. M. (2011). Trait versus situation-specific intolerance of uncertainty in a clinical sample with anxiety and depressive disorders. *Cognitive Behaviour Therapy, 41*, 26–39. doi:10.1080/16506073.2011.622131

Mahoney, A. E. J., & McEvoy, P. M. (2012). A transdiagnostic examination of intolerance of uncertainty across anxiety and depressive disorders. *Cognitive Behaviour Therapy., 41*, 212–222. doi:10.1080/16506073.2011.622130

Manber Ball, T., Ramsawh, H. J., CampbellSills, L., Paulus, M. P., & Stein, M. B. (2013). Prefrontal dysfunction during emotion regulation in generalized anxiety and panic disorders. *Psychological Medicine, 1*, 1–12. doi:10.1017/S0033291712002383

Mathews, A. (1990). Why worry? A cognitive function of anxiety. *Behaviour Research and Therapy, 28*, 455–468. http://dx.doi.org/10.1016/0005-7967(90)90132-3

Mathews, A., & MacLeod, C. (2005). Cognitive vulnerability to emotional disorders. *Annual Review of Clinical Psychology, 1*, 167–195. doi:10.1146/annurev.clinpsy.1.102803.143916

McEvoy, P. M., & Mahoney, A. E. (2012). To be sure, to be sure: Intolerance of uncertainty mediates symptoms of various anxiety disorders and depression. *Behavior Therapy, 43*, 533–545. http://dx.doi.org/10.1016/j.beth.2011.02.007

McEvoy, P. M., & Mahoney, A. (2013). Intolerance of uncertainty and negative metacognitive beliefs as transdiagnostic mediators of repetitive negative thinking in a clinical sample with anxiety disorders. *Journal of Anxiety Disorders, 27*, 216–224. http://dx.doi.org/10.1016/j.janxdis.2013.01.006

Mennin, D. S., Heimberg, R. G., Turk, C. L., & Fresco, D. M. (2005). Preliminary evidence for an emotion dysregulation model of generalized anxiety disorder. *Behaviour Research and Therapy, 43*, 1281–1310. doi:10.1016/j.brat.2004.08.008

Mitte, K. (2008). Memory bias for threatening information in anxiety and anxiety disorders: A meta-analytic review. *Psychological Bulletin, 134*, 886–911. http://dx.doi.org/10.1037/a0013343

Mogg, K., & Bradley, B. P. (1998). A cognitive motivational analysis of anxiety. *Behaviour Research and Therapy, 36*, 809–848. http://dx.doi.org/10.1016/S0005-7967(98)00063-1

Nelson, B. D., & Shankman, S. A. (2011). Does intolerance of uncertainty predict anticipatory startle responses to uncertain threat? *International Journal of Psychophysiology, 81*, 107–115. doi:10.1016/j.ijpsycho.2011.05.003

Nelson, B. D., Shankman, S. A., & Proudfit, G. H. (2014). Intolerance of uncertainty mediates reduced reward anticipation in major depressive disorder. *Journal of Affective Disorders, 158*, 108–113. http://dx.doi.org/10.1016/j.jad.2014.02.014

Nitschke, J. B., Sarinopoulos, I., Oathes, D. J., Johnstone, T., Whalen, P. J., Davidson, R. J., & Kalin, N. H. (2009). Anticipatory activation in the amygdala and anterior cingulate in generalized anxiety disorder and prediction of treatment response. *American Journal of Psychiatry, 166*, 302–310. http://dx.doi.org/10.1176/appi.ajp.2008.07101682

Norr, A. M., Oglesby, M. E., Capron, D. W., Raines, A. M., Korte, K. J., & Schmidt, N. B. (2013). Evaluating the unique contribution of intolerance of uncertainty relative to other cognitive vulnerability factors in anxiety psychopathology. *Journal of Affective Disorders, 151*, 136–142. http://dx.doi.org/10.1016/j.jad.2013.05.063

Ottaviani, C., Borlimi, R., Brighetti, G., Caselli, G., Favaretto, E., Giardini, I., ... Sassaroli, S. (2014). Worry as an adaptive avoidance strategy in healthy controls but not in pathological worriers. *International Journal of Psychophysiological, 93*, 349–355. doi:10.1016/j.ijpsycho.2014.05.010

Palm, M. E., Elliott, R., McKie, S., Deakin, J. F. W., & Anderson, I. M. (2011). Attenuated responses to emotional expressions in women with generalized anxiety disorder. *Psychological Medicine, 41*, 1009–1018. doi:10.1017/S0033291710001455

Paulesu, E., Sambugaro, E., Torti, T., Danelli, L., Ferri, F., Scialfa, G., ... Sassaroli, S. (2010). Neural correlates of worry in generalized anxiety disorder and in normal controls: A functional MRI study. *Psychological Medicine, 40*, 117–124. http://dx.doi.org/10.1017/S0033291709005649

Pawluk, E. J., & Koerner, N. (2013). A preliminary investigation of impulsivity in generalized anxiety disorder. *Personality and Individual Differences, 54*, 732–737. http://dx.doi.org/10.1016/j.paid.2012.11.027

Prencipe, A., Kesek, A., Cohen, J., Lamm, C., Lewis, M., & Zelazo, P. (2011). Development of hot and cool executive function during the transition to adolescence. *Journal of Experimental Child Psychology, 108*, 621–637. http://dx.doi.org/10.1016/j.jecp.2010.09.008

Radomsky, A. S., Ashbaugh, A. R., & Gelfand, L. A. (2007). Relationships between anger, symptoms and cognitive factors in OCD checkers. *Behaviour Research and Therapy, 45*, 2712–2725. http://dx.doi.org/10.1016/j.brat.2007.07.009

Reuther, E. T., Davis, T. E., Rudy, B. M., Jenkins, W. S., Whiting, S. E., & May, A. C. (2013). Intolerance of uncertainty as a mediator of the relationship between perfectionism and obsessive-compulsive symptom severity. *Depression and Anxiety, 30*, 773–777. doi:10.1002/da.22100

Robichaud, M. (2013). Cognitive behavior therapy targeting intolerance of uncertainty: Application to a clinical case of generalized anxiety disorder. *Cognitive and Behavioral Practice, 20*, 251–263. http://dx.doi.org/10.1016/j.cbpra.2012.09.001

Robinson, O. J., Vytal, K., Cornwell, B. R., & Grillon, C. (2013). The impact of anxiety upon cognition: perspectives from human threat of shock studies. *Frontiers in Human Neurosciences, 7*, 1–21. doi:10.3389/fnhum.2013.00203

Rosen, N. O., Ivanova, E., & Knäuper, B. (2013). Differentiating intolerance of uncertainty from three related but distinct constructs. *Anxiety, Stress & Coping, 27*, 55–73.

Ruggiero, G. M., Stapinski, L., Caselli, G., Fiore, F., Gallucci, M., Sassaroli, S., & Rapee, R. M. (2012). Beliefs over control and meta-worry interact with the effect of intolerance of uncertainty on worry. *Personality and Individual Differences, 53*, 224–230. doi:10.1016/j.paid.2012.03.016

Sternheim, L., Konstantellou, A., Startup, H., & Schmidt, U. (2011). What does uncertainty mean to women with anorexia nervosa? An interpretative phenomenological analysis. *European Eating Disorders Review, 19*, 12–24. http://dx.doi.org/10.1002/erv.v19.1

Taylor, S., McKay, D., & Abramowitz, J. (2005). Hierarchical structure of dysfunctional beliefs in obsessive-compulsive disorder. *Cognitive Behaviour Therapy, 34*, 216–228. http://dx.doi.org/10.1080/16506070510041167

van der Heiden, C., Melchior, K., Muris, P., Bouwmeester, S., Bos, A. E. R., & van der Molen, H. T. (2010). A hierarchical model for the relationships between general and specific vulnerability factors and symptom levels of generalized anxiety disorder. *Journal of Anxiety Disorders, 24*, 284–289. http://dx.doi.org/10.1016/j.janxdis.2009.12.005

Wells, A. (2000). *Emotional disorders and metacognition: Innovative cognitive therapy*. Chichester: Wiley.

Wells, A. (2007). Cognition about cognition: Metacognitive therapy and change in generalized anxiety disorder and social phobia. *Cognitive and Behavioral Practice, 14*, 18–25. doi:1077-7229/07/18-25$1.00/0

Wells, A., & Matthews, G. (1994). *Attention and emotion: A clinical perspective*. Hillsdale, NJ: Erlbaum.

Whalen, P. J., Johnstone, T., Somerville, L. H., Nitschke, J. B., Polis, S., Alexander, A. L., ... Kalin, N. H. (2008). A functional magnetic resonance imaging predictor of treatment response to venlafaxine in generalized anxiety disorder. *Biological Psychiatry, 63*, 858–863. http://dx.doi.org/10.1016/j.biopsych.2007.08.019

Williams, A. D., & Grisham, J. R. (2013). Cognitive bias modification (CBM) of obsessive-compulsive beliefs. *BMC Psychiatry, 13*, 256. doi:10.1186/1471-244X-13-256

Williams, J. M. G., Watts, F. N., MacLeod, C., & Mathews, A. (1997). *Cognitive psychology and emotional disorders*. New York, NY: Wiley.

Yiend, J., & Mathews, A. (2001). Anxiety and attention to threatening pictures. *The Quarterly Journal of Experimental Psychology, 54A*, 665–681. http://dx.doi.org/10.1080/713755991

Yook, K., Kim, K. H., Suh, S. Y., & Lee, K. S. (2010). Intolerance of uncertainty, worry, and rumination in major depressive disorder and generalized anxiety disorder. *Journal of Anxiety Disorders, 24*, 623–628. http://dx.doi.org/10.1016/j.janxdis.2010.04.003

Zentner, M., & Bates, J. E. (2008). Child temperament: An integrative review of concepts, research programs, and measures. *European Journal of Developmental Sciences, 2*, 7–37.

Zlomke, K. R., & Jeter, K. M. (2014). Stress and worry: Examining intolerance of uncertainty's moderating effect. *Anxiety, Stress & Coping: An International Journal, 27*, 202–215. doi:10.1080/10615806.2013.835400

11

Cognitive decline in normal aging and early Alzheimer's disease: A continuous or discontinuous transition?

Pauline E.J. Spaan[1,2]*

*Corresponding author: Pauline E.J. Spaan, Department of Brain and Cognition, University of Amsterdam, Weesperplein 4, 1018 XA Amsterdam, The Netherlands; Department of Psychiatry & Medical Psychology, Onze Lieve Vrouwe Gasthuis (OLVG, Hospital), Amsterdam, The Netherlands

E-mail: paulinee.j.spaan@gmail.com

Reviewing editor: Peter Walla, University of Newcastle, Australia

Abstract: A longstanding debate in dementia research has been whether normal aging and Alzheimer's disease (AD) are extremes that lie along the same continuum (*continuity view*), or whether AD is categorically different from normal aging (*discontinuity view*). In other words, do only *quantitative* differences in neuropsychological test performance exist between normal aging and AD, or are there also *qualitative* differences? This question has been dominating dementia research for a century now and is characterized by inconsistent results and differences in methodological approach. In this review, I discuss studies that draw conclusions in terms of a continuous transition from normal aging to AD, followed by a discussion of studies that draw conclusions in terms of a discontinuous transition. In addition, several methodological issues are discussed that may explain the contrasting findings. This led to a proposal for investigating this topic in further research. I argue that only a latent variable (structural equation modeling) approach testing for measurement equivalence may or may not reveal structural (i.e. qualitative) differences in

ABOUT THE AUTHOR

Pauline E.J. Spaan works part-time as an assistant professor in clinical neuropsychology at the University of Amsterdam, and part-time as a senior clinical neuropsychologist, conducting neuropsychological assessment and treatment, at the Department 'Psychiatry and Medical Psychology' of the OLVG hospital, Amsterdam, and in her private practice.

Her research (PhD 2003) focuses on the early assessment of dementia and how various memory components may improve prediction. In particular, she is interested in the nature of semantic processing deficits in (early stage) Alzheimer's disease and how this may contribute to more reliable differential assessment.

Furthermore, she is interested in explaining patterns of age-related cognitive deficits within the *normal* aging spectrum: from young-old (55+) to very old age (up to 96 years old). More specifically, she studies (by means of SEM) the interplay between episodic and semantic memory components, on the one hand, and processing speed and executive functioning, on the other hand.

PUBLIC INTEREST STATEMENT

Alzheimer's disease (AD) may already occur at age 50 (or before), but occurs more frequently when we get older. Especially at very old age, it is difficult to determine what is normal and what is not. Besides, we do not even know whether the transition from normal aging to AD is continuous or discontinuous. Normal aging and AD could be two extremes on the same continuum: people simply differ at a *quantitative* level. Or: Does AD represent a *qualitatively* different entity--a disease that could be acquired by some but not by others, even when they grow very old?

This review summarizes research results that seem to adhere the *continuity* or the *discontinuity hypothesis*. Various methodological factors are discussed that may explain the contrasting findings. To finally answer this longstanding debate, it seems crucial to choose a more advanced statistical approach that may specify whether differences are quantitative or also qualitative.

neuropsychological test performance between normal aging and AD. This outcome has important implications for the selection of optimal procedures of early AD assessment, particularly at very old age.

Subjects: Aging and Health; Dementia; Dementia & Alzheimer's Disease; Statistics for Social Sciences

Keywords: Alzheimer's disease; normal aging; cognitive decline; continuity view; discontinuity view; structural equation modeling; metric invariance

1. Introduction

A longstanding debate in dementia research (e.g. Berrios, 1994; Huppert & Kopelman, 1989) has been whether normal aging and Alzheimer's disease (AD) are extremes that lie along the same continuum (*continuity view*), or whether AD is categorically different from normal aging (*discontinuity view*). Thus, does everyone who lives long enough eventually develop dementia or AD in particular, or not? Berrios (1994) described this debate in historical context that exists for approximately a century now. Alois Alzheimer himself allegedly adhered the continuity view (1907), whereas Kraepelin, Barclay, and Robertson (1919) may rather have supported the discontinuity view (Berios).

The debate most likely originates from a large variability regarding course of the disease and age of onset (Fratiglioni et al., 2000; Harvey, Skelton-Robinson, & Rossor, 2003; Lobo et al., 2000). There are wide individual differences in the rate at which memory and other cognitive decline occurs in AD (Mayeux, Stern, & Spanton, 1985; Wilson, Gilley, Bennett, Beckett, & Evans, 2000). Concerning age of onset, Braak and Braak (1997) concluded that AD is an age-related, but not an age-dependent disease. On the one hand, AD may already occur in persons in their 50s, or, although highly uncommonly, even in their 30s, in persons without, for example, Down's syndrome. On the other hand, there are anecdotal reports of individuals, defined as "SuperAgers", who seem immune to both age-related memory impairment and age-related changes in cortical volume (Harrison, Weintraub, Mesulam, & Rogalski, 2012).

Nonetheless, Wilson et al. (2000) stated that as age is the most robust risk factor for developing AD, any attempt to account for the heterogeneity of AD should probably begin with age. In addition, it is important to be aware of the methodological characteristics of the research being conducted. Inconsistent findings regarding the rate of cognitive decline in relation to age may be influenced by, for example, sample sizes, the number or spacing of observations over time, follow-up participation, floor and ceiling effects on measures of cognitive function, and statistical methods to analyze longitudinal cognitive data (Wilson et al., 2000). Wilson (2008) concluded that controversy prevails in aging research whether or not neurological factors contributing to late life dementia are different from the factors contributing to subtle changes in memory and cognition seen in old people without dementia.

This debate is not only of scientific importance, but has also become more and more relevant for clinical practice considering increased average life expectancy and, consequently, increased prevalence of AD (e.g. Fratiglioni et al., 2000; Lobo et al., 2000). Evidence in favor of the discontinuity hypothesis emphasizes the importance of developing tests that are able to detect the precise nature of the cognitive problems characteristic of early AD, up to very old age (e.g. Spaan, Raaijmakers, & Jonker, 2005). In contrast, evidence in favor of the continuity hypothesis would recommend efforts of improving normative data or determining optimal cut-off scores of (existing) neuropsychological tests. Obviously, both types of efforts to improve clinical neuropsychological assessment of AD are dependent on thorough and systematic scientific research.

To further elucidate this long-lasting debate, first, it is crucial to clearly specify the research concepts that are related to the one and to the other hypothesis. (1) The continuity hypothesis states that normal aging and AD are extremes that lie along the same continuum. In other words, everyone who lives long enough will eventually develop AD. In this case, cognitive changes at (very) old age are *not really* different from cognitive decline in (early) AD. Thus, these changes only differ in *degree*, at a *quantitative* level (e.g. Berg, 1985). (2) The discontinuity hypothesis, however, states that AD is categorically different from normal aging. Therefore, the cognitive changes at (very) old age do not only differ in degree but also in *kind*, at a *qualitative* level (e.g. Little, 1997). More specifically, the central research question is: Do only quantitative differences in neuropsychological test performance exist between normal aging and AD, or also qualitative differences? This question can be extended to quantitative or also qualitative differences in AD relevant neuroanatomical variables.

My approach to answer this research question is to critically review[1] studies that draw conclusions in terms of a continuous transition from normal aging to AD (Section 2), followed by a similarly critical review of studies that draw conclusions in terms of a discontinuous transition (Section 3). In Section 4, several methodological issues will be discussed that may explain the contrasting findings. This will lead to a proposal for investigating this topic in further research (Section 5).

2. A continuous transition from normal aging to Alzheimer's disease

Berg (1985) posed the question whether AD represents just an exaggeration of normal aging, which would be consistent with the continuity hypothesis. He encouraged researchers to investigate this question to provide a definite answer (which, in fact, still has not been found). To facilitate research, he formulated the following criteria in case AD is indeed just an exaggeration of normal aging: (1) normal aging and AD have the same causes and mechanisms; (2) there are only quantitative differences between the two; (3) given sufficient longevity, everyone will develop AD; (4) the study of one may lead to the solution of both; (5) when caretakers of an elderly, demented person seek our advice only after the illness is advanced and explain "We thought it was just old age," they are closer to the truth than we thought; (6) normal aging of the brain represents very mild or subclinical AD. Criteria 1, 2, and 6 have been investigated.

Regarding the first and sixth criterion (i.e. normal aging and AD have the same causes and mechanisms; normal aging of the brain represents very mild or subclinical AD), the following research findings are relevant. First of all, the neuropathology that is common for AD (plaques and tangles) is not specific for AD, but also occurs in normal aging, as was found by Price, Davis, Morris, and White (1991). In addition, they found that the location of the brain where particularly tangles were found differed along with the presence and severity of dementia (as was clinically determined by the Clinical Dementia Rating (CDR); Berg, 1988; Hughes, Berg, Danziger, Coben, & Martin, 1982), as well as with age. Tangles were present in all of the brains examined (also non-demented), and appear during aging in the anterior olfactory nucleus, the parahippocampal gyrus and the hippocampus, but are rare in the neocortex except in demented brains. Conversely plaques may develop first in the neocortex. Unlike tangles, plaques are not a consistent feature of aging, at least up to age 80. It should be noted that sample sizes of the various clinical groups were rather small.

Sample sizes were much larger in the study by Schneider, Arvanitakis, Leurgans, and Bennett (2009). Similar to Price et al., Schneider et al. concluded that clinically diagnosed probable AD and mild cognitive impairment (MCI; e.g. Petersen et al., 1999), even amnestic MCI, are pathologically heterogeneous disorders, with many persons exhibiting mixed pathologies. Richards and Brayne (2010) summarized that although plaques and tangles are rarely absent in patients with a clinical diagnosis of AD, these brain features are not pathognomonic, and some people with postmortem evidence of these were cognitively spared at death. Thus, neuropathology seems heterogeneous or diffuse, considering that too many qualitative differences are found among AD patients, whereas the classical pathological features may also occur in non-demented individuals. Therefore, Richards and Brayne concluded, in line with the previous studies, that AD is unlikely to refer to a discrete neuropathological entity and may represent a syndrome rather than a disease.

The second criterion formulated by Berg (1985) was that there are only quantitative differences between normal aging and AD. As Buckner (2004) reviewed, within a unitary factor framework, mild memory decline common in aging exists along a single continuum with memory impairment associated with dementia. Dementia is considered as an acceleration of the same processes that affect cognition in all individuals. Many epidemiological, longitudinal, aging studies seem to adhere to this principle, consistent with the continuity view. These studies (e.g. Brayne & Calloway, 1988; Huppert & Brayne, 1994) assume a gradual, continuous transition from normal aging to AD, without sudden accelerations (or "dents") in the course of decline. According to Bäckman, Jones, Berger, Laukka, and Small (2005), labels such as "normal aging," "preclinical AD," "MCI," and "early AD" are best viewed as instances on a dimension of brain and cognitive functioning rather than discrete categories.

However, the previously discussed neuropathological patterns found in AD as well as normal aging cannot automatically be translated to a similar distribution of cognitive functioning in AD and normal aging. As Salthouse (2011) discussed, inferences that age-related brain changes *cause* age-related cognitive changes, may not be true, when these are based on correlational information. For this reason, more advanced statistical models may provide useful information: *structural equation modeling* (SEM; e.g. LISREL 8.80; Jöreskog & Sörbom, 2007). SEM is a statistical technique for building and testing statistical models, which are often causal models. It is a hybrid technique that encompasses aspects of confirmatory factor analysis (CFA), path analysis, and regression. SEM encourages confirmatory, rather than exploratory, modeling; thus, it is suited to theory testing, rather than theory development. It usually starts with a hypothesis, represents it as a model, operationalizes the constructs of interest with a measurement instrument and tests the model. Among its strengths is the ability to model constructs as *latent variables*--variables which are not measured directly (e.g. cognitive functions), but are estimated in the model from measured variables (e.g. neuropsychological tests) which are assumed to "tap into" the latent variables. This allows the modeler to explicitly capture unreliability of measurement in the model, in theory allowing the structural relations between latent variables to be accurately estimated. SEM is an extension of the general linear model that simultaneously estimates relationships between multiple independent, dependent, and latent variables.

Salthouse and Becker (1998) argued that although performance of AD patients is significantly impaired relative to that of healthy elderly controls on various cognitive measures, the extent to which the effects of AD on different variables are independent of one another is not yet known. By means of single common factor analysis, they found that the majority of effects of AD was shared among different cognitive variables. Their results indicated that if an adjustment was made for the general effects of AD, then there were no remaining effects of AD on nearly 75% of the variables and consistent independent effects only on variables assessing episodic memory.

Similar results, using CFA, were found by Johnson, Storandt, Morris, Langford, and Galvin (2008). After controlling for AD-specific changes in episodic memory, the same hybrid model was found applicable to both AD and normal aging. This model contained one general factor that maximized detection of dementia, and three specific factors (verbal memory, visuospatial ability, and working memory) that revealed the heterogeneity of dementia's associated cognitive deficits. Johnson et al. (2008) stated that this hybrid CFA model allows for direct (quantitative) comparisons of cognitive abilities between different disorders or normal aging.

Chapman et al. (2010) also found, using principal components analysis, that qualitatively the same model of cognitive performance fitted to both AD and normal aging. Chapman et al. concluded that the close similarities across clinical groups (AD, MCI, normal aging) in their underlying neuropsychological dimensions support the use of a common metric system for measuring neuropsychological factors in all these elderly individuals. They argue that a common metric system is a useful and powerful measurement tool for gauging neuropsychological performance in AD, MCI, and normal elderly. The factor scores derived from this metric may then be used to diagnose patients with AD or predict progression to AD in MCI patients, under the assumption that neuropsychological performance only differs at a quantitative level.

3. A discontinuous transition from normal aging to Alzheimer's disease

The above-mentioned criteria by Berg (1985) were proposed to examine whether AD represents just an exaggeration of normal aging, which would be consistent with the continuity hypothesis. In this section, research findings will be discussed that reported contrasting findings in AD, compared to normal aging, which would be consistent with the discontinuity hypothesis. These findings may be interpreted in accordance with nosological thinking that has dominated the previous century (Berrios, 1994): AD represents a separate diagnostic category, apart from the normal aging process, with also a separate neuropathology (e.g. medial temporal lobe atrophy, etc. Braak & Braak, 1991).

The first criterion (Berg, 1985) was: normal aging and AD have the same causes and mechanisms. The study of Ritchie and Kildea (1995) argues oppositely. In their meta-analysis of nine epidemiological studies, also including sufficient numbers of very old people (over age 80), they fitted the prevalence of dementia curve. This curve was best described as a flattened S curve that fitted a modified logistic function rather than an exponential pattern. They concluded that senile dementia seems better conceptualized as an "age-related" (i.e. occurring within a specific age range) rather than as an "aging-related" disorder (i.e. caused by the aging process itself). Very elderly survivors may be at a diminished risk of dementia.

In addition, contrasting findings are described in the following studies, regarding both the first criterion of Berg and his sixth criterion, i.e. normal aging of the brain represents very mild or subclinical AD. In these studies (rather), selective neuropathology is found in AD. West, Coleman, Flood, and Troncoso (1994) found that the most distinctive AD-related neuron loss was seen in the CA1 region of the hippocampus. In the normal aging group, there was almost no neuron loss in this region. West et al. concluded that the neurodegenerative processes associated with normal aging and with AD are qualitatively different and that AD is not accelerated by aging, but is a distinct pathological process.

Furthermore, Krasuski et al. (1998) found that by means of MRI, measured volumes of the anterior–posterior parahippocampal gyrus, which contains the entorhinal cortex, were reduced, but the amygdala and hippocampal volumes show greater reduction, relative to healthy controls. Nonetheless, despite significant differences in group means, particularly the hippocampal volumes of their control subjects overlapped with those of AD patients. Golomb et al. (1993) found that a third of their cognitively normal elderly sample had MRI evidence of hippocampal atrophy, which was associated with subclinical memory deficits. Whether these supposedly control subjects with reductions in hippocampal size are in fact at risk for future cognitive decline explained by dementia is unclear.

This overlap may indeed be explained by not all controls really being controls, considering Raz and Rodrigue's (2006) review that the entorhinal cortex is affected almost exclusively in those who showed significant ante-mortem cognitive decline. In contrast, the effects of normal aging on the volume of the entorhinal cortex are negligible. In addition, reduced hippocampal volume is a good predictor of a concurrent AD and of AD-type pathology in (supposedly) non-demented individuals.

This selective neuropathology in AD, in contrast to normal aging, may also be associated with selective behavioral problems, as Serra et al. (2010) examined. They found associations in regions implicated by AD neuropathology and behavioral problems, such as mood disorders, anxiety, agitation, psychotic symptoms, disinhibition, and delusions, rather than these problems representing a psychological reaction to cognitive disabilities. This suggested that these behavioral problems are likely to represent clinical features of AD and should be regarded for their diagnostic and prognostic value.

To conclude, Buckner (2004) reviewed that frontal-striatal change may underlie mild memory difficulties in aging that are most apparent on tasks demanding high levels of attention and controlled processing. In contrast, through separate mechanisms, AD preferentially affects the medial temporal lobe and cortical networks, including posterior cingulate and retrosplenial cortex early in its progression, often before clinical symptoms are recognized. Disruption of the medial temporal lobe memory system leads directly to memory impairment. This seems inconsistent with the criteria of Berg (1985) that normal aging and AD have the same causes and mechanisms, and that normal aging of the brain represents very mild or subclinical AD. This also suggests the existence of not only quantitative but also qualitative differences in cognitive performance. This would be in contrast with the second criterion formulated by Berg (1985), which will be further discussed below.

There are many studies, conducting *cross-sectional* research, that report specifically disturbed cognitive processes in AD patients on tests of episodic memory, verbal and spatial span, and semantic encoding, including qualitative differences in performance characteristics, relative to even *very old* non-demented controls (e.g. Carlesimo et al., 1998; Perri, Serra, Carlesimo, & Caltagirone, 2007; Spaan, Raaijmakers, & Jonker, 2003; Spaan et al., 2005). However, these cross-sectional studies do not provide insight into the nature of decline over time in the same individuals.

In contrast with the *longitudinal* studies discussed in the previous section (e.g. Bäckman et al., 2005; Brayne & Calloway, 1988; Huppert & Brayne, 1994), the longitudinal study by Grober et al. (2008) did *not* find a gradual, continuous transition from normal aging to AD. Grober et al. found from seven years before the assessment of AD, several accelerations in the course of decline: first in episodic memory functioning, and several years later in executive functioning. Johnson, Storandt, Morris, and Galvin (2009) found similar results in their longitudinal study with better statistical methodology. The best-fitting model for each of four cognitive factors in a group of 310 elderly individuals that stayed non-demented was linear. In contrast, Johnson et al. (2009) found a sharp "inflection point" followed by accelerating decline in multiple domains of cognition (including memory and visuospatial ability) in the course of decline in a group of 134 elderly individuals who were assessed with AD during follow-up. These results were also obtained when data were limited to a subset ($N = 44$) with autopsy-confirmed AD.

The findings discussed above seem consistent with the multiple factor framework, as was reviewed by Buckner (2004). In this model, separate factors are hypothesized to affect cognition in aging, each with distinct causes, risk factors, anatomic targets, and cognitive sequelae. This is also supported by the study of Siedlecki, Honig, and Stern (2008), adopting a more advanced SEM approach. They performed exploratory factor analysis and a series of confirmatory factor analyses to, ultimately, find a five-factor model of cognitive functioning that fitted well across three clinical groups: cognitively healthy older adults, patients diagnosed with questionable dementia, and patients diagnosed with probable AD. This model, thus, obtained *configural invariance* across the three groups, similar to the approach and findings of studies that were discussed in Section 2 (Chapman et al., 2010; Johnson et al., 2008; Salthouse & Becker, 1998). For a model to demonstrate configural invariance, the relations among the latent constructs (i.e. cognitive factors) and their measured variables (i.e. cognitive tests) should be the same across different groups (Horn, McArdle, & Mason, 1983). That is, the *structure* of the model should be invariant.

Although a structurally same cognitive model may be applicable to both (early) AD and normal aging, there may *still be consistent qualitative differences* across separate diagnostic groups. Thus, configural invariance of a model across different groups does not necessarily imply that this model and each cognitive construct within it are measuring the same constellation of cognitive abilities in the various clinical groups that are investigated. There may still be differences in relations among variables and, thus, differences in what the variables may be measuring. In other words, the cognitive profile derived from a model may represent a different set of cognitive processes in (early) AD than in normal aging. If there are qualitative differences (such that the model is not invariant), then differences across groups are difficult to interpret because the meaning of the construct may be changing (e.g. Horn & Mcardle, 1992; Little, 1997).

To further investigate the existence of qualitative differences, Siedlecki et al. subsequently performed an analysis of *metric invariance*. Metric invariance is established when the *magnitude of the unstandardized coefficients*--i.e. the factor loadings of each measured variable (i.e. cognitive test) on its respective latent construct (i.e. cognitive factor)--is not significantly different across groups (Horn & Mcardle, 1992). This is tested by constraining the factor loadings to be the same across the groups and comparing the fit of the constrained (metric invariance) model to the baseline (configural) model. If the metric model does not fit significantly worse, then it can be argued that the model demonstrates metric invariance. Note that this does not imply that the group means are identical across groups.

However, the analysis performed by Siedlecki et al. did *not* show metric invariance. Specifically, their memory construct may have represented something different in the questionable dementia and AD groups as compared to the healthy older adult group. They interpret this specific finding as consistent with the underlying pathology in early AD.

Similar results, using a similar statistical approach, were found by Mitchell, Shaughnessny, Shirk, Yang, and Atri (2012). They conducted CFA to test a four-factor model of cognitive functioning in a group of amnestic MCI and AD patients vs. a group of cognitively healthy older adults. This model obtained adequate configural invariance across groups, but their metric invariance model showed significantly reduced fit, relative to their baseline (configural) model. Therefore, as was found by Siedlecki et al., the model of Mitchell et al. was *not* metric invariant either.

These results (Mitchell et al., 2012; Siedlecki et al., 2008) suggest that not only quantitative but also qualitative differences in cognitive performance exist between (early) AD and normal aging. This provides support for the discontinuity hypothesis.

4. Methodological explanations for the contrasting findings

As Wilson et al. (2000) discussed, inconsistent research findings regarding the nature of decline in relation to age and in AD may be influenced by, for example, (small) sample sizes (e.g. Carlesimo et al., 1998; Krasuski et al., 1998; Price et al., 1991; West et al., 1994), the number (or spacing) of observations over time (if any: e.g. Carlesimo et al., 1998; Perri et al., 2007; Spaan et al., 2005), dropout at follow-up participation (e.g. Spaan et al., 2005), floor and ceiling effects on measures of cognitive function, and statistical methods to analyze data (the latter two are discussed below). Therefore, the discrepancy of research findings and conclusions, as described in Sections 2 and 3, may be explained by these and several other methodological issues that will be further discussed in the current section.

First of all, the characteristics of the contrasted clinical groups may differ a lot. For example, various studies that were discussed in Section 2 or *3[2] investigated differences in performance between very healthy and clearly demented participants, and thus did *not include a preclinical AD or MCI group* (of whom the majority may be in a preclinical stage of AD; Albert et al., 2011): e.g. *Carlesimo et al. (1998), Johnson et al. (2008), Price et al. (1991), Salthouse & Becker (1998), and *Siedlecki et al. (2008). Fortunately, in the past 10 years, the inclusion of a preclinical AD group or at least a MCI group has become rather common practice: e.g. Bäckman et al. (2005); Chapman et al. (2010), *Grober et al. (2008), *Johnson et al. (2009), *Krasuski et al., (1998), *Mitchell et al. (2012); *Perri et al. (2007), Schneider et al. (2009); *Serra et al. (2010), *Spaan et al. (2005).

In addition, the age range of the participants that are involved in several studies is often rather narrow and does *not (or hardly) include (particularly) cognitive healthy elderly individuals that are of very old age* (i.e. over age 80): e.g. Brayne & Calloway (1988), *Krasuski et al. (1998), *Perri et al. (2007), Salthouse & Becker (1998), *Serra et al. (2010). However, a growing number of studies do include participants of very old age: e.g. Bäckman et al. (2005), *Carlesimo et al. (1998), Chapman et al. (20100, *Harrison et al. (2012), Johnson et al. (2008), *(2009); Price et al. (1991), *Ritchie & Kildea (1995), Schneider et al. (2009), *Siedlecki et al. (2008), *West et al. (1994).

When the characteristics of the contrasted clinical groups differ a lot and/or "the very old" are not included, this *may cause a bias in favor of the* ***discontinuity*** *view*. Nonetheless, group differences may still be merely quantitative, rather than qualitative. It is therefore important to examine all aspects of normal vs. pathological aging that may or may not precede the development of AD. As Bäckman, Small, Wahlin, and Larsson (2000) discussed, prevalence and incidence of various diseases related to cognitive functioning (e.g. dementia, circulatory disease, and diabetes) greatly increase with advancing age. What should define "normal aging" in very late life? The influence of various concomitant conditions (e.g. sensory deficits, depression, and vitamin deficiency) on cognitive performance may be magnified, reduced, or unchanged at very old age. Bäckman et al. (2000) stated that delineating conditions that follow these patterns is another way of addressing the issue of continuity vs. discontinuity of cognitive functioning across the adult life span.

In addition, Raz and Rodrigue (2006) reviewed that--independent of dementia--the human brain shrinks with age and brain shrinkage is selective and differential, not uniform, or randomly distributed. They found that the subcortical white matter and the hippocampus show substantial shrinkage in the older old and the rate of shrinkage may be accelerated by hypertension. They stated that the evidence suggesting that a large share of age-related changes is accounted by vascular pathology continues to accumulate. The hippocampus appears especially vulnerable to multiple negative modifiers of aging. Other putative negative modifiers are stress and hormonal depletion.

Secondly, *reduced construct validity of the administered neuropsychological tests* (i.e. one test often represents the influence of more than one cognitive process) complicates the detection of specific patterns of cognitive performance or deficits (e.g. Spaan et al., 2003). This may also enhance the probability that a certain cognitive construct measures a different constellation of cognitive abilities in different clinical groups that are investigated. For example, Siedlecki et al. found that their cognitive model was not metric invariant across (early) AD and normal aging, most likely because their memory construct may have represented something different in the one vs. the other group.

Thirdly, in many studies, only a few tests (i.e. measuring one or a few cognitive functions) or even only cognitive screening tests--such as the *Mini-Mental State Examination* (MMSE; Folstein, Folstein, & McHugh, 1975), the *Cambridge Examination of Mental Disorders of the Elderly* (CAMDEX; e.g. Roth, Huppert, Mountjoy, & Tym, 1998), or CDR--were administered (e.g. Brayne & Calloway, 1988; Huppert & Brayne, 1994; Price et al., 1991). This limits the possibility to derive a sufficiently broad cognitive profile from the results. Obviously, conclusions drawn in each study, in terms of which cognitive functions show greatest decline with age and in AD, are always dependent on the battery of specific cognitive tests or tasks that were administered. In addition, and more importantly, particularly the cognitive screening test method reduces the reliability of the clinical diagnosis that has been determined. This is also acknowledged by Price et al. (1991): it is possible that some subjects in their study that were assessed as non-demented were, in fact, in an early stage of dementia. It is therefore difficult to determine whether the density and distribution of tangles and plaques in non-demented cases are related to incipient AD, or to the normal aging process (Price et al., 1991).

Also, Krasuski et al. (1998) and Golomb et al. (1993) acknowledged the possibility that *not all controls were actually controls*. As Buckner (2004) reviewed, it is difficult to obtain a sample of older adults free from AD. He summarized that in many studies, participants are assumed to be spared from AD if they achieve a certain level of performance on a global cognitive screening test (e.g. MMSE). Such methods eliminate severely impaired individuals but lead to the inclusion of older adults in the early stages of the disease who, because of high baseline functioning and other mitigating factors, retain average global cognition during the initial progression of the disease. The relevance of this issue is that several studies of non-demented aging have found correlations between atrophy of the medial temporal lobe, or substructures within the medial temporal lobe, and memory performance (e.g. Krasuski et al., 1998).

Both the second and the third issue, concerning the cognitive tests that were used, *may lead to conclusions in favor of the* ***continuity*** *view.*

Finally, studies often differ in the adopted statistical approach. Commonly, the investigation is at the level of individual *tests* but conclusions are drawn at the latent level of cognitive *functions* (e.g. Bäckman et al., 2005; Brayne & Calloway, 1988; Carlesimo et al., 1998; Grober et al., 2008; Huppert & Brayne, 1994; Perri et al., 2007; Spaan et al., 2003, 2005). This also disregards the examination of the *interrelations* between the cognitive (measured *and* latent) variables (e.g. Spaan, 2015). This more complete examination, also taking into account the impact of measurement errors of the individual tests (i.e. particularly relevant when construct validity is reduced), is possible with SEM (e.g. LISREL 8.80; Jöreskog & Sörbom, 2007; Chapman et al., 2010; Johnson et al., 2008, 2009; Mitchell et al., 2012; Salthouse, 2011; Salthouse & Becker, 1998; Siedlecki et al., 2008).

In fact, all these data together represent the *qualitative* performance profile of the tested subjects of each clinical group. Moreover, these types of analyses correspond nicely with the interpretation of the cognitive profile that is done in adequate neuropsychological assessment of each individual patient. We should never base our assessment of cognitive functioning of a patient on the results of only one or a few neuropsychological tests. Instead, we attempt to link performance on tests that aim to measure the same cognitive function, as well as to make cross-connections between different cognitive functions.

In this respect, it should be noted that two studies that draw conclusions in terms of the continuity hypothesis (Johnson et al., 2008; Salthouse & Becker, 1998), beforehand, made a *qualitative* adjustment to the model they claimed was invariant across normal aging and AD. Salthouse and Becker (1998), first, adjusted for the general effects of AD; *then* they found that there were no remaining effects of AD on nearly 75% of the variables and consistent independent effects only on variables assessing episodic memory. In addition, Johnson et al. (2008) reported that *after* controlling for AD-specific changes in episodic memory, their hybrid CFA model allowed for direct (*quantitative*) comparisons of cognitive abilities between different disorders or normal aging. These adjustments probably *created a bias toward the* ***continuity*** *view.*

Configural and metric invariance are two different levels of measurement invariance. As was argued by the end of Section 3, the investigation whether a cognitive model has configural invariance across normal aging and AD is not enough to answer the question of continuity vs. discontinuity. Despite configural invariance, there may still be differences in relations among variables and, thus, differences in what the variables may be measuring: i.e. *qualitative* differences (e.g. Little, 1997). Therefore, also metric invariance should be tested across groups (e.g. Horn & Mcardle, 1992). If this analysis is neglected, this may *bias toward the* ***continuity*** *view* as well.

Subsequently, if configural as well as metric invariance are always investigated in a study, it may be of reduced importance to the question of continuity vs. discontinuity, which specific cognitive functions are examined. In advanced research, it would be more interesting when studies vary in their test approach, instead of always administering the same battery of tests.

5. Conclusions and suggestions for further research

In this review, an attempt was made to shed some light on a longstanding debate in dementia research: Are normal aging and AD extremes that lie along the same continuum (*continuity view*), or is AD categorically different from normal aging (*discontinuity view*)? In other words, do only *quantitative* differences in neuropsychological test performance exist between normal aging and AD, or are there also *qualitative* differences?

As was summarized in the previous section, this debate is characterized by inconsistent results and differences in methodological approach. Several methodological explanations for the contrasting findings were discussed in Section 4. This discussion leads to the following proposal for investigating this topic in further research. I argue that only a latent variable approach testing for measurement equivalence is appropriate to investigate whether *also* qualitative--rather than *only* quantitative--differences in neuropsychological test performance exist between normal aging and AD (e.g. Horn & Mcardle, 1992; Little, 1997). The few studies that used this approach seem to provide support for the discontinuity hypothesis. Moreover, alternative (methodological) explanations were extensively described for the outcome of studies that draw conclusions in favor of the continuity hypothesis (see Section 4).

The study by Spaan and Dolan (2010) is another example that used the same statistical approach. We attempted to avoid the methodological disadvantages that were discussed in the previous section. We investigated the hypotheses of continuity vs. discontinuity by means of a multi-group SEM approach, testing for configural as well as metric invariance. We used data collected in a sample of 80 early or preclinical AD patients and 80 age-, education-, and gender-matched controls, of a broad age range (55–87 years), on a newly developed computerized neuropsychological test battery with refined construct validity (for a more extensive description of this test battery, see Spaan, 2015; for a more extensive description of the study sample, see Spaan, 2016). The results of our study showed adequate configural invariance across the two groups (RMSEA = .063), but no metric invariance (RMSEA = .085; reduced fit: $\Delta\chi^2 = 75.02$, $\Delta df = 12$, $p < .001$). Our results were, therefore, in favor of the discontinuity hypothesis.

Nonetheless, far more studies using this measurement invariance approach should be conducted to try to replicate the previously found results that seem consistent with the discontinuity hypothesis. Moreover, it may relevant to clinical practice to investigate the boundaries of this hypothesis. A suggestion would be to not only involve AD patients but also other type of dementia patients. In addition, the investigation of the influence of various diseases related to cognitive functioning and (advanced) aging (circulatory or cardiovascular system disease, hypertension, diabetes, etc.; e.g. Bäckman et al., 2000; Raz & Rodrigue, 2006) would be interesting.

In sum, this long lasting continuity vs. discontinuity debate is not only of scientific relevance, but also has large consequences for our actions in clinical practice. The preliminary evidence, described in this review, which seems in favor of the discontinuity hypothesis, emphasizes the importance of developing tests that are able to detect the precise nature of the cognitive problems characteristic of early AD (e.g. Spaan, 2016; Spaan et al., 2005). Nonetheless, efforts of improving normative data or determining optimal cut-off scores of (existing) neuropsychological tests are still very important, especially at very old age, in order to reliably answer the question what is normal and what is not when we grow older.

Acknowledgments

The results of an empirical study related to the literature review described in this manuscript were presented both at the 2010 Mid-Year Meeting of the International Neuropsychological Society, Krakow, Poland, July 2010, and at the Second Meeting of the Federation of European Societies of Neuropsychology, Amsterdam, the Netherlands, September 2010. The results of this empirical study were subsequently published: Spaan, P. E. J., & Dolan, C. V. (2010). Cognitive decline in normal ageing and early Alzheimer's disease: A continuous or discontinuous transition? *Behavioural Neurology, 23*, 203–206.

Funding

The author received no direct funding for this research.

Competing Interests

The author declares no competing interests.

Author details

Pauline E.J. Spaan[1,2]

E-mail: paulinee.j.spaan@gmail.com

ORCID ID: http://orcid.org/0000-0001-5858-2419

[1] Department of Brain and Cognition, University of Amsterdam, Weesperplein 4, 1018 XA Amsterdam, The Netherlands.

[2] Department of Psychiatry & Medical Psychology, Onze Lieve Vrouwe Gasthuis (OLVG, Hospital), Amsterdam, The Netherlands.

Notes

1. Journal articles were obtained from computerized database searches of PsycINFO, PubMed and Google Scholar (no year limit). The key words were: "Alzheimer's disease"; "continuity" or "continuous"; "discontinuity" or "discontinuous"; "quantitative"; "qualitative"; "measurement invariance"; "metric invariance". Some articles

were also located by citation. Criteria for inclusion were rather broad. Studies were included if a group of AD patients was directly compared with an appropriate control group, *and* if the results were explicitly *or* implicitly relevant to the continuity or the discontinuity hypothesis. I.e. not all studies made explicit interpretations in terms of these hypotheses, but were included anyway, if their results seemed relevant to the debate. Studies were excluded if they concerned a completely different research topic. Relevant results are described in this review.

2. Studies that draw conclusions in terms of a discontinuous transition from normal aging to AD (discussed in Section 3) are noted by means of a *-symbol in this section of the text. Studies that draw conclusions in terms of a continuous transition (discussed in Section 2) are noted without a *-symbol.

References

Albert, M. S., DeKosky, S. T., Dickson, D., Dubois, B., Feldman, H. H., Fox, N. C., ... Phelps, C. H. (2011). The diagnosis of mild cognitive impairment due to Alzheimer's disease: Recommendations from the National Institute on Aging-Alzheimer's Association workgroups on diagnostic guidelines for Alzheimer's disease. *Alzheimer's & Dementia, 7*, 270–279.

Bäckman, L., Jones, S., Berger, A. K., Laukka, E. J., & Small, B. J. (2005). Cognitive impairment in preclinical Alzheimer's disease: A meta-analysis. *Neuropsychology, 19*, 520–531. http://dx.doi.org/10.1037/0894-4105.19.4.520

Bäckman, L., Small, B. J., Wahlin, A., & Larsson, M. (2000). Cognitive functioning in very old age. In F. I. M. Craik & T. A. Salthouse (Eds.), *The handbook of aging and cognition* (2nd ed., pp. 499–558). Mahwah, NJ: Lawrence Erlbaum.

Berg, L. (1985). Does Alzheimer's disease represent an exaggeration of normal aging? *Archives of Neurology, 42*, 437–439.

Berg, L. (1988). Clinical dementia rating (CDR). *Psychopharmacological Bulletin, 25*, 637–639.

Berrios, G. F. (1994). Dementia and aging since the nineteenth century. In F. A. Huppert, C. Brayne, & D. W. O'Connor (Eds.), *Dementia and normal aging* (pp. 15–40). Cambridge: Cambridge University Press.

Braak, H., & Braak, E. (1991). Neuropathological stageing of Alzheimer-related changes. *Acta Neuropathologica, 82*, 239–259. http://dx.doi.org/10.1007/BF00308809

Braak, H., & Braak, E. (1997). Frequency of stages of Alzheimer-related lesions in different age categories. *Neurobiology of Aging, 18*, 351–357. http://dx.doi.org/10.1016/S0197-4580(97)00056-0

Brayne, C., & Calloway, P. (1988). Normal ageing, impaired cognitive function, and senile dementia of the Alzheimer's type: A continuum? *The Lancet, 331*, 1265–1267. http://dx.doi.org/10.1016/S0140-6736(88)92081-8

Buckner, R. L. (2004). Memory and executive function in aging and AD: Multiple factors that cause decline and reserve factors that compensate. *Neuron, 44*, 195–208. http://dx.doi.org/10.1016/j.neuron.2004.09.006

Carlesimo, G. A., Mauri, M., Graceffa, A. M. S., Fadda, L., Loasses, A., Lorusso, S., & Caltagirone, C. (1998). Memory performances in young, elderly, and very old healthy individuals versus patients with Alzheimer's disease: Evidence for discontinuity between normal and pathological aging. *Journal of Clinical and Experimental Neuropsychology, 20*, 14–29. http://dx.doi.org/10.1076/jcen.20.1.14.1482

Chapman, R. M., Mapstone, M., McCrary, J. W., Gardner, M. N., Bachus, L. E., DeGrush, E., ... Guillily, M. D. (2010). Cognitive dimensions in Alzheimer's disease, mild cognitive impairment, and normal elderly: Developing a common metric. *The Open Geriatric Medicine Journal, 3*, 1–10. http://dx.doi.org/10.2174/1874827901003010001

Folstein, M. F., Folstein, S. F., & McHugh, P. R. (1975). "Mini-Mental State": A practical method for grading the cognitive state of patients for the clinician. *Journal of Psychiatric Research, 12*, 189–198. http://dx.doi.org/10.1016/0022-3956(75)90026-6

Fratiglioni, L., Launer, L. J., Andersen, K., Breteler, M. M., Copeland, J. R., Dartigues, J. F., ... Hofman, A. (2000). Incidence of dementia and major subtypes in Europe: A collaborative study of population-based cohorts. Neurologic Diseases in the Elderly Research Group. *Neurology, 54*, S10–S15.

Golomb, J., deLeon, M. J., Kiger, A., George, A. E., Tarshish, C., & Ferris, S. H. (1993). Hippocampal atrophy in normal aging: An association with recent memory impairment. *Archives of Neurology, 50*, 967–973. http://dx.doi.org/10.1001/archneur.1993.00540090066012

Grober, E., Hall, C. B., Lipton, R. B., Zonderman, A. B., Resnick, S. M., & Kawas, C. (2008). Memory impairment, executive dysfunction, and intellectual decline in preclinical Alzheimer's disease. *Journal of the International Neuropsychological Society, 14*, 266–278.

Harrison, T. M., Weintraub, S., Mesulam, M. M., & Rogalski, E. (2012). Superior memory and higher cortical volumes in unusually successful cognitive aging. *Journal of the International Neuropsychological Society, 18*, 1081–1085. http://dx.doi.org/10.1017/S1355617712000847

Harvey, R. J., Skelton-Robinson, M., & Rossor, M. N. (2003). The prevalence and causes of dementia in people under the age of 65 years. *Journal of Neurology, Neurosurgery and Psychiatry, 74*, 1206–1209. http://dx.doi.org/10.1136/jnnp.74.9.1206

Horn, J. L., & Mcardle, J. J. (1992). A practical and theoretical guide to measurement invariance in aging research. *Experimental Aging Research, 18*, 117–144. http://dx.doi.org/10.1080/03610739208253916

Horn, J. L., McArdle, J. J., & Mason, R. (1983). When is invariance not invariant: A practical scientist's look at the ethereal concept of factor invariance. *Southern Psychologist, 1*, 179–188.

Hughes, C. P., Berg, L., Danziger, W. L., Coben, L. A., & Martin, R. L. (1982). A new clinical scale for the staging of dementia. *The British Journal of Psychiatry, 140*, 566–572. http://dx.doi.org/10.1192/bjp.140.6.566

Huppert, F. A., & Brayne, C. (1994). What is the relationship between dementia and normal aging? In F. A. Huppert, C. Brayne, & D. W. O'Connor (Eds.), *Dementia and normal aging* (pp. 3–12). Cambridge: Cambridge University Press.

Huppert, F. A., & Kopelman, M. D. (1989). Rates of forgetting in normal ageing: A comparison with dementia. *Neuropsychologia, 27*, 849–860. http://dx.doi.org/10.1016/0028-3932(89)90008-0

Johnson, D. K., Storandt, M., Morris, J. C., & Galvin, J. E. (2009). Longitudinal study of the transition from healthy aging to Alzheimer disease. *Archives of Neurology, 66*, 1254–1259.

Johnson, D. K., Storandt, M., Morris, J. C., Langford, Z., & Galvin, J. E. (2008). Cognitive profiles in dementia: Alzheimer disease vs healthy brain aging. *Neurology, 71*, 1783–1789. http://dx.doi.org/10.1212/01.wnl.0000335972.35970.70

Jöreskog, K. G., & Sörbom, D. (2007). *LISREL 8* (Version 8.80) [Computer software]. Chicago, IL: Scientific Software International.

Kraepelin, E., Barclay, R. M., & Robertson, G. M. (1919). *Dementia praecox.*

Krasuski, J. S., Alexander, G. E., Horwitz, B., Daly, E. M., Murphy, D. G. M., Rapoport, S. I., & Schapiro, M. B. (1998). Volumes of medial temporal lobe structures in patients with Alzheimer's disease and mild cognitive impairment (and in healthy controls). *Biological Psychiatry, 43*, 60–68. http://dx.doi.org/10.1016/S0006-3223(97)00013-9

Little, T. D. (1997). Mean and covariance structures (MACS) analyses of cross-cultural data: Practical and theoretical issues. *Multivariate Behavioral Research, 32*, 53–76. http://dx.doi.org/10.1207/s15327906mbr3201_3

Lobo, A., Launer, L. J., Fratiglioni, L., Andersen, K., Di Carlo, A., Breteler, M. M., ... Hofman, A. (2000). Prevalence of dementia and major subtypes in Europe: A collaborative study of population-based cohorts. Neurologic Diseases in the Elderly Research Group. *Neurology, 54*, S4–S9.

Mayeux, R., Stern, Y., & Spanton, S. (1985). Heterogeneity in dementia of the Alzheimer type: Evidence of subgroups. *Neurology, 35*, 453–461. http://dx.doi.org/10.1212/WNL.35.4.453

Mitchell, M. B., Shaughnessny, L. W., Shirk, S. D., Yang, F. M., & Atri, A. (2012). Neuropsychological test performance and cognitive reserve in healthy aging and the Alzheimer's disease spectrum: A theoretically driven factor analysis. *Journal of the International Neuropsychological Society, 18*, 1–10.

Perri, R., Serra, L., Carlesimo, G. A., & Caltagirone, C. (2007). Amnestic mild cognitive impairment: Difference of memory profile in subjects who converted or did not convert to Alzheimer's disease. *Neuropsychology, 21*, 549–558. http://dx.doi.org/10.1037/0894-4105.21.5.549

Petersen, R. C., Smith, G. E., Waring, S. C., Ivnik, R. J., Tangalos, E. G., & Kokmen, E. (1999). Mild cognitive impairment: Clinical characterization and outcome. *Archives of Neurology, 56*, 303–308. http://dx.doi.org/10.1001/archneur.56.3.303

Price, J. L., Davis, P. B., Morris, J. C., & White, D. L. (1991). The distribution of tangles, plaques and related immunohistochemical markers in healthy aging and Alzheimer's disease. *Neurobiology of Aging, 12*, 295–312. http://dx.doi.org/10.1016/0197-4580(91)90006-6

Raz, N., & Rodrigue, K. M. (2006). Differential aging of the brain: Patterns, cognitive correlates and modifiers. *Neuroscience and Biobehavioral Reviews, 30*, 730–748. http://dx.doi.org/10.1016/j.neubiorev.2006.07.001

Richards, M., & Brayne, C. (2010). What do we mean by Alzheimer's disease? *British Medical Journal, 341*, 865–867.

Ritchie, K., & Kildea, D. (1995). Is senile dementia "age-related" or "ageing-related"?—Evidence from meta-analysis of dementia prevalence in the oldest old. *The Lancet, 346*, 931–934. http://dx.doi.org/10.1016/S0140-6736(95)91556-7

Roth, M., Huppert, F. A., Mountjoy, C. Q., & Tym, E. (1998). *The Cambridge examination of mental disorders of the elderly revised: CAMDEX-R.* Cambridge: Cambridge University Press.

Salthouse, T. A. (2011). Neuroanatomical substrates of age-related cognitive decline. *Psychological Bulletin, 137*, 753–784. http://dx.doi.org/10.1037/a0023262

Salthouse, T. A., & Becker, J. T. (1998). Independent effects of Alzheimer's disease on neuropsychological functioning. *Neuropsychology, 12*, 242–252. http://dx.doi.org/10.1037/0894-4105.12.2.242

Schneider, J. A., Arvanitakis, Z., Leurgans, S. E., & Bennett, D. A. (2009). The neuropathology of probable Alzheimer disease and mild cognitive impairment. *Annals of Neurology, 66*, 200–208. http://dx.doi.org/10.1002/ana.v66:2

Serra, L., Perri, R., Cercignani, M., Spano, B., Fadda, L., Marra, C., ... Bozzali, M. (2010). Are the behavioral symptoms of Alzheimer's disease directly associated with neurodegeneration? *Journal of Alzheimer's Disease, 21*, 627–639.

Siedlecki, K. L., Honig, L. S., & Stern, Y. (2008). Exploring the structure of a neuropsychological battery across healthy elders and those with questionable dementia and Alzheimer's disease. *Neuropsychology, 22*, 400–411. http://dx.doi.org/10.1037/0894-4105.22.3.400

Spaan, P. E. J. (2015). Episodic and semantic memory functioning in very old age: Explanations from executive functioning and processing speed theories. *Cogent Psychology, 2*, 1109782. http://dx.doi.org/10.1080/23311908.2015.1109782

Spaan, P. E. J. (2016). Episodic and semantic memory impairments in (very) early Alzheimer's disease: The diagnostic accuracy of paired-associate learning formats. *Cogent Psychology, 3*, 1125076. http://dx.doi.org/10.1080/23311908.2015.1125076

Spaan, P. E. J., & Dolan, C. V. (2010). Cognitive decline in normal ageing and early Alzheimer's disease: A continuous or discontinuous transition? *Behavioural Neurology, 23*, 203–206. http://dx.doi.org/10.1155/2010/946315

Spaan, P. E. J., Raaijmakers, J. G. W., & Jonker, C. (2003). Alzheimer's disease versus normal ageing: A review of the efficiency of clinical and experimental memory measures. *Journal of Clinical and Experimental Neuropsychology, 25*, 216–233. http://dx.doi.org/10.1076/jcen.25.2.216.13638

Spaan, P. E. J., Raaijmakers, J. G. W., & Jonker, C. (2005). Early assessment of dementia: The contribution of different memory components. *Neuropsychology, 19*, 629–640. http://dx.doi.org/10.1037/0894-4105.19.5.629

West, M. J., Coleman, P. D., Flood, D. G., & Troncoso, J. C. (1994). Differences in the pattern of hippocampal neuronal loss in normal ageing and Alzheimer's disease. *The Lancet, 344*, 769–772. http://dx.doi.org/10.1016/S0140-6736(94)92338-8

Wilson, R. S. (2008). Neurological factors in cognitive aging. In S. M. Hofer & D. F. Alwin (Eds.), *Handbook of cognitive aging: Interdisciplinary perspectives* (pp. 298–307). Thousand Oaks, CA: Sage. http://dx.doi.org/10.4135/9781412976589

Wilson, R. S., Gilley, D. W., Bennett, D. A., Beckett, L. A., & Evans, D. A. (2000). Person-specific paths of cognitive decline in Alzheimer's disease and their relation to age. *Psychology and Aging, 15*, 18–28. http://dx.doi.org/10.1037/0882-7974.15.1.18

12

Neuropsychiatric symptoms and their impact on quality of life in multiple system atrophy

R. Ceponiene[1,2], S.D. Edland[1,3,4], T.N. Reid[5], A. Al Rizaiza[1] and I. Litvan[1,5]*

*Corresponding author: I. Litvan, Department of Neurosciences, University of California, San Diego, 8950 Villa La Jolla Drive, Suite C112, La Jolla, CA 92037, USA; University of Louisville, 1911 S 3rd Street, Louisville, KY 40208, USA

E-mail: ilitvan@ucsd.edu

Reviewing editor: Peter Walla, University of Newcastle, Australia

Abstract: *Background*: Multiple system atrophy (MSA) is a sporadic neurodegenerative disorder characterized by severe dysautonomia and atypical Parkinsonism or cerebellar dysfunction. Disease-modifying treatment is not available and the mainstream of care is supportive. Neuropsychiatric symptoms are frequent in MSA and their successful management can improve patients' quality of life (QOL). This study aimed to define a comprehensive neuropsychiatric profile in MSA patients in relation to QOL. *Methods*: In 48 MSA patients and 40 controls neuropsychiatric symptoms were assessed using Neuropsychiatric Inventory. MSA patients completed Beck Depression Inventory and QOL questionnaire (SF12), including Mental and Physical subscales. *Results*: Eighty-seven percent of MSA patients had neuropsychiatric symptoms as compared with 10.4% of controls. Depression (56%), apathy (48%), anxiety (27%), and agitation (27%) predominated. The Physical SF-12 scores were lower in the patients as compared with the controls. Neuropsychiatric Inventory (NPI) scores did not correlate with QOL measures. Depression, as reflected by the BDI, correlated with the mental component score of the SF-12 in MSA patients. *Conclusions*: Neuropsychiatric symptoms are very frequent in patients with MSA and are dominated by depression and apathy. They appear independent from physical disability and loosely map onto the known brain pathology of MSA. Only depression,

ABOUT THE AUTHORS

This study was done under the lead of professor I. Litvan, a world-renowned expert in movement disorders and a director of the University of California, San Diego National Parkinson Foundation Center of Excellence. The Center does clinical, basic, and cutting edge technology research aiming at the improvement of the diagnosis, understanding etiopathogenesis of motor, autonomic, and cognitive manifestations of parkinsonian disorders, as well as developing new treatments and comprehensive care models. Atypical parkinsonian disorders is special interest and expertise of Litvan's. This study examined the neuropsychiatric aspects of Multiple System Atrophy, a relatively neglected aspect of the disorder with a potential to affect quality of life. R. Ceponiene has published extensively in the field of cognitive neurodevelopmental neurophysiology and aging. During preparation of this manuscript, she acted as a movement disorders fellow in the Center and now works as a movement disorders specialist at Kaiser Permanente, San Diego.

PUBLIC INTEREST STATEMENT

Multiple system atrophy (MSA) is an atypical parkinsonian condition manifested by severe autonomic dysfunction and movement difficulties. No treatments are available to slow down the disease, and patient care focuses on symptom treatment. Neuropsychiatric symptoms have been reported in MSA however their extent and nature has not been investigated. In this study, we showed that these symptoms affect almost 90% of MSA patients, the most frequent being depression, apathy, anxiety, and agitation. Depression showed a strong negative impact on mental quality of life, when assessed by a patient-reported questionnaire. Therefore, it will be important to evaluate the relationships between all neuropsychiatric symptoms and quality of life using self-reported measures. Awareness of the prevalence and nature of the neuropsychiatric symptoms in MSA will help to detect and treat them, as well as counsel the patients and their families, thereby improving the quality of life in individuals with this unforgiving disorder.

as reflected by the BDI, negatively affected mental QOL. The discrepancy between the BDI and NPI-depression scores likely stems from the different approaches to symptoms by these questionnaires.

Subjects: Bioscience; Health and Social Care; Medicine, Dentistry, Nursing & Allied Health

Keywords: apathy; depression; multiple system atrophy; Parkinsonism; neuropsychiatric symptoms

1. Introduction

Multiple system atrophy (MSA) is a sporadic, adult-onset neurodegenerative disorder manifesting primarily with autonomic dysfunction and an atypical Parkinsonism or ataxia (Gilman et al., 2008). The prevalence of MSA is 2–5 per 100,000 and average life expectancy is 7–9 years from diagnosis. At this time no disease-modifying treatments are available and the mainstream of care is supportive. Mood and behavioral symptoms are potentially modifiable and their successful management may improve the quality of life (QOL) of the MSA patients and help to understand the underlying pathophysiology. In previous studies, we were able to delineate distinct neuropsychiatric impairment profiles in related neurodegenerative disorders including corticobasal degeneration (CBD) and progressive supranuclear palsy (PSP) (Litvan, Cummings, & Mega, 1998; Litvan, Mega, Cummings, & Fairbanks, 1996; Litvan, Paulsen, Mega, & Cummings, 1998), and these profiles paralleled the known structural and functional abnormalities of CBD and PSP.

Depression is the best studied neuropsychiatric symptom in MSA. Its prevalence is as high as 40–86% (Balas, Balash, Giladi, & Gurevich, 2010; Kao et al., 2009; Schrag et al., 2010; Siri et al., 2013; Tison, Yekhlef, & Chrysostome, 2006), and its impact on QOL in MSA patients was found to be comparable to that of motor and autonomic symptoms (Benrud-Larson, Sandroni, Schrag, & Low, 2005; Schrag et al., 2006, 2010). Only two studies so far studied a broader neuropsychiatric symptom profile in MSA (Kao et al., 2009; Siri et al., 2013). They used the Neuropsychiatric Inventory (NPI) to assess the frequency and severity of 10 behavioral and 2 neurovegetative symptoms (Cummings et al., 1994). In a multi-center European study Siri et al. (2013) found that in their MSA patients with Parkinsonism (MSA-P, n = 39) the highest NPI scores were for depression, irritability, and anxiety, while in the MSA patients with ataxia (MSA-C, n = 22) the highest scores were for apathy, agitation, and depression. Further, the NPI-depression scores were comparable between the MSA (n = 61) and Parkinson disease (PD) patients (n = 20) but the self-reported Geriatric Depression Scale (GDS) scores were higher in the MSA than in the PD patients of that study. In the second study that utilized NPI, Kao et al. (2009) compared cognitive and psychiatric profiles between patients with PD, MSA, and LBD. In their 10 patients with MSA the most prevalent symptoms were depression, apathy, and anxiety. The NPI-depression scores were significantly lower in the MSA than in the other patient groups, while the GDS did not differ among the three groups.

Therefore, while several neuropsychiatric symptoms appear to be frequent in MSA, including depression, irritability, anxiety, and apathy, more studies are needed to determine their relative prevalence and impact on QOL in MSA. Further, the comparison groups in the aforementioned studies were patients with PD and Lewy Body Dementia, without an inclusion of a healthy control group. Using healthy peers as controls would minimize the reference group variability and increase generalizability of the results. Finally, the self-reported (GDS) vs. caregiver-reported (NPI) measures yielded somewhat different results in these previous studies, warranting further inquiry into these measures. Therefore, the main aims of the present study were to determine a comprehensive neuropsychiatric profile in patients with MSA using the NPI (Cummings et al., 1994), in comparison with a healthy peer control group; to investigate the relationships between the neuropsychiatric symptoms captured by the NPI vs. BDI and QOL; and to compare the patient (self) and caregiver assessments of the depressive symptoms.

2. Methods

2.1. Subjects

This study included 48 consecutive MSA patients evaluated at the University of Louisville Movement Disorders Clinic between 2003 and 2008 who met the second consensus criteria for probable ($n = 21$) or possible ($n = 27$) MSA (Gilman et al., 2008). Forty-six patients had MSA-P and two patients had MSA-C. With patients' informed consent, their caregivers completed a NPI questionnaire (Cummings et al., 1994). The caregivers were spouses or other family members who interacted with the patients on a daily basis.

Forty healthy participants, similar to the MSA patients in age, gender, education, and ethnicity, served as controls. Control participant data were published previously (Litvan et al., 1996; Litvan, Cummings et al., 1998). Control participants were residents of a Southern California retirement community. They were administered the Mini-Mental State Examination (MMSE) and had to score 25 or above to be included in the study. In addition, their spouses were asked about any concerns regarding any signs of dementia or memory loss. If these concerns were denied, the spouses filled out the NPI questionnaire. All participants signed institutional informed consents. The study was approved by the IRBs of the University of Louisville and UCLA.

2.2. Measures

The Mini-Mental State Examination (MMSE) (Folstein, Folstein, & McHugh, 1975) was administered to each study participant. Patients completed the *Beck Depression Inventory-II (BDI-II)*, which is a 21-item scale assessing the behavioral, cognitive, somatic, and affective symptoms of depression within the past two weeks (Beck & Steer, 1993). BDI-II scores ≥14 indicate mild depression, ≥20 moderate depression, and those ≥29 indicate severe depression. The caregivers of the MSA patients (spouses or other family members) completed the *NPI* (Cummings et al., 1994), which assesses the frequency and severity of 10 behavioral (depression, apathy, anxiety, agitation, irritability, disinhibition, hallucinations, delusions, euphoria, and aberrant motor behavior) and two neurovegetative domains. The original, 10-item behavioral version was used in this study since it has been validated for content and reliability and avoided confounds with vegetative symptoms of MSA. Symptom frequency was rated using a 1–4 scale and the severity is rated using a 1–3 scale (higher scores for more severe). The composite score for each behavioral domain is the product of the frequency and severity subscores for that particular behavior and can attain a maximum value of 12. The total NPI score is the sum of the subscale scores. The *Unified Parkinson's Disease Rating Scale (UPDRS)* (Movement Disorder Society Task Force on Rating Scales for Parkinson's Disease, 2003) was administered to all MSA patients to assess the severity of motor and non-motor symptoms. The UPDRS is the main standardized clinical assessment tool in Parkinson's disease and atypical parkinsonian disorders. Of the four subscales of the UPDRS, we obtained the non-motor daily living subscale, UPDRS-1, which is obtained from the patient with help from a caregiver if needed. The motor subscale, UPDRS-3, is obtained during examination by a health care provider and assesses rigidity, bradykinesia, tremor, gait, and balance. Although there are now specific scales for MSA, those were not available when the study was conducted. To assess health-related QOL in the MSA patients, the Physical Component score and Mental Component score of the *Twelve-item Short-Form Health Survey (SF-12)* (Ware, Kosinski, Turner-Boweker, & Gandeck, 2007), were used. The SF-12 is a US 1998 population-normed instrument allowing placement of an individual in a population-based reference framework. In this scale, the mean is 50 and the standard deviation is 10 (higher score means better QOL). The SF-12 was completed by the patients themselves.

2.3. Statistical analyses

The between-group comparisons of demographic characteristics and composite NPI scores were done using t-tests for continuous variables and Fisher's exact test for discrete variables. Correlation analyses assessing for associations between NPI scores, BDI scores, UPDRS, disease duration, and QOL measures from SF-12 Mental component and SF-12 Physical component scores in MSA cases were performed using the non-parametric Spearman Rank Correlation coefficient. Non-parametric correlation coefficients were used to accommodate skewed distributions and the lack of linear association between some of the variables.

3. Results

Descriptive subject characteristics are presented in Table 1. There was between-group age difference ($p = .05$) and there were relatively more males in the MSA group. However, there was no between-group difference in the MMSE scores. Of the QOL measures, the distribution of SF-12 Mental component score of the MSA group was similar to that of the instrument population norms: 49.83 ± 9.29 vs. 50 ± 10, respectively. The SF-12 Physical component score was significantly lower in the MSA group than that in the general population: 32 ± 8.7 vs. 50 ± 10. The SF-12 Physical component score correlated negatively with the UPDRS motor examination score ($r = -.339$, $p < .02$; Table 2). The SF-12 Mental component score correlated negatively with disease duration ($r = -.293$, $p < .04$), UPDRS non-motor symptom subscale ($r = -.291$, $p < .02$), as well as BDI scores as noted in Table 2.

The BDI showed that 37.5% of patients with MSA had symptoms of depression, mild in 27% (13/48) of patients, moderate in 10.4% (5/48), and no patient had a BDI score in the severe range. However, nine patients reported having had recent suicidal ideations. The BDI scores correlated positively with the disease duration ($r = .337$, $p < .02$) and strongly and negatively with SF-12 Mental component scores ($r = -.542$, $p < .0001$).

According to NPI, 87% of MSA patients had at least one neuropsychiatric symptom, as compared with 10.4% of controls. In both groups, the most prevalent symptom was depression. In addition to depression (56%), MSA patients showed significantly more apathy (48%), anxiety (27%), agitation (27%), and hallucinations (15%) than controls (Table 3, Figure 1). There was a trend for apathy and depression to co-occur: of 27 patients with depression, 16 showed apathy (59%) while out of 21 patients without depression, 7 showed apathy (33%, Fisher's exact test $p = .09$).

The total NPI scores in the MSA group did not correlate with either the physical or mental component scores of SF-12 questionnaire (Table 2). There were no significant correlations between the NPI scores of depression, apathy, or anxiety and the BDI scores. The NPI depression scores correlated weakly but significantly with UPDRS non-motor symptom subscale that assesses cognitive, mood, sleep, and autonomic symptoms. The NPI apathy scores correlated significantly and positively with age while NPI anxiety scores tended to correlate negatively with age. Agitation correlated with irritability, and significantly and negatively with the UPDRS non-motor symptom subscale. Hallucinations correlated with delusions and the total NPI score. UPDRS motor examination score correlated negatively with SF-12 Physical component score and showed a trend for negative correlation with SF-12 Mental component score. The BDI scores correlated positively with the disease duration and strongly and negatively with SF-12 Mental component scores.

Table 1. Demographic characteristics and MMSE of MSA and control study groups (Mean ± SD)

Characteristics	MSA (n = 48)	Controls (n = 40)
Age, years	69.75 ± 10.58	73.55 ± 5.97 *
Gender, M/F	35/13	20/20 *
Disease duration, years	5.56 ± 3.55	na
MMSE	28.75 ± 1.58	28.43 ± 1.34
UPDRS-1 (out of 55)	2.04 ± 1.54	n/a
UPDRS-2 (out of 55)	16.81 ± 10.23	n/a
UPDRS-3 (out of 72)	24.21 ± 10.11	n/a
UPDRS-total (out of 199)	41.73 ± 15.89	n/a

*$p < .05$.

Table 2. Correlations that were significant or showed strong trends between the NPI, BDI, SF-12, UPDRS, disease duration in the MSA patient group. (*r* value/*p* value)

	Age	DUR	SF12-M	SF-P	U-1	U-3	DEP	HAL	IRR	DEL
BDI	−.201	**.337**	**−.542**	−.204	.128	.205	.111	.117	.036	.091
	.20	**.02**	**.0001**	.16	.39	.16	.45	.43	.80	.54
APA	**.327**	−.108	−.045	−.011	.004	.185	.225	.187	.250	.029
	.023	.47	.76	.93	.98	.21	.12	.20	.08	.85
DEP	−.103	−.186	−.065	−.065	**.285**	−.143	1	−.052	.083	.201
	.48	.21	.96	.66	**.05**	.33		.72	.57	.17
ANX	−.274	−.042	−.203	.065	−.262	−.049	.062	−.022	−.014	−.125
	.06	.78	.17	.66	.26	.74	.67	.88	.92	.40
AGI	−.099	−.073	.039	−.143	**−.340**	.003	.007	.174	**.298**	.148
	.50	.62	.79	.33	**.02**	.98	.93	.24	**.04**	.31
HAL	.151	.045	−.160	−.238	.124	.159	−.053	1	.247	**.510**
	.30	.76	.28	.10	.40	.28	.72		.09	**.0002**
SF12-P	.190	−.071	−.028	1	−.096	**−.339**	−.065	−.238	.003	−.187
	.20	.63	.85		.52	**.02**	.66	.10	.99	.20
SF12-M	.092	**−.293**	1	−.028	**−.291**	−.254	−.008	−.169	−.062	.022
	.54	**.04**		.85	**.045**	.08	.96	.28	.68	.88
U-2	.067	.255	−.193	−.145	.241	**.590**	−.238	.113	.038	−.034
	.65	.08	.19	.32	.10	**.00001**	.10	.45	.80	.82

Notes: AGE: age, AGI: agitation, ANX: anxiety, APA-apathy, BDI: Beck depression inventory, DEL: delusions, DEP: depression, DUR: disease duration, HAL: hallucinations, IRR: irritability, NPI-T: total NPI score, SF12-P: SF12 Physical score, SF12-M: SF12 Mental score, U-1: UPDRS part I (non-motor daily living score), U-3: UPDRS part III (motor score).

Table 3. Neuropsychiatric inventory (NPI) composite scores (maximum 12) in patients with MSA and their controls (Mean ± SD, % of patients)

Behavior	MSA (*n* = 48)	Controls (*n* = 40)
Depression/Dysphoria	1.56 ± 2.31, 56.3%**	.23 ± 1.06, 5.1%
Apathy/Indifference	1.65 ± 2.54, 47.9% ***	0
Anxiety	.60 ± 1.28, 27.1%**	0
Agitation/Aggression	.60 ± 1.41, 27.1%**	0
Hallucination	.21 ± .54, 14.6%*	0
Disinhibition	.52 ± 1.97, 12.5%	.13 ± .656, 5%
Irritability/Lability	.21 ± .68, 10.4%	.05 ± .32, 2.5%
Delusions	.06 ± .32, 4.25%	0
NPI, total	5.42 ± 5.46, 87.55***	.41 ± 1.68, 10.35

*$p < .05$.

**$p < .01$.

***$p < .001$.

The frequency of depressive symptoms was higher (56.3%) when assessed by the NPI than by the self-reported BDI (37.5%). In the NPI, 39.5% (19/48) of patients showed mild, 12.5% (6/48) showed moderate, and 4% (2/48) showed severe symptoms, while in the BDI, no patient showed severe depression.

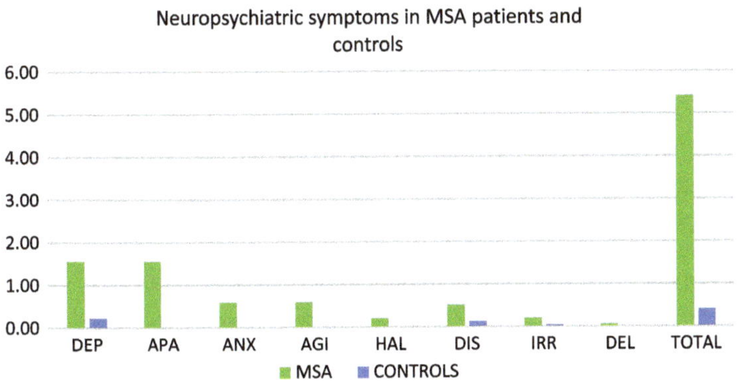

Figure 1. Total neuropsychiatric inventory scores (symptom severity x frequency) in MSA patients and controls.

Notes: AGI: agitation, ANX: anxiety, APA-apathy, DEL: delusions, DEP: depression, DIS: disinhibition, HAL: hallucinations, IRR: irritability, TOTAL: total NPI score.

4. Discussion

In summary, our study found that neuropsychiatric symptoms are very frequent in cognitively intact patients with MSA. Depression and apathy dominated profile, followed by anxiety and agitation. Depression, but only as reflected by BDI, correlated negatively with the mental QOL. In addition, mental QOL, as reflected by the SF-12 Mental component scores, correlated negatively with disease duration and with UPDRS non-motor symptom subscale. None of the NPI scores, including the NPI-depression score, correlated with any of the QOL measures. Physical QOL, as measured by the SF-12 Physical component scores, correlated negatively with UPDRS motor examination scores.

The high incidence of neuropsychiatric symptoms in MSA in our study was comparable to that in other parkinsonian disorders, and the symptom profile was most reminiscent of that in CBD which is also dominated by depression, apathy, irritability, and agitation (Litvan, Cummings, et al., 1998; Litvan, Paulsen, et al., 1998). The frequency of depression in MSA found in our study (56%) was within the 40–80% range reported in previous studies (Balas et al., 2010; Kao et al., 2009; Schrag et al., 2010; Siri et al., 2013; Tison et al., 2006). The strong negative correlation between the BDI and SF-12 Mental component scores suggests that depression worsens the QOL in these patients. Further, the fact that the BDI scores did not correlate with the SF-12 Physical component scores argues against the idea of physical disability being a significant contributor to the depression in MSA (or vice versa). Moreover, while both the depression (per the BDI) and mental QOL worsened with disease duration, physical QOL did not show such correlations. Even though the Physical QOL correlated with the objective measures of UPDRS motor examination scores, at least in this patient sample, neither correlated with the disease duration. This underscores the increasing impact of non-motor symptoms on the QOL as the disease progresses over time. Granted, patients with a progressive and potentially life-ending condition have strong objective reasons to feel depressed. However, less than half of our patients did not report depression; this suggests a range in the biologically based vulnerability to depression, which likely interacts with the pathological changes specific to MSA, resulting in the development of depression irrespective of motor or autonomic impairment. Specifically, depression in MSA can be mediated by the degeneration of noradrenergic and dopaminergic neurons of the brainstem (Lewis et al., 2012; Matsuura et al., 2013), as well as the prefrontal lobe and limbic systems (Balas et al., 2010; Herting et al., 2007; Siri et al., 2013; Stankovic et al., 2014).

In addition to depression (per the BDI), the mental QOL correlated with the UPDRS non-motor living subscale. The latter is mostly patient reported and assesses cognitive impairment, hallucinations, depression, anxiety, agitation, apathy, and impulsiveness (symptoms of dopamine dysregulation syndrome). However, these same symptoms, as measured by the NPI, did not correlate with the SF-12 Mental component scores. Further, there were no correlations between the BDI and the NPI scores of depression, anxiety, or apathy. It therefore appears that the BDI and NPI measure different aspects of depression; conceivably, the BDI is more reflective of the inner experiences (self-report) whereas the NPI is more reflective of the behavioral manifestations (caregiver report). The non-demented patients, such as those with MSA, while being aware of their depression, may also be able and willing to conceal it from their caregivers. On the other hand, the caregivers themselves can be influenced by their observational skills, relationship with the patient, and their own distress. Low agreement rates between the self and caregiver reports have been reported earlier (McKinlay et al., 2008) and could explain the discrepancy between the different measures in this study as well as in the earlier studies that used NPI along with the self-reported measures (Siri et al., 2013). Interestingly however, the NPI depression scores correlated with the mostly self-reported UPDRS non-motor symptom subscale, suggesting that some symptoms from the self-reported UPDRS are reflected in the NPI as well, possibly those that are more readily observable. However, in non-demented populations such as MSA patients, self-reports might be preferable due to the better correlation with self-perceived QOL, as suggested by the findings of the present study. Clearly, further studies are needed to clarify these complex relationships between the self vs. caregiver reports. Larger numbers of healthy participants as well as patients with Parkinson spectrum disorders with and without cognitive impairment will need to be assessed using caregiver and self-reported questionnaires, including caregivers as a study population. This would also shed light onto the impact of a caregiver burden onto the QOL of MSA patients.

Apathy was the second most frequent neuropsychiatric feature of MSA in our study, affecting almost half of the patients. It was previously reported in PSP (91% of 22 patients (Litvan et al., 1996)) and CBD (40% of 12 patients (Litvan, Cummings, et al., 1998)). While apathy was previously reported in MSA (Fetoni, Soliveri, Monza, Testa, & Girotti, 1999; Kao et al., 2009; Siri et al., 2013), it had not been considered a salient aspect of the MSA profile. Nonetheless, in Siri et al. study (2013), the NPI apathy score was the fourth highest in their MSA-P patients, and it was the highest score in their 22 MSA-C patients. Further, Kao et al. (2009) found that 4 of their 10 patients with MSA exhibited apathy which was the second frequent symptom after depression. Finally, Fetoni et al. (1999) found that 11 out of 12 patients had blunted affect on a Brief Psychiatric Rating scale which may suggest apathy. The neuropathologic substrate of apathy/abulia is medial-opercular frontal lobe—basal ganglia circuit (Jorge, Starkstein, & Robinson, 2010). In addition, in a review of 240 stroke cases, basal ganglia lesions most frequently manifested with apathy, and the majority of abulia cases were associated with lesions in the caudate nucleus (Bhatia & Marsden, 1994). Deficiency in dopaminergic and cholinergic transmission has been implicated in apathy as well (Allain, Bentue-Ferrer, & Lacomblez, 2004). Therefore, apathy appears a frequent feature of MSA, and there is a substantial overlap between the neural bases of apathy and those of MSA. Given the involvement of frontal–subcortical networks in both, future studies should assess apathy in MSA in relation to executive functioning rather than in relation to MMSE that is insensitive to frontal lobe dysfunction.

In our study, apathy did not correlate with measures of QOL. It tended to correlate with irritability, as previously found in CBD (Litvan, Cummings, et al., 1998). While the NPI-apathy scores did not correlate with NPI-depression scores, there was a tendency for the patients who appeared depressed to also appear apathetic—more frequently than for those patients who did not appear depressed. This could be a true phenomenon but could also be caused by the overlapping overt manifestations of apathy and depression. Therefore, future studies should assess the impact of apathy on QOL using caregiver as well as self-reported measures, such as Apathy Evaluation Scale (Marin, Biedrzycki, & Firinciogullari, 1991) or a Dimensional apathy scale (Radakovic & Abrahams, 2014). Finally, in our study apathy worsened with age but not with the disease duration. This is puzzling since the disease duration increases with age. One possible explanation is smaller variance of the disease duration (standard deviation of 7 years) as compared with that of age (20 years). Alternatively, the diverging trajectories of apathy, anxiety, as well as depression with age may suggest differential susceptibilities of the respective underlying networks to aging and the disease process. However, clarification of the underpinnings of these different trajectories would require further, longitudinal studies, and utilization of functional imaging tools. Differentiating apathy from depression or physical symptoms of illness is very important due to their differential impact on prognosis and management. Specifically, apathy, and not depression, was associated with lower cognitive functioning, progressive decline, and lower QOL in patients with stroke and neurodegenerative disorders (Jorge et al., 2010; Levy et al., 1998;

Tang, Lau, Mok, Ungvari, & Wong, 2013). Further, apathy is a potential side effect of SSRI therapy (Zahodne et al., 2012) and therefore consideration should be given to treating apathy and depression in MSA with SNRIs (rather than SSRIs), cholinesterase inhibitors (Figiel & Sadowsky, 2008), MAO-B inhibitors, D2/D3 agonists (Thobois et al., 2013), or stimulants.

In our patient sample, over a quarter of patients exhibited symptoms of anxiety and over a quarter of patients exhibited symptoms of agitation. This is somewhat less than the earlier reported frequency of 33–37% (Kao et al., 2009; Schrag et al., 2010; Siri et al., 2013). In our study, these symptoms did not correlate with QOL. In contrast, Schrag et al. (2010) found a correlation between anxiety and health-related QOL in their large group of MSA patients (n = 286), however they used a self-reported questionnaire. Anxiety is always a rather disabling symptom and should be considered and treated in MSA patients. Hallucinations and delusions are unusual in MSA (Kao et al., 2009; Siri et al., 2013) and in our study, they were rare and explained by dopaminergic medications in all but one patient who had a concurrent urinary tract infection. Thus, presence of hallucinations in MSA points to medications, infections, or metabolic disorders.

The strengths of the present study are that it provides the full neuropsychiatric symptom profile in a relatively large group of well-characterized MSA patients, in comparison with their healthy peers. It emphasizes the high incidence of treatable neuropsychiatric symptoms in patients with MSA, including depression, apathy, anxiety, and agitation, offering the potential to improve their QOL. A variety of treatments are available including education, medications, support groups, and cognitive behavioral therapies, allowing for clinical intervention studies. One study limitation is a small number of MSA-C patients, since their neuropsychiatric profile may be different. Further, this study revealed the need for further research to characterize the relationships between the self vs caregiver reported neuropsychiatric symptoms in cognitively intact populations such as patients with MSA.

In summary, this study was the first to assess the frequency of neuropsychiatric symptoms in MSA in relation to healthy controls. It showed that these symptoms affect almost 90% of patients. Depression and apathy were encountered in about half of the patients each and anxiety and agitation were encountered in about a quarter of patients each. The neural bases of these symptoms appear to loosely map onto those of MSA, however further functional neuroimaging studies are needed to clarify the neural underpinnings. Neuropsychiatric symptoms did not correlate with objective measures of physical disability or subjective physical QOL, making the causal link between them unlikely. Depression showed a strong negative correlation with mental QOL, however only when assessed by a patient-reported instrument (BDI) and not when assessed by a caregiver reported instrument (NPI). Therefore, in the future it is important to evaluate the relationships between all neuropsychiatric symptoms and QOL using self-reported measures, which could be preferred in non-demented populations. Clinician's awareness of the prevalence and nature of the neuropsychiatric symptoms in MSA will help to detect and treat them as well as counsel the patients and their families, thereby improving the QOL in individuals with this unforgiving disorder.

Acknowledgments
We thank all MSA patients and their caregivers for participating in this study, as well as David Houghton, MD and Jay Ferrara, MD for patient referral. We thank Dr. Jeffrey Cummings for contributing control participant's data.

Funding
This work was supported by National Institute on Aging [grant number AG005131].

Competing interest
The authors declare no competing interest.

Author details

R. Ceponiene[1,2]
E-mail: rita.ceponiene@kp.org
ORCID ID: http://orcid.org/0000-0003-2417-8180
S.D. Edland[1,3,4]
E-mail: sedland@ucsd.edu
T.N. Reid[5]
E-mail: tnreid01@gmail.com
A. Al Rizaiza[1]
E-mail: adeeb15@gmail.com
I. Litvan[1,5]
E-mail: ilitvan@ucsd.edu
[1] Department of Neurosciences, University of California, San Diego, 8950 Villa La Jolla Drive, Suite C112, La Jolla, CA 92037, USA.
[2] Southern California Physician Medical Group, Kaiser Permanente, 4405 Vandever Ave, San Diego, CA 92120, USA.
[3] Department of Family and Preventive Medicine, Division of Biostatistics and Bioinformatics, University of California, San Diego, 9500 Gilman Dr. La Jolla, La Jolla, CA, USA.

[4] Department of Neurosciences, University of California, San Diego, 9500 Gilman Dr. La Jolla, La Jolla, CA, USA.

[5] University of Louisville, 1911 S 3rd Street, Louisville, KY 40208, USA.

References

Allain, H., Bentue-Ferrer, D., & Lacomblez, L. (2004). Biology of motivation. *Psychologie & Neuropsychiatrie du Vieillissement, 2*, 167–172.

Balas, M., Balash, Y., Giladi, N., & Gurevich, T. (2010). Cognition in multiple system atrophy: Neuropsychological profile and interaction with mood. *Journal of Neural Transmission, 117*, 369–375. http://dx.doi.org/10.1007/s00702-009-0365-z

Beck, A. T., & Steer, R. A. (1993). *Beck depression inventory manual*. San Antonio, TX: Psychological Corporation.

Benrud-Larson, L. M., Sandroni, P., Schrag, A., & Low, P. A. (2005). Depressive symptoms and life satisfaction in patients with multiple system atrophy. *Movement Disorders, 20*, 951–957. http://dx.doi.org/10.1002/(ISSN)1531-8257

Bhatia, K. P., & Marsden, C. D. (1994). The behavioural and motor consequences of focal lesions of the basal ganglia in man. *Brain, 117*, 859–876. http://dx.doi.org/10.1093/brain/117.4.859

Cummings, J. L., Mega, M., Gray, K., Rosenberg-Thompson, S., Carusi, D. A., & Gornbein, J. (1994). The neuropsychiatric inventory: Comprehensive assessment of psychopathology in dementia. *Neurology, 44*, 2308–2308. http://dx.doi.org/10.1212/WNL.44.12.2308

Fetoni, V., Soliveri, P., Monza, D., Testa, D., & Girotti, F. (1999). Affective symptoms in multiple system atrophy and Parkinson's disease: Response to levodopa therapy. *Journal of Neurology, Neurosurgery & Psychiatry, 66*, 541–544. http://dx.doi.org/10.1136/jnnp.66.4.541

Figiel, G., & Sadowsky, C. (2008). A systematic review of the effectiveness of rivastigmine for the treatment of behavioral disturbances in dementia and other neurological disorders. *Current Medical Research and Opinion, 24*, 157–166. http://dx.doi.org/10.1185/030079908X260961

Folstein, M. F., Folstein, S. E., & McHugh, P. R. (1975). "Mini-mental state". *Journal of Psychiatric Research, 12*, 189–198. http://dx.doi.org/10.1016/0022-3956(75)90026-6

Gilman, S., Wenning, G. K., Low, P. A., Brooks, D. J., Mathias, C. J., Trojanowski, J. Q., ... Vidailhet, M. (2008). Second consensus statement on the diagnosis of multiple system atrophy. *Neurology, 71*, 670–676. http://dx.doi.org/10.1212/01.wnl.0000324625.00404.15

Herting, B., Beuthien-Baumann, B., Pöttrich, K., Donix, M., Triemer, A., Lampe, J. B., ... Holthoff, V. A. (2007). Prefrontal cortex dysfunction and depression in atypical parkinsonian syndromes. *Movement Disorders, 22*, 490–497. http://dx.doi.org/10.1002/(ISSN)1531-8257

Jorge, R. E., Starkstein, S. E., & Robinson, R. G. (2010). Apathy following stroke. *Canadian Journal of psychiatry revue Canadienne de Psychiatrie, 55*, 350–354.

Kao, A. W., Racine, C. A., Quitania, L. C., Kramer, J. H., Christine, C. W., & Miller, B. L. (2009). Cognitive and neuropsychiatric profile of the synucleinopathies. *Alzheimer Disease & Associated Disorders, 23*, 365–370. http://dx.doi.org/10.1097/WAD.0b013e3181b5065d

Levy, M. L., Cummings, J. L., Fairbanks, L. A., Masterman, D., Miller, B. L., Craig, A. H., ... Litvan, I. (1998). Apathy is not depression. *The Journal of Neuropsychiatry and Clinical Neurosciences, 10*, 314–319. http://dx.doi.org/10.1176/jnp.10.3.314

Lewis, S. J., Pavese, N., Rivero-Bosch, M., Eggert, K., Oertel, W., Mathias, C. J., & Gerhard, A. (2012). Brain monoamine systems in multiple system atrophy: A positron emission tomography study. *Neurobiology of Disease, 46*, 130–136. http://dx.doi.org/10.1016/j.nbd.2011.12.053

Litvan, I., Cummings, J. L., & Mega, M. (1998). Neuropsychiatric features of corticobasal degeneration. *Journal of Neurology, Neurosurgery & Psychiatry, 65*, 717–721. http://dx.doi.org/10.1136/jnnp.65.5.717

Litvan, I., Mega, M. S., Cummings, J. L., & Fairbanks, L. (1996). Neuropsychiatric aspects of progressive supranuclear palsy. *Neurology, 47*, 1184–1189. http://dx.doi.org/10.1212/WNL.47.5.1184

Litvan, I., Paulsen, J. S., Mega, M. S., & Cummings, J. L. (1998). Neuropsychiatric assessment of patients with hyperkinetic and hypokinetic movement disorders. *Archives of Neurology, 55*, 1313–1319. http://dx.doi.org/10.1001/archneur.55.10.1313

Marin, R. S., Biedrzycki, R. C., & Firinciogullari, S. (1991). Reliability and validity of the apathy evaluation scale. *Psychiatry Research, 38*, 143–162. http://dx.doi.org/10.1016/0165-1781(91)90040-V

Matsuura, K., Maeda, M., Yata, K., Ichiba, Y., Yamaguchi, T., Kanamaru, K., & Tomimoto, H. (2013). Neuromelanin magnetic resonance imaging in Parkinson's disease and multiple system atrophy. *European Neurology, 70*, 70–77. http://dx.doi.org/10.1159/000350291

McKinlay, A., Grace, R. C., Dalrymple-Alford, J. C., Anderson, T. J., Fink, J., & Roger, D. (2008). Neuropsychiatric problems in Parkinson's disease: Comparisons between self and caregiver report. *Aging & Mental Health, 12*, 647–653.

Movement Disorder Society Task Force on Rating Scales for Parkinson's Disease. (2003). The Unified Parkinson's Disease Rating Scale (UPDRS): Status and recommendations. *Movement Disorders: Official Journal of the Movement Disorder Society, 18*, 738–750.

Radakovic, R., & Abrahams, S. (2014). Developing a new apathy measurement scale: Dimensional apathy scale. *Psychiatry Research, 219*, 658–663. http://dx.doi.org/10.1016/j.psychres.2014.06.010

Schrag, A., Geser, F., Stampfer-Kountchev, M., Seppi, K., Sawires, M., Köllensperger, M., ... European MSA-Study Group. (2006). Health-related quality of life in multiple system atrophy. *Movement Disorders, 21*, 809–815. http://dx.doi.org/10.1002/mds.20808

Schrag, A., Sheikh, S., Quinn, N. P., Lees, A. J., Selai, C., Mathias, C., ... Jahanshahi, M. (2010). A comparison of depression, anxiety, and health status in patients with progressive supranuclear palsy and multiple system atrophy. *Movement Disorders, 25*, 1077–1081. http://dx.doi.org/10.1002/mds.22794

Siri, C., Duerr, S., Canesi, M., Delazer, M., Esselink, R., Bloem, B. R., ... Antonini, A. (2013). A cross-sectional multicenter study of cognitive and behavioural features in multiple system atrophy patients of the parkinsonian and cerebellar type. *Journal of Neural Transmission, 120*, 613–618. http://dx.doi.org/10.1007/s00702-013-0997-x

Stankovic, I., Krismer, F., Jesic, A., Antonini, A., Benke, T., Brown, R. G., on behalf of the Movement Disorders Society MSA (MODIMSA) Study Group. (2014). Cognitive impairment in multiple system atrophy: A position statement by the neuropsychology task force of the MDS multiple system atrophy (MODIMSA) study group. *Movement Disorders, 29*, 857–867. http://dx.doi.org/10.1002/mds.v29.7

Tang, W. K., Lau, C. G., Mok, V., Ungvari, G. S., & Wong, K. S. (2013). Apathy and health-related quality of life in stroke. *Archives of Physical Medicine and Rehabilitation, 95*, 857–861.

Thobois, S., Lhommee, E., Klinger, H., Ardouin, C., Schmitt, E., Bichon, A., ... Krack, P. (2013). Parkinsonian apathy responds to dopaminergic stimulation of D2/D3 receptors with piribedil. *Brain, 136*, 1568–1577. http://dx.doi.org/10.1093/brain/awt067

Tison, F., Yekhlef, F., & Chrysostome, V. (2006). Depression and self-reported depressive symptoms in multiple system atrophy compared to Parkinson's disease. *Movement Disorders, 21*, 1056–1057. http://dx.doi.org/10.1002/(ISSN)1531-8257

Ware, J. E., Kosinski, M., Turner-Boweker, D., & Gandeck, B. (2007). *User's manual for the SF-12v2 Health Survey.* Lincoln, RI: Quality Metrics Incorporated and Health Assessment Lab.

Zahodne, L. B., Bernal-Pacheco, O., Bowers, D., Ward, H., Oyama, G., Limotai, N., ... Okun, M. S. (2012). Are selective serotonin reuptake inhibitors associated with greater apathy in Parkinson's disease? *The Journal of Neuropsychiatry and Clinical Neurosciences, 24*, 326–330. http://dx.doi.org/10.1176/appi.neuropsych.11090210

13

Hierarchy and dynamics of self-referential processing: The non-personal Me1 and the personal Me2 elicited via single words

Peter Walla[1,2] and Cornelia Herbert[3,4,5,6]*

*Corresponding author: Cornelia Herbert, Department of Psychology and Education, University of Ulm, Ulm, Germany; Department of Psychiatry, University of Tübingen, Tübingen, Germany; Department of Biomedical Resonance Imaging, University of Tübingen, Tübingen, Germany; Department of Psychology, University of Würzburg, Würzburg, Germany

E-mail: cornelia.herbert@psychologie. uni-wuerzburg.de

Reviewing editor: Sirous Mobini, University of East London, UK

Abstract: Recent electroencephalography (EEG) studies accumulated evidence that support a dynamic view of the self (multiple aspect theory). In this study, we test the specific hypothesis of the multiple aspect theory of the self by using EEG data from the HisMine paradigm. In the HisMine paradigm German pronouns are visually presented in a stream of additional stimuli, while changes in brain activity are determined by means of EEG. At an early cortical processing stage, the presentation of the possessive pronouns “mein” (“my”), “sein” (“his”) and “dein” (“your”) elicited significantly different brain activities when compared to the non-personal pronoun “ein” (“a”). At a later processing stage, cortical processing of the self-related possessive pronoun ("mein") differed from the processing of all other possessive and the non-personal pronoun. In line with previous observations (and the multiple aspect theory of the self), the early effect (here referred to as Me1) was found at specifically left occipito-parietal electrode locations (e.g. PO9), whereas the later effect (here referred to as Me2) occurred specifically at the left fronto-temporal electrode site, F7. This finding supports the idea that the human self is consisting of multiple aspects. Potential implications are discussed.

Subjects: Behavioral Sciences; Development Studies; Neuroscience

Keywords: self; self-referential processing; electroencephalography; language

ABOUT THE AUTHORS

Cornelia Herbert and Peter Walla form a cooperative partnership. Both authors contributed equally to this manuscript (shared first authorship and correspondence). Cornelia’s own individual neurophysiological focus is on the self, language and emotion, and the development of novel paradigms. Peter’s long-term interest focuses on an evolutionary perspective related to the development of the self. Their common applied interest is to unravel the boundary conditions of self-referential processing to contribute to a better understanding of clinical conditions with disordered self-aspects. In the present paper, EEG data from the HisMine paradigm was analysed with regard to the hypothesis of the multiple aspect theory of the self to test the validity and boundary conditions of this theoretical approach. The HisMine paradigm was developed by Cornelia Herbert within the framework of her grant HE5880/3-1.

PUBLIC INTEREST STATEMENT

The present study confirms previous findings supporting the idea that the human self is not a singular construct, but consists of at least two aspects that are processed by separate brain structures as part of a hierarchy. A Me1 represents any personal engagement (more like a We), while a Me2 then forms the proper self that is distinct and different from other. Those two aspects could represent developmental stages during early childhood. Further, respective knowledge might help to better diagnose and treat clinical conditions that are associated with disordered self-concepts.

1. Introduction

Since William James, the self has been a central topic in science and philosophy. With the advent of neuroimaging techniques, researchers started to investigate those brain structures involved in self-referential processing to better understand how brain activity contributes to the phenomenon of the self. Northoff and colleagues (2006) conducted a meta-analysis including nearly almost all studies on self-referential processing that were published between 2000 and 2004. The studies included in the meta-analysis used functional magnetic resonance imaging or positron emission tomography in combination with a broad range of tasks. The meta-analysis revealed the so-called cortical midline structures (CMS) as a network commonly activated in association with self-referential processing independently from task and stimulus modality. A more recent meta-analysis of 107 neuroimaging studies confirmed that especially the ventral medial prefrontal cortex as part of the CMS as well as the left ventrolateral prefrontal cortex and the left anterior insula are frequently activated during self-processing tasks that require participants to judge whether a stimulus is related to the self or somebody else (Denny, Kober, Wager, & Ochsner, 2012).

While those imaging studies answered the question which brain structures are associated with self-referential processing, a number of recent studies have explored the time course of self-referential processing by means of electroencephalography (EEG) or magnetencephalography. The results of these studies support the idea that self-referential processing is a dynamic process and related to different aspects of the self.

Walla et al., for instance, conducted a series of EEG and MEG studies whose results confirmed a multiple aspect theory of the self. The studies used language stimuli such as possessive pronouns combined with nouns (e.g. "my garden", "his garden" and "a garden") to elicit self-referential versus other-referential processing (e.g. Walla, Duregger, Greiner, Thurner, & Ehrenberger, 2008; Walla, Greiner, Duregger, Deecke, & Thurner, 2007). By doing so, it could be shown that at around 200 ms post-stimulus onset, self related stimuli such as "my garden" are processed similarly to other-related stimuli ("his garden") but that self- and other-related stimuli are processed differently from stimuli having no personal reference ("a garden"). Later though brain activity patterns elicited by self-related stimuli ("my garden") differed significantly from other-related stimuli ("his garden") as well as from personally unrelated stimuli ("a garden") at around 400 ms post-stimulus onset especially over left fronto-temporal areas. Taken together the results are in line with the ideas of the multiple aspect theory of the self (Walla et al., 2007). This theory assumes that the human brain first processes the self just as somebody else (other), but different from an un-personal condition (non- or un-personal self, Me1; more like a "We"), whereas only later then it considers information related to the self as distinct from information related to the other. This latter step might indicate the theoretical concept of an elaborate or proper self (personal self, Me2). The idea of two different aspects of the self is consistent with very early views about separate self-aspects such as the "Me" and the "I" that were suggested by James (1890) and that distinguish between at least two aspects of the self.

So far, a number of further EEG studies that all used pronoun–noun pairs (e.g. Herbert, Herbert, Ethofer, & Pauli, 2011; Herbert, Pauli, & Herbert, 2010) or pronouns as stimuli (Blume & Herbert, 2014; Shi, Zhou, Liu, Zhang, & Han, 2010; Zhou et al., 2010) have accumulated evidence in support of a dynamic and multiple aspect view of the self. Nevertheless, the results of these studies have been mixed with regard to the processing stages at which discrimination between self from non-self and self from other occurs: Herbert, Herbert, Ethofer, and Pauli (2011) used pronoun–noun pairs as stimuli. In contrast to Walla et al., pronoun–noun pairs could be of emotional or neutral content and self-referential or not (e.g. *my fear, his fear, the fear, my garden, his garden* and *the garden*). Participants' task was to read the words silently while EEG was recorded. Modulation of early brain potentials differentiated self- and other-related pronoun–noun pairs from those without personal reference, but showed—as predicted from the multiple aspect theory—no differentiation between self- and other-related pronoun–noun pairs. Moreover and again in line with the multiple aspect theory, modulation of late event-related brain potentials showed a clear processing advantage for self-related emotional pronoun–noun pairs as compared to other-related or unreferenced emotional word pairs at about 500 ms after stimulus onset. However, notably all other stimuli including self-related neutral pronoun–noun pairs did not elicit any significant event-related potential (ERP) amplitude changes in later time windows.

Shi et al. (2010) and Zhou et al. (2010) as well as Blume and Herbert (2014) investigated whether pronouns related to the self would be processed differently from pronouns unrelated to the self when these are presented visually either as rare stimuli in an oddball task or with the same presentation frequency amongst other stimuli in an RSVP design. While in the oddball tasks, Shi et al. and Zhou et al. found no generally significant differentiation between self- and other-related pronouns at early processing stages in line with the idea of a non-personal self, a near-significant trend towards larger P2 amplitudes for self- vs. other-related pronouns was observed at specifically the left frontal electrode site F7. Blume and Herbert (2014) could demonstrate that when stimuli are presented in rapid streams at a rate of for instance 2.5 Hz, self-related pronouns are spontaneously processed preferentially compared to other-related pronouns already during initial processing stages starting as early as in the P1 time window. The latter findings challenge the assumption that processing of simple self-related stimuli such as possessive pronouns would always reliably elicit the two prior described self- aspects (including the Me1 as a non-personal self, unable to discriminate self from other and an elaborate self, the Me2 able to discriminate self from other and self from non-self). However, in all three pronoun studies mentioned before, no comparisons between self-related with unrelated pronouns were included for why it is unclear whether and if so at which processing stage differentiation between personal and non-personal information might have taken place. Similarly, all three studies focused on the analyses of robust ERP effects, whereas Walla et al. analysed the whole time frame of cortical activity without looking at discrete ERP modulation patterns. Perhaps then, locally more refined temporal analyses of ERP effects as reported by Walla et al. (2007) could help reveal subtle temporal differences in stimulus processing that might have gone unnoticed in previous analyses focusing on modulation of ERP amplitudes.

The aim of the present paper therefore was to investigate the boundary conditions of the multiple aspect theory by determining whether or not simple visual presentations of pronouns would elicit the two prior described self-aspects (Me1 and Me2) when compared to un-personal pronouns. In particular, by using EEG data from the HisMine paradigm (Blume & Herbert, 2014), which comprises all personal and possessive as well as non-personal pronouns and articles of the German language will allow us to test the specific hypothesis of the multiple aspect theory of the self (Walla et al., 2007): Firstly, whether visual presentations of the German possessive pronouns "mein" (my) and "sein" (his) would elicit similar brain activity at early stages around 200 ms post-stimulus that differs from the non-personal pronoun ("ein") (a). Secondly, whether processing of the possessive pronoun "mein" would enhance brain activity at around 400 ms post-stimulus separating self- from other-referential processing at left frontal areas.

2. Methods

2.1. Participants

Data from 28 native speakers of German (23 female, 5 male) with a mean age of 22.9 years (SD = 3.8) were analysed. Participants had normal or corrected-to-normal vision, and none of them had a history of prior somatic, neurological or psychiatric disorders. The study was conducted in accordance with the Declaration of Helsinki. All participants provided written informed consent. They were reimbursed financially or received course credit for their participation.

2.2. Stimuli

Stimuli consisted of the German pronouns "ich" ("I"), "du ("you")", "er" ("he"), (personal pronouns) and "mein" ("my"), "dein" ("your"), "sein" ("his") (possessive pronouns) which were presented together with the pronoun "ein" ("a") and the articles "es" ("it") and "das" ("the") containing no self- or other-reference. For the purpose of this study, we only analysed the "ein", "mein", "sein" and "dein" conditions. Previous analyses showed that visual presentation of the possessive pronoun "dein" might contain both, self- and other-reference, depending on the specificities of the task and the reader's perspective (Blume & Herbert, 2014). In the present analysis, the "dein" condition was therefore also included as a further control and compared against non-personal pronouns. In line with the multiple aspect theory, it could be expected that the second-person possessive pronoun "dein" elicits brain activity similar to the first- and third-person possessive pronouns "mein" and "sein" at early stages, while also eliciting brain activity that differs from the "mein" condition at later stages.

2.3. Procedure

All words were presented visually in black font (Times font, 40 points) at the centre of a white computer screen. Stimuli were presented for 1,000 ms (1 Hz) in a serial visual stream. Each word was presented 60 times in a random sequence which controlled for frequency of occurrence such that each stimulus had the same transition probability. Participants were instructed to silently read the words. The experiment was programmed and controlled by Presentation® software (Neurobehavioral Systems, Inc.).

The processing condition under examination here was part of a larger experimental set-up consisting of different processing conditions that comprised passive viewing conditions that were followed by active counting conditions (for an overview see Blume & Herbert, 2014), which are not part of the present analysis. Here, data from only the 1 Hz passive viewing condition were reanalysed with regard to the hypothesis of the multiple aspect theory (Walla et al., 2007; 2008) to validate, if the different processing stages of the two aspects of the Me proposed by the multiple aspect theory of the self occur for the self-referential and other-referential possessive pronouns "mein" ("my"), "dein" ("your") and "sein" ("his") in relation to the non-personal pronoun "ein" ("a"). To this end, effects of interest were analysed at exactly the same electrode positions as suggested and previously reported by Walla and colleagues (see Walla et al., 2007).

2.4. Electroencephalography

Participants were seated on a comfortable chair at a distance of about 70 cm from the computer screen. Thirty-two active Ag/AgCl electrodes were placed on the scalp according to the international 10–20 system using an actiCAP® system (Brain Products GmbH). The electro-oculogram (EOG) was recorded from two Ag/AgCl electrodes placed above and below the participant's right eye (VEOG) and from two electrodes that were fixed laterally to the outer canthus of each eye (HEOG). Impedance was kept below 10 kΩ and raw EEG signals were continuously recorded at a sampling rate of 500 Hz using a BrainVision BrainAmp® DC amplifier. Electrodes were connected to ground and referenced to the vertex (Cz).

2.5. Analysis

All EEG data were processed with EEGDISPLAY, a custom-made software package to process EEG data of various different formats (Ross Fulham). Raw EEG data files were downsampled from 500 to 256 samples per second. Then, data were visually inspected and a band pass filter from .1 to 30 Hz was applied. An EEGDISPLAY inbuilt algorithm was used for eye blink correction and epochs were generated by using a 100 ms baseline (for baseline correction) and a 1,000 ms post-stimulus period. Finally, averages were calculated across single trials for each of the four conditions of interest ("mein", "sein", "dein" and "ein") corresponding to "my", "his" "your" and "a".

ERPs were generated to display brain potential changes over time for all four conditions of interest at two selected electrode sites (F7 and PO9) (see Figure 1). For the purpose of statistical analysis, the post-stimulus epoch was split into 39 × 26 ms time windows and all data points within these time windows were averaged to result in single amplitude values. Short intervals were chosen to keep statistical temporal resolution at a high level. The mean amplitudes were then taken as dependent variables and subjected to a 4 (factor *condition*: "ein", "mein", "sein", "dein") × 2 (factor *electrode*: PO9, F7) repeated measures (RM) analysis of variance (ANOVA). One RM ANOVA was calculated for each time interval separately. Also, topographical maps were created for all four conditions and

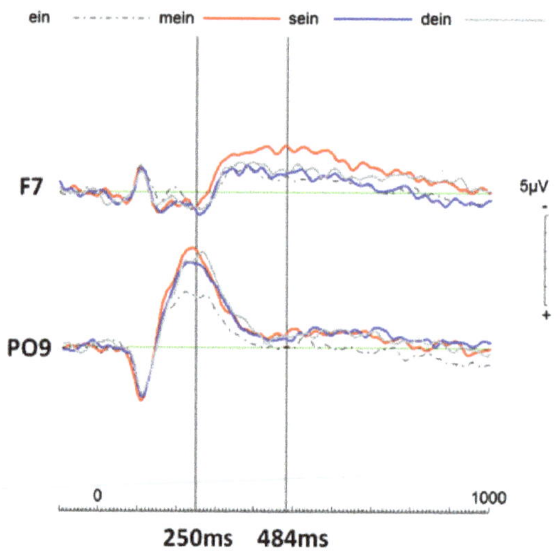

Figure 1. Event-related potentials (ERPs) of all four pronouns of interest (possessive pronouns: "mein" (my), "sein" (his), "dein" (your) and non-personal pronoun "ein" (a)).

Notes: Around 250 ms post-stimulus onset all possessive pronouns elicited more negative going electrophysiological activity compared to the non-personal pronoun "ein" (a) over the left parieto-occipital area (i.e. PO9 electrode location). This finding is here referred to as the Me1, which simply reflects any personal engagement. Later, starting at about 350 ms post-stimulus, "mein" elicited more negative going activity than the rest over the left frontal cortical area. This finding is here referred to as the Me2, the proper (elaborate) self.

t-maps were calculated to show significant differences between the conditions. As already mentioned, the selection of electrodes was based on previous EEG and MEG studies (see for an overview Walla et al., 2007, 2008) which revealed that the Me1 and Me2 effects are particularly pronounced at these two electrodes.

3. Results

3.1. EEG

The ERPs shown in Figure 1 clearly demonstrate that at electrode location PO9 (left occipito-parietal), the possessive pronouns "mein" ("my"), "dein" ("your") and "sein" ("his") elicited similar brain activity that differs from the non-personal pronoun "ein" ("a"). This difference between any person and no person starts before 200 ms post-stimulus onset (see Figure 1). This early neural phenomenon is here referred to as the Me1 (non-personal self). At the left frontal electrode (F7), brain activity elicited by the self-related possessive pronoun "mein" ("my") differed from brain activity elicited by all other pronouns ("ein" ("a"), "dein" ("your") and "sein" ("his")) from about 250 ms until about 700 ms post-stimulus onset (maxim effect at around 484 ms post-stimulus onset). This later phenomenon is here referred to as the Me2 (proper and actual self).

The repeated measure ANOVAs revealed condition main effects starting from 224 ms after stimulus onset until the end of the entire epoch (1,000 ms). This result confirms that the conditions of interest indeed elicited significantly different brain activities. Further, condition × electrode interactions occurred between 146 ms and 328 ms post-stimulus (see Table 1). The early condition × electrode interactions are resulting from PO9-specific Me1 effects, whereas the later condition main effects without electrode interactions result from differences in electrophysiological activity at both electrode locations. However, the expected pattern of distinct brain activity differences was only found at F7 (see Figures 1 and 2).

T-tests comparing the no-person condition ("ein" (a)) with all person conditions separately ("ein-dein" (a-your), "ein-mein" (a-my) and "ein-sein" (a-his)) for every single time interval revealed that indeed all personal possessive pronouns elicited different electrophysiological activity compared to the no-personal pronoun at the left occipito-parietal electrode (PO9) at an early stage (exemplified for maximum effects at 250 ms post-stimulus in Figure 1), whereas the exclusive difference between the no-personal pronoun "ein" (a) and the self-possessive pronoun "mein" (my) clearly occurred at a later stage of

Table 1. Consecutive repeated measures ANOVA results for every single post-stimulus time interval showing *p*-values (including *F* value and observed power) related to main effects (cond) and cond × electrode interactions (c × ele)

F7 and PO9		
Post-stimulus interval	***p*-values (*F*); observed power (η^2)**	
ms	**cond**	**c × ele**
146	.609 (F = .527); η^2 = .137	.032 (F = 3.231); η^2 = .683
172	.130 (F = 1.994); η^2 = .462	.015 (F = 3.795); η^2 = .781
198	.423 (F = .905); η^2 = .212	.002 (F = 5.981); η^2 = .931
224	.000 (F = 8.603); η^2 = .984	.001 (F = 7.432); η^2 = .952
250	.000 (F = 13.576); η^2 = 1	.000 (F = 7.557); η^2 = .965
276	.000 (F = 12.613); η^2 = 1	.008 (F = 4.587); η^2 = .830
302	.000 (F = 7.366); η^2 = .972	.008 (F = 4.641); η^2 = .824
328	.001 (F = 6.215); η^2 = .948	.034 (F = 3.412); η^2 = .656
354	.002 (F = 5.637); η^2 = .920	.225 (F = 1.509); η^2 = .347
380	.001 (F = 6.069); η^2 = .944	.163 (F = 1.797); η^2 = .414
406	.002 (F = 5.612); η^2 = .911	.480 (F = .810); η^2 = .206
432	.000 (F = 10.147); η^2 = .996	.129 (F = 1.999); η^2 = .463
458	.000 (F = 10.187); η^2 = .994	.242 (F = 1.445); η^2 = .323
484	.000 (F = 8.823); η^2 = .992	.203 (F = 1.603); η^2 = .369
510	.000 (F = 9.938); η^2 = .992	.472 (F = .826); η^2 = .210
536	.001 (F = 6.475); η^2 = .936	.108 (F = 2.215); η^2 = .477
562	.000 (F = 8.276); η^2 = .979	.055 (F = 2.773); η^2 = .608
588	.002 (F = 6.074); η^2 = .907	.138 (F = 1.937); η^2 = .451
614	.001 (F = 6.829); η^2 = .953	.555 (F = .677); η^2 = .179
640	.016 (F = 4.073); η^2 = .757	.594 (F = 1.934); η^2 = .155
666	.004 (F = 5.114); η^2 = .887	.255 (F = 1.394); η^2 = .316
692	.001 (F = 6.750); η^2 = .955	.489 (F = .765); η^2 = .186
718	.003 (F = 5.540); η^2 = .906	.170 (F = 1.792); η^2 = .389
744	.015 (F = 3.871); η^2 = .777	.199 (F = 1.617); η^2 = .377
770	.001 (F = 6.447); η^2 = .942	.529 (F = .709); η^2 = .182
796	.003 (F = 5.273); η^2 = .893	.374 (F = 1.030); η^2 = .243
822	.006 (F = 4.668); η^2 = .861	.271 (F = 1.335); η^2 = .314
848	.025 (F = 3.314); η^2 = .726	.340 (F = 1.130); η^2 = .280
874	.002 (F = 5.575); η^2 = .917	.286 (F = 1.283); η^2 = .320
900	.012 (F = 4.061); η^2 = .803	.222 (F = 1.533); η^2 = .337
926	.010 (F = 4.357); η^2 = .816	.283 (F = 1.295); η^2 = .297
952	.039 (F = 2.981); η^2 = .667	.474 (F = .811); η^2 = .201
978	.008 (F = 4.254); η^2 = .835	.203 (F = 1.592); η^2 = .378

Notes: Condition main effects occurred from 224 ms post-stimulus until the end of the entire epoch, whereas condition × electrode interactions occurred between 146 and 328 ms post-stimulus.

processing at the left frontal area (see Figure 2). Finally, separate topographies for every single pronoun condition of interest show that around the early time period (250 ms post-stimulus) all three possessive pronouns are associated with increased left occipito-parietal negative going ERPs. Later, at around 484 ms the self-possessive pronoun "mein" (my) elicits stronger negativity as compared to all other conditions at the left frontal electrode site F7, replicating Walla et al. (2007) (Figure 3).

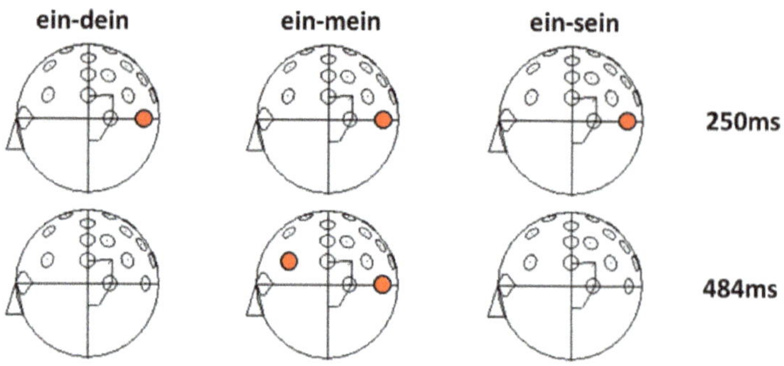

Figure 2. Sample *t*-maps demonstrating that at early time intervals all possessive pronouns elicited significantly different electrophysiological activity compared to the no-personal pronoun "ein" (a). Later, here exemplified at the maximum effect (484 ms), only processing of the self possessive pronoun "mein" (my) differs from the processing of the non-personal pronoun "ein" (a).

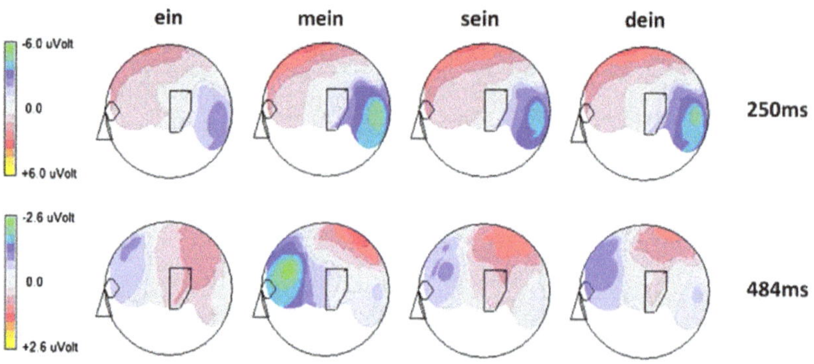

Figure 3. Brain topographic maps revealed that at early times (250 ms) the pronouns "mein" (my), "sein" (his) and "dein" (your) all elicited similar brain activities that differed from "ein" (a). On the other hand, later at 484 ms "mein" (my) elicited different brain activity than all other pronouns ("ein" (a), "sein" (his) and "dein" (your), respectively.

4. Discussion

4.1. General

The present paper analysed data from the HisMine Paradigm (Blume & Herbert, 2014) in order to test the boundary conditions of the multiple aspect theory of the self proposed by Walla et al. (2007, 2008). As predicted from this theory, the current analysis revealed two distinct spatiotemporally separate effects distinguishing self- and other-related pronouns from non-personal pronouns in early time windows and self from other-related pronouns in later time windows. Moreover, in line with previous observations (e.g. Walla et al., 2007), the early effect occurred at specifically left occipito-parietal electrode locations (e.g. PO9), whereas the later effect was found specifically at the left fronto-temporal electrode site, F7. Although the present analysis was restricted to a few sensors, it exactly replicates findings of previous studies of Walla and colleagues who, using similar analyses strategies, observed identical cortical activity patterns during processing of pronoun–noun pairs. Thus, the present observations might provide support for the previously stated multiple aspect theory (Walla et al., 2007, 2008). This dynamic self-model assumes two different aspects of the self, the Me1 and the Me2. The Me1 is like a first low-level processing stage of the self that exists in the brain and understands the self as simply being personal or non-personal, but not different to other. Perhaps, this aspect of the self could also be seen as a "We" reflecting any personal versus no personal engagement. In contrast, the Me2 is defined as the personal self that clearly distinguishes between self and other.

In the literature, many distinctions between two and even more kinds (e.g. Neisser, 1988) of self have been made previously (e.g. minimal versus narrative self; pre-reflective versus reflective self; see Dor-Ziderman, Berkovich-Ohana, Glicksohn, & Goldstein, 2013 for definitions of other multiple aspects of the self). One such distinction was put forward by Esslen, Metzler, Pascual-Marqui, and Jancke (2008) who additionally provided neurophysiological evidence to support a dynamic and multiple aspect view of the self by what the authors call a pre-reflective self and a reflective self (for a detailed distinction see Legrand, 2007). What they report does widely confirm to the notion of distinct aspects of self-processing as suggested by the multiple aspect theory, although their idea of pre-reflective and reflective self is conceptually different from the idea of a Me1 and Me2. Esslen et al. (see also Legrand, 2007) aimed to draw the distinction between a non-conscious, but distinctively self-related (pre-reflective) and a conscious (reflective) aspect of the self, which they investigated by means of sentences starting with the personal pronouns "I" or "He/She" to examine the pre-reflective self on one hand, and the reflective self on the other hand by asking subjects to judge trait adjectives as self- or other-related. Shi et al. (2010) and Blume and Herbert (2014) investigated the extent to which pre-reflective and reflective self is reflected in event-related brain potential (ERP) modulation patterns elicited by personal and possessive pronouns, but unexpectedly no significant difference in pre-reflective and reflective temporal processing of personal and possessive pronouns was found. Shi et al. reported only a marginally significant trend while in the study by Blume and Herbert self-related pronouns were processed preferentially regardless of pronoun type. Moreover, during early processing stages, ERP modulation also indicated that processing of possessive pronouns was more pronounced than processing of personal pronouns. Thus, whereas the extent to which the pre-reflective self and the reflective self is reflected in the processing of pronouns might be up to future research, more evidence from especially pronoun studies seems to exist for the distinction between a Me1 and Me2, although the observation of preferential processing of self-related possessive pronouns compared to other-related pronouns during initial processing stages are a challenge for both theories and should be addressed in future studies.

What could be the implications of a multiple and hierarchical aspect theory of self that distinguishes between a Me1 and a Me2?

4.2. Impact of multiple and hierarchical self-aspect theory and future research

The concept of a Me1 means only being a person (no difference between self and other). It forms an important basis for a more elaborate form of self, the Me2 and its underlying spatiotemporal dynamics. Decety and Sommerville (2003) put together pieces from developmental and social psychology as well as neuroscience leading to the idea of a shared network between self and other whereby among others the inferior parietal cortex seems to play a crucial role. This goes well in line with previous findings (e.g. Herbert, Herbert, Ethofer, & Pauli, 2011; Walla et al., 2007), and the present observation showing similar brain activity at the occipito-parietal electrode PO9 for self- and other-related pronouns as compared to the non-personal pronoun "a" supporting the suggestion of a more primitive, non-personal Me1.

Theoretically, these two self-aspects interact, but still are distinct. The non-personal self (Me1) might exist without the personal self (Me2). The personal self however might not exist without the non-personal self, which can be interpreted as representing a hierarchical structure. Thinking in terms of evolutionary lineage, the Me1 might have evolved earlier than the Me2. This could mean that the Me1 might also exist in non-human mammals and also that a human being during early childhood starts off with only the Me1, while later on the Me2 develops. Future developmental studies using the HisMine paradigm (or similar approaches) will test this idea. In addition, besides further strengthening the multiple aspect theory of the human self, investigating the self from a dynamic point of view may also provide useful implications for clinical investigations.

Various psychological and neurological diseases are associated with disordered self-concepts or malfunctioning theory of mind capacities (e.g. Korkmaz, 2011). Disordered self in the schizophrenia spectrum (Parnas & Henriksen, 2014), self-defeating personality disorder (Reich, 1987) and autism (Uddin, 2011) are just a few of many more such diseases. Patients with disordered self-concepts may demonstrate selectively disordered Me1 or Me2 functions. Early lesion studies have shown deficient self-awareness and self-control in lesions of the right inferior parietal lobe (Posner & Rothbart,

1998; Stuss & Levine, 2002), which could be seen as an index for selective Me1 impairments. In such cases, it would be predicted that Me2 functions are affected as well. On the other hand, it is predicted that Me2 impairments can occur while leaving Me1 functions intact. Future EEG or MEG studies could test this prediction. The HisMine paradigm (Blume & Herbert, 2014) comprising all pronouns of the first, second and third person as well as non-personal pronouns would be perfectly suited to this end. Due to its simplicity, it could be even administered to severely impaired patients groups.

Previous imaging research showed that the CMS play an important role in self-referential processing. However, the precise role of this network is still unclear, especially with regard to the concepts of consciousness and awareness. Activation of CMS including the anterior cingulate cortex (ACC) has been found in a number of tasks including pronoun processing (e.g. Herbert, Herbert & Pauli, 2011; Shi et al., 2010). It might be related to attention (Carter et al., 1998; Elliott & Dolan, 1998; Devinsky, Morrell, & Vogt, 1995; Paus, Koski, Caramanos, & Westbury, 1998; Peterson et al., 1999; Posner & Rothbart, 1998; Weissman et al., 2004; Whalen et al., 1998). Given that attention is crucial for conscious processing, it might be that activations of CMS such as the ACC are mediating consciousness in concert with other networks or brain structures. One such other structure could be the insular cortex as suggested by Walla et al. (2007). When both structures are simultaneously active self-awareness might be generated.

Although the present results are based on very locally restricted single electrode analyses and therefore cannot tell us anything about the localisation of the observed effects in the brain, they do support the idea that changes in brain activity and thus in self-referential processing do occur within the millisecond range. Importantly, these changes might have a crucial influence on whether midline structures are active simultaneously to self-referential processing (see Herbert, Herbert, Ethofer, Pauli, 2011; Herbert, Herbert, & Pauli, 2011; Northoff, 2013; Qin & Northoff, 2011) and whether or not self-referential processing is associated with self-awareness.

While this is only speculation, future research using the present design and following a dynamic approach of the self could reveal insight into various clinical conditions that are associated with disordered self-concepts including research on self-awareness and consciousness.

Acknowledgements
Many thanks to Ross Fulham for his highly appreciated data analysis contribution.

Funding
This study was supported by the German Research Foundation (DFG HE5880/3-1) and the Gustav-A. Lienert-Stiftung.

Competing Interests
The authors declare no competing interest.

Author details
Peter Walla[1,2]
E-mail: peter.walla@newcastle.edu.au
Cornelia Herbert[3,4,5,6]
E-mail: cornelia.herbert@psychologie.uni-wuerzburg.de
[1] Department of Psychology, Webster University Vienna, Palais Wenkheim, Vienna, Austria.
[2] School of Psychology, Centre for Translational Neuroscience and Mental Health Research, University of Newcastle, Callaghan, New South Wales, Australia.
[3] Department of Psychology and Education, University of Ulm, Ulm, Germany.
[4] Department of Psychiatry, University of Tübingen, Tübingen, Germany.
[5] Department of Biomedical Resonance Imaging, University of Tübingen, Tübingen, Germany.
[6] Department of Psychology, University of Würzburg, Würzburg, Germany.

Author contribution
This manuscript is a shared first authorship and correspondence.

References

Blume, C., & Herbert, C. (2014). The HisMine-paradigm: A new paradigm to investigate self-awareness employing pronouns. *Social Neuroscience, 9*, 289–299. http://dx.doi.org/10.1080/17470919.2014.886616

Carter, C. S., Braver, T. S., Barch, D. M., Botvinick, M. M., Noll, D., & Cohen, J. D. (1998). Anterior cingulate cortex, error detection, and the online monitoring of performance. *Science, 280*, 747–749. http://dx.doi.org/10.1126/science.280.5364.747

Decety, J., & Sommerville, J. A. (2003). Shared representations between self and other: A social cognitive neuroscience view. *Trends in Cognitive Sciences, 7*, 527–533. http://dx.doi.org/10.1016/j.tics.2003.10.004

Denny, B. T., Kober, H., Wager, T. D., & Ochsner, K. N. (2012). A meta-analysis of functional neuroimaging studies of self- and other judgments reveals a spatial gradient for mentalizing in medial prefrontal cortex. *Journal of Cognitive Neuroscience, 24*, 1742–1752. http://dx.doi.org/10.1162/jocn_a_00233

Devinsky, O., Morrell, M. J., & Vogt, B. A. (1995). Review article. *Brain, 118*, 279–306. http://dx.doi.org/10.1093/brain/118.1.279

Dor-Ziderman, Y., Berkovich-Ohana, A., Glicksohn, J., & Goldstein, A. (2013). Mindfulness-induced selflessness: A MEG neurophenomenological study. *Frontiers in Human Neuroscience, 7*, 582. doi:10.3389/fnhum.2013.00582

Elliott, R., & Dolan, R. J. (1998). Activation of different anterior cingulate foci in association with hypothesis testing and response selection. *NeuroImage, 8*, 17–29. http://dx.doi.org/10.1006/nimg.1998.0344

Esslen, M., Metzler, S., Pascual-Marqui, R., & Jancke, L. (2008). Pre-reflective and reflective self-reference: A spatiotemporal EEG analysis. *NeuroImage, 42*, 437–449. http://dx.doi.org/10.1016/j.neuroimage.2008.01.060

Herbert, C., Herbert, B. M., Ethofer, T., & Pauli, P. (2011). His or mine? The time course of self-other discrimination in emotion processing. *Social Neuroscience, 6*, 277–288. http://dx.doi.org/10.1080/17470919.2010.523543

Herbert, C., Herbert, B. M., & Pauli, P. (2011). Emotional self-reference: Brain structures involved in the processing of words describing one's own emotions. *Neuropsychologia, 49*, 2947–2956. http://dx.doi.org/10.1016/j.neuropsychologia.2011.06.026

Herbert, C., Pauli, P., & Herbert, B. M. (2010). Self-reference modulates the processing of emotional stimuli in the absence of explicit appraisal instructions. *Social Cognitive and Affective Neuroscience, 6*, 653–661.

James, W. (1890). *The principles of psychology*. New York, NY: Holt. http://dx.doi.org/10.1037/11059-000

Korkmaz, B. (2011). Theory of mind and neurodevelopmental disorders of childhood. *Pediatric Research, 69*, 101R–108R. http://dx.doi.org/10.1203/PDR.0b013e318212c177

Legrand, D. (2007). Pre-reflective self-as-subject from experiential and empirical perspectives. *Consciousness and Cognition, 16*, 583–599. http://dx.doi.org/10.1016/j.concog.2007.04.002

Neisser, U. (1988). Five kinds of self-knowledge. *Philosophical Psychology, 1*, 35–59. http://dx.doi.org/10.1080/09515088808572924

Northoff, G. (2013). *Unlocking the brain: Consciousness* (Vol. 2). Oxford: Oxford University Press.

Northoff, G., Heinzel, A., de Greck, M., Bermpohl, F., Dobrowolny, H., & Panksepp, J. (2006). Self-referential processing in our brain—A meta-analysis of imaging studies on the self. *NeuroImage, 31*, 440–457. http://dx.doi.org/10.1016/j.neuroimage.2005.12.002

Parnas, J., & Henriksen, M. G. (2014). Disordered self in the schizophrenia spectrum. *Harvard Review of Psychiatry, 22*, 251–265. http://dx.doi.org/10.1097/HRP.0000000000000040

Paus, T., Koski, L., Caramanos, Z., & Westbury, C. (1998). Regional differences in the effects of task difficulty and motor output on blood flow response in the human anterior cingulate cortex. *NeuroReport, 9*, R37–R47. http://dx.doi.org/10.1097/00001756-199806220-00001

Peterson, B. S., Skudlarski, P., Gatenby, J. C., Zhang, H. P., Anderson, A. W., & Gore, J. C. (1999). An fMRI study of stroop word-color interference: Evidence for cingulate subregions subserving multiple distributed attentional systems. *Biological Psychiatry, 45*, 1237–1258. http://dx.doi.org/10.1016/S0006-3223(99)00056-6

Posner, M. I. & Rothbart, M. K. (1998). Attention, self-regulation and consciousness. *Philosophical Transactions of the Royal Society B: Biological Sciences, 353*, 1915–1927. http://dx.doi.org/10.1098/rstb.1998.0344

Qin, P., & Northoff, G. (2011). How is our self related to midline regions and the default-mode network? *Neuroimage, 57*, 1221–1233.

Reich, J. (1987). Prevalence of DSM-III-R self-defeating (masochistic) personality disorder in normal and outpatient populations. *The Journal of Nervous and Mental Disease, 175*, 52–54. http://dx.doi.org/10.1097/00005053-198701000-00009

Shi, Z., Zhou, A., Liu, P., Zhang, P., & Han, W. (2010). An EEG study on the effect of self-relevant possessive pronoun: Self-referential content and first-person perspective. *Neuroscience Letters, 494*, 174–179.

Stuss, D. T., & Levine, B. (2002). Adult clinical neuropsychology: Lessons from studies of the frontal lobes. *Annual Review of Psychology, 53*, 401–433. http://dx.doi.org/10.1146/annurev.psych.53.100901.135220

Uddin, L. Q. (2011). The self in autism: An emerging view from neuroimaging. *Neurocase, 17*, 201–208.

Walla, P., Duregger, C., Greiner, K., Thurner, S., & Ehrenberger, K. (2008). Multiple aspects related to self-awareness and the awareness of others: An electroencephalography study. *Journal of Neural Transmission, 115*, 983–992. http://dx.doi.org/10.1007/s00702-008-0035-6

Walla, P., Greiner, K., Duregger, C., Deecke, L., & Thurner, S. (2007). Self-awareness and the subconscious effect of personal pronouns on word encoding: A magnetoencephalography (MEG) study. *Neuropsychologia, 45*, 796–809. http://dx.doi.org/10.1016/j.neuropsychologia.2006.08.017

Weissman, D. H., Gopalakrishnan, A., Hazlett, C. J., & Woldorff, M. G. (2004). Dorsal anterior cingulate cortex resolves conflict from distracting stimuli by boosting attention toward relevant events. *Cerebral Cortex, 15*, 229–237. http://dx.doi.org/10.1093/cercor/bhh125

Whalen, P. J., Bush, G., McNally, R. J., Wilhelm, S., McInerney, S. C., Jenike, M. A., & Rauch, S. L. (1998). The emotional counting Stroop paradigm: A functional magnetic resonance imaging probe of the anterior cingulate affective division. *Biological Psychiatry, 44*, 1219–1228.

Zhou, A. B., Shi, Z., Zhang, P. Y., Liu, P. R., Han, W., Wu, H. F., ... Xia, R. X. (2010). An ERP study on the effect of self-relevant possessive pronoun. *Neuroscience Letters, 480*, 162–166. http://dx.doi.org/10.1016/j.neulet.2010.06.033

Permissions

All chapters in this book were first published in CS&N, by Cogent OA; hereby published with permission under the Creative Commons Attribution License or equivalent. Every chapter published in this book has been scrutinized by our experts. Their significance has been extensively debated. The topics covered herein carry significant findings which will fuel the growth of the discipline. They may even be implemented as practical applications or may be referred to as a beginning point for another development.

The contributors of this book come from diverse backgrounds, making this book a truly international effort. This book will bring forth new frontiers with its revolutionizing research information and detailed analysis of the nascent developments around the world.

We would like to thank all the contributing authors for lending their expertise to make the book truly unique. They have played a crucial role in the development of this book. Without their invaluable contributions this book wouldn't have been possible. They have made vital efforts to compile up to date information on the varied aspects of this subject to make this book a valuable addition to the collection of many professionals and students.

This book was conceptualized with the vision of imparting up-to-date information and advanced data in this field. To ensure the same, a matchless editorial board was set up. Every individual on the board went through rigorous rounds of assessment to prove their worth. After which they invested a large part of their time researching and compiling the most relevant data for our readers.

The editorial board has been involved in producing this book since its inception. They have spent rigorous hours researching and exploring the diverse topics which have resulted in the successful publishing of this book. They have passed on their knowledge of decades through this book. To expedite this challenging task, the publisher supported the team at every step. A small team of assistant editors was also appointed to further simplify the editing procedure and attain best results for the readers.

Apart from the editorial board, the designing team has also invested a significant amount of their time in understanding the subject and creating the most relevant covers. They scrutinized every image to scout for the most suitable representation of the subject and create an appropriate cover for the book.

The publishing team has been an ardent support to the editorial, designing and production team. Their endless efforts to recruit the best for this project, has resulted in the accomplishment of this book. They are a veteran in the field of academics and their pool of knowledge is as vast as their experience in printing. Their expertise and guidance has proved useful at every step. Their uncompromising quality standards have made this book an exceptional effort. Their encouragement from time to time has been an inspiration for everyone.

The publisher and the editorial board hope that this book will prove to be a valuable piece of knowledge for researchers, students, practitioners and scholars across the globe.

List of Contributors

Gina A. Glanc
Department of Psychology & Sociology, Texas A&M University Corpus Christi, 6300 Ocean Drive, Corpus Christi, TX 78412, USA

Rawshan Zannat
Department of Psychology, University of Chittagong, Chittaagong 4334, Bangladesh

Mir Muhammad Nasir Uddin
Department of Pharmacy, University of Chittagong, Chittagong 4331, Bangladesh

Md. Atiar Rahman and Jannatul Aklima
Department of Biochemistry and Molecular Biology, University of Chittagong, Chittagong 4331, Bangladesh

Md. Mamun Al Amin
Queensland Brain Institute, University of Queensland, Queensland, Australia

Marieclaire Overton, Mats Pihlsgård and Sölve Elmståhl
Division of Geriatric Medicine, Lunds University, Skånes University Hospital, Jan Waldenströms gata 35, CRC Building 28, fl.13, SE-205 02 Malmö, Sweden

Patric Schubert, Stephanie Kersten and Christian T. Haas
Faculty of Health and Social Sciences, Institute of Complex Health Research, Hochschule Fresenius, University of Applied Sciences, Idstein, Germany

Magnus Liebherr
Faculty of Health and Social Sciences, Institute of Complex Health Research, Hochschule Fresenius, University of Applied Sciences, Idstein, Germany
Department of General Psychology, University of Duisburg- Essen, Duisburg, Germany

Johannes Schiebener
Department of General Psychology, University of Duisburg- Essen, Duisburg, Germany

Lola L. Cuddy, Ritu Sikka, Kristen Silveira, Sean Bai and Ashley Vanstone
Department of Psychology, Queen's University, 62 Arch Street, Humphrey Hall, Room 232, Kingston, Ontario, Canada

Pierre Flor-Henry and Yakov Shapiro
Department of Psychiatry, University of Alberta, Edmonton, Canada

Corine Sombrun
Les Beaux Arts, Paris, France

David Hensel and Judith Znanewitz
Institute of Marketing, Helmut Schmidt University/ University of the Federal Armed Forces Hamburg, Hamburg, Germany

Ana Iorga
Buyer Brain, Bucharest, Romania

Lisa Wolter
Hamburg Media School, Hamburg, Germany

Joseph E. Robinson and John Kiely
School of Sport and Wellbeing, Institute of Coaching and Performance, University of Central Lancashire, Preston, Lancashire PR1 2HE, UK

Carlo Abbate and Silvia Inglese
Geriatric Unit, Fondazione IRCCS Ca' Granda, Ospedale Maggiore Policlinico, via Pace 9, 20122 Milan, Italy

Beatrice Arosio
Geriatric Unit, Fondazione IRCCS Ca' Granda, Ospedale Maggiore Policlinico, via Pace 9, 20122 Milan, Italy
Department of Medical Sciences and Community Health, University of Milan, via Francesco Sforza 35, 20122 Milan, Italy

Pietro Davide Trimarchi, Fabrizio Giunco and Renzo Bagarolo
Alzheimer's Assessment Unit, S. Maria Nascente, Fondazione IRCCS Don Carlo Gnocchi, via Alfonso Capecelatro 66, 20148 Milan, Italy

Laura Manzoni, Anna Maria Quarenghi and Gian Pietro Salvi
Istituto Clinico Quarenghi, via San Carlo 70, 24016 San Pellegrino Terme, Italy

Daniela Mari
Department of Medical Sciences and Community Health, University of Milan, via Francesco Sforza 35, 20122 Milan, Italy

Marie Vander Haegen and Anne-Marie Etienne
Unit of Health Psychology, Université de Liège, Quartier Village 2, Rue de l'Aunaie 30, Liège 4000, Belgium

Pauline E. J. Spaan
Department of Brain and Cognition, University of Amsterdam, Weesperplein 4, 1018 XA Amsterdam, The Netherlands
Department of Psychiatry & Medical Psychology, Onze Lieve Vrouwe Gasthuis (OLVG, Hospital), Amsterdam, The Netherlands

A. Al Rizaiza
Department of Neurosciences, University of California, San Diego, 8950 Villa La Jolla Drive, Suite C112, La Jolla, CA 92037, USA
Southern California Physician Medical Group, Kaiser Permanente, 4405 Vandever Ave, San Diego, CA 92120, USA

R. Ceponiene
Department of Neurosciences, University of California, San Diego, 8950 Villa La Jolla Drive, Suite C112, La Jolla, CA 92037, USA
Southern California Physician Medical Group, Kaiser Permanente, 4405 Vandever Ave, San Diego, CA 92120, USA

S. D. Edland
Department of Neurosciences, University of California, San Diego, 8950 Villa La Jolla Drive, Suite C112, La Jolla, CA 92037, USA
Department of Family and Preventive Medicine, Division of Biostatistics and Bioinformatics, University of California, San Diego, 9500 Gilman Dr. La Jolla, La Jolla, CA, USA
Department of Neurosciences, University of California, San Diego, 9500 Gilman Dr. La Jolla, La Jolla, CA, USA

I. Litvan
Department of Neurosciences, University of California, San Diego, 8950 Villa La Jolla Drive, Suite C112, La Jolla, CA 92037, USA
University of Louisville, 1911 S 3rd Street, Louisville, KY 40208, USA

T. N. Reid
University of Louisville, 1911 S 3rd Street, Louisville, KY 40208, USA

Peter Walla
Department of Psychology, Webster University Vienna, Palais Wenkheim, Vienna, Austria
School of Psychology, Centre for Translational Neuroscience and Mental Health Research, University of Newcastle, Callaghan, New South Wales, Australia

Cornelia Herbert
Department of Psychology and Education, University of Ulm, Ulm, Germany
Department of Psychiatry, University of Tübingen, Tübingen, Germany
Department of Biomedical Resonance Imaging, University of Tübingen, Tübingen, Germany
Department of Psychology, University of Würzburg, Würzburg, Germany

Index

CPSIA information can be obtained
at www.ICGtesting.com
Printed in the USA
LVHW060900030122
707669LV00002B/274

9 781647 261580